Data-Driven Intelligent Modeling and Optimization Algorithms for Industrial Processes

Data-Driven Intelligent Modeling and Optimization Algorithms for Industrial Processes

Guest Editors

Li Jin
Sheng Du
Zixin Huang
Xiongbo Wan

Basel • Beijing • Wuhan • Barcelona • Belgrade • Novi Sad • Cluj • Manchester

Guest Editors

Li Jin	Sheng Du	Zixin Huang
China University of Geosciences	China University of Geosciences	Wuhan Institute of Technology
Wuhan	Wuhan	Wuhan
China	China	China

Xiongbo Wan
China University of
Geosciences
Wuhan
China

Editorial Office
MDPI AG
Grosspeteranlage 5
4052 Basel, Switzerland

This is a reprint of the Special Issue, published open access by the journal *Algorithms* (ISSN 1999-4893), freely accessible at: https://www.mdpi.com/journal/algorithms/special_issues/8255D33H50.

For citation purposes, cite each article independently as indicated on the article page online and as indicated below:

Lastname, A.A.; Lastname, B.B. Article Title. *Journal Name* **Year**, *Volume Number*, Page Range.

ISBN 978-3-7258-2985-9 (Hbk)
ISBN 978-3-7258-2986-6 (PDF)
https://doi.org/10.3390/books978-3-7258-2986-6

© 2025 by the authors. Articles in this book are Open Access and distributed under the Creative Commons Attribution (CC BY) license. The book as a whole is distributed by MDPI under the terms and conditions of the Creative Commons Attribution-NonCommercial-NoDerivs (CC BY-NC-ND) license (https://creativecommons.org/licenses/by-nc-nd/4.0/).

Contents

About the Editors vii

Sheng Du, Zixin Huang, Li Jin and Xiongbo Wan
Recent Progress in Data-Driven Intelligent Modeling and Optimization Algorithms for Industrial Processes
Reprinted from: *Algorithms* 2024, 17, 569, https://doi.org/10.3390/a17120569 1

Duby Castellanos-Cárdenas, Norha L. Posada, Andrés Orozco-Duque, Lina M. Sepúlveda-Cano, Fabio Castrillón, Oscar E. Camacho and Rafael E. Vásquez
A Review on Data-Driven Model-Free Sliding Mode Control
Reprinted from: *Algorithms* 2024, 17, 543, https://doi.org/10.3390/a17120543 7

Fengwei Jing, Fenghe Li, Yong Song, Jie Li, Zhanbiao Feng and Jin Guo
Root Cause Tracing Using Equipment Process Accuracy Evaluation for Looper in Hot Rolling
Reprinted from: *Algorithms* 2024, 17, 102, https://doi.org/10.3390/a17030102 36

Borut Buchmeister and Natasa Vujica Herzog
Advancements in Data Analysis for the Work-Sampling Method
Reprinted from: *Algorithms* 2024, 17, 183, https://doi.org/10.3390/a17050183 55

Jaciel David Hernandez-Resendiz, Edgar Tello-Leal and Marcos Sepúlveda
A Data-Driven Approach to Discovering Process Choreography
Reprinted from: *Algorithms* 2024, 17, 188, https://doi.org/10.3390/a17050188 72

Wen Ying, Zhaohui Wang, Hui Li, Sheng Du and Man Zhao
Intelligent Ship Scheduling and Path Planning Method for Maritime Emergency Rescue
Reprinted from: *Algorithms* 2024, 17, 197, https://doi.org/10.3390/a17050197 94

Tarik Zarrouk, Mohammed Nouari, Jamal-Eddine Salhi, Mohammed Abbadi and Ahmed Abbadi
Three-Dimensional Finite Element Modeling of Ultrasonic Vibration-Assisted Milling of the Nomex Honeycomb Structure
Reprinted from: *Algorithms* 2024, 17, 204, https://doi.org/10.3390/a17050204 104

João Pedro Costa Violante, Marcela A. G. Machado, Amanda dos Santos Mendes and Túlio S. Almeida
An Interface to Monitor Process Variability Using the Binomial ATTRIVAR SS Control Chart
Reprinted from: *Algorithms* 2024, 17, 216, https://doi.org/10.3390/a17050216 118

Guangqiang Tian and Fuzhong Wang
Data-Driven Load Frequency Control for Multi-Area Power System Based on Switching Method under Cyber Attacks
Reprinted from: *Algorithms* 2024, 17, 233, https://doi.org/10.3390/a17060233 131

Bishwajit Dey, Gulshan Sharma and Pitshou N. Bokoro
A Novel Hybrid Crow Search Arithmetic Optimization Algorithm for Solving Weighted Combined Economic Emission Dispatch with Load-Shifting Practice
Reprinted from: *Algorithms* 2024, 17, 313, https://doi.org/10.3390/a17070313 147

Andrés Tobón, Carlos Andrés Ramos-Paja, Martha Lucía Orozco-Gutíerrez, Andrés Julián Saavedra-Montes and Sergio Ignacio Serna-Garcés
Adaptive Sliding-Mode Controller for a Zeta Converter to Provide High-Frequency Transients in Battery Applications
Reprinted from: *Algorithms* 2024, 17, 319, https://doi.org/10.3390/a17070319 176

Amalia Moutsopoulou, Markos Petousis, Georgios E. Stavroulakis, Anastasios Pouliezos and Nectarios Vidakis
Novelty in Intelligent Controlled Oscillations in Smart Structures
Reprinted from: *Algorithms* **2024**, *17*, 505, https://doi.org/10.3390/a17110505 . . . . **201**

Wentao Xu, Jin Qian, Yueyang Wu, Shaowei Yan, Yongling Ni and Guangjin Yang
A VIKOR-Based Sequential Three-Way Classification Ranking Method
Reprinted from: *Algorithms* **2024**, *17*, 530, https://doi.org/10.3390/a17110530 . . . . **224**

About the Editors

Li Jin

Li Jin received a B.S. in Automation and a Ph.D. in Control Science and Engineering from China University of Geosciences, Wuhan, China, in 2016 and 2021, respectively. She was a joint Ph.D. student with the Department of Electrical Engineering and Electronics, University of Liverpool, Liverpool, U.K., from 2018 to 2020. She was a Postdoctoral Fellow in Control Science and Engineering, China University of Geosciences, Wuhan, China, from 2022 to 2024. She is currently a Professor at the School of Automation, China University of Geosciences, Wuhan, China. Her current research interests include power system stability analysis and control, time-delay systems, and robust theory and application.

Sheng Du

Sheng Du received a B.S. in Measurement & Control Technology and Instruments and a Ph.D. in Control Science and Engineering from China University of Geosciences, Wuhan, China, in 2016 and 2021, respectively. He was a joint Ph.D. student with the Department of Electrical and Computer Engineering, University of Alberta, Edmonton, Canada, from 2019 to 2021. He was a Postdoctoral Fellow in Control Science and Engineering, China University of Geosciences, Wuhan, China, from 2021 to 2023. He is currently a Professor with the School of Automation, China University of Geosciences, Wuhan, China. His research interests include process control, intelligent control, intelligent optimization, computational intelligence, and artificial intelligence. Dr. Du is a Senior Member of the Chinese Association of Automation (CAA) and a winner of the Outstanding Doctoral Thesis Nomination Award of the CAA. He is an Associate Editor of Measurement and Control.

Zixin Huang

Zixin Huang received his B.S. and M.S. in engineering from Wuhan Textile University, Wuhan, China, in 2013 and 2016, respectively; received his Ph.D. from the School of Automation, China University of Geosciences, Wuhan, China, in 2020; and became a postdoctoral fellow at Nankai University, Tianjin, China, in 2023. He is currently a postdoctoral fellow with Shanghai Jiao Tong University, Shanghai, China. He is a senior visiting scholar at the University of Science and Technology of China, Anhui, China. He is currently an associate professor with the School of Electrical and Information Engineering, Wuhan Institute of Technology. His current research interests include nonlinear system control and intelligent control. Dr. Huang is a senior member of the Chinese Association of Automation.

Xiongbo Wan

Xiongbo Wan received a B.S. in information and computing science from Huazhong Agricultural University, Wuhan, China, in 2006, an M.S. in probability theory and mathematical statistics, and a Ph.D. in control theory and engineering from Huazhong University of Science and Technology, Wuhan, in 2008 and 2011, respectively. From 2012 to 2013, he was a Visiting Scholar with Akita Prefectural University, Akita, Japan. From 2011 to 2014, he was a Lecturer and then an Associate Professor with the College of Engineering, Huazhong Agricultural University. From 2016 to 2017, he was a Visiting Scholar with the Department of Computer Science, Brunel University London, Uxbridge, U.K. Since 2015, he has been with the China University of Geosciences, Wuhan, where he is currently a Professor with the School of Automation. His research interests include fault diagnosis, state estimation, and model predictive control of complex industrial systems.

Editorial

Recent Progress in Data-Driven Intelligent Modeling and Optimization Algorithms for Industrial Processes

Sheng Du [1,2,3], Zixin Huang [4], Li Jin [1,2,3],* and Xiongbo Wan [1,2,3]

1. School of Automation, China University of Geosciences, Wuhan 430074, China; dusheng@cug.edu.cn (S.D.); xbwan23@cug.edu.cn (X.W.)
2. Hubei Key Laboratory of Advanced Control and Intelligent Automation for Complex Systems, Wuhan 430074, China
3. Engineering Research Center of Intelligent Technology for Geo-Exploration, Ministry of Education, Wuhan 430074, China
4. School of Electrical and Information Engineering, Wuhan Institute of Technology, Wuhan 430205, China; huangzx@wit.edu.cn
* Correspondence: jinli@cug.edu.cn

Abstract: This editorial discusses recent progress in data-driven intelligent modeling and optimization algorithms for industrial processes. With the advent of Industry 4.0, the amalgamation of sophisticated data analytics, machine learning, and artificial intelligence has become pivotal, unlocking new horizons in production efficiency, sustainability, and quality assurance. Contributions to this Special Issue highlight innovative research in advancements in work-sampling data analysis, data-driven process choreography discovery, intelligent ship scheduling for maritime rescue, process variability monitoring, hybrid optimization algorithms for economic emission dispatches, and intelligent controlled oscillations in smart structures. These studies collectively contribute to the body of knowledge on data-driven intelligent modeling and optimization, offering practical solutions and theoretical frameworks to address complex industrial challenges.

Keywords: data-driven modeling; industrial processes; machine learning algorithms; optimization algorithms; adaptive learning

1. Introduction

As industrial systems become increasingly complex, traditional mechanistic modeling methods are struggling to address the significant challenges posed by modern production processes. This is especially true for systems characterized by strong multivariable coupling, nonlinearity, and time-variance, where the limitations of expert-based and traditional modeling methods have become increasingly evident. As a result, data-driven modeling approaches have gradually become the focus of research. By mining the vast amounts of data embedded in industrial production processes and combining data-driven models with optimization algorithms, the real-time monitoring, state prediction, control, optimization scheduling, and fault diagnosis of industrial processes can be achieved. This provides solid technical support for the intelligent transformation of modern manufacturing, while ensuring the stability of production processes and product quality [1–3].

Traditional data-driven modeling and optimization algorithms primarily include multivariate statistical methods and machine learning models. Multivariate statistical methods, such as the use of one-way ANOVA for the detection of abnormalities in the sintering process [4] and Gaussian process regression for performance prediction in sintering [5], establish statistically based models to provide reliable decision support for industrial operations. With the rapid development of technologies such as big data, cloud computing, and the Internet of Things, researchers have become increasingly interested in the application of machine learning models in industrial production. Examples include resource allocation decision support systems that combine multi-objective optimization and meta-learning [6], artificial neural network optimization for solar energy multi-supply systems [7], and dynamic compressive strength prediction models for freeze–thaw rock based on a swarm intelligence optimization of hybrid support vector regression [8]. Machine learning has significant advantages in handling complex, dynamically changing data by automatically learning and adapting to different data patterns.

As modern industry continues to advance toward automation and intelligence, advanced artificial intelligence techniques, such as deep learning, reinforcement learning, and ensemble learning, have become mainstream in data-driven intelligent modeling. Examples include the development of optimal control strategies for nonlinear industrial production systems using spatiotemporal graph convolutional networks [9] and reinforcement learning [10], as well as bearing fault detection methods using convolutional neural networks [11] and sintering endpoint prediction models [12]. Artificial intelligence methods are highly effective in processing high-dimensional, nonlinear, temporal, and dynamically changing data. They possess strong feature extraction and learning capabilities, enabling them to adapt to real-time and complex optimization problems in big data environments.

Moreover, hybrid methods combining physical models with data-driven models can effectively integrate the advantages of physical models in causal analysis with the efficiency of data-driven methods in correlation analysis. For example, seismic damage prediction methods using finite element calculations in conjunction with multi-particle swarm optimization algorithms [13], integrated machine learning methods combined with physics-based empirical models for ship operation status recognition [14], and energy control strategies that combine mechanistic modeling with machine learning [15] all demonstrate the unique advantages of hybrid physical and data-driven models in addressing practical problems.

However, numerous challenges have yet to be addressed, particularly when tackling high-dimensional, nonlinear, and multi-scale industrial problems. Therefore, further research efforts are essential to advance both the theoretical and practical developments in this critical field.

2. An Overview of Published Articles

In the ever-evolving landscape of industrial process modeling and optimization, data-driven intelligent algorithms have emerged as a transformative force. This Special Issue aims to explore the intersection of data-driven approaches, intelligent modeling, and optimization algorithms in the context of industrial processes. With the relentless growth of Industry 4.0, the integration of advanced data analytics, machine learning, and artificial intelligence has become imperative to opening up new possibilities to improve production efficiency, sustainability, and quality assurance in industrial processes.

This Special Issue aims to explore the multifaceted aspects of data-driven intelligent modeling and optimization algorithms for industrial processes. The main objectives are to harness the power of data to improve control, decision making, and parameter optimization, and to drive industrial systems to unprecedented levels of efficiency, reliability, and adaptability. The research areas of this Special Issue include data-driven modeling, intelligent data representation, integration/hybrid modeling, machine learning and optimization, advanced machine learning algorithms, hybrid models with optimization algorithms, adaptive learning algorithms, intelligent process monitoring, real-time data monitoring and analysis, soft sensing technologies, operating mode perception and recognition, decision support systems, intelligent decision support systems, the integration of optimization algorithms, and human–machine collaboration for enhanced decision making.

The analysis of the papers published in this Special Issue is shown in Table 1. A considerable amount of research has been conducted on data-driven modeling and optimization algorithms, covering a wide range of research areas related to automatic control. References [16–19] focus on optimization algorithms in data-driven models, while References [20–22] examine the decision support strategies in industrial production. References [23–25] explore the control strategies, Reference [26] investigates process optimization, and Reference [26] addresses process monitoring.

Table 1. Analysis of the published contributions in the Special Issue.

No.	DOI	Research Area	Focus	Type of Research	Industry	Country
1	10.3390/a17030102	Optimization algorithms	hot strip rolling; looper; production stability; root cause traceability	Mathematical modeling	Manufacturing	China
2	10.3390/a17050204	Process optimization	modeling finite elements; cutting tool; surface quality; stress and strain distribution; chip size	Mathematical modeling	Aerospace	Morocco
3	10.3390/a17070313	Optimization algorithms	combined economic emission dispatch; load shifting; demand side management; crow search algorithm; arithmetic optimization algorithm	Mathematical modeling	Power systems	South Africa
4	10.3390/a17070319	Optimization algorithms	hybrid energy storage system; adaptive sliding-mode controller; battery degradation; supercapacitor; Zeta converter	Mathematical modeling	Power systems	Colombia
5	10.3390/a17050183	Decision support strategies	work sampling; observations; proportions; interdependence between activities	Empirical research	Production management	Slovenia
6	10.3390/a17050188	Decision support strategies	process choreography; data-driven; process mining	Mathematical modeling	Production management	Mexico
7	10.3390/a17110530	Decision support strategies	ideal solution; sequential three-way decisions; muti-attribute decision making	Mathematical modeling	Production management	China
8	10.3390/a17060233	Control strategies	load frequency control; switching system; event-triggered; model-free adaptive control	Mathematical modeling	Power systems	China
9	10.3390/a17110505	Control strategies	vibration; intelligent control; piezoelectric structures; H_2 criterion; H-infinity criterion	Mathematical modeling	Manufacturing	Greece
10	10.3390/a17120543	Control strategies	Sliding mode control; data-driven techniques; intelligent algorithms	Review	Manufacturing	Colombia

Table 1. Cont.

No.	DOI	Research Area	Focus	Type of Research	Industry	Country
11	10.3390/a17050216	Process monitoring	control chart; variability; variance; interface; Shiny package	Mathematical modeling	Manufacturing	Brazil
12	10.3390/a17050204	Optimization algorithms	maritime emergency rescue; intelligent navigation; path planning; A* algorithm; B-spline interpolation; regional search	Mathematical modeling	Maritime rescue	China

It is worth noting that References [16,23,27] all involve the application of fault detection methods. Reference [16] investigates an optimization algorithm for fault tracking in hot rolling processes, using an equipment process accuracy evaluation to trace the root causes of failures. Reference [23] applies data-driven methods to detect faults in power systems and proposes an effective load frequency control strategy to address potential fault scenarios. Reference [27] employs real-time process monitoring techniques to assess fluctuations in the production process and combines these with statistical analysis to provide early warnings for fault detection, ensuring production stability.

References [18,24,25] all involve the application of system control strategies. Reference [18] proposes an effective battery management strategy that uses controllers to mitigate battery aging and manage high-frequency transients. Reference [24] explores the application of intelligent control strategies in piezoelectric structures, employing smart piezoelectric patches and advanced control methods to effectively suppress vibrations in engineering structures. Reference [25] introduces the application of data-driven, model-free sliding mode control techniques.

References [20–22] focus on the application of decision support strategies. Reference [20] presents a data analysis method based on the work sampling technique, studying work activities and their interrelationships in production management and providing decision-makers with more accurate production optimization tools. Reference [21] helps production managers optimize workflows by discovering the process choreography. Reference [22] proposes a sequential three-way classification ranking method based on the VIKOR method, aiding decision-makers in making optimal choices.

In addition, Reference [19] introduces real-time monitoring in maritime rescue missions through path planning and intelligent scheduling methods. Reference [26] utilizes finite element modeling to simulate surface quality and stress distribution in the ultrasonic vibration-assisted milling process, optimizing material processing. Reference [17] presents a hybrid crow search arithmetic optimization algorithm for solving the weighted combined economic emission dispatch problem in power systems, optimizing emissions and cost issues in the power scheduling process.

Finally, the industries covered in these studies include manufacturing, power systems, maritime rescue, and aerospace. The authors are mainly from China, but scholars from Slovenia, Mexico, Morocco, Brazil, South Africa, Colombia, and Greece also contributed to our Special Issue.

3. Conclusions

This Editorial presents the latest advancements in data-driven intelligent modeling and optimization algorithms, with a particular focus on the application of cutting-edge methods and technologies in recent years. These powerful intelligent algorithms leverage data for control, decision making, and parameter optimization, driving industrial systems to unprecedented levels of efficiency, reliability, and adaptability. The research indicates that with the rapid development of Industry 4.0, data-driven intelligent modeling and optimization algorithms have become a key driving force in enhancing production efficiency, promoting sustainability, and ensuring product quality.

Funding: This research was funded by the Natural Science Foundation of Wuhan under Grant No. 2024040801020280, the China Postdoctoral Science Foundation under Grant No. 2023M733306, the Hubei Provincial Natural Science Foundation of China under Grant No. 2022CFB582, the 111 Project under Grant No. B17040, and in part by the Fundamental Research Funds for the Central Universities, China University of Geosciences under Grant No. 2021237.

Conflicts of Interest: The authors declare no conflicts of interest.

References

1. Du, S.; Huang, C.; Ma, X.; Fan, H. A review of data-driven intelligent monitoring for geological drilling processes. *Processes* **2024**, *12*, 2478. [CrossRef]
2. Liu, P.; Wang, L.; Ranjan, R.; He, G.; Zhao, L. A survey on active deep learning: From model driven to data driven. *ACM Comput. Surv.* **2022**, *54*, 1–34. [CrossRef]
3. Zheng, Z.; Wang, F.; Gong, G.; Yang, H.; Han, D. Intelligent technologies for construction machinery using data-driven methods. *Autom. Constr.* **2023**, *147*, 104711. [CrossRef]
4. Du, S.; Ma, X.; Wu, M.; Cao, W.; Pedrycz, W. Time series anomaly detection via rectangular information granulation for sintering process. *IEEE Trans. Fuzzy Syst.* **2024**, *32*, 4799–4804. [CrossRef]
5. Du, S.; Wu, M.; Chen, L.; Jin, L.; Cao, W.; Pedrycz, W. Operating performance improvement based on prediction and grade assessment for sintering process. *IEEE Trans. Cybern.* **2022**, *52*, 10529–10541. [CrossRef]
6. Mahmoodi, E.; Fathi, M.; Tavana, M.; Ghobakhloo, M.; Ng, A.H. Data-driven simulation-based decision support system for resource allocation in Industry 4.0 and smart manufacturing. *J. Manuf. Syst.* **2024**, *72*, 287–307. [CrossRef]
7. Yang, C.; Nutakki, T.U.K.; Alghassab, M.A.; Alkhalaf, S.; Alturise, F.; Alharbi, F.S.; Elmasry, Y.; Abdullaev, S. Optimized integration of solar energy and liquefied natural gas regasification for sustainable urban development: Dynamic modeling, data-driven optimization, and case study. *J. Clean. Prod.* **2024**, *447*, 141405. [CrossRef]
8. Zhou, S.; Zhang, Z.X.; Luo, X.; Huang, Y.; Yu, Z.; Yang, X. Predicting dynamic compressive strength of frozen-thawed rocks by characteristic impedance and data-driven methods. *J. Rock Mech. Geotech. Eng.* **2024**, *16*, 2591–2606. [CrossRef]
9. Chi, Z.; Chen, X.; Xia, H.; Liu, C.; Wang, Z. An adaptive control system based on spatial–temporal graph convolutional and disentangled baseline-volatility prediction of bellows temperature for iron ore sintering process. *J. Process Control* **2024**, *140*, 103254. [CrossRef]
10. Mattera, G.; Caggiano, A.; Nele, L. Optimal data-driven control of manufacturing processes using reinforcement learning: An application to wire arc additive manufacturing. *J. Intell. Manuf.* **2024**. [CrossRef]
11. Mahesh, T.R.; Chandrasekaran, S.; Ram, V.A.; Kumar, V.V.; Vivek, V.; Guluwadi, S. Data-driven intelligent condition adaptation of feature extraction for bearing fault detection using deep responsible active learning. *IEEE Access* **2024**, *12*, 45381–45397. [CrossRef]
12. Chen, X.; Liu, C.; Xia, H.; Chi, Z. Burn-through point prediction and control based on multi-cycle dynamic spatio-temporal feature extraction. *Control Eng. Pract.* **2025**, *154*, 106165. [CrossRef]
13. Sun, B.; Guo, T. Mechanism-driven and data-driven fusion prediction of seismic damage evolution of concrete structures based on cooperative multi-particle swarm optimization. *Eng. Appl. Artif. Intell.* **2024**, *133*, 108659. [CrossRef]
14. Zeng, X.; Chen, M.; Li, H.; Wu, X. A data-driven intelligent energy efficiency management system for ships. *IEEE Intell. Transp. Syst. Mag.* **2022**, *15*, 270–284. [CrossRef]
15. Cai, Q.; Luo, X.; Wang, P.; Gao, C.; Zhao, P. Hybrid model-driven and data-driven control method based on machine learning algorithm in energy hub and application. *Appl. Energy* **2022**, *305*, 117913. [CrossRef]
16. Jing, F.; Li, F.; Song, Y.; Li, J.; Feng, Z.; Guo, J. Root Cause Tracing Using Equipment Process Accuracy Evaluation for Looper in Hot Rolling. *Algorithms* **2024**, *17*, 102. [CrossRef]
17. Dey, B.; Sharma, G.; Bokoro, P. A Novel Hybrid Crow Search Arithmetic Optimization Algorithm for Solving Weighted Combined Economic Emission Dispatch with Load-Shifting Practice. *Algorithms* **2024**, *17*, 313. [CrossRef]
18. Tobón, A.; Ramos-Paja, C.; Orozco-Gutíerrez, M.; Saavedra-Montes, A.; Serna-Garcés, S. Adaptive Sliding-Mode Controller for a Zeta Converter to Provide High-Frequency Transients in Battery Applications. *Algorithms* **2024**, *17*, 319. [CrossRef]
19. Ying, W.; Wang, Z.; Li, H.; Du, S.; Zhao, M. Intelligent Ship Scheduling and Path Planning Method for Maritime Emergency Rescue. *Algorithms* **2024**, *17*, 197. [CrossRef]
20. Buchmeister, B.; Herzog, N. Advancements in Data Analysis for the Work-Sampling Method. *Algorithms* **2024**, *17*, 183. [CrossRef]
21. Hernandez-Resendiz, J.; Tello-Leal, E.; Sepúlveda, M. A Data-Driven Approach to Discovering Process Choreography. *Algorithms* **2024**, *17*, 188. [CrossRef]
22. Xu, W.; Qian, J.; Wu, Y.; Yan, S.; Ni, Y.; Yang, G. A VIKOR-Based Sequential Three-Way Classification Ranking Method. *Algorithms* **2024**, *17*, 530. [CrossRef]

23. Tian, G.; Wang, F. Data-Driven Load Frequency Control for Multi-Area Power System Based on Switching Method under Cyber Attacks. *Algorithms* **2024**, *17*, 233. [CrossRef]
24. Moutsopoulou, A.; Petousis, M.; Stavroulakis, G.; Pouliezos, A.; Vidakis, N. Novelty in Intelligent Controlled Oscillations in Smart Structures. *Algorithms* **2024**, *17*, 505. [CrossRef]
25. Castellanos-Cárdenas, D.; Posada, N.L.; Orozco-Duque, A.; Sepúlveda-Cano, L.M.; Castrillón, F.; Camacho, O.; Vásquez, R.E. A Review on Data-Driven Model-Free Sliding Mode Control. *Algorithms* **2024**, *17*, 543. [CrossRef]
26. Zarrouk, T.; Nouari, M.; Salhi, J.; Abbadi, M.; Abbadi, A. Three-Dimensional Finite Element Modeling of Ultrasonic Vibration-Assisted Milling of the Nomex Honeycomb Structure. *Algorithms* **2024**, *17*, 204. [CrossRef]
27. Violante, J.; Machado, M.; Mendes, A.; Almeida, T. An Interface to Monitor Process Variability Using the Binomial ATTRIVAR SS Control Chart. *Algorithms* **2024**, *17*, 216. [CrossRef]

Disclaimer/Publisher's Note: The statements, opinions and data contained in all publications are solely those of the individual author(s) and contributor(s) and not of MDPI and/or the editor(s). MDPI and/or the editor(s) disclaim responsibility for any injury to people or property resulting from any ideas, methods, instructions or products referred to in the content.

Review

A Review on Data-Driven Model-Free Sliding Mode Control

Duby Castellanos-Cárdenas [1,*], Norha L. Posada [2], Andrés Orozco-Duque [1], Lina M. Sepúlveda-Cano [3], Fabio Castrillón [2], Oscar E. Camacho [4] and Rafael E. Vásquez [2]

[1] Faculty of Engineering, Universidad de Medellín, Carrera 87 # 30-65, Medellín 050026, Colombia; aforozco@udemedellin.edu.co

[2] School of Engineering, Universidad Pontificia Bolivariana, Circular 1 # 70-01, Medellín 050031, Colombia; norha.posada@upb.edu.co (N.L.P.); fabio.castrillon@upb.edu.co (F.C.); rafael.vasquez@upb.edu.co (R.E.V.)

[3] Business School, Universidad EAFIT, Carrera 49 # Calle 7 Sur-50, Medellín 050022, Colombia; lmsepulvec@eafit.edu.co

[4] Colegio de Ciencias e Ingenierías "El Politécnico", Universidad San Francisco de Quito USFQ, Quito 170157, Ecuador; ocamacho@usfq.edu.ec

* Correspondence: dcastellanos@udemedellin.edu.co; Tel.: +57-604-5904870 (ext. 11012)

Abstract: Sliding mode control (SMC) has been widely used to control linear and nonlinear dynamics systems because of its robustness against parametric uncertainties and matched disturbances. Although SMC design has traditionally addressed process model-based approaches, the rapid advancements in instrumentation and control systems driven by Industry 4.0, coupled with the increased complexity of the controlled processes, have led to the growing acceptance of controllers based on data-driven techniques. This review article aims to explore the landscape of SMC, focusing specifically on data-driven techniques through a comprehensive systematic literature review that includes a bibliometric analysis of relevant documents and a cumulative production model to estimate the deceleration point of the scientific production of this topic. The most used SMC schemes and their integration with data-driven techniques and intelligent algorithms, including identifying the leading applications, are presented.

Keywords: sliding mode control; data-driven techniques; systematic literature review; intelligent algorithms; applications

1. Introduction

Sliding mode control (SMC) has been applied in diverse fields, including engineering disciplines such as mechanical, electrical, chemical, electronics, and telecommunications, and topics such as robotics, chaos theory, power converters, etc. [1–4]. Despite being a technique whose origins date back to the 1950s [5,6], sliding mode control continues to be of interest to the scientific community [1,7,8].

SMC has been recognized for its robustness, especially in complex nonlinear systems; insensitivity to unmodeled uncertainties and external disturbances; utilization of reduced-order sliding mode equations; zero-error convergence in closed-loop systems; and simplicity of implementation [9,10]. Likewise, SMC has shown its ability to efficiently manage systems characterized by the features mentioned above, outperforming other control techniques like $H\infty$, backstepping control, and proportional–integral–derivative (PID) controller [1,2,10,11]. Furthermore, it has been successfully applied to control time-varying systems [12–14].

The main obstacle to applying a sliding mode strategy is chattering [1,7,15,16]. This phenomenon results in high-frequency oscillations with finite amplitude generated by imperfections in switching devices, unmodeled dynamics, and the discrete-time implementation of the control strategy [1,8,15]. It should be noted that chattering can be detrimental to the performance of processes that require smooth and oscillation-free control action [2,17].

The design of SMC can be addressed using the model-based or model-free approach. Although model-based control (MBC) has been the predominant framework, it has limitations, such as dependence on a plant model, which, in many cases, becomes a time-consuming task, especially when dealing with complex or nonlinear systems [18,19]. Furthermore, the system modeling process is always subject to a modeling error that directly affects the performance of MBC [18–20]. On the other hand, MBC can become inefficient when dealing with disturbances and scenarios not considered during the design stage [19,21]. The model-based SMC design is illustrated in Figure 1.

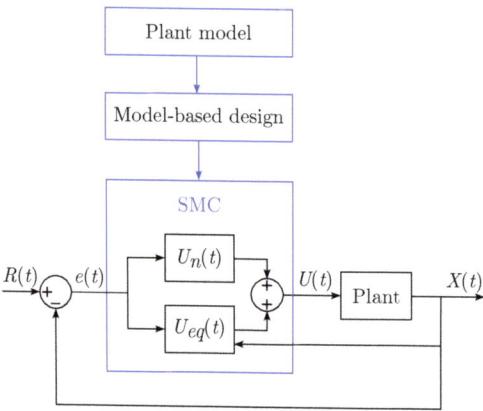

Figure 1. Model-based SMC design.

In contrast, the model-free control (MFC) approach, which operates without explicit system models, has emerged as a viable alternative to mitigate the inherent limitations of MBC. The above is mainly due to its adaptability in formulating control laws and its ability to leverage the advancements of Industry 4.0, which has substantially increased the number of interconnected instruments that provide a large amount of information in real time [18,19,22–25]. Nonetheless, this approach presents certain drawbacks concerning stability, convergence analysis, and computational overhead during controller implementation [19,26]. Despite these challenges, integrating MFC and MBC frameworks can enhance the overall performance of the control system, using the strengths of both methodologies and offering a promising option to address the shortcomings while taking advantage of the benefits of each technique [18,19].

The data-driven framework encompasses process modeling, controller design, and performance evaluation tasks, assuming high data availability [19,27,28]. Two of the most prominent data-driven control strategies are model predictive and adaptive control [21,29–32]. Model predictive control (MPC) was devised to employ dynamic models to forecast the future behavior of the process and optimize the variable manipulated under process constraints, distinct from predictive control based on raw data for prediction, avoiding the need for an explicit model of process [32,33]. Otherwise, adaptive control embraces a set of techniques that can learn and dynamically adjust the control strategy based on the measured plant data [29,30]. Some versions of model-based adaptive control rely on a plant or a disturbance model, while data-driven adaptive control only requires the measurements obtained from the system [21,29]. In addition, there are other data-driven control techniques, such as model-free schemes. The iPID (intelligent PID) controller is a designation for model-free controllers that incorporate elements of the traditional PID controller, including iterative feedback tuning [21,34–36], and hybrid schemes, such as the proposal by Rsetam et al. [37], which combined an active disturbance rejection controller SMC with nonlinear gains that are a function of the tracking error and an adaptive extended state observer for temperature regulation in an electric furnace. Nevertheless, this article emphasizes adaptive, predictive, iPID, and model-free schemes because they are frequently found in reviewed articles.

MFC exploits the measured input–output data of the process for the controller designing, and it does not concern the dynamics process since it treats it as a black box [19,21,28,29,38]. MFC can be designed through a training process employing machine learning techniques, learning from plant behavior, and using approximate dynamic programming or reinforcement learning. Consequently, intelligent algorithms, including neural networks, optimization algorithms, and fuzzy systems, are strongly connected to data-driven techniques [19,28,29]. Regarding SMC based on a model-free approach, there are several proposals for different sliding mode schemes, each offering unique insights and methodologies [39–45]. Moreover, optimization and learning algorithms have gained attention in SMC research due to improving controller performance and adaptability under various process operating conditions [46–49]. Furthermore, adaptive techniques, which allow controllers to adjust to system uncertainties and variations, and predictive strategies, have been integrated into SMC frameworks [50–55]. Moreover, incorporating observers has enhanced SMC design and performance, facilitating state estimation and feedback control in real-time applications [56–58]. Figure 2 illustrates the fundamental structure of SMC design in a model-free framework. Unlike traditional SMC approaches, this method does not rely on a mathematical model of the system. Instead, it utilizes input–output data from the process and the reference signal to formulate the control law.

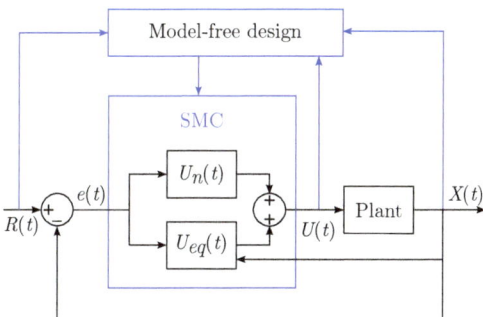

Figure 2. Model-free SMC design.

The theory and applications of SMC have been documented in recent surveys. Gambhire et al. [10] focused on terminal SMC (TSMC) combined with intelligent and adaptive schemes, addressing some examples of SMC applications. Xiao et al. [59] contributed a comprehensive review article, essentially serving as a tutorial for the development of sliding mode predictive control, a hybrid control strategy taking advantage of the strengths of both MPC and SMC. Furthermore, Hamza et al. [60] explored hybrid control systems that incorporate fuzzy logic systems, computational intelligence algorithms, and SMC. On the other hand, George et al. [61] provided an overview of SMC based on an adaptive neuro-fuzzy inference system (ANFIS) for nonlinear systems and that it helps to limit high-frequency chattering. Yu et al. [62] presented a complete review of the theory and applications of TSMC, examining the technical aspects and the challenges and future opportunities of TSMC in the context of technologies such as cyber–physical, artificial intelligence, and networking systems.

There are SMC review articles that examine specific applications or processes. Some of these articles explore using SMC in networked control systems, highlighting SMC schemes designed to handle challenges such as time delays, packet losses, quantization, uncertainty, and disturbances [63,64]. In another line, it is possible to find works that address the application of sliding mode surfaces in the design of observers and controllers for synchronous motors [65–68]. Another area of interest is using SMC in treating photovoltaic systems and power converters [69–72]. Pilloni et al. [73] presented the characteristics of variable structure control with sliding modes to design robust consensus controllers for multi-agent systems using nonsmooth analysis tools. Riaz et al. [74] described the advantages and disadvantages of SMC and discussed the chattering problem while reviewing SMC in the field of fault-tolerant control. Liu et al. [75] presented the advances in research and development of switched systems, combining them with SMC, which allows researchers to work with complex and changing systems, improving their efficiency and stability. Mat-Noh et al. [76] reviewed advances in SMC in autonomous underwater vehicles.

To the best of our knowledge, there is currently no comprehensive review specifically addressing data-driven approaches within the context of sliding mode control (SMC). This work aims to fill this gap by providing an extensive overview of trends and developments in data-driven sliding mode control (DDSMC) techniques. The key contributions of this research are as follows:

1. A detailed bibliometric analysis is carried out, highlighting publication trends and introducing a cumulative production model that predicts both the deceleration point in scientific output and the stabilization point for research in DDSMC. This offers valuable foresight into the evolution of this research area.
2. An in-depth identification of the primary applications of SMC enhanced by data-driven techniques is achieved, offering a clearer understanding of how these methods have been successfully applied across various domains.
3. A critical evaluation of the most widely adopted SMC schemes is performed, focusing on their integration with data-driven techniques and intelligent algorithms and thus paving the way for more robust and adaptive control strategies.

This article not only provides practical insights into the most frequently utilized algorithms but also guides researchers and practitioners in balancing simulation-based testing with real-world prototype implementation when choosing control schemes. Moreover, it emphasizes the performance metrics commonly employed, serving as a reference for improving the efficiency and robustness of systems controlled through DDSMC techniques.

This paper is structured as follows: Section 2 introduces the fundamentals of SMC and describes some of the most relevant schemes. Section 3 presents the systematic literature review methodology, and Section 4 shows the findings derived from bibliometric analysis. Section 5 shows the analysis of SMC schemes, applications, and intelligent algorithms under the data-driven framework; the main highlights of the findings are also discussed. Finally, Section 6 provides the conclusions.

2. Preliminaries for Designing a Sliding Mode Controller

This section describes some of the most relevant versions of sliding mode control. From basic concepts to mathematical foundations, the objective is to provide readers with the fundamental information required to deal with SMC theory. Although continuous-time approaches of SMC are explored in more detail, it is important to acknowledge that discrete-time versions of SMC are also highly significant.

2.1. Methodology Principles

The sliding mode control methodology, called variable structure control, is a nonlinear control method. The design of an SMC consists of two steps.

- In the initial stage, a custom surface must be designed. Later, it is called the choice of sliding surface.
- In the second phase, a feedback control must be designed to ensure the convergence of a system's trajectory to the sliding surface; hence, the sliding surface must be achieved in a finite amount of time. The motion of the system on a sliding surface is known as the sliding mode [1].

Once on the sliding surface, the dynamics of the plant is constrained to the equations of the custom surface, and they are robust to internal and external disturbances. Furthermore, they are insensitive to variations in control parameters [1].

To illustrate the methodology, the following parts show the steps to obtain the controller: choosing the sliding surface; determining the control law; and finally, establishing a convergence or reaching condition.

2.1.1. Sliding Surface Choice

Different sliding surfaces have been suggested in the literature, and each one works better for a specific application. The most common way to obtain the sliding regime that guarantees that the state will move toward its reference is to use the following surface variable [1,77,78]:

$$\sigma(t) = \left(\frac{d}{dt} + \lambda\right)^n \int e(t)dt, \qquad (1)$$

where $e(t)$ is the difference between the reference $R(t)$ and the controlled variable $X(t)$, $e(t) = R(t) - X(t)$; the objective of control is to keep the sliding surface at zero. λ is a tuning parameter that determines the performance of the system on the sliding surface, n is the order of the system, and $\sigma(t)$ is the sliding surface chosen by the designer [77,78].

2.1.2. Control Law Determination

The structure of a sliding mode controller consists of two parts: one called the continuous part ($U_{eq}(t)$) and the second one named the discontinuous or nonlinear part $U_n(t)$; hence,

$$U(t) = U_{eq}(t) + U_n(t), \qquad (2)$$

where $U_{eq}(t)$ is obtained from the equivalent control method [6,77] and is used to control the variable on the sliding surface $\sigma(t) = 0$. Moreover, $U_{eq}(t)$ is obtained by combining the previous equation and the process model, which could be expressed by a differential equation such as the following:

$$\frac{dx(t)}{dt} = f(t, x(t), u(t, x(t))), \quad t \in \mathbb{R}, \qquad (3)$$

where $x(t) \in \mathbf{R}^n$ denotes the vector of system states; $u(t) \in \mathbf{R}^m$ represents the vector of control inputs, which depends on time and state, and it can be discontinuous in its arguments but locally bounded; and f is a continue function for simplicity.

Thus, the equivalent control is deduced, considering that the derivative of the surface is zero. Therefore, the sliding condition is given as follows:

$$\frac{d\sigma(t)}{dt} = 0. \qquad (4)$$

Moreover, $U_{eq}(t)$ is derived by combining the previous equation and the process system model. The equivalent control method involves determining a control law that makes the system's dynamics on the sliding surface equivalent to a more straightforward system. It transforms the original system into an equivalent system with simplified dynamics, making it easier to design and analyze the controller. This equivalent system typically exhibits simpler behavior on the sliding surface, facilitating the application of control strategies. In summary, the equivalent control method in sliding mode control aims to simplify the analysis and design of the control law by transforming the system dynamics on the sliding surface into an equivalent and more manageable form.

On the other hand, $U_n(t)$ is the discontinuous control part; it allows the system to reach the sliding surface. $U_n(t)$ incorporates a nonlinear element that includes a switching element of the control law and is given as follows:

$$U_n(t) = K_D \operatorname{sgn}(\sigma(t)). \qquad (5)$$

Finally, K_D is a tuning parameter responsible for the reaching mode.

The chattering phenomenon is the main concern in SMC due to the jumps of the sliding surface [1]. In practice, chattering produces inadmissible effects, such as neglected excitation of system dynamics in modeling, wear-induced vibration of actuators, and performance degradation. Several approaches have been proposed to reduce such effects. One of these possibilities lies in smoothing the nonlinear switching function using soft logistic activation functions, as the sigmoid function preferentially [78]. Therefore, the discontinuous part of the proposed controller uses the sigmoid function as follows:

$$U_n(t) = K_D \frac{\sigma(t)}{|\sigma(t)| + \delta}, \tag{6}$$

where the parameter δ is associated with the chattering effect; because of this, it is necessary to assign an appropriate value.

2.1.3. Convergence Condition

The convergence condition, often known as attractiveness, ensures that the system dynamics will always converge on the sliding surface [1,77]. Formulating a Lyapunov function $V(t) > 0$ with finite energy is necessary. The candidate Lyapunov function is defined as follows:

$$V(t) = 1/2\sigma^2(t). \tag{7}$$

It is sufficient to make sure that the derivative of the function $V(t)$ is negative for it to be possible for the function $V(t)$ to diminish. Therefore, the condition of convergence can be written as follows:

$$\frac{dV(t)}{dt} = \frac{d\sigma(t)}{dt}\sigma(t) < 0. \tag{8}$$

If t is the finite reaching time for the sliding surface, then one can conclude that $t \leq \frac{|\sigma(0)|}{\eta}$ and the sliding surface can be reached [79].

2.2. SMC Schemes

The literature reports different SMC schemes that address the main problems of this type of controller. Some of the most important ones are presented below.

2.2.1. Higher-Order Sliding Mode Control

In a higher-order sliding mode (HOSM), the control input drives the sliding variable and its $(r-1)$ initial higher-order derivatives to zero, acting discontinuously on the r-th time derivative of the sliding function [1,80]. The parameter r is called the sliding mode order and is defined as the relative degree of the sliding function with respect to the control variable. The case $r = 1$ corresponds to the well-known first-order SMC; for $r > 1$, it is considered a HOSM [81,82].

HOSMC helps face the disadvantages of first-order SMC; therefore, its use reduces chattering, eliminates the restriction of relative degree, reaches the finite-time converge and improves sample time accuracy for discrete implementations [1,80,83]. However, implementing HOSMC requires knowing the values of the sliding variable and its derivatives to $r - 1$ order; for this reason, it has been necessary to design accurate and robust differentiators to determine the correct value of derivatives [84,85].

One of the most well-known HOSM algorithms is super-twisting, a second-order SMC [1,86–88]. When a super-twisting controller (STC) is used for relative degree systems equal to one, the continuous control action reduces the chattering effects [85,88]. However, some variants of STC, such as the integral SMC (ISMC), allow the STC to be extended to systems of an arbitrary relative degree [89]. The ISMC eliminates the reaching phase and drives nominal controllers, usually designed without considering uncertainties, to improve robustness against matched disturbances [87].

The design of the SMC of $r > 3$ becomes a more challenging task due to the order of the system [81,82]. To implement HOSMC, it is necessary to know only the relative degree and derivative boundaries of the system [82,84]; due to this, the concept of black-box HOSM arises [82,90,91].

Despite the advantages of the HOSMC, it is important to consider that its performance can be affected by unmodeled dynamics and disturbances. Hence, for some systems, a first-order SMC can achieve better results than a HOSMC, benefiting from the simplicity of the former [83].

2.2.2. Terminal SMC

TSMC originated in terminal attractor theory, a nonlinear term with fractional power included in the sliding function [2,62]. Unlike the classic SMC, TSMC provides fast finite-time convergence to the origin for continuous-time controllers and robustness against uncertainties [2,62,92]. Ref. [93] introduced TSMC for second-order systems, which developed a controller for a rigid links robot based on second-order systems. Consider the next single-input affine system [62]:

$$\dot{\mathbf{x}} = \mathbf{f}(\mathbf{x},t) + \mathbf{b}(\mathbf{x},t)u + \lambda(\mathbf{x},t), \quad (9)$$

where $\mathbf{x} \in \mathbb{R}^n$ is the system state, $u \in \mathbb{R}$ is the control law, $\mathbf{b}(\mathbf{x},t) \neq 0$, and $\lambda(\mathbf{x},t) \in \mathbb{R}^n$ lumps internal uncertainties and external disturbances. The sliding function defined by the authors and used subsequently in other studies [10,62,94,95] was as follows:

$$\sigma(\mathbf{x},t) = \frac{d\mathbf{x}(t)}{dt} + \beta |\mathbf{x}(t)|^\lambda \operatorname{sgn}(\mathbf{x}(t)), \quad (10)$$

where $\beta > 0$, and $0 < \lambda < 1$. For $x(0) \neq 0$ and $\sigma = 0$ the sliding dynamics reaches the $x = 0$ equilibrium point in the time given by

$$t_{eq} = \beta^{-1}(1-\lambda)^{-1}|x(0)|^{1-\lambda}. \quad (11)$$

Nonsingular TSMC (NTSMC) was designed to address singularity problems that can arise when the sliding surface derivative exhibits negative powers, leading to a controller that cannot be implemented [10,62]. In the case of systems of one relative degree, a modification was introduced in (10) by incorporating the integral of the fractional power term to address the singularity issue presented in the TSMC; this version is called integral TSMC (ITSMC) [62,96].

On the other hand, both NTSMC and TSMC have a slow convergence rate when the states are far from the equilibrium point [10,97]. For this reason, the fast TSMC (FTSMC) was introduced to reduce the convergence time [10,62]. Furthermore, TSMC was extended to high-order systems arising higher-order TSMC (HOTSMC) [98,99].

The characteristics of each TSMC have been combined in different studies to take advantage of their strengths and deal with complex dynamics [58,100–102]. However, the design of terminal sliding mode observers and controllers is more challenging than classical SMC due to the nonlinearity of the terminal sliding mode function, as well as the control of multi-input–multi-output (MIMO) systems, the optimal tuning of TSMC parameters, and its implementation [62].

2.2.3. Fractional-Order SMC

Fractional-order calculus extends the derivative and integration operations to fractional exponents [103,104]. It has been widely used for the design of control systems and process modeling [103,105–107]. Fractional-order controllers provide designers with flexibility in choosing a fractional power order and additional parameters for the tuning process that can enhance performance and robustness concerning integer-order controllers [105,107]. Regarding fractional-order models, they can obtain better approximations of processes that exhibit inherent fractional-order behavior, for instance, phenomena of viscoelasticity, chaos systems, robotics, cell diffusion process, voltage–current relation of semi-infinite transmission lines, fractals, resonant systems, HIV infection resistance, chemical processes, etc. [104–106,108,109].

Thanks to the advances in computational tools, the number of fractional-order controllers has increased in automatic control systems with a high degree of complexity [106,107]. The most common structures of fractional-order controllers include combinations such as integer order plant and controller, integer order plant and fractional-order controller, fractional-order plant and IO controller, and fractional-order plant and controller [105]. Moreover, fractional-order controller design can be approached from both the time and frequency domains, where the time domain uses optimization techniques more frequently. In contrast, the frequency domain methods are based on $H\infty$ norm, isodamping, and loop-shaping [105].

Various fractional-order control strategies have been documented, such as Tilted Integral Derivative (TID) controllers [110–113], CRONE (Contrôle Robuste d'Ordre Non-Entier translating to non-integer robust control in French) controllers [114–117], fractional-order PID controller [118–121], fractional-order lead–leag compensators [122–124]. Additionally, there are proposals for fractional-order adaptive controllers based on model reference, fuzzy systems, and neural networks, among others [125–129].

Within the field fractional-order SMC (FOSMC), the fractional order can be approached using the sliding surface and switching functions of the fractional order or the derivatives and integrals of the fractional order in the control law [130–132]. Some proposals combine fractional-order HOSMC or TSMC with adaptive techniques, fuzzy and neural network systems, observers, etc. [133–138].

Despite the increasing number of publications on fractional-order controllers [105,107, 139–141], some significant aspects must be considered. The implementation of fractional-order function models exhibits a higher degree of complexity than IO controllers [105,107,109] due to the memory requirement for fractional-order functions, which need past values of signals, that is, a long memory effect [109,139]. In addition, it is also common to use approximate models of integer order to implement fractional-order transfer function models [105,139]. Furthermore, the mathematical operations and calculations of fractional-order control systems are inherently more complex than those of integer order [97,105,139].

3. Methodology of the Systematic Literature Review

This study followed a four-stage systematic literature review methodology: article search process, definition of inclusion criteria, exhaustive screening of articles, and final selection of articles [142]. The first step in this literature review was to generate the search equation. For this stage, the articles were initially explored to identify the keywords and synonyms related to the topic of interest. The search equation was defined as follows: ((("DATA DRIVEN" OR "MODEL FREE" OR "MODEL INDEPENDENT") AND "SLIDING MODE" AND CONTROL*). This equation was used in two of the most widely used scientific databases for engineering. Scopus and WOS (Web of Science) [143,144]. This process resulted in 812 documents from Scopus and 551 WOS. Duplicate records were removed from the database, resulting in a final set of 747 papers. These articles formed the primary literary space and covered 1992 and 2023.

Given the substantial volume of documents, it became imperative to establish exclusion criteria to delimit the literary space and select the most relevant papers for the analysis; this represented the second stage. Only articles, conference papers, journal-type sources, and English-language publications published after 2018 were considered for this review, resulting in a final dataset that contains 265 documents for analysis.

Subsequently, in the third stage, the quality of the documents was assessed to refine the selection further and reduce the number of articles. The title and abstract of articles were analyzed to discard articles that were not related initially; this process eliminated 23 articles. Following this, the articles underwent a systematic grading process based on their suitability to the research question, methodological quality, accessibility, and citation count, particularly for older articles. For articles published in the early years (2018–2020), a minimum of 10 citations was required. As a result of this full-text screening process, a final set of 116 articles was selected for this study. Figure 3 shows the stages of the systematic literature review methodology.

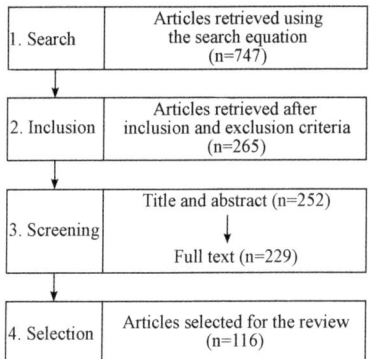

Figure 3. Methodology of systematic literature review.

4. Bibliometric Analysis

The bibliometric analysis allows for extracting relevant information on trends and quantitative data of the research topic through mathematical tools [145–147]. The initial step aligns with the first stage of the systematic literature review methodology, in which a search equation was developed based on identified keywords, yielding a set of 812 documents. The second step involved selecting appropriate scientific bibliographic databases; as previously mentioned, SCOPUS and WoS were chosen. Following this, a data segregation process was implemented to organize, classify, and separate the dataset, resulting in the primary literary space of 747 papers, which included all articles selected for the bibliometric analysis. Subsequently, the Rstudio Bibliometrix package was selected for metadata analysis due to the facilities to develop thematic mapping and analysis, such as clustering; keywords; and the productivity of authors, sources, and institutions, among others [148]. Given the extensive outputs provided by Bibliometrix, the final step was to select the most relevant results for presentation. The methodology of the bibliometric analysis is illustrated in Figure 4.

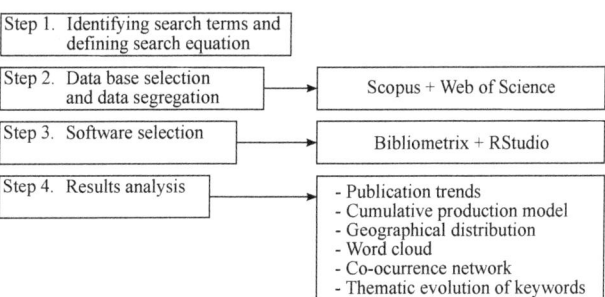

Figure 4. Methodology of bibliometric analysis.

4.1. Publication Trends

This method involves knowing the trends in publication and finding measurable indicators of interest from the academic community [146]. Furthermore, it is interesting to determine whether cumulative production exhibits an exponential growth phase. Once this phase is reached, the number of publications tends to decrease, indicating a potential consolidation process within a technology or research topic under examination [149].

Figure 5 shows the annual production of DDSMC. The yearly count of articles only exceeded the 10-mark threshold after 2008, and most of the articles emerged within the last five years. Furthermore, the exponential trend line exceeds the cumulative growth of the thematic interest production. As a result, a nonlinear regression process was performed to fit a sigmoidal model.

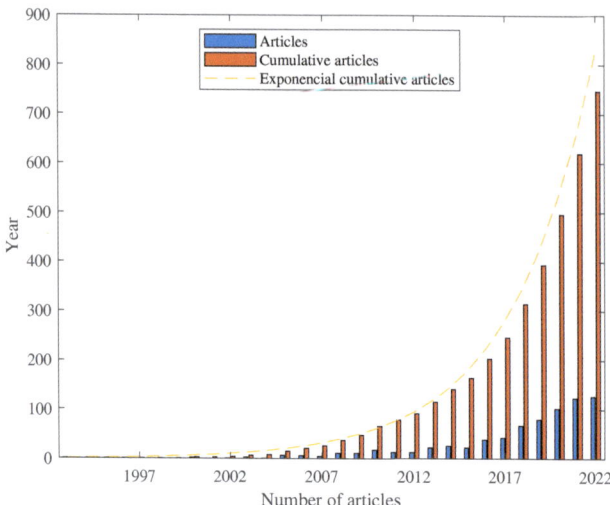

Figure 5. Annual scientific production trend of 747 articles.

S curves are used in the analysis of technology life cycles and innovation. Through these curves, it becomes feasible to estimate the inflection point, providing insight into the current state of technology and the time when production growth starts to decelerate. This information is valuable in determining whether it is an opportune moment to develop products such as patents, software registrations, etc. [150].

The cumulative production was characterized using the three-parameter model given by

$$f(t) = \frac{a}{1 + e^{-\frac{(t - t_0)}{b}}}, \quad (12)$$

where $f(t)$ is the cumulative production function; a represents the upper limit of scientific production, serving as the horizontal asymptote; t is the time measured in years; t_0 is the inflection point; and b is a scale factor. The model parameters for this function were determined using RStudio as follows:

$$f(t) = \frac{2621.22}{1 + e^{-\frac{(t - 2025.75)}{3.99}}}, \quad (13)$$

The model's coefficient of determination was $R^2 = 99.82\%$, and all statistical assumptions regarding the model were verified. Figure 6 shows the extended model until 2070. The model indicates an asymptote of 2621 articles, expected to be reached by 2048. Additionally, the inflection point is estimated to occur around 2026, so the deceleration of scientific production has not yet begun.

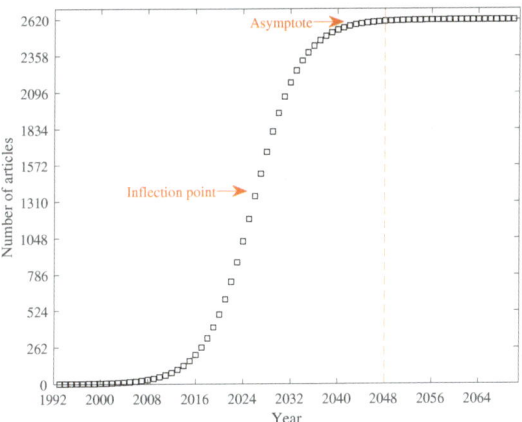

Figure 6. Cumulative production model.

4.2. Analysis of Publications

The Bibliometrix package in R simplifies conducting a comprehensive analysis of the document dataset, enabling the identification of key concepts and terms that frequently appear in elements such as the title, abstract, and body of each article [145,148]. This analysis reveals research trends and provides insight into the evolving dynamics of the topic of interest over time [145,146].

The relationships between terms are visualized in the co-occurrence network in Figure 7. There are five main nodes, each uniquely identified by a different color. The purple node represents core concepts of sliding mode control, integrating terms like robustness, neural networks, and finite-time convergence. The green node highlights data-driven control techniques, including model-free adaptive control and prescribed performance. Meanwhile, the blue node focuses on model-free control approaches, linked to tracking control and sliding mode observers. The red node groups topics related to time-delay estimation and adaptive control strategies.

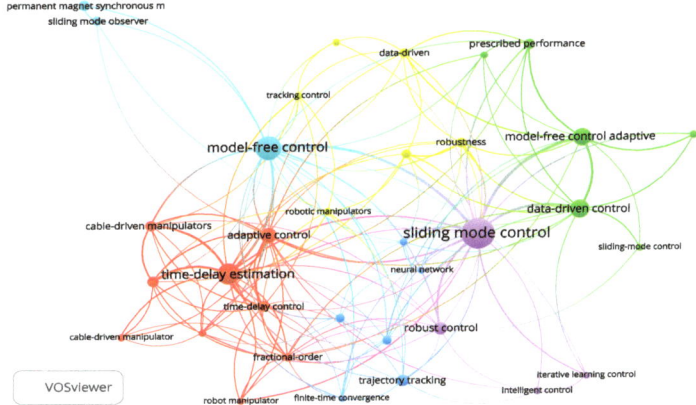

Figure 7. Co-occurrence network of keyword plus. Performed with VOSviewer 1.6.20.

The thematic evolution graph facilitates the construction of a historical context by delineating keyword relationships over a specific time frame. This information identifies emerging research topics and discerning temporal trends [145]. The analysis was segmented into four periods, a shown in Figure 8. The initial period involved the design of the control system based on the mathematical model. In the second period, the focus shifted to model-free control techniques, alongside a focus on SMC and robust control, mainly applied to vehicles. The third period spotlighted SMC and tracking control, with additional attention on topics such as adaptive control, the design of sliding mode observers, and higher-order SMC. The most recent period, the fourth, showcased diversified research interests, emphasizing topics such as terminal sliding mode, optimization methods, discrete-time controller design, and the development of controllers for disturbance rejection and fail detection systems.

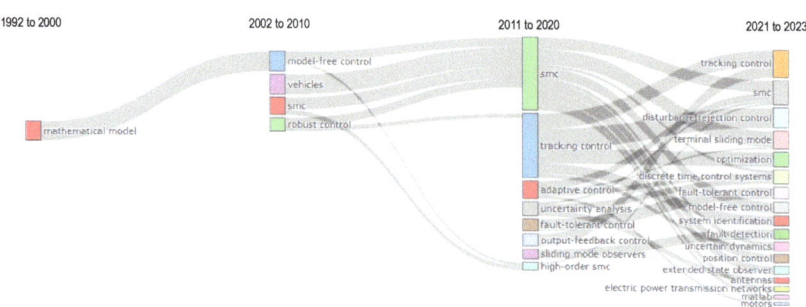

Figure 8. Thematic evolution of keyword plus.

The thematic map is a coordinate system of two axes based on co-words and keyword cluster analysis. The abscissa axis is the centrality or relevance grade and is a measure of the intensity of connections among clusters. On the other hand, the ordinate axis is the degree of density or development and characterizes the strength of the links that connect words within the cluster [151,152].

Figure 9 shows the thematic map of the dataset. In motor themes (quadrant 1), which are highly relevant and well developed, model-free SMC takes precedence, followed by data-driven control and learning systems. The design and implementation of data-driven control techniques involve discrete-time system analysis. Within the same quadrant is a group focusing on applications of electrical systems, including motors.

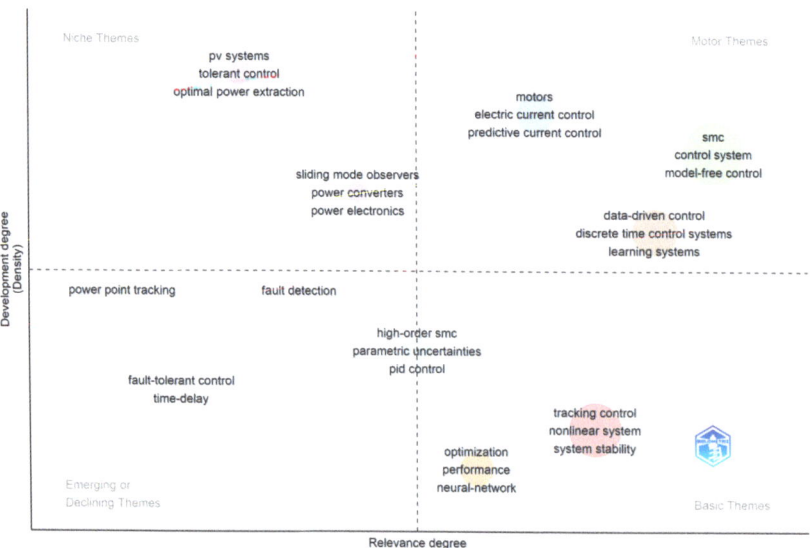

Figure 9. Thematic map of keyword plus.

Quadrant 2 (basic themes) encompasses pertinent topics that have yet to reach a high level of development. The first group includes analysis of nonlinear systems, stability, and trajectory control. Closely following is another cluster where the focus shifts to optimization and neural networks, emphasizing system performance metrics.

Quadrant 3 (niche themes) is dedicated to specific applications characterized by substantial technological development, including photovoltaic systems, power converters, and power systems. Meanwhile, quadrant 4, where emerging or declining themes are found, encompasses subjects such as fault detection systems, analysis of delayed systems, and power point tracking systems.

5. Results

In order to conduct a comprehensive analysis of DDSMC, the 116 selected articles in the systematic literature review (Section 4) were categorized according to the SMC schemes, data-driven techniques, intelligent algorithms and applications. Figure 10 shows how each category is classified, and all articles were analyzed this way.

Initially, the analysis focused on determining the applications and identifying their relationships with SMC schemes and data-driven techniques. Both relationships are presented in Tables 1 and 2. Classic SMC includes the sliding mode methodology presented by Utkin [6] or Slotine et al. [77].

According to the information in Table 1, the most popular application is robotics. This category included air, ground, underwater and surface vehicles; manipulators; and various types of robots. The second category covers applications for electromechanical systems such as engines and machines. Third, the generic systems category appears, including applications that do not fit into the main categories or those that do not describe a specific application, such as MIMO (multi-input–multi-output) systems, high-order systems, and multi-agent systems, among others. The fourth place is in energy conversion systems applications. Fifth, chemical processes are presented, including tank systems, heat exchanges, and reactors. Finally, medical applications appear last, including glycemia regulation systems, neuronal disorders treatment, etc. Figure 11 presents the percentage of each application according to Table 1.

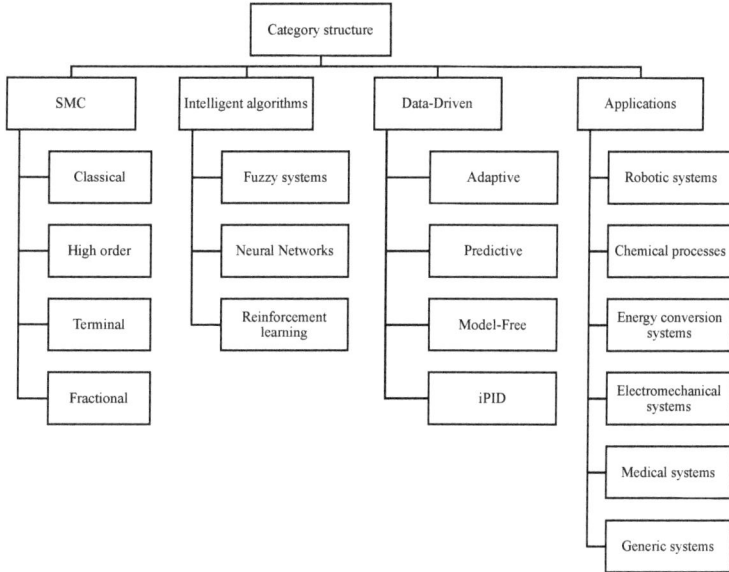

Figure 10. Classification of techniques and applications DDSMC.

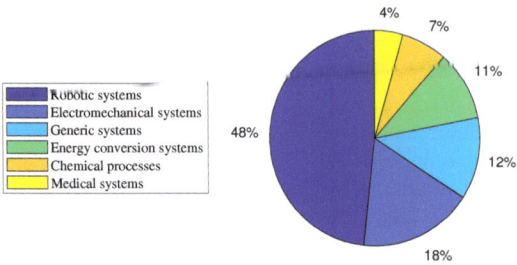

Figure 11. Applications of DDSMC.

Table 1. Applications and SMC schemes.

Application		Classical	High Order	Fractional Order	Terminal
Robotics	Vehicles	[153–168]	[169–175]		
	Manipulators	[171,176–182]		[53,183,184]	[53,99,101, 102,183–192]
	Robots	[193–197]	[198]	[56,199]	
Electromechanical systems	Electric generation		[200]	[201]	[202–204]
	Turbines	[205]			[206]
	Electric loaders	[207]			
	Engines	[208,209]	[210,211]		[48,212,213]
	Filters	[214]		[51]	[215]
	Machines	[216–220]			[52]
Generic systems	Based on a nonlinear model	[46,221–226]		[227,227,228]	
	General theory with examples	[54,229,230]	[231]	[232]	[232]
Energy conversion systems	Batteries	[233]			
	Converters	[47]	[234]		[235]
Chemical processes	Tank systems			[44,236]	[237]
	Heat exchanges	[238]			
	Seeded batch crystallizer	[49]			
	Reactors	[239]			
	Gas collectors	[240]			
Medical applications	Glycemia regulation systems		[241]		
	Medical images	[242]			
	Other medical applications	[243]	[244]		[245]

Continuing with the analysis of Table 1, the most widely used control scheme is the classical approach, followed by terminal, fractional-order SMC, and high-order SMC. It should be noted that the TSMC, NTSMC, FTSMC, ITSMC, and HOTSMC schemes were grouped into the terminal category. TSMC has gained interest, especially the most frequently reported combination of nonsingular and fast terminal approaches, followed by integral TSMC. Some proposals combine TSMC with fractional order for applications such as robotics, electromechanical, and generic systems.

The data-driven techniques are presented in Table 2. This study considered four main techniques. The first is adaptive control, which offers significant advantages for enhancing the performance of industrial processes. It allows systems to respond agilely to dynamic environments by automatically adjusting parameters based on real-time data analysis. Furthermore, by incorporating machine learning algorithms, the system continuously improves its accuracy and efficiency, learning from both historical and current data patterns [53,153,155,157,177,180,208,227].

The second is the MPC approach, which uses advanced algorithms and predictive models to foresee how variations in process conditions will influence its behavior and adjust parameters to maintain the desired performance. This approach improves resource utilization by preventing unwanted variations and dynamically adjusting parameters to maximize efficiency. In complex industrial environments, MPC increases productivity and promotes more intelligent management [209,220,226,233,246]. It must be considered that, usually, MPC assumes some known information about the process [59].

The third is the model-free approach, which eliminates the need for a detailed and complex mathematical model of the system and instead uses a generic model whose parameters are estimated online through continuous analysis of the data measured in the process. This feature simplifies implementation in complex or difficult-to-model systems while allowing for greater flexibility, as it can quickly adapt to unexpected changes in environmental or process conditions [209,220,226,233,246].

Finally, the iPID controller extends classical PID control by utilizing an ultra-local model. This model is valid in a small time window, and its parameters are updated based on the input and output data of the process. The ultra-local model uses derivatives of the process's input and output signals to capture the system's local behavior, which is helpful in the control of systems with fast and changing dynamics [49,154,161,193]. However, its implementation involves greater complexity compared to the traditional PID control. In general, the four strategies report the use of significant computational resources for the forecasting and online parameter-adjusting processes [10,59].

Regarding data-driven techniques, according to Table 2, the most commonly used approach is model-free [247], followed by adaptive. Some proposals employ the adaptive scheme to adjust the controller, estimator, or plant model parameters. The iPID controller appears only in robotics, chemical processes, and electromechanical systems applications. In addition, MPC has the lowest number of associated items and has been used for robotics, chemical processes, and medical applications. The adaptive and model-free approaches have been used combined in all applications. Currently, iPID controllers, mixed with adaptive and model-free schemes, have also been employed in robotics, chemical processes, and electromechanical systems. Additionally, the predictive scheme has been integrated with the model-free approach in robotics and other applications.

Table 2. Applications and data-driven techniques.

Application	Adaptive	Predictive	Model-Free	iPID
Robotics	[53,99,102,153,155–160,162,165,167,171,173,175–177,179–181,183–187,189,192,194,195,199,248]	[55]	[55,56,99,101,153,157–167,169,170,172,174,175,177,180,182,186,187,191–197,199,248,249]	[154,161,182,193]
Chemical processes	[49,238–240,250]	[237]	[44,236,238–240,250]	[44,49,236]
Energy conversion systems	[200–206,213,234]		[47,203,204,213,233,234,251]	
Electromechanical systems	[51,52,57,208,214,215,217–219,246]		[48,51,52,57,58,207–212,215–220,235,246]	[211]
Generic systems	[46,221–224,227,228,230]	[54]	[46,54,221,222,224–227,229,231,232]	
Medical applications	[241,242]	[241,242,244]	[245]	

The second part of the analysis focused on SMC schemes and data-driven techniques, as illustrated in Table 3. The classical SMC remains predominant and has been successfully integrated into all data-driven techniques. Also, terminal- and fractional-order schemes have been combined with adaptive and model-free approaches. Further, the iPID controller has been utilized with high-order and fractional-order schemes. Again, the model-free approach has more publications, followed by adaptive, iPID, and predictive approaches.

Table 3. SMC and data-driven techniques.

Data-Driven Technique	Classical	High Order	Fractional Order	Terminal
Adaptive	[46,49,153,155–160,162, 165,171,176,177,179–181,194,195,205,208,214, 217–219,221–224,230,238–240,242,248]	[200,234,241]	[51,53,183,201,227,252]	[51–53,99,102,173,175,183–187,189,192,199,202–204,206,213,215,227, 228,246,250]
Predictive	[54]			[237]
Model-Free	[46,47,54,153,157–163,165,166,177,180,182, 193–196,207–209,216–222,224–226,229,233,238–240,242,248]	[169,170,197,210,211, 231,234,241,244,249]	[44,51,172,211,227,232, 236]	[48,51,52,56,99,101,174, 175,186,187,191,192,199, 203,204,212,213,215, 227,232,235,246,250]
iPID	[49,154,161,182,193]	[211]	[44,211,236]	

As indicated in Table 4, the SMC schemes and intelligent algorithms were also analyzed. It is worth highlighting that only some articles explicitly report the intelligent algorithm used; because of this, Table 4 reports fewer documents. In this case, neural networks are the most algorithm employed, followed by fuzzy and reinforcement learning algorithms. The adaptive, recurrent fuzzy, radial basis function, and adaptive radial basis function neural networks are some reported types. Among these, radial basis function neural networks emerge as the most frequently cited instances.

Within the intelligent algorithms, reinforcement learning stands out for its potential in implementing model-free control schemes. One of the most interesting works that used this technique is the one proposed by Azad et al. [178], which successfully employed it in parallel robots. In this case, reinforcement learning was employed to select the dynamical model of the process with variable parameters, improving its performance and robustness, reducing chattering, and maintaining stability in the presence of external disturbances. On the other hand, Li et al. [153] utilized SMC to maintain an underwater vehicle's normal operating state and incorporated an auxiliary controller that combined reinforcement learning with a dynamic programming algorithm. It is noted that the proposed strategy learns from the control actions and, in addition, includes a prioritized experience replay (PER(λ)) that allows it to prioritize some experiences during the training process. Additionally, Zhang et al. [201] used deep reinforcement learning to self-tune the FOSMC parameters, using a data-driven dynamic model of the static VAR compensator in a wind generation system. The use of reinforcement learning enhanced the robustness against disturbances thanks to the FOSMC's self-tuning abilities. It should be noted that reinforcement learning adapts to environments with parameter variations models caused by external factors [178,201,253].

Table 4. SMC and intelligent algorithms.

Intelligent Algorithm	Classical	High Order	Fractional Order	Terminal
Fuzzy	[156,171,179,193,221]		[198]	[188,215,235,246]
Neural networks	[158,165,168,207,214,219]		[51]	[51,173,174,185,235,250]
Reinforcement learning	[47,153,178,207,224,229,248]		[201]	[48]

Additionally, the performance indexes were analyzed, finding that the most used are based on error measures, such as RMSE (root mean square error), MAE (mean absolute error), MSE (mean square error), ITAE (integral time absolute error), IAE (integral absolute error), ISE (integral square error), ITSE (integral time square error), and steady-state error; settling time and overshoot have also been used. Few articles review the convergence time and control effort or define customized error functions.

Furthermore, the articles were classified according to their tests, determining whether they were simulated or implemented through a real or scaled prototype. The analysis revealed that 56% of the articles employed simulation software. In contrast, 18% used prototypes, while 26% incorporated a combination of simulation and prototype testing. The following analysis considered only the total number of articles that realized implementation. The classical SMC was implemented in 30.9% of cases, followed by ITSMC and NTSMC each at 16.4%, FOSMC at 14.5%, and both HOSMC and FTSMC at 9.1% each. TSMC and HOTSMC had the lowest implementation rates, each comprising 1.8% of the cases. The most implemented data-driven techniques were the model-free approach at 31.6% and the adaptive one at 23.7%, followed by the iPID controller at 5.9% and the predictive approach at 1.5%. On the other hand, fuzzy and neural network algorithms were the most implemented with an equal number, 38.9% each. By contrast, reinforcement learning was the least implemented, 22.2%. In particular, neither fuzzy logic nor reinforcement learning algorithms have been reported to be implemented in chemical processes.

Regarding the reported prototypes, the hardware in the loop (HIL) technique was utilized in various studies to test embedded control systems in applications such as converters in energy systems, robotic manipulators, spacecraft, and motors applications [47,217,234,243,248,250]. The dSPACE hardware platform was combined with Matlab® to streamline the design, testing, and simulation of real-time systems, specifically in dSPACE real-time control boards DS1103, DS1104, DS1105, and DS1202. Other prototypes were implemented using NI DAQ systems connected, in most cases to Matlab/Simulink® and a smaller number to LabVIEW® [53,188,202,246]. On the other hand, Zhao et al. [213] employed a different HIL platform named LINKS-RT that is also compatible with Matlab®-Simulink. The reported NI DAQ devices included the NI PCI6225e, NI PXIe-1078, and NI PC 6229. Concerning robotics systems, two prototypes were implemented with Raspberry Pi or commercial robots executing ROS (robot operating system), again combined with a controller designed in Matlab® [56,170]. It is worth highlighting the prototype developed by Babaei et al. [198], who used a DELTA PLC-DVP-10SX for data acquisition and LabVIEW® to implement a FOSMC for a sun-tracking system. Similarly, Ding et al. [217] employed a SIEMENS 840D to control a CNC lathe, where the model-free adaptive SMC was designed in Matlab®-Simulink and subsequently downloaded to a dSPACE 1103 controller board.

About software, Matlab® was the primary choice for both prototyping and simulation implementations. Optimizer, Simulink Real-Time, Aerospace, Simmechanics, and Simscape were the most commonly used toolboxes [154,173,183,210]. Notably, there is an important trend of using auxiliary platforms to implement the process model, which is then connected to Matlab® for the design and implementation of the controller. Some examples of this kind of platform are TruckSim, JMAG-Designer, CarSim, SolidWorks, and ANSYS Workbench [160,162,172,173,187,195,216]. Finally, some simulation platforms different from Matlab are CopeliaSim, CRH380 EMU driving simulator, and Gazebo simulation environment [168,185,208].

Chattering is the most significant issue in implementing SMC, which has led many studies to propose methods for mitigating this effect. Approximately 60% of the documents reviewed reported incorporating strategies to address chattering. Of these, about 24% employed the boundary layer method, which involves replacing the discontinuous sign function with smooth, continuous functions such as the sigmoid, hyperbolic tangent, or saturation. As expected, the primary SMC scheme utilizing this strategy was classical, followed by fractional-order and nonsingular. It is also noteworthy that the literature reports that strategies like HOSMC and FOSMC have been shown to reduce chattering effectively, and this was observed in articles such as Ding et al. [53], Wang et al. [197], Babaei et al. [198], Zhang et al. [201], Sami and Ro [234], Saied et al. [249], among others. Additionally, some authors have reported using dynamic switching gains to mitigate chattering [181,220], while others such as Onen [154], Esmaeili et al. [227] highlighted the use of observers.

In addition, the relevance of using observers in DDSMC should be mentioned. For instance, around 46% of the articles incorporated an observer within their control system design, with 3.5% falling under the sliding mode type. In some cases, observers handled unmeasured variables, but others were the primary component of the model-free control strategy. Observers can be utilized to estimate lumped uncertainty and time-varying parameters by compensating for the poorly understood dynamics of the system, besides reducing chattering. Observers have been used for various applications and can be improved using adaptive techniques and intelligent algorithms, such as fuzzy or neural networks. In addition, high-gain, extended-state, finite-time, and nonlinear disturbance observers were employed.

In terms of the latest advancements in SMC design, studies like that of Zhang et al. [254] propose a novel framework combining ISMC with MPC to address the consensus problem in continuous interconnected linear heterogeneous systems. This approach enhances the system's disturbance rejection performance by employing a distributed iterative optimization algorithm to determine the steady-state solutions of interconnected systems, representing a step forward in resolving the consensus issue in networked systems. Another contribution comes from Yonezawa et al. [255], who utilized a virtual controlled object (VCO) to simplify the SMC design. This approach uses a Tsukamoto-type fuzzy inference system to mitigate the chattering. Finally, Wang et al. [256] introduce a multistate fractional-order terminal sliding surface that improves the anti-swing capabilities of cargo transfer systems, reducing the chattering and providing robust control in complex dynamic environments. Deep learning models were employed to forecast the swings of the cargo, and at the same time, they helped define constrained workspaces. To summarize, there is a clear trend toward combining SMC structures with intelligent algorithms to provide a model-free framework and reduce chattering.

6. Conclusions

Despite the numerous advances in data acquisition, processing, analysis systems, and intelligent algorithms, the design of sliding mode control (SMC) based on data-driven techniques continues to captivate the academic community's interest. This subject shows no signs of slowing down in scientific production, with projections indicating that research output will continue to climb, possibly reaching its zenith by 2048.

Although the classical approach to SMC is still widely used because of its simplicity in implementation and the availability of mathematical tools for analysis, there has been a noticeable increase in research works that focus on terminal sliding mode control. This trend shows the advantages offered by this scheme, particularly in terms of robustness and convergence properties.

Articles that focus on the treatment of generic systems are very useful for addressing specific applications through tailored models and methodologies. They establish foundations of system dynamics and control principles that can be adapted and applied to a wide range of practical scenarios. This approach facilitates the translation of theoretical advancements into practical solutions in the field of SMC.

Robotics is the primary field where data-driven techniques have been used recently in order to enhance control performance and autonomy. This leads to opportunities to apply these techniques in fields such as industrial chemical processes and medical applications, where precise and robust control is paramount.

The exploration of alternatives that facilitate the implementation of TSMC and FOSMC controllers is important given the existing constraints in integrating them into industrial/commercial controllers like programmable logic controllers (PLCs), microcontrollers, single-board computers, and others. The constraints associated with compatibility and scalability need to be addressed to facilitate the widespread adoption of these advanced control techniques.

Author Contributions: Conceptualization, D.C.-C., O.E.C. and R.E.V.; methodology, D.C.-C., N.L.P. and L.M.S.-C.; validation, O.E.C., F.C. and R.E.V.; formal analysis, D.C.-C., N.L.P., A.O.-D., L.M.S.-C., F.C., O.E.C. and R.E.V.; investigation, D.C.-C., N.L.P., A.O.-D., L.M.S.-C., F.C., O.E.C. and R.E.V.; writing—original draft preparation, D.C.-C., N.L.P. and O.E.C.; writing—review and editing, D.C.C. and R.E.V.; supervision, A.O.-D., F.C., O.E.C. and R.E.V. All authors have read and agreed to the published version of the manuscript.

Funding: This work was developed with the funding of Universidad de Medellín UdeM, Universidad Pontificia Bolivariana UPB, Universidad Eafit, and Universidad San Francisco de Quito USFQ.

Institutional Review Board Statement: Not applicable.

Informed Consent Statement: Not applicable.

Data Availability Statement: Data are available upon request from the authors.

Conflicts of Interest: The authors declare no conflicts of interest.

Abbreviations

The following abbreviations are used in this manuscript:

ANFIS	Neuro-Fuzzy Inference System
CRONE	Contrôle Robuste d'Ordre Non-Entier
DDSMC	Data-Driven Sliding Mode Control
FOSMC	Fractional-Order Sliding Mode Control
FTSMC	Fast Terminal Sliding Mode Control
HIL	Hardware In the Loop
HOSM	Higher-Order Sliding Mode
HOSMC	Higher-Order Sliding Mode Control
HOTSMC	Higher-Order Terminal Sliding Mode Control
iPID	Intelligent Proportional–Integral–Derivative
IAE	Integral Absolute Error
ISE	Integral Square Error
ISMC	Integral Sliding Mode Control
ITAE	Integral Time Absolute Error
ITSE	Integral Time Square Error
ITSMC	Integral Terminal Sliding Mode Control
MAE	Mean Absolute Error
MBC	Model-Based Control
MFC	Model-Free Control
MPC	Model Predictive Control
MIMO	Multi-Input–Multi-Output
NTSMC	Nonsingular Terminal Sliding Mode Control
PID	Proportional–Integral–Derivative
PLC	Programmable Logic Controller
RMSE	Root Mean Square Error

ROS	Robot Operating System
SMC	Sliding Mode Control
STC	Super-Twisting Controller
TID	Tilted Integral Derivative
TSMC	Terminal Sliding Mode Control
VCO	Virtual Controlled Object

References

1. Utkin, V.; Poznyak, A.; Orlov, Y.; Polyakov, A. *Road Map for Sliding Mode Control Design*; Springer Briefs in Mathematics; Springer International Publishing: Berlin/Heidelberg, Germany, 2020.
2. Vaidyanathan, S.; Lien, C. *Applications of Sliding Mode Control in Science and Engineering*; Studies in Computational Intelligence; Springer International Publishing: Berlin/Heidelberg, Germany, 2017.
3. Espin, J.; Castrillon, F.; Leiva, H.; Camacho, O. A modified Smith predictor based–Sliding mode control approach for integrating processes with dead time. *Alex. Eng. J.* **2022**, *61*, 10119–10137. [CrossRef]
4. Morales, L.; Aguilar, J.; Camacho, O.; Rosales, A. An intelligent sliding mode controller based on LAMDA for a class of SISO uncertain systems. *Inf. Sci.* **2021**, *567*, 75–99. [CrossRef]
5. Emelyanov, S.V. Control of first order delay systems by means of an astatic controller and nonlinear correction. *Autom Remote Control* **1959**, *8*, 212–222.
6. Utkin, V.I. Variable Structure Systems with Sliding Modes. *IEEE Trans. Autom. Control* **1977**, *22*, 212–222. [CrossRef]
7. Steinberger, M.; Horn, M.; Fridman, L. *Variable-Structure Systems and Sliding-Mode Control: From Theory to Practice*; Studies in Systems, Decision and Control; Springer International Publishing: Berlin/Heidelberg, Germany, 2020.
8. Liu, J.; Gao, Y.; Yin, Y.; Wang, J.; Luo, W.; Sun, G. *Sliding Mode Control Methodology in the Applications of Industrial Power Systems*; Studies in Systems, Decision and Control; Springer International Publishing: Berlin/Heidelberg, Germany, 2020.
9. Singh, A.; Ghosh, A. Comparison of Quantitative Feedback Theory Dependent Controller with Conventional PID and Sliding Mode Controllers on DC-DC Boost Converter for Microgrid Applications. *Technol. Econ. Smart Grids Sustain. Energy* **2022**, *7*, 11. [CrossRef]
10. Gambhire, S.J.; Kishore, D.R.; Londhe, P.S.; Pawar, S.N. Review of sliding mode based control techniques for control system applications. *Int. J. Dyn. Control* **2021**, *9*, 363–378. [CrossRef]
11. Bandyopadhyay, B.; Deepak, F.; Kim, K.S.; Bandyopadhyay, B.; Deepak, F.; Kim, K.S. Introduction. In *Sliding Mode Control Using Novel Sliding Surfaces*; Springer: Berlin/Heidelberg, Germany, 2009; pp. 1–15. [CrossRef]
12. Cao, J.; Zhou, J.; Chen, J.; Hu, A.; Hu, M. Sliding Mode Control for Discrete-Time Systems with Randomly Occurring Uncertainties and Nonlinearities Under Hybrid Cyber Attacks. *Circuits Syst. Signal Process.* **2021**, *40*, 5864–5885. [CrossRef]
13. Wang, J.; Chen, M.Z.; Zhang, L. Observer-based discrete-time sliding mode control for systems with unmatched uncertainties. *J. Frankl. Inst.* **2021**, *358*, 8470–8484. [CrossRef]
14. Dehri, K.; Messaoud, A.; Abdennour, R.B. A discrete output feedback 2-SMC using Linear Matrix Inequalities and adaptive switching gain approaches: Real application on a chemical reactor. *J. Vib. Control* **2022**, *29*, 2116–2128. [CrossRef]
15. Lee, H.; Utkin, V.I. Chattering suppression methods in sliding mode control systems. *Annu. Rev. Control* **2007**, *31*, 179–188. [CrossRef]
16. Shtessel, Y.; Edwards, C.; Fridman, L.; Levant, A. *Sliding Mode Control and Observation*; Control Engineering; Springer: New York, NY, USA, 2014.
17. Castellanos-Cárdenas, D.; Castrillán, F.; Vásquez, R.E.; Smith, C. PID Tuning Method Based on IMC for Inverse-Response Second-Order Plus Dead Time Processes. *Processes* **2020**, *8*, 1183. [CrossRef]
18. Hou, Z.S.; Wang, Z. From model-based control to data-driven control: Survey, classification and perspective. *Inf. Sci.* **2013**, *235*, 3–35. [CrossRef]
19. Prag, K.; Woolway, M.; Celik, T. Toward Data-Driven Optimal Control: A Systematic Review of the Landscape. *IEEE Access* **2022**, *10*, 32190–32212. [CrossRef]
20. Brunton, S.; Kutz, J. *Data-Driven Science and Engineering: Machine Learning, Dynamical Systems, and Control*; Cambridge University Press: Cambridge, UK, 2022.
21. Precup, R.; Roman, R.; Safaei, A. *Data-Driven Model-Free Controllers*; CRC Press: Boca Raton, FL, USA, 2022.
22. Lamnabhi-Lagarrigue, F.; Annaswamy, A.; Engell, S.; Isaksson, A.; Khargonekar, P.; Murray, R.M.; Nijmeijer, H.; Samad, T.; Tilbury, D.; Van den Hof, P. Systems & Control for the future of humanity, research agenda: Current and future roles, impact and grand challenges. *Annu. Rev. Control* **2017**, *43*, 1–64. [CrossRef]
23. Ivanov, D.; Sethi, S.; Dolgui, A.; Sokolov, B. A survey on control theory applications to operational systems, supply chain management, and Industry 4.0. *Annu. Rev. Control* **2018**, *46*, 134–147. [CrossRef]
24. Smarra, F.; Jain, A.; de Rubeis, T.; Ambrosini, D.; D́Innocenzo, A.; Mangharam, R. Data-driven model predictive control using random forests for building energy optimization and climate control. *Appl. Energy* **2018**, *226*, 1252–1272. [CrossRef]
25. Guo, D.; Ling, S.; Rong, Y.; Huang, G.Q. Towards synchronization-oriented manufacturing planning and control for Industry 4.0 and beyond. *IFAC-PapersOnLine* **2022**, *55*, 163–168. [CrossRef]

26. De Persis, C.; Tesi, P. Formulas for Data-Driven Control: Stabilization, Optimality, and Robustness. *IEEE Trans. Autom. Control* **2020**, *65*, 909–924. [CrossRef]
27. Huang, B.; Kadali, R. *Dynamic Modeling, Predictive Control and Performance Monitoring: A Data-driven Subspace Approach*; Lecture Notes in Control and Information Sciences; Springer: London, UK, 2008.
28. Tang, W.; Daoutidis, P. Data-Driven Control: Overview and Perspectives. In Proceedings of the 2022 American Control Conference (ACC), Atlanta, GA, USA, 8–10 June 2022; pp. 1048–1064. [CrossRef]
29. Benosman, M. Model-based vs data-driven adaptive control: An overview. *Int. J. Adapt. Control Signal Process.* **2018**, *32*, 753–776. [CrossRef]
30. Middleton, R.H. Adaptive Control: Overview. In *Encyclopedia of Systems and Control*; Baillieul, J., Samad, T., Eds.; Springer International Publishing: Cham, Switzerland, 2021; pp. 18–20. [CrossRef]
31. Badgwell, T.A.; Qin, S.J. Model Predictive Control in Practice. In *Encyclopedia of Systems and Control*; Baillieul, J., Samad, T., Eds.; Springer International Publishing: Cham, Switzerland, 2021; pp. 1239–1252. [CrossRef]
32. Verheijen, P.; Breschi, V.; Lazar, M. Handbook of linear data-driven predictive control: Theory, implementation and design. *Annu. Rev. Control* **2023**, *56*, 100914. [CrossRef]
33. Ljung, L. System Identification: An Overview. In *Encyclopedia of Systems and Control*; Baillieul, J., Samad, T., Eds.; Springer International Publishing: Cham, Switzerland, 2021; pp. 2302–2317. [CrossRef]
34. Åström, K.; Hang, C.; Persson, P.; Ho, W. Towards intelligent PID control. *Automatica* **1992**, *28*, 1–9. [CrossRef]
35. Yamamoto, T.; Kurozumi, R.; Fujisawa, S. A Design of CMAC Based Intelligent PID Controllers. In Proceedings of the Artificial Neural Networks and Neural Information Processing—ICANN/ICONIP 2003; Kaynak, O., Alpaydin, E., Oja, E., Xu, L., Eds.; Springer: Berlin/Heidelberg, Germany, 2003; pp. 471–478.
36. Fliess, M.; Join, C. Intelligent PID controllers. In Proceedings of the 2008 16th Mediterranean Conference on Control and Automation, Ajaccio, France, 25–27 June 2008; pp. 326–331. [CrossRef]
37. Rsetam, K.; Al-Rawi, M.; Cao, Z. Robust adaptive active disturbance rejection control of an electric furnace using additional continuous sliding mode component. *ISA Trans.* **2022**, *130*, 152–162. [CrossRef] [PubMed]
38. Hou, Z.; Jin, S. *Model Free Adaptive Control: Theory and Applications*; CRC Press: Boca Raton, FL, USA, 2014.
39. Hou, M.; Wang, Y. Data-driven adaptive terminal sliding mode control with prescribed performance. *Asian J. Control* **2021**, *23*, 774–785. [CrossRef]
40. An, C.; Jia, S.; Zhou, J.; Wang, C. Fast Model-Free Learning for Controlling a Quadrotor UAV with Designed Error Trajectory. *IEEE Access* **2022**, *10*, 79669–79680. [CrossRef]
41. Esmaeili, B.; Madani, S.S.; Salim, M.; Baradarannia, M.; Khanmohammadi, S. Model-free adaptive iterative learning integral terminal sliding mode control of exoskeleton robots. *J. Vib. Control* **2022**, *28*, 3120–3139. [CrossRef]
42. Hou, Z.; Yu, X.; Lu, P. Terminal Sliding Mode Control for Quadrotors with Chattering Reduction and Disturbances Estimator Theory and Application. *J. Intell. Robot. Syst.* **2022**, *105*, 71. [CrossRef]
43. Yu, Y.; Liu, X. Model-Free Fractional-Order Sliding Mode Control of Electric Drive System Based on Nonlinear Disturbance Observer. *Fractal Fract.* **2022**, *6*, 603. [CrossRef]
44. Ardjal, A.; Bettayeb, M.; Mansouri, R. Improved model-free fractional-order intelligent proportional–integral fractional-order sliding mode control with anti-windup compensator. *Trans. Inst. Meas. Control* **2022**, *44*, 3092–3106. [CrossRef]
45. Johansyah, M.D.; Sambas, A.; Mobayen, S.; Vaseghi, B.; Al-Azzawi, S.F.; Sukono; Sulaiman, I.M. Dynamical Analysis and Adaptive Finite-Time Sliding Mode Control Approach of the Financial Fractional-Order Chaotic System. *Mathematics* **2023**, *11*, 100. [CrossRef]
46. Ebrahimi, N.; Ozgoli, S.; Ramezani, A. Data-driven sliding mode control: A new approach based on optimization. *Int. J. Control* **2020**, *93*, 1980–1988. [CrossRef]
47. Gheisarnejad, M.; Akhbari, A.; Rahimi, M.; Andresen, B.; Khooban, M.H. Reducing Impact of Constant Power Loads on DC Energy Systems by Artificial Intelligence. *IEEE Trans. Circuits Syst. II Express Briefs* **2022**, *69*, 4974–4978. [CrossRef]
48. Zhang, Y.; Ma, L.; Yang, C.; Dai, W. Reinforcement Learning-Based Sliding Mode Tracking Control for the Two-Time-Scale Systems: Dealing with Actuator Attacks. *IEEE Trans. Circuits Syst. II Express Briefs* **2022**, *69*, 3819–3823. [CrossRef]
49. Afsi, N.; Bakir, T.; Sakly, A.; Othman, S. Two concurrent β-variable adaptive model-free controls of a seeded batch crystallizer. *Trans. Inst. Meas. Control* **2023**, *45*, 533–545. [CrossRef]
50. Yuan, D.; Wang, Y. Data Driven Model-Free Adaptive Control Method for Quadrotor Formation Trajectory Tracking Based on RISE and ISMC Algorithm. *Sensors* **2021**, *21*, 1289. [CrossRef] [PubMed]
51. Hou, S.; Wang, C.; Chu, Y.; Fei, J. Neural network–based adaptive fractional-order terminal sliding mode control. *Trans. Inst. Meas. Control* **2022**, *44*, 3107–3117. [CrossRef]
52. Liu, H.; Cheng, Q.; Xiao, J.; Hao, L. Data-driven adaptive integral terminal sliding mode control for uncertain SMA actuators with input saturation and prescribed performance. *ISA Trans.* **2022**, *128*, 624–632. [CrossRef]
53. Ding, L.; Liu, K.; Zhu, G.; Wang, Y.; Li, Y. Adaptive Robust Control via a Nonlinear Disturbance Observer for Cable-driven Aerial Manipulators. *Int. J. Control. Autom. Syst.* **2023**, *21*, 604–615. [CrossRef]
54. Tian, Y.; Su, B. Model-Free Predictive Control for a Kind of High Order Nonlinear Systems. *J. Harbin Inst. Technol.* **2022**, *29*, 62–69. [CrossRef]

55. Jiang, X.; Huang, L.; Peng, M.; Li, Z.; Yang, K.j. Nonlinear model predictive control using symbolic computation on autonomous marine surface vehicle. *J. Mar. Sci. Technol.* **2022**, *27*, 482–491. [CrossRef]
56. Song, T.; Fang, L.; Wang, H. Model-free finite-time terminal sliding mode control with a novel adaptive sliding mode observer of uncertain robot systems. *Asian J. Control* **2022**, *24*, 1437–1451. [CrossRef]
57. Li, Z.; Zhang, Z.; Feng, S.; Wang, J.; Guo, X.; Sun, H. A new sensorless control strategy of the PMLSM based on an ultra-local model velocity control system. *Mech. Sci.* **2022**, *13*, 761–770. [CrossRef]
58. Sun, Z.; Deng, Y.; Wang, J.; Yang, T.; Wei, Z.; Cao, H. Finite Control Set Model-Free Predictive Current Control of PMSM with Two Voltage Vectors Based on Ultralocal Model. *IEEE Trans. Power Electron.* **2023**, *38*, 776–788. [CrossRef]
59. Xiao, H.; Zhao, D.; Gao, S.; Spurgeon, S.K. Sliding mode predictive control: A survey. *Annu. Rev. Control* **2022**, *54*, 148–166. [CrossRef]
60. Hamza, M.F.; Yap, H.J.; Choudhury, I.A.; Chiroma, H.; Kumbasar, T. A survey on advancement of hybrid type 2 fuzzy sliding mode control. *Neural Comput. Appl.* **2018**, *30*, 331–353. [CrossRef]
61. George, J.; Mani, G.; Alexander Stonier, A. An extensive critique of sliding mode control and adaptive neuro-fuzzy inference system for nonlinear system. *Asian J. Control* **2022**, *24*, 2548–2564. [CrossRef]
62. Yu, X.; Feng, Y.; Man, Z. Terminal Sliding Mode Control—An Overview. *IEEE Open J. Ind. Electron. Soc.* **2021**, *2*, 36–52. [CrossRef]
63. Hu, J.; Zhang, H.; Liu, H.; Yu, X. A survey on sliding mode control for networked control systems. *Int. J. Syst. Sci.* **2021**, *52*, 1129–1147. [CrossRef]
64. Zhou, W.; Wang, Y.; Liang, Y. Sliding mode control for networked control systems: A brief survey. *ISA Trans.* **2022**, *124*, 249–259. [CrossRef]
65. Ganapathy, A.; Santha, K. Review of sliding mode observers for sensorless control of permanent magnet synchronous motor drives. *Int. J. Power Electron. Drive Syst.* **2018**, *9*, 46–54. [CrossRef]
66. Zaihidee, F.M.; Mekhilef, S.; Mubin, M. Robust speed control of pmsm using sliding mode control (smc)-a review. *Energies* **2019**, *12*, 1669. [CrossRef]
67. Zuo, Y.; Lai, C.; Iyer, K.L.V. A Review of Sliding Mode Observer Based Sensorless Control Methods for PMSM Drive. *IEEE Trans. Power Electron.* **2023**, *38*, 11352–11367. [CrossRef]
68. Yu, L.; Huang, J.; Luo, W.; Chang, S.; Sun, H.; Tian, H. Sliding-Mode Control for PMLSM Position Control—A Review. *Actuators* **2023**, *12*, 31. [CrossRef]
69. Ahmad, F.F.; Ghenai, C.; Hamid, A.K.; Bettayeb, M. Application of sliding mode control for maximum power point tracking of solar photovoltaic systems: A comprehensive review. *Annu. Rev. Control* **2020**, *49*, 173–196. [CrossRef]
70. Komurcugil, H.; Biricik, S.; Bayhan, S.; Zhang, Z. Sliding Mode Control: Overview of Its Applications in Power Converters. *IEEE Ind. Electron. Mag.* **2021**, *15*, 40–49. [CrossRef]
71. Sami, I.; Ullah, S.; Khan, L.; Al-Durra, A.; Ro, J.S. Integer and Fractional-Order Sliding Mode Control Schemes in Wind Energy Conversion Systems: Comprehensive Review, Comparison, and Technical Insight. *Fractal Fract.* **2022**, *6*, 447. [CrossRef]
72. Wu, L.; Liu, J.; Vazquez, S.; Mazumder, S.K. Sliding Mode Control in Power Converters and Drives: A Review. *IEEE/CAA J. Autom. Sin.* **2022**, *9*, 392–406. [CrossRef]
73. Pilloni, A.; Franceschelli, M.; Pisano, A.; Usai, E. On the variable structure control approach with sliding modes to robust finite-time consensus problems: A methodological overview based on nonsmooth analysis. *Annu. Rev. Control* **2023**, *55*, 338–355. [CrossRef]
74. Riaz, U.; Tayyeb, M.; Amin, A.A. A review of sliding mode control with the perspective of utilization in fault tolerant control. *Recent Adv. Electr. Electron. Eng.* **2021**, *14*, 312–324. [CrossRef]
75. Liu, Q.; Jiang, B.; Wu, Z.; Chen, Z.; Hao, W. Sliding Mode Control and Its Application in Switched Systems: A Survey. *Discret. Contin. Dyn. Syst.-Ser. S* **2023**, *16*, 1856–1875. [CrossRef]
76. Mat-Noh, M.; Mohd-Mokhtar, R.; Arshad, M.; Zain, Z.M.; Khan, Q. Review of sliding mode control application in autonomous underwater vehicles. *Indian J. Geo-Mar. Sci.* **2019**, *48*, 973–984.
77. Slotine, J.J.E.; Li, W. *Applied Nonlinear Control*; Prentice Hall: Englewood Cliffs, NJ, USA, 1991; Volume 199.
78. Camacho, O.; Smith, C.A. Sliding mode control: An approach to regulate nonlinear chemical processes. *ISA Trans.* **2000**, *39*, 205–218. [CrossRef] [PubMed]
79. Karami-Mollaee, A.; Barambones, O. Dynamic sliding mode control of dc-dc converter to extract the maximum power of photovoltaic system using dual sliding observer. *Electronics* **2022**, *11*, 2506. [CrossRef]
80. Sharma, N.K.; Sivaramakrishnan, J. *Discrete-Time Higher Order Sliding Mode: The Concept and the Control*; Springer: Berlin/Heidelberg, Germany, 2019; pp. 1–96. [CrossRef]
81. Fridman, L.; Levant, A. Higher-Order Sliding Modes. In *Sliding Mode Control in Engineering*; Automation and Control Engineering; CRC Press: Boca Raton, FL, USA, 2002; pp. 53–102.
82. Bartolini, G.; Fridman, L.; Pisano, A.; Usai, E. Discontinuous Homogeneous Control. In *Modern Sliding Mode Control Theory: New Perspectives and Applications*; Lecture Notes in Control and Information Sciences; Springer: Berlin/Heidelberg, Germany, 2008; pp. 71–96.
83. Utkin, V. Discussion Aspects of High-Order Sliding Mode Control. *IEEE Trans. Autom. Control* **2016**, *61*, 829–833. [CrossRef]
84. Fridman, L.; Barbot, J.P.; Plestan, F. *Recent Trends in Sliding Mode Control*; Institution of Engineering and Technology: London, UK, 2016; pp. 1–419. [CrossRef]

85. Moreno, J.A.; Fridman, L. Lyapunov-based HOSM control. *Rev. Iberoam. Autom. Inform. Ind.* **2022**, *19*, 394–406. [CrossRef]
86. Levant, A. Sliding order and sliding accuracy in sliding mode control. *Int. J. Control* **1993**, *58*, 1247–1263. [CrossRef]
87. Ferrara, A. *Sliding Mode Control of Vehicle Dynamics*; Institution of Engineering and Technology: London, UK, 2017; pp. 1–295. [CrossRef]
88. Moreno, J.A. *Discontinuous Integral Control for Systems with Relative Degree Two*; Springer International Publishing: Berlin/Heidelberg, Germany, 2018; pp. 187–218. [CrossRef]
89. Pérez-Ventura, U.; Fridman, L. When is it reasonable to implement the discontinuous sliding-mode controllers instead of the continuous ones? Frequency domain criteria. *Int. J. Robust Nonlinear Control* **2019**, *29*, 810–828. [CrossRef]
90. Gallardo Hernández, A.G.; Fridman, L.; Levant, A.; Shtessel, Y.; Leder, R.; Revilla Monsalve, C.; Islas Andrade, S. High-Order Sliding-Mode control of blood glucose concentration via practical relative degree identification. In Proceedings of the 2011 50th IEEE Conference on Decision and Control and European Control Conference, Orlando, FL, USA, 12–15 December 2011; pp. 5786–5791. [CrossRef]
91. Rosales, A.; Fridman, L.; Shtessel, Y. Practical relative degree in SMC systems: Frequency domain approach. In Proceedings of the 2014 13th International Workshop on Variable Structure Systems (VSS), Nantes, France, 29 June–2 July 2014; pp. 1–5. [CrossRef]
92. Fridman, L.; Moreno, J.; Iriarte, R. (Eds.) Sliding Mode Enforcement after 1990: Main Results and Some Open Problems. In *Sliding Modes after the First Decade of the 21st Century: State of the Art*; Springer: Berlin/Heidelberg, Germany, 2012; Chapter 1, pp. 3–57. [CrossRef]
93. Venkataraman, S.T.; Gulati, S. Control of Nonlinear Systems Using Terminal Sliding Modes. In Proceedings of the 1992 American Control Conference, New York, NY, USA, 24–26 June1992; pp. 891–893. [CrossRef]
94. Wijaya, A.A.; Darsivan, F.J.; Solihin, M.I.; Wahyudi; Akmeliawati, R. Terminal sliding mode control for active engine mounting system. In Proceedings of the 2009 IEEE/ASME International Conference on Advanced Intelligent Mechatronics, Singapore, 14–17 July 2009; pp. 417–420. [CrossRef]
95. Lee, S.H.; Park, J.B.; Choi, Y.H. Finite time control of nonlinear underactuated systems using terminal sliding surface. In Proceedings of the 2009 IEEE International Symposium on Industrial Electronics, Seoul, Republic of Korea, 5–8 July 2009; pp. 626–631. [CrossRef]
96. Chiu, C.S. Derivative and integral terminal sliding mode control for a class of MIMO nonlinear systems. *Automatica* **2012**, *48*, 316–326. [CrossRef]
97. Eray, O.; Tokat, S. The design of a fractional-order sliding mode controller with a time-varying sliding surface. *Trans. Inst. Meas. Control* **2020**, *42*, 3196–3215. [CrossRef]
98. Feng, Y.; Yu, X.; Han, F. High-Order Terminal Sliding-Mode Observer for Parameter Estimation of a Permanent-Magnet Synchronous Motor. *IEEE Trans. Ind. Electron.* **2013**, *60*, 4272–4280. [CrossRef]
99. Ahmed, S.; Wang, H.; Tian, Y. Adaptive High-Order Terminal Sliding Mode Control Based on Time Delay Estimation for the Robotic Manipulators with Backlash Hysteresis. *IEEE Trans. Syst. Man, Cybern. Syst.* **2021**, *51*, 1128–1137. [CrossRef]
100. Van, M.; Ge, S.S.; Ren, H. Finite Time Fault Tolerant Control for Robot Manipulators Using Time Delay Estimation and Continuous Nonsingular Fast Terminal Sliding Mode Control. *IEEE Trans. Cybern.* **2017**, *47*, 1681–1693. [CrossRef] [PubMed]
101. Duong, T.T.C.; Nguyen, C.C.; Tran, T.D. Synchronization Sliding Mode Control of Closed-Kinematic Chain Robot Manipulators with Time-Delay Estimation. *Appl. Sci.* **2022**, *12*, 5527. [CrossRef]
102. Ding, L.; Ma, R.; Wu, Z.; Qi, R.; Ruan, W. Optimal Joint Space Control of a Cable-Driven Aerial Manipulator. *Comput. Model. Eng. Sci.* **2023**, *135*, 441–464. [CrossRef]
103. Das, S. *Functional Fractional Calculus for System Identification and Controls*; Springer: Berlin/Heidelberg, Germany, 2008; pp. 1–240. [CrossRef]
104. Pisano, A.; Rapaić, M.; Usai, E. Second-Order Sliding Mode Approaches to Control and Estimation for Fractional Order Dynamics. In *Sliding Modes After the First Decade of the 21st Century: State of the Art*; Springer: Berlin/Heidelberg, Germany, 2012; Chapter 6, pp. 169–197. [CrossRef]
105. Dastjerdi, A.A.; Vinagre, B.M.; Chen, Y.; HosseinNia, S.H. Linear fractional order controllers: A survey in the frequency domain. *Annu. Rev. Control* **2019**, *47*, 51–70. [CrossRef]
106. Gude, J.J.; García Bringas, P.; Herrera, M.; Rincón, L.; Di Teodoro, A.; Camacho, O. Fractional-order model identification based on the process reaction curve: A unified framework for chemical processes. *Results Eng.* **2024**, *21*, 101757. [CrossRef]
107. Shah, P.; Sekhar, R.; Sharma, D.; Penubadi, H.R. Fractional order control: A bibliometric analysis (2000–2022). *Results Control Optim.* **2024**, *14*, 100366. [CrossRef]
108. Pinto, C.M.; Carvalho, A.R. Effect of drug-resistance in a fractional complex-order model for HIV infection. *IFAC-PapersOnLine* **2015**, *48*, 188–189. [CrossRef]
109. Varga, B.; Tar, J.K.; Horváth, R. Fractional order inspired iterative adaptive control. *Robotica* **2024**, *42*, 482–509. [CrossRef]
110. Lurie, B.J. Three-Parameter Tunable Tilt-Integral-Derivative (TID) Controller. U.S. Patent 5 371 670, NASA-CASE-NPO-18492-1-CU, 6 December 1994.
111. Morsali, J.; Zare, K.; Tarafdar Hagh, M. MGSO optimised TID-based GCSC damping controller in coordination with AGC for diverse-GENCOs multi-DISCOs power system with considering GDB and GRC non-linearity effects. *IET Gener. Transm. Distrib.* **2017**, *11*, 193–208. [CrossRef]

112. Guha, D.; Roy, P.K.; Banerjee, S. Maiden application of SSA-optimised CC-TID controller for load frequency control of power systems. *IET Gener. Transm. Distrib.* **2019**, *13*, 1110–1120. [CrossRef]
113. Ahmed, M.; Magdy, G.; Khamies, M.; Kamel, S. Modified TID controller for load frequency control of a two-area interconnected diverse-unit power system. *Int. J. Electr. Power Energy Syst.* **2022**, *135*, 107528. [CrossRef]
114. Oustaloup, A. *Systèmes Asservis Linéaires D'ordre Fractionnaire: Théorie et Pratique*; Elsevier Masson: Paris, France, 1983.
115. Yousfi, N.; Melchior, P.; Lanusse, P.; Derbel, N.; Oustaloup, A. Decentralized CRONE control of nonsquare multivariable systems in path-tracking design. *Nonlinear Dyn.* **2014**, *76*, 447–457. [CrossRef]
116. Lanusse, P.; Sabatier, J.; Oustaloup, A. Fractional Order PID and First Generation CRONE Control System Design. In *Fractional Order Differentiation and Robust Control Design: CRONE, H-infinity and Motion Control*; Springer: Dordrecht, The Netherlands, 2015; pp. 63–105. [CrossRef]
117. Yessef, M.; Bossoufi, B.; Taoussi, M.; Motahhir, S.; Lagrioui, A.; Chojaa, H.; Lee, S.; Kang, B.G.; Abouhawwash, M. Improving the Maximum Power Extraction from Wind Turbines Using a Second-Generation CRONE Controller. *Energies* **2022**, *15*, 3644. [CrossRef]
118. Podlubny, I. *Fractional-Order Systems and Fractional-Order Controllers*; Institute of Experimental Physics, Slovak Academy of Sciences, Kosice: Košice, Slovakia, 1994; Volume 12, pp. 1–18.
119. Sharma, R.; Rana, K.; Kumar, V. Performance analysis of fractional order fuzzy PID controllers applied to a robotic manipulator. *Expert Syst. Appl.* **2014**, *41*, 4274–4289. [CrossRef]
120. Zeng, G.Q.; Chen, J.; Dai, Y.X.; Li, L.M.; Zheng, C.W.; Chen, M.R. Design of fractional order PID controller for automatic regulator voltage system based on multi-objective extremal optimization. *Neurocomputing* **2015**, *160*, 173–184. [CrossRef]
121. Hekimoglu, B. Optimal Tuning of Fractional Order PID Controller for DC Motor Speed Control via Chaotic Atom Search Optimization Algorithm. *IEEE Access* **2019**, *7*, 38100–38114. [CrossRef]
122. Monje, C.A.; Calderón, A.J.; Vinagre, B.M.; Feliu, V. The fractional order lead compensator. In Proceedings of the ICCC 2004—Second IEEE International Conference on Computational Cybernetics, Vienna, Austria, 30 August–1 September 2004; pp. 347–352.
123. Zhang, X.; Lai, L.J.; Zhu, L.M. Data-driven fractional order phase-lead and proportional–integral feedback control strategy with application to a reluctance-actuated compliant micropositioning system. *Sens. Actuators A Phys.* **2022**, *348*, 113988. [CrossRef]
124. Mondal, R.; Dey, J. An Extended Experimental Study on Control of Unstable and Non-Minimum Phase Plants with the Cascaded Form of a Fractional Order Compensator. *IEEE Trans. Ind. Appl.* **2023**, *59*, 3086–3097. [CrossRef]
125. Liu, H.; Pan, Y.; Li, S.; Chen, Y. Adaptive Fuzzy Backstepping Control of Fractional-Order Nonlinear Systems. *IEEE Trans. Syst. Man Cybern. Syst.* **2017**, *47*, 2209–2217. [CrossRef]
126. Nikdel, N.; Badamchizadeh, M.; Azimirad, V.; Nazari, M.A. Fractional-Order Adaptive Backstepping Control of Robotic Manipulators in the Presence of Model Uncertainties and External Disturbances. *IEEE Trans. Ind. Electron.* **2016**, *63*, 6249–6256. [CrossRef]
127. Bouzeriba, A.; Boulkroune, A.; Bouden, T. Projective synchronization of two different fractional-order chaotic systems via adaptive fuzzy control. *Neural Comput. Appl.* **2016**, *27*, 1349–1360. [CrossRef]
128. Gong, P.; Lan, W. Adaptive robust tracking control for uncertain nonlinear fractional-order multi-agent systems with directed topologies. *Automatica* **2018**, *92*, 92–99. [CrossRef]
129. Fang, Y.; Fei, J.; Cao, D. Adaptive Fuzzy-Neural Fractional-Order Current Control of Active Power Filter with Finite-Time Sliding Controller. *Int. J. Fuzzy Syst.* **2019**, *21*, 1533–1543. [CrossRef]
130. Monje, C.; Chen, Y.; Vinagre, B.; Xue, D.; Feliu, V. *Fractional-Order Systems and Controls*; Springer: London, UK, 2010. [CrossRef]
131. Yin, C.; Chen, Y.; Zhong, S.M. Fractional-order sliding mode based extremum seeking control of a class of nonlinear systems. *Automatica* **2014**, *50*, 3173–3181. [CrossRef]
132. Bandyopadhyay, B.; Kamal, S. *Stabilization and Control of Fractional Order Systems: A Sliding Mode Approach*; Springer International Publishing: Berlin/Heidelberg, Germany, 2015; Volume 317, pp. 1–54. [CrossRef]
133. Wang, J.; Shao, C.; Chen, Y.Q. Fractional order sliding mode control via disturbance observer for a class of fractional order systems with mismatched disturbance. *Mechatronics* **2018**, *53*, 8–19. [CrossRef]
134. Wang, Y.; Chen, J.; Yan, F.; Zhu, K.; Chen, B. Adaptive super-twisting fractional-order nonsingular terminal sliding mode control of cable-driven manipulators. *ISA Trans.* **2019**, *86*, 163–180. [CrossRef]
135. Ma, Z.; Ma, H. Adaptive Fuzzy Backstepping Dynamic Surface Control of Strict-Feedback Fractional-Order Uncertain Nonlinear Systems. *IEEE Trans. Fuzzy Syst.* **2020**, *28*, 122–133. [CrossRef]
136. Song, S.; Zhang, B.; Xia, J.; Zhang, Z. Adaptive Backstepping Hybrid Fuzzy Sliding Mode Control for Uncertain Fractional-Order Nonlinear Systems Based on Finite-Time Scheme. *IEEE Trans. Syst. Man Cybern. Syst.* **2020**, *50*, 1559–1569. [CrossRef]
137. Fanaee, N. Adaptive finite time high-order sliding mode observer for non-linear fractional order systems with unknown input. *Asian J. Control* **2021**, *23*, 1083–1096. [CrossRef]
138. Fang, Y.; Li, S.; Fei, J. Adaptive Intelligent High-Order Sliding Mode Fractional Order Control for Harmonic Suppression. *Fractal Fract.* **2022**, *6*, 482. [CrossRef]
139. Deniz, F.N.; Alagoz, B.B.; Tan, N.; Koseoglu, M. Revisiting four approximation methods for fractional order transfer function implementations: Stability preservation, time and frequency response matching analyses. *Annu. Rev. Control* **2020**, *49*, 239–257. [CrossRef]

140. Mehta, U.; Bingi, K.; Saxena, S. *Applied Fractional Calculus in Identification and Control*; Studies in Infrastructure and Control; Springer Nature Singapore: Singapore, 2022. [CrossRef]
141. Gude, J.J.; Di Teodoro, A.; Herrera, M.; Rincón, L.; Camacho, O. Sliding Mode Control Design Using a Generalized Reduced-Order Fractional Model for Chemical Processes. *Results Eng.* **2024**, *24*, 103032. [CrossRef]
142. Akindele, N.; Taiwo, R.; Sarvari, H.; Oluleye, B.I.; Awodele, I.A.; Olaniran, T.O. A state-of-the-art analysis of virtual reality applications in construction health and safety. *Results Eng.* **2024**, *23*, 102382. [CrossRef]
143. Lytridis, C.; Kaburlasos, V.G.; Pachidis, T.; Manios, M.; Vrochidou, E.; Kalampokas, T.; Chatzistamatis, S. An Overview of Cooperative Robotics in Agriculture. *Agronomy* **2021**, *11*, 1818. [CrossRef]
144. Peng, Y.; Lei, Y.; Tekler, Z.D.; Antanuri, N.; Lau, S.K.; Chong, A. Hybrid system controls of natural ventilation and HVAC in mixed-mode buildings: A comprehensive review. *Energy Build.* **2022**, *276*, 112509. [CrossRef]
145. Marín-Rodríguez, N.J.; González-Ruiz, J.D.; Botero Botero, S. Dynamic Co-Movements among Oil Prices and Financial Assets: A Scientometric Analysis. *Sustainability* **2022**, *14*, 12796. [CrossRef]
146. Kumari, A.; Singh, M.P. A journey of social sustainability in organization during MDG & SDG period: A bibliometric analysis. *Socio-Econ. Plan. Sci.* **2023**, *88*, 101668. [CrossRef]
147. Tharayil, J.M.; Chinnaiyan, P.; John, D.M.; Kishore, M.S. Environmental sustainability of FO membrane separation applications—Bibliometric analysis and state-of-the-art review. *Results Eng.* **2024**, *21*, 101677. [CrossRef]
148. Aria, M.; Cuccurullo, C. Bibliometrix: An R-tool for comprehensive science mapping analysis. *J. Inf.* **2017**, *11*, 959–975. [CrossRef]
149. Yamaguchi, N.U.; Bernardino, E.G.; Ferreira, M.E.C.; de Lima, B.P.; Pascotini, M.R.; Yamaguchi, M.U. Sustainable development goals: A bibliometric analysis of literature reviews. *Environ. Sci. Pollut. Res.* **2023**, *30*, 5502–5515. [CrossRef]
150. Yepes, S.; Martínez, M.; Restrepo, S.; Palacio, J.; Ríos, A.; Zartha, J. Technological Surveillance and Technology Life Cycle Analysis—Application in Food Drying. *Int. J. Appl. Eng. Res.* **2018**, *13*, 7273–7288.
151. Callon, M.; Courtial, J.P.; Laville, F. Co-word analysis as a tool for describing the network of interactions between basic and technological research: The case of polymer chemsitry. *Scientometrics* **1991**, *22*, 155–205. [CrossRef]
152. Yu, J.; Muñoz-Justicia, J. A Bibliometric Overview of Twitter-Related Studies Indexed in Web of Science. *Future Internet* **2020**, *12*, 91. [CrossRef]
153. Li, T.; Yang, D.; Xie, X. Prioritized experience replay based reinforcement learning for adaptive tracking control of autonomous underwater vehicle. *Appl. Math. Comput.* **2023**, *443*, 127734. [CrossRef]
154. Onen, U. Model-Free Controller Design for Nonlinear Underactuated Systems with Uncertainties and Disturbances by Using Extended State Observer Based Chattering-Free Sliding Mode Control. *IEEE Access* **2023**, *11*, 2875–2885. [CrossRef]
155. Oh, K.; Seo, J. Development of a Sliding-Mode-Control-Based Path-Tracking Algorithm with Model-Free Adaptive Feedback Action for Autonomous Vehicles. *Sensors* **2022**, *23*, 405. [CrossRef]
156. Zhong, Y.; Yu, C.; Wang, R.; Liu, C.; Lian, L. Adaptive depth tracking of underwater vehicles considering actuator saturation: Theory, simulation and experiment. *Ocean. Eng.* **2022**, *265*, 112517. [CrossRef]
157. Yuan, D.; Wang, Y. Data Driven Model-Free Adaptive Control Method for Quadrotor Trajectory Tracking Based on Improved Sliding Mode Algorithm. *J. Shanghai Jiaotong Univ. (Sci.)* **2022**, *27*, 790–798. [CrossRef]
158. Guo, X.; Niu, P.; Zhao, D.; Li, X.; Wang, S.; Chang, A. Model-free Controls of Manipulator Quadrotor UAV Under Grasping Operation and Environmental Disturbance. *Int. J. Control. Autom. Syst.* **2022**, *20*, 3689–3705. [CrossRef]
159. Weng, Y.; Wang, N. SMC-based model-free tracking control of unknown autonomous surface vehicles. *ISA Trans.* **2022**, *130*, 684–691. [CrossRef]
160. Jiang, Y.; Meng, H.; Chen, G.; Yang, C.; Xu, X.; Zhang, L.; Xu, H. Differential-steering based path tracking control and energy-saving torque distribution strategy of 6WID unmanned ground vehicle. *Energy* **2022**, *254*, 124209. [CrossRef]
161. Lv, X.; Zhang, G.; Wang, G.; Zhu, M.; Shi, Z.; Bai, Z.; Alexandrov, I.V. Numerical Analyses and a Nonlinear Composite Controller for a Real-Time Ground Aerodynamic Heating Simulation of a Hypersonic Flying Object. *Mathematics* **2022**, *10*, 3022. [CrossRef]
162. Zhang-qi, F.; Hao-bin, J.; Qi-zhi, W.; Yang-ke, H.; Abiodun Oluwaleke, O. Model-free adaptive sliding mode control for intelligent vehicle longitudinal dynamics. *Adv. Mech. Eng.* **2022**, *14*, 168781322211101. [CrossRef]
163. Xu, K.T.; Ge, M.F.; Liang, C.D.; Ding, T.F.; Zhan, X.S. Predefined-time time-varying formation control of networked autonomous surface vehicles: A velocity- and model-free approach. *Nonlinear Dyn.* **2022**, *108*, 3605–3622. [CrossRef]
164. Weng, Y.; Wang, N. Finite-time observer-based model-free time-varying sliding-mode control of disturbed surface vessels. *Ocean. Eng.* **2022**, *251*, 110866. [CrossRef]
165. Zhang, Y.; Wang, X.; Wang, S.; Tian, X. Three-dimensional formation–containment control of underactuated AUVs with heterogeneous uncertain dynamics and system constraints. *Ocean. Eng.* **2021**, *238*, 109661. [CrossRef]
166. Weng, Y.; Wang, N. Data-driven robust backstepping control of unmanned surface vehicles. *Int. J. Robust Nonlinear Control* **2020**, *30*, 3624–3638. [CrossRef]
167. Weng, Y.; Wang, N.; Guedes Soares, C. Data-driven sideslip observer-based adaptive sliding-mode path-following control of underactuated marine vessels. *Ocean. Eng.* **2020**, *197*, 106910. [CrossRef]
168. Patel, S.; Sarabakha, A.; Kircali, D.; Kayacan, E. An Intelligent Hybrid Artificial Neural Network-Based Approach for Control of Aerial Robots. *J. Intell. Robot. Syst.* **2020**, *97*, 387–398. [CrossRef]

169. González-García, J.; Narcizo-Nuci, N.A.; Gómez-Espinosa, A.; García-Valdovinos, L.G.; Salgado-Jiménez, T. Finite-Time Controller for Coordinated Navigation of Unmanned Underwater Vehicles in a Collaborative Manipulation Task. *Sensors* **2022**, *23*, 239. [CrossRef]
170. González-García, J.; Gómez Espinosa, A.; García-Valdovinos, L.G.; Salgado-Jiménez, T.; Cuan-Urquizo, E.; Cabello, J.A.E. Model-Free High-Order Sliding Mode Controller for Station-Keeping of an Autonomous Underwater Vehicle in Manipulation Task: Simulations and Experimental Validation. *Sensors* **2022**, *22*, 4347. [CrossRef] [PubMed]
171. Peng, F.; Wen, H.; Zhang, C.; Xu, B.; Li, J.; Su, H. Adaptive Robust Force Position Control for Flexible Active Prosthetic Knee Using Gait Trajectory. *Appl. Sci.* **2020**, *10*, 2755. [CrossRef]
172. Lv, X.; Zhang, G.; Zhu, M.; Shi, Z.; Bai, Z.; Alexandrov, I.V. Aerodynamic Heating Ground Simulation of Hypersonic Vehicles Based on Model-Free Control Using Super Twisting Nonlinear Fractional Order Sliding Mode. *Mathematics* **2022**, *10*, 1664. [CrossRef]
173. Lv, X.; Zhang, G.; Zhu, M.; Ouyang, H.; Shi, Z.; Bai, Z.; Alexandrov, I.V. Adaptive Neural Network Global Nonsingular Fast Terminal Sliding Mode Control for a Real Time Ground Simulation of Aerodynamic Heating Produced by Hypersonic Vehicles. *Energies* **2022**, *15*, 3284. [CrossRef]
174. Ye, D.; Xiao, Y.; Sun, Z.; Xiao, B. Neural Network Based Finite-Time Attitude Tracking Control of Spacecraft with Angular Velocity Sensor Failures and Actuator Saturation. *IEEE Trans. Ind. Electron.* **2022**, *69*, 4129–4136. [CrossRef]
175. Xu, D.; Zhang, W.; Shi, P.; Jiang, B. Model-Free Cooperative Adaptive Sliding-Mode-Constrained-Control for Multiple Linear Induction Traction Systems. *IEEE Trans. Cybern.* **2020**, *50*, 4076–4086. [CrossRef]
176. Zhang, R.; Hou, S.; Sun, H.; Li, Z.; Tang, X. An adaptive sliding mode control algorithm for flexibly supported Stewart mechanism. *J. Braz. Soc. Mech. Sci. Eng.* **2022**, *44*, 578. [CrossRef]
177. Baek, S.; Baek, J.; Kwon, W.; Han, S. An Adaptive Model Uncertainty Estimator Using Delayed State-Based Model-Free Control and Its Application to Robot Manipulators. *IEEE/ASME Trans. Mechatronics* **2022**, *27*, 4573–4584. [CrossRef]
178. Azad, F.A.; Rad, S.A.; Arashpour, M. Back-stepping control of delta parallel robots with smart dynamic model selection for construction applications. *Autom. Constr.* **2022**, *137*, 104211. [CrossRef]
179. Ghafarian, M.; Shirinzadeh, B.; Al-Jodah, A.; Das, T.K. Adaptive Fuzzy Sliding Mode Control for High-Precision Motion Tracking of a Multi-DOF Micro/Nano Manipulator. *IEEE Robot. Autom. Lett.* **2020**, *5*, 4313–4320. [CrossRef]
180. Garcia-Rodriguez, R.; Parra-Vega, V.; Ramos-Velasco, L.E.; Dominguez-Ramirez, O.A. Neuro-controller for antagonistic bi-articular muscle actuation in robotic arms based on terminal attractors. *Trans. Inst. Meas. Control* **2020**, *42*, 2031–2043. [CrossRef]
181. Lee, J.; Chang, P.H.; Yu, B.; Seo, K.H.; Jin, M. An Effective Adaptive Gain Dynamics for Time-Delay Control of Robot Manipulators. *IEEE Access* **2020**, *8*, 192229–192238. [CrossRef]
182. Elleuch, D.; Damak, T. Robust Model-Free Control for Robot Manipulator under Actuator Dynamics. *Math. Probl. Eng.* **2020**, *2020*, 1–11. [CrossRef]
183. Ding, L.; Yao, Y.; Ma, R. Observer-Based Control for a Cable-Driven Aerial Manipulator under Lumped Disturbances. *Comput. Model. Eng. Sci.* **2023**, *135*, 1539–1558. [CrossRef]
184. Wang, Y.; Yan, F.; Chen, J.; Ju, F.; Chen, B. A New Adaptive Time-Delay Control Scheme for Cable-Driven Manipulators. *IEEE Trans. Ind. Inform.* **2019**, *15*, 3469–3481. [CrossRef]
185. Zeng, H.; Lyu, Y.; Qi, J.; Zou, S.; Qin, T.; Qin, W. Adaptive finite-time model estimation and control for manipulator visual servoing using sliding mode control and neural networks. *Adv. Robot.* **2023**, *37*, 576–590. [CrossRef]
186. Chen, Z.; Wang, X.; Cheng, Y. Model free based finite time fault-tolerant control of robot manipulators subject to disturbances and input saturation. *Int. J. Robust Nonlinear Control* **2022**, *32*, 5281–5303. [CrossRef]
187. Wu, Z.; Chen, Y.; Geng, Y.; Wang, X.; Xuan, B. Model-free robust adaptive integral sliding mode impedance control of knee-ankle-toe active transfemoral prosthesis. *Int. J. Med. Robot. Comput. Assist. Surg.* **2022**, *18*, e2378. [CrossRef]
188. Zhao, J.; Wang, Y.; Wang, D.; Ju, F.; Chen, B.; Wu, H. Practical continuous nonsingular terminal sliding mode control of a cable-driven manipulator developed for aerial robots. *Proc. Inst. Mech. Eng. Part I J. Syst. Control Eng.* **2020**, *234*, 1011–1023. [CrossRef]
189. Wang, Y.; Yan, F.; Jiang, S.; Chen, B. Adaptive nonsingular terminal sliding mode control of cable-driven manipulators with time delay estimation. *Int. J. Syst. Sci.* **2020**, *51*, 1429–1447. [CrossRef]
190. Wang, Y.; Zhang, R.; Ju, F.; Zhao, J.; Chen, B.; Wu, H. A light cable-driven manipulator developed for aerial robots: Structure design and control research. *Int. J. Adv. Robot. Syst.* **2020**, *17*, 172988142092642. [CrossRef]
191. Wang, Y.; Zhu, K.; Chen, B.; Jin, M. Model-free continuous nonsingular fast terminal sliding mode control for cable-driven manipulators. *ISA Trans.* **2020**, *98*, 483–495. [CrossRef] [PubMed]
192. Choi, J.; Baek, J.; Lee, W.; Lee, Y.S.; Han, S. Adaptive Model-Free Control with Nonsingular Terminal Sliding-Mode for Application to Robot Manipulators. *IEEE Access* **2020**, *8*, 169897–169907. [CrossRef]
193. Precup, R.E.; Roman, R.C.; Hedrea, E.L.; Petriu, E.M.; Bojan-Dragos, C.A. Data-Driven Model-Free Sliding Mode and Fuzzy Control with Experimental Validation. *Int. J. Comput. Commun. Control* **2021**, *16*, 4076. [CrossRef]
194. Qiu, X.; Hua, C.; Chen, J.; Zhang, L.; Guan, X. Model-free adaptive iterative sliding mode control for a robotic exoskeleton trajectory tracking system. *Int. J. Syst. Sci.* **2020**, *51*, 1782–1797. [CrossRef]
195. Meng, K.; Jia, Y.; Yang, H.; Niu, F.; Wang, Y.; Sun, D. Motion Planning and Robust Control for the Endovascular Navigation of a Microrobot. *IEEE Trans. Ind. Inform.* **2020**, *16*, 4557–4566. [CrossRef]

196. Chen, L.; Duan, H.; Dian, S.; Hoang, S. Event-based model-free sliding mode control for an inspection robot. *Adv. Control Appl.* **2020**, *2*, e33. [CrossRef]
197. Wang, W.; Ma, J.; Li, X.; Zhu, H.; Silva, C.W.D.; Lee, T.H. Hybrid Active–Passive Robust Control Framework of a Flexure-Joint Dual-Drive Gantry Robot for High-Precision Contouring Tasks. *IEEE Trans. Ind. Electron.* **2023**, *70*, 1676–1686. [CrossRef]
198. Babaei, S.M.; Yahyazadeh, M.; Fatehi Marj, H. Novel MPPT for Linear-Rotational Sun-Tracking System Using Fractional Fuzzy Grey-Based Sliding Mode Control. *Iran. J. Sci. Technol. Trans. Electr. Eng.* **2020**, *44*, 1379–1401. [CrossRef]
199. Ebrahimi, N.; Ozgoli, S.; Ramezani, A. Model-free high-order terminal sliding mode controller for Lipschitz nonlinear systems. Implemented on Exoped® exoskeleton robot. *Int. J. Syst. Sci.* **2021**, *52*, 1061–1073. [CrossRef]
200. Li, Y.; Pei, P.; Ma, Z.; Ren, P.; Huang, H. Method for system parameter identification and controller parameter tuning for super-twisting sliding mode control in proton exchange membrane fuel cell system. *Energy Convers. Manag.* **2021**, *243*, 114370. [CrossRef]
201. Zhang, G.; Zhao, J.; Hu, W.; Cao, D.; Tan, B.; Huang, Q.; Chen, Z. A Novel Data-Driven Self-Tuning SVC Additional Fractional-Order Sliding Mode Controller for Transient Voltage Stability with Wind Generations. *IEEE Trans. Power Syst.* **2023**, *38*, 5755–5767. [CrossRef]
202. Yin, L.; Li, Q.; Breaz, E.; Chen, W.; Gao, F. Net Power Enhancement of PEMFC System Based on Dual Loop Multivariable Coordinated Management. *IEEE Trans. Ind. Electron.* **2023**, *70*, 11216–11230. [CrossRef]
203. Am, O.A.; Wang, H.; Tian, Y. Enhanced Model-Free Discrete-Time Adaptive Terminal Sliding-Mode Control for SOFC Power Plant with Input Constraints. *Arab. J. Sci. Eng.* **2022**, *47*, 2851–2864. [CrossRef]
204. Omer Abbaker, A.M.; Wang, H.; Tian, Y. Robust Model-Free Adaptive Interval Type-2 Fuzzy Sliding Mode Control for PEMFC System Using Disturbance Observer. *Int. J. Fuzzy Syst.* **2020**, *22*, 2188–2203. [CrossRef]
205. Verij Kazemi, M.; Sadati, S.J.; Gholamian, S.A. Adaptive frequency control support of a DFIG based on second-order derivative controller using data-driven method. *Int. Trans. Electr. Energy Syst.* **2020**, *30*, e12424. [CrossRef]
206. Mazare, M.; Taghizadeh, M.; Ghaf-Ghanbari, P. Pitch actuator fault-tolerant control of wind turbines based on time delay control and disturbance observer. *Ocean. Eng.* **2021**, *238*, 109724. [CrossRef]
207. Mosayebi, M.; Fathollahi, A.; Gheisarnejad, M.; Farsizadeh, H.; Khooban, M.H. Smart Emergency EV-to-EV Portable Battery Charger. *Inventions* **2022**, *7*, 45. [CrossRef]
208. Zhou, L.; Li, Z.; Yang, H.; Fu, Y.; Yan, Y. Data-Driven Model-Free Adaptive Sliding Mode Control Based on FFDL for Electric Multiple Units. *Appl. Sci.* **2022**, *12*, 10983. [CrossRef]
209. Zheng, Z.; Zhang, H.; Vo, D.T. Analysis of model-free sliding mode control of permanent magnet synchronous motor. *Int. J. Mechatronics Appl. Mech.* **2020**, *2*, 217–224.
210. Chen, G.; Xu, L. Ultra-local model-free speed prediction control based on high-order sliding mode compensation for PMSM drives. *Adv. Mech. Eng.* **2022**, *14*, 168781322211142. [CrossRef]
211. Gao, P.; Lv, X.; Ouyang, H.; Mei, L.; Zhang, G. A Novel Model-Free Intelligent Proportional-Integral Supertwisting Nonlinear Fractional-Order Sliding Mode Control of PMSM Speed Regulation System. *Complexity* **2020**, *2020*, 1–15. [CrossRef]
212. Yan, G.; Abidi, K. A practical application of sliding mode control in the motion control of a high precision piezoelectric motor. *J. Braz. Soc. Mech. Sci. Eng.* **2022**, *44*, 201. [CrossRef]
213. Zhao, Y.; Liu, X.; Yu, H.; Yu, J. Model-free adaptive discrete-time integral terminal sliding mode control for PMSM drive system with disturbance observer. *IET Electr. Power Appl.* **2020**, *14*, 1756–1765. [CrossRef]
214. Zhang, H.; Liu, Y. Adaptive RBF neural network based on sliding mode controller for active power filter. *Int. J. Power Electron.* **2020**, *11*, 460. [CrossRef]
215. Hou, S.; Chu, Y.; Fei, J. Adaptive Type-2 Fuzzy Neural Network Inherited Terminal Sliding Mode Control for Power Quality Improvement. *IEEE Trans. Ind. Inform.* **2021**, *17*, 7564–7574. [CrossRef]
216. wDhale, S.B.; Mobarakeh, B.N.; Nalakath, S.; Emadi, A. Digital Sliding Mode Based Model-Free PWM Current Control of Switched Reluctance Machines. *IEEE Trans. Ind. Electron.* **2022**, *69*, 8760–8769. [CrossRef]
217. Ding, L.; Sun, Y.; Xiong, Z. Model-Free Adaptive Sliding Mode Control-Based Active Chatter Suppression by Spindle Speed Variation. *J. Dyn. Syst. Meas. Control* **2022**, *144*, 071002. [CrossRef]
218. Liu, M.; Zhao, Z.; Hao, L. Prescribed performance model-free adaptive sliding mode control of a shape memory alloy actuated system. *ISA Trans.* **2022**, *123*, 339–345. [CrossRef]
219. Yang, W.; Meng, F.; Meng, S.; Man, S.; Pang, A. Tracking Control of Magnetic Levitation System Using Model-Free RBF Neural Network Design. *IEEE Access* **2020**, *8*, 204563–204572. [CrossRef]
220. Yonezawa, A.; Kajiwara, H.; Yonezawa, H. Novel Sliding Mode Vibration Controller with Simple Model-Free Design and Compensation for Actuator's Uncertainty. *IEEE Access* **2020**, *9*, 4351–4363. [CrossRef]
221. Rahmani, B.; Ziaiefar, A.; Hashemi, S. Output feedback-based adaptive fuzzy sliding mode control for seismic response reduction of base-isolated buildings. *ISA Trans.* **2022**, *126*, 94–108. [CrossRef] [PubMed]
222. Gao, C.; Zhang, W.; Xu, D.; Yang, W.; Pan, T. Event-Triggered Based Model-Free Adaptive Sliding Mode Constrained Control for Nonlinear Discrete-Time Systems. *Int. J. Innov. Comput. Inf. Control* **2022**, *18*, 525–536. [CrossRef]
223. Zhang, Y.; Song, J. Nonlinear leader-following MASs control: A data-driven adaptive sliding mode approach with prescribed performance. *Nonlinear Dyn.* **2022**, *108*, 349–361. [CrossRef]

224. Cao, L.; Gao, S.; Zhao, D. Data-driven model-free sliding mode learning control for a class of discrete-time nonlinear systems. *Trans. Inst. Meas. Control* **2020**, *42*, 2533–2547. [CrossRef]
225. Chen, L.; Yan, Y.; Sun, C. A novel modeling and controlling approach for high-order nonlinear systems. *Asian J. Control* **2020**, *22*, 1295–1305. [CrossRef]
226. Yu, J.; Jin, S.; Wang, X.; Xiong, X.; Lv, Z.; Jin, Y. A Variable Gain Sliding Mode Tracking Differentiator for Derivative Estimation of Noisy Signals. *IEEE Access* **2020**, *8*, 148500–148509. [CrossRef]
227. Esmaeili, B.; Salim, M.; Baradarannia, M. Predefined performance-based model-free adaptive fractional-order fast terminal sliding-mode control of MIMO nonlinear systems. *ISA Trans.* **2022**, *131*, 108–123. [CrossRef]
228. Shen, H.; Pan, Y.J. Improving Tracking Performance of Nonlinear Uncertain Bilateral Teleoperation Systems with Time-Varying Delays and Disturbances. *IEEE/ASME Trans. Mechatronics* **2020**, *25*, 1171–1181. [CrossRef]
229. Zhou, J.; Huang, L.; Song, J.; Wang, H. Partial model-free sliding mode control design for a class of disturbed systems via computational learning algorithm. *Optim. Control Appl. Methods* **2021**, *44*, 1278–1289. [CrossRef]
230. Song, J.; Huang, L.Y.; Karimi, H.R.; Niu, Y.; Zhou, J. ADP-Based Security Decentralized Sliding Mode Control for Partially Unknown Large-Scale Systems Under Injection Attacks. *IEEE Trans. Circuits Syst. I Regul. Pap.* **2020**, *67*, 5290–5301. [CrossRef]
231. Wang, R.; Wei, Y.; Chi, R. Enhanced data-driven optimal iterative learning control for nonlinear non-affine discrete-time systems with iterative sliding-mode surface. *Trans. Inst. Meas. Control* **2020**, *42*, 1923–1934. [CrossRef]
232. Taheri, M.; Zhang, C.; Berardehi, Z.R.; Chen, Y.; Roohi, M. No-chatter model-free sliding mode control for synchronization of chaotic fractional-order systems with application in image encryption. *Multimed. Tools Appl.* **2022**, *81*, 24167–24197. [CrossRef]
233. Xu, D.; Zhang, W.; Jiang, B.; Shi, P.; Wang, S. Directed-Graph-Observer-Based Model-Free Cooperative Sliding Mode Control for Distributed Energy Storage Systems in DC Microgrid. *IEEE Trans. Ind. Inform.* **2020**, *16*, 1224–1235. [CrossRef]
234. Sami, I.; Ro, J.S. Adaptive supertwisting sliding mode control of multi-converter MVDC power systems. *Energy Rep.* **2022**, *8*, 467–479. [CrossRef]
235. Wang, Y.; Yang, Y.; Liang, R.; Geng, T.; Zhang, W. Adaptive Current Control for Grid-Connected Inverter with Dynamic Recurrent Fuzzy-Neural-Network. *Energies* **2022**, *15*, 4163. [CrossRef]
236. Ardjal, A.; Bettayeb, M.; Mansouri, R.; Zouak, B. Design and implementation of a Model-Free Fractional Order Intelligent PI Fractional Order Sliding Mode Controller for water level tank system. *ISA Trans.* **2022**, *127*, 501–510. [CrossRef]
237. Wang, Y.; Hou, M. Model-free adaptive integral terminal sliding mode predictive control for a class of discrete-time nonlinear systems. *ISA Trans.* **2019**, *93*, 209–217. [CrossRef]
238. Huang, X.; Dong, Z.; Zhang, F.; Zhang, L. Discrete-time extended state observer-based model-free adaptive sliding mode control with prescribed performance. *Int. J. Robust Nonlinear Control* **2022**, *32*, 4816–4842. [CrossRef]
239. Gao, S.; Zhao, D.; Yan, X.; Spurgeon, S.K. Linearized Bregman iteration based model-free adaptive sliding mode control for a class of non-linear systems. *IET Control Theory Appl.* **2021**, *15*, 281–296. [CrossRef]
240. Gao, X.; Weng, Y. Chattering-free model free adaptive sliding mode control for gas collection process with data dropout. *J. Process Control* **2020**, *93*, 1–13. [CrossRef]
241. Ebrahimi, N.; Ozgoli, S.; Ramezani, A. Model free sliding mode controller for blood glucose control: Towards artificial pancreas without need to mathematical model of the system. *Comput. Methods Programs Biomed.* **2020**, *195*, 105663. [CrossRef] [PubMed]
242. Chen, Y.; Tang, C.; Roohi, M. Design of a model-free adaptive sliding mode control to synchronize chaotic fractional-order systems with input saturation: An application in secure communications. *J. Frankl. Inst.* **2021**, *358*, 8109–8137. [CrossRef]
243. Gheisarnejad, M.; Faraji, B.; Esfahani, Z.; Khooban, M.H. A Close Loop Multi-Area Brain Stimulation Control for Parkinson's Patients Rehabilitation. *IEEE Sens. J.* **2020**, *20*, 2205–2213. [CrossRef]
244. Lee, J.; Deshpande, N.; Caldwell, D.G.; Mattos, L.S. Microscale Precision Control of a Computer-Assisted Transoral Laser Microsurgery System. *IEEE/ASME Trans. Mechatronics* **2020**, *25*, 604–615. [CrossRef]
245. Tian, Y.; Wang, H.; Wu, Q.; Hu, M.; Christov, N. Nonsingular Fast Terminal Sliding Mode Based Model-Free Control: Application to Glycemia Regulation Systems. *Inf. Technol. Control.* **2019**, *48*, 602–617. [CrossRef]
246. Kang, S.; Wu, H.; Yang, X.; Li, Y.; Wang, Y. Model-free robust finite-time force tracking control for piezoelectric actuators using time-delay estimation with adaptive fuzzy compensator. *Trans. Inst. Meas. Control* **2020**, *42*, 351–364. [CrossRef]
247. Fliess, M.; Join, C. Model-free control. *Int. J. Control* **2013**, *86*, 2228–2252. [CrossRef]
248. Wang, W.; Ma, J.; Cheng, Z.; Li, X.; Silva, C.W.D.; Lee, T.H. Global Iterative Sliding Mode Control of an Industrial Biaxial Gantry System for Contouring Motion Tasks. *IEEE/ASME Trans. Mechatronics* **2022**, *27*, 1617–1628. [CrossRef]
249. Saied, M.; Lussier, B.; Fantoni, I.; Shraim, H.; Francis, C. Active versus passive fault-tolerant control of a redundant multirotor UAV. *Aeronaut. J.* **2020**, *124*, 385–408. [CrossRef]
250. Yin, F.C.; Ji, Q.Z.; Wen, C.W. An adaptive terminal sliding mode control of stone-carving robotic manipulators based on radial basis function neural network. *Appl. Intell.* **2022**, *52*, 16051–16068. [CrossRef]
251. Gheisarnejad, M.; Farsizadeh, H.; Tavana, M.R.; Khooban, M.H. A Novel Deep Learning Controller for DC–DC Buck–Boost Converters in Wireless Power Transfer Feeding CPLs. *IEEE Trans. Ind. Electron.* **2021**, *68*, 6379–6384. [CrossRef]
252. Wang, Y.; Zhou, W.; Luo, J.; Yan, H.; Pu, H.; Peng, Y. Reliable Intelligent Path Following Control for a Robotic Airship Against Sensor Faults. *IEEE/ASME Trans. Mechatronics* **2019**, *24*, 2572–2582. [CrossRef]
253. Mosayebi, M.; Gheisarnejad, M.; Khooban, M.H. An intelligent sliding mode control for stabilization of parallel converters feeding CPLs in DC-microgrid. *IET Power Electron.* **2022**, *15*, 1596–1606. [CrossRef]

254. Zhang, Y.; Li, F.; Gao, S.; Zhao, D.; Yan, X.G.; Spurgeon, S.K. Output consensus for interconnected heterogeneous systems via a combined model predictive control and integral sliding mode control with application to CSTRs. *Control Eng. Pract.* **2024**, *153*, 106100. [CrossRef]
255. Yonezawa, H.; Yonezawa, A.; Kajiwara, I. Experimental verification of model-free active damping system based on virtual controlled object and fuzzy sliding mode control. *Mech. Syst. Signal Process.* **2025**, *224*, 111961. [CrossRef]
256. Wang, Y.; Lu, X.; Gao, Y.; Chen, Y. An anti-swing control method combining deep learning prediction models with a multistate fractional-order terminal sliding mode controller for wave motion compensation devices. *Mech. Syst. Signal Process.* **2025**, *223*, 111819. [CrossRef]

Disclaimer/Publisher's Note: The statements, opinions and data contained in all publications are solely those of the individual author(s) and contributor(s) and not of MDPI and/or the editor(s). MDPI and/or the editor(s) disclaim responsibility for any injury to people or property resulting from any ideas, methods, instructions or products referred to in the content.

Article

Root Cause Tracing Using Equipment Process Accuracy Evaluation for Looper in Hot Rolling

Fengwei Jing [1], Fenghe Li [2], Yong Song [1], Jie Li [1], Zhanbiao Feng [1] and Jin Guo [2,*]

[1] National Engineering Research Center for Advanced Rolling Technology and Intelligent Manufacturing, University of Science and Technology Beijing, Beijing 100083, China; jingfengwei@nercar.ustb.edu.cn (F.J.); songyong@ustb.edu.cn (Y.S.); lijiefh@126.com (J.L.); fengzhanbiao0926@gmail.com (Z.F.)

[2] School of Automation and Electrical Engineering, University of Science and Technology Beijing, Beijing 100083, China; li_fenghe@outlook.com

* Correspondence: guojin@ustb.edu.cn

Abstract: The concept of production stability in hot strip rolling encapsulates the ability of a production line to consistently maintain its output levels and uphold the quality of its products, thus embodying the steady and uninterrupted nature of the production yield. This scholarly paper focuses on the paramount looper equipment in the finishing rolling area, utilizing it as a case study to investigate approaches for identifying the origins of instabilities, specifically when faced with inadequate looper performance. Initially, the paper establishes the equipment process accuracy evaluation (EPAE) model for the looper, grounded in the precision of the looper's operational process, to accurately depict the looper's functioning state. Subsequently, it delves into the interplay between the EPAE metrics and overall production stability, advocating for the use of EPAE scores as direct indicators of production stability. The study further introduces a novel algorithm designed to trace the root causes of issues, categorizing them into material, equipment, and control factors, thereby facilitating on-site fault rectification. Finally, the practicality and effectiveness of this methodology are substantiated through its application on the 2250 hot rolling equipment production line. This paper provides a new approach for fault tracing in the hot rolling process.

Keywords: hot strip rolling; looper; EPAE; production stability; root cause traceability

Citation: Jing, F.; Li, F.; Song, Y.; Li, J.; Feng, Z.; Guo, J. Root Cause Tracing Using Equipment Process Accuracy Evaluation for Looper in Hot Rolling. *Algorithms* **2024**, *17*, 102. https://doi.org/10.3390/a17030102

Academic Editor: Mircea-Bogdan Radac

Received: 22 January 2024
Revised: 17 February 2024
Accepted: 20 February 2024
Published: 26 February 2024

Copyright: © 2024 by the authors. Licensee MDPI, Basel, Switzerland. This article is an open access article distributed under the terms and conditions of the Creative Commons Attribution (CC BY) license (https://creativecommons.org/licenses/by/4.0/).

1. Introduction

In the contemporary industrial, agricultural, and construction sectors, hot-rolled strip products have become increasingly vital, leading to their production volume representing a significant portion of total steel output for steel companies. This has positioned the hot-rolled production line as a foundational element for these companies [1]. Advancements in traditional production methods, combined with the progression of computer technology, have markedly increased automation within the hot continuous rolling process [2], enhancing both the volume and quality of rolling output. Nevertheless, there has been a growing demand for higher quality in hot-rolled strip products in recent years. This surge in demand imposes more rigorous requirements on the hot-rolling production process and the precision of the equipment used. The challenge of improving the quality of plates and strips while simultaneously reducing the scrap rate represents a crucial developmental direction for steel companies and the plate and strip production industry [3].

As shown in Figure 1, the hot rolling process is inherently complex, exhibiting dynamic and nonlinear attributes. It involves numerous control loops and thousands of process variables that critically influence product quality, epitomizing a sophisticated industrial process [4]. When issues arise in any part of the process or equipment, it can significantly impact the entire production line, ultimately affecting the company's profitability. Therefore, promptly identifying and analyzing these problematic links or equipment is essential.

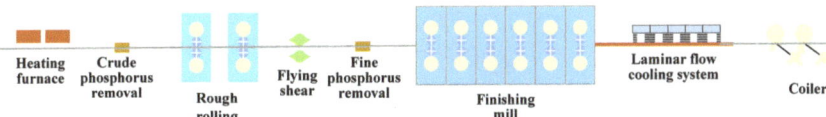

Figure 1. Hot rolling process.

Modern hot tandem rolling technology is characterized by its complexity, particularly in controlling temperature and rolling force [5], which can lead to fluctuations in product quality. To improve the stability of hot continuous rolling production, typical strategies involve focusing on critical stability-affecting factors and exploring enhancements for processes and equipment performance. Various research methodologies have been employed to address these challenges. For instance, a data-driven dynamic concurrent kernel canonical correlation analysis (DCKCCA) method was utilized for diagnosing CAP-thickness-related faults [6]. Additionally, ref. [7] developed a fault diagnosis method using two-dimensional time–frequency images and data enhancement, training a convolutional neural network (CNN)-based model for this purpose. A combination of continuous wavelet transform and a deep convolutional generative adversarial network (DCGAN) was proposed for tackling uneven data distribution in rolling bearing fault diagnosis [8]. Modified independent component analysis (MICA) was used to construct a multivariate statistical process monitoring model for detecting and analyzing chatter in hot strip mill processes [9]. Furthermore, a data-driven key performance indicator (KPI) prediction and diagnosis scheme was developed [10], offering a simplified alternative to the standard partial least squares (PLS) method.

However, most existing methods primarily focus on surface data characteristics, inferring the superficial causes of faults based on data traits. Consequently, while these methods can locate the faulty link or equipment, they often fail to identify the underlying root cause. This paper seeks to address this limitation by analyzing the problem from the perspectives of production continuity, product quality stability, and extreme specification production capacity. By examining the issue from exterior to interior layers, this study aims to identify the fundamental cause of faults. Specifically, the finishing rolling area of the hot tandem rolling production line is used as a case study, categorizing production stability factors into material, equipment, and control aspects in Table 1.

Table 1. Factors related to production stability in finishing rolling area.

Object	Name
Control factors	Final temperature hit Plate type Mechanical equipment
Material factors	Roll gap setting accuracy Surface quality Electrical equipment
Equipment factors	Roll force setting accuracy Width, thickness Water, gas, and thermal equipment

There is much related equipment involved in the finishing rolling area, and the looper can ensure the stability of the strip during the rolling process, control the shape and size of the strip, and reduce surface defects of the strip, etc. [11]; so, here we take the looper as a case study to trace its root cause. When identifying a low EPAE score for the looper during production, as Figure 2 shows, instead of examining surface-level faults and errors such as looper angle and looper tension, the focus shifts towards investigating the more profound issues depicted in the figure below. Based on the EPAE model, this paper designs a root-cause-traceability algorithm to analyze material factors, equipment factors, and control factors, to ensure that the root cause of the problem can be quickly located after an abnormality occurs.

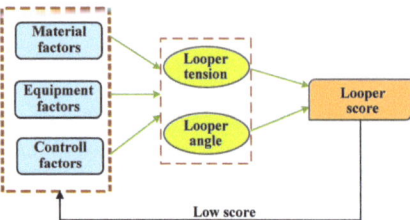

Figure 2. Root cause tracing.

This paper considers the problem of root cause traceability in looper equipment under the framework of production stability in the hot rolling area, inspired by the [12–14]. First, this paper elucidates the physical structure and operational principles of the looper. Subsequently, it delineates the precision indices for controlling the looper in each operational process and establishes the EPAE model for the looper. Then, an analysis is conducted to explore the relationship between the EPAE model of the looper and production stability. Based on this, a root-cause-traceability algorithm is proposed. In addition, actual data pertaining to loopers within the 2250 hot rolling equipment production line were used to trace the root cause, identifying the primary factors most likely contributing to a low looper score. The main contributions of the paper can be summarized as the following points.

- This paper initiates its approach from the foundational layer of production stability and analyzes problems that may arise in the production process, which is different from most existing work on fault diagnosis.
- An EPAE model based on the actual working process of the looper is proposed. This model aims to improve the interpretability of subsequent causal relationship modeling.
- A root-cause-tracing algorithm is proposed and its viability is assessed by using available actual production data.

The root-cause-tracing algorithm is a brand-new diagnostic algorithm proposed by this paper for industrial processes. It consists of data processing, building neural networks, and calculating weights. Different from previous fault diagnosis algorithms, this algorithm is committed to finding deeper problems, rather than just locating the device where the fault occurred. The calculation of weights is the highlight of this algorithm, this part converts the problem of fault location into a problem of solving a system of equations, and converts the possibility of fault occurrence into the weight of each eigenvalue. And when constructing the system of equations, both new data and past data are used to construct the system of equations. With past data as a reference, the solution is more reliable.

The remainder of the paper is structured as follows: Section 2 starts from the control accuracy of the looper and then constructs the EPAE model of the looper; Section 3 analyzes the relationship between the EPAE score and production stability and proposes a root-cause-traceability algorithm; Section 4 uses existing data to verify the root-cause-tracing algorithm and analyze its feasibility; Section 5 summarizes the findings of this paper and suggests some potential future directions.

2. EPAE Model of Looper

2.1. Physical Structure of the Looper

In the rolling process of hot-rolled plate and strip, the looper plays an important role. It stabilizes the tension between the stands, adjusts the flow rate between the stands, and ensures a constant set amount. Precisely controlling the tension and sleeve volume of the finishing rolling loop contributes to enhanced production stability, reduces the risk of accidents, and reduces the shear loss caused by the reduction in strip width [15].

Especially when rolling thin strips, precise control of the looper is crucial. Figure 3 illustrates its structure.

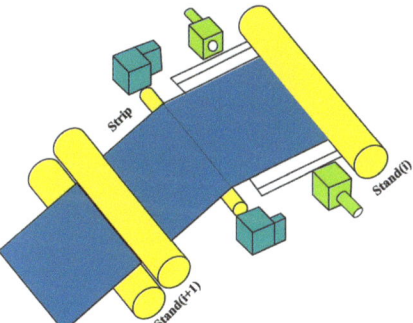

Figure 3. Schematic diagram of looper structure.

The end of the looper rod is connected to the looper arm on the transmission side, keeping a certain distance from the hinge point [16]. The looper shaft is installed on the exit side of the previous stand, below the rolling line. When the looper moves to the highest position, there is a moderate movement space between the inlet and outlet of the rolling mill to ensure that the looper is reliably in place.

2.2. Working Principle of the Looper

In the finishing rolling unit, the rolling process is usually carried out in the order of steel biting, continuous rolling formation, continuous rolling tension establishment, stable continuous rolling, and steel throwing. The looper control can be divided into three main stages: from looping to strip tension formation (entry process), looper small tension continuous rolling (steady-state process), and exit process [17].

The entry process mainly refers to the short period of time from the head of the strip being bitten by the roller until the strip establishes tension between the frames, which is about 1 s [18]. In the entire continuous rolling process, this period of time is very short. As shown in Figure 4, there are two important positions in the process: mechanical zero position α_0 and working zero position α_{ref}, which directly affect the quality and performance of the product during the rolling process.

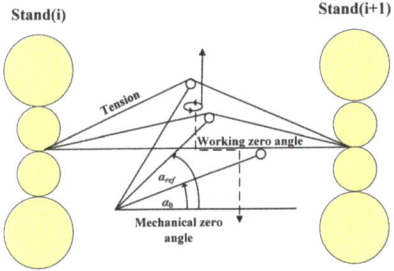

Figure 4. Starting process of the looper.

The steady-state process refers to maintaining a slight tension during the rolling process, so that the rolled piece can maintain a stable shape and movement between the rollers without deformation or other problems caused by excessive tension [19]. This is usually achieved through a highly closed loop control system to ensure that the force and tension exerted on the rolled piece during the rolling process are effectively controlled. The existence of this stage helps improve the stability of the rolling and the quality of the finished product.

The exit process is a key step in the finishing rolling process. It refers to adjusting the position of the rolling mill roll sleeve so that it gradually decreases to the minimum value and finally ends the rolling process [20]. At this stage, the rolling mill gradually lowers the position of the roller sleeve and reduces the tension, finally achieving a smooth end of rolling. This process requires careful control to ensure that the shape and size of the final rolled piece meet product specifications.

2.3. Control Accuracy of the Looper

The EPAE model of the looper calculates various control indicators of the looper to obtain the control accuracy of each looper in each rolling process. As a standard to measure the operating status of the looper, the detailed control indicators are shown in Table 2.

Table 2. Evaluation index of process accuracy of the looper.

Object	Name	Symbol
Entry process	Starting angle	$\Delta \alpha$
	Rising time	t
	Steady-state time	t_n
Steady-state process	Oscillation amplitude	a
	Number of oscillations	f_s
	Looper tension	T_f
Exit process	Falling time	d_t
	Steel-throwing tension	T_t
	Small set time	t_s
	Small set angle	a_s

The looper equipment process accuracy evaluation system mainly focuses on various control indicators related to the looper angle and looper tension during the three processes of looper operation. The looper control system mainly includes the looper volume calculation model, looper torque calculation model, looper height control, looper tension control, etc. The above contents will be described in detail below.

2.3.1. Entry Process

The starting process mainly focuses on three indicators, the starting angle, the rising time and the time to enter the steady state.

(1) Starting angle

This is the average value of the looper within 3–8 m of the head of the strip. The maximum value of the difference between the measured angle of the loop and the set value within the range of 3–8 m from the head of the rolling plate strip on the lower frame of the loop is calculated. The calculation process is as follows.

The defined length of the strip head is 3–8 m. The starting and ending points of the head are calculated according to the rolling speed and sampling period:

$$\sum_{t=0}^{N_3}[v_i[t]T = 3]$$
$$\sum_{t=0}^{N_8}[v_i[t]T = 8]$$
(1)

where v_i is the rolling speed of the finishing rolling F_i stand, T is the data sampling interval, N_3 is the head 3 m data point, N_8 is the head 8 m data point. When the rolling section reaches the 3 m data point and the 8 m data point, the lifting angles at both positions as α_i and α_i', respectively, are recorded.

The starting angle is calculated based on the obtained h_3 and h_8:

$$\Delta \alpha_i = \max(|\alpha_i - \alpha_i'|) \tag{2}$$

where α_i is a vector composed of measured angles of the looper LP_i, α_i' is a vector composed of set angles of the looper LP_i, and $\Delta \alpha$ is the starting angle of the looper.

(2) Rising time

The time it takes for the looper to rise during the set-up phase. The time it takes for the actual measured value of the looper angle to go from the set value 10% to the set value 90% is calculated. The calculation method is as follows:

$$\begin{aligned} \alpha_{i\_set} \times 10\% &= \alpha_i[t_1] \\ \alpha_{i\_set} \times 90\% &= \alpha_i[t_2] \\ t_i &= t_2 - t_1 \end{aligned} \tag{3}$$

where α_{i_set} is the set value of the looper angle, t_i is the rise time of the looper LP_i, t_1 is the data point reaching the 10% set value, and t_2 is the time to reach 90% of the data points for the set values.

(3) Steady-state time

The time it takes for the looper to reach steady state. The time it takes for the looper to bite the steel from the lower frame until the actual measured value of the looper enters the ±2° error band of the looper set value is calculated.

All points where the upper and lower error bands of the measured value of the looper angle intersect with the set value of the looper are calculated:

$$\alpha_i[\Xi[i]] = (\alpha_i' + 2) || (\alpha_i' - 2) \tag{4}$$

where Ξ is the set of all points where the upper and lower error bands of the measured value of the looper angle intersect with the set value of the looper, and "||" is the "OR" operation.

The two points with the largest distance in the set, which are the steady-state start time and steady-state end time is calculated:

$$\begin{aligned} \Xi[k+1] - \Xi[k] &= \max(\Xi[i+1] - \Xi[i]) \\ d_u &= \Xi[k] \\ d_e &= \Xi[k+1] \end{aligned} \tag{5}$$

where d_u is the start data point of steady state, and d_e is the end data point of steady state. The time it takes to reach steady state is calculated:

$$t_{n,i} = d_u - t_b \tag{6}$$

where t_n is the time it takes to enter the steady state, and t_b is the moment when the looper starts the signal.

2.3.2. Steady State Process

Since the most important thing for a looper in the steady-state process is stability, the steady-state process mainly focuses on three indicators: oscillation amplitude, number of oscillations, and looper tension. These three indicators can well reflect the stability of the looper during the steady-state process.

(1) Oscillation amplitude

The maximum amplitude of the oscillation within the steady-state range. The maximum difference between the actual measured value of the loop and the set value of the loop during the time interval from when the looper enters steady state to when the small loop signal turns ON is calculated.

$$a_i = \max(\alpha_i - \alpha_i')[d_u : d_s^s] \tag{7}$$

where a_i is the oscillation amplitude of the looper, d_u is the time it takes to enter steady state, d_s^s is a small set of signal ON data points, α_i is the measured angle of the looper LP_i, and α_i' is the set angle of the looper LP_i.

(2) Number of oscillations

The number of oscillations of the looper within the steady state interval. The number of times the oscillation amplitude of the actual measured value of the loop exceeds the set value ±1° in the time interval from when the looper enters the steady state to when the small loop signal turns ON is calculated.

$$\alpha_i[\Xi_s[i]] = (\alpha_i' + 1) || (\alpha_i' - 1), \; i \in [d_u : d_s^s] \\ f_{s,i} = \lfloor \text{len}(\alpha_i[\Xi_s[i]])/2 \rfloor \tag{8}$$

where $f_{s,i}$ is the number of oscillations of the looper, Ξ_s is the set of data points where the actual measured value of the looper exceeds the set value ±1°, and $\text{len}(\Xi_s)$ is the number of data, the number of oscillations f_s is the number of data in Ξ_s divisible by 2, and $\lfloor \cdot \rfloor$ represents rounding down.

(3) Looper tension

The maximum amplitude of loop tension oscillation within the steady-state range. The maximum difference between the actual measured value of the looper tension and the set value of the looper tension in the time interval from when the looper enters steady state to when the small looper signal turns ON is calculated.

$$T_{f,i} = \max\{(T_i - T_i')\} \tag{9}$$

where $T_{f,i}$ is the looper tension, T_i is the measured tension of the i-th frame, and T_i' is the set tension of the i-th frame.

2.3.3. Exit Process

During the setting process, we mainly focus on the relevant indicators of small setting control, setting time, steel throwing tension, small setting time, and small setting angle.

(1) Falling time

The time it takes for the looper to actually fall into place. The time it takes from the small set of signals OFF to the upstream rack load OFF is calculated:

$$d_{t,i} = d_{t,i-1} - d_{s,i}^e \tag{10}$$

where $d_{t,i}$ is the falling time, $d_{t,i-1}$ is the steel throwing data point of the corresponding upstream rack, and $d_{s,i}^e$ is the data point of the small set of signal OFF.

(2) Steel throwing tension

The tension at the moment when the looper starts to fall. The measured tension of the looper at the moment when the small set signal is ON and OFF is calculated:

$$T_{t,i} = T_i[d_s^e] \tag{11}$$

where $T_{t,i}$ is the steel throwing tension, and T_i is the measured tension of the i-th frame.

(3) Small set of time

The time when the looper performs the control of the small loop. The duration of the small set of signals ON is calculated:

$$t_{s,i} = d_{s,i}^e - d_{s,i}^s \tag{12}$$

where $t_{s,i}$ is the small set of time, and $d_{s,i}^s$ is a small set of signal ON data points.

(4) Small set of angle

The angle of the looper when performing small set control. The looper angle at the moment when the small set signal turns ON and OFF is calculated:

$$a_{s,i} = \alpha_i [d_s^e] \tag{13}$$

where $a_{s,i}$ is the small set of the angle.

The looper equipment process accuracy evaluation system represents the precision of the looper within the real production process, influenced by the collective impact of relevant equipment and control models. The looper equipment process accuracy evaluation system evaluates the operating status of the looper in real time. If the evaluation result is low, which can reflect an abnormality in the current looper operation status, then fault diagnosis is conducted.

2.4. EPAE Model Construction of Looper

The division and distribution of functional areas of the hot rolling production lines have multi-level characteristics. Therefore, we considered designing a multi-level analytic hierarchy process based on the level division, to recursively deduce the global index weights. Then, the entropy weight method is used to adjust the weights, aiming to obtain subjective and objective comprehensive weights. Finally, the fuzzy comprehensive evaluation method and the membership gravity center defuzzification method are used to achieve an accurate evaluation of the equipment process accuracy. Still taking the looper area as an example, its level can be divided into: finishing rolling area, finishing rolling unit, looper, equipment process accuracy, and evaluation index (starting angle, rising time, etc.).

Firstly, a hierarchical structure model of an analytic hierarchy process (AHP) is constructed [21], stipulating that t is the specific functional index under the looper component. The hierarchical structure can be divided upward into component-level, equipment-level, regional-level, and factory-level. The EPAE results are represented by the symbols e, m, g, P, and then a judgment matrix is constructed according to the relative importance of the indicators at each level. The subjective weight of each level of indicators is obtained by AHP:

$$\begin{cases} e = A_1(t) \otimes E_1(t) \\ m = A_2(e) \otimes E_2(e) \\ g = A_3(m) \otimes E_3(m) \\ P = A_4(g) \otimes E_4(g) \end{cases} \tag{14}$$

where A_n is the index weight of the current level, E_n is the evaluation index of the current level, and $\otimes$ is the hierarchical analysis operation process of weights and evaluation indicators.

Secondly, the entropy weight method [22] is used to assist in the indicator weight assignment of the AHP model. Information entropy is an important indicator that reflects the degree of order and chaos of the system. According to information entropy theory, the entropy value $H(x)$ can be expressed as

$$H(x) = -\sum_{i=1}^{k} [p(x_i) \ln p(x_i)] \tag{15}$$

where k is the number of source messages, and $p(x_i)$ is the probability of occurrence of event x_i. The entropy weight method essentially uses the entropy value to judge the degree of dispersion of its indicators.

Afterwards, the results obtained by multi-layer AHP need to be combined with the entropy weight method. AHP mainly determines the evaluation scheme based on expert experience, which makes the judgment of the relative importance of each indicator highly subjective, so entropy becomes necessary. The weight method assists in achieving objective assignment of indicator weights. The weight values of each indicator, derived through the multi-layer AHP and entropy weight method, are brought into the following formula to calculate the comprehensive weight of the evaluation indicator β_i.

$$\beta_i = \mu \omega_i + (1-\mu)\epsilon_i \tag{16}$$

where μ represents the preference factor, determined by expert experience according to the importance of subjective and objective factors; ω_i is the subjective weight of various indicators obtained by multi-layer AHP; and ϵ_i is the various items obtained by the entropy weight method. The indicators are objectively weighted.

Finally, the fuzzy relationship matrix R is established based on the equipment process evaluation index and the evaluation set. Subsequently, utilizing a combined evaluation method integrating AHP and entropy weight methods, the weight vector of the evaluation factors $W = (\beta_1, \beta_2, \ldots, \beta_n)$ is determined, resulting in the ultimate evaluation outcome.

$$result = fuzzy(W, R) \tag{17}$$

The membership centroid method is applied to defuzzify the above results [23], and the multiple evaluation indicators of the looper are weighted and summed to obtain the final evaluation score.

3. Root-Cause-Tracing Algorithm

Due to the large scale and complexity of the hot rolling, when the system crashes it is difficult for operation and maintenance personnel to find the root cause of the faults in a short time, so the system will be in an unstable state, even causing irreversible losses. Therefore, the process of finding the root cause of large-scale system faults becomes particularly important. To solve this problem, there are some automated fault diagnosis and root-cause-analysis technologies, such as data mining and model-based fault prediction, which can find the cause of the fault, but the speed and efficiency of fault repair are low. Therefore, this section proposes a root-cause-traceability analysis algorithm to analyze the production stability of the finishing rolling area.

3.1. Correlation Analysis between EPAE and Production Stability

Taking the finishing rolling area as an example, the EPAE score in this area includes five aspects: side guides, loopers, AGC, bending rolls, and shifting rolls. Simultaneously, abnormal conditions in the finishing rolling area include the head of the finishing rolling area abnormalities, body abnormalities in the finishing rolling area, and tail abnormalities in the finishing rolling area.

The strip production process is complex and involves many parameters, so the same anomaly in the finishing rolling area may occur multiple times. In this section, the total number of abnormalities in the finishing rolling area of each strip is used as an indicator of production stability, and the correlation between the total number of abnormalities and the EPAE score is analyzed.

The Pearson correlation coefficient, also known as the Pearson product–moment correlation coefficient, is used to measure the linear correlation between two sets of data X and Y, and its value ranges from -1 to 1 [24]. The calculation formula is

$$r = \frac{\sum_{i=1}^{n}(X_i - \bar{X})(Y_i - \bar{Y})}{\sqrt{\sum_{i=1}^{n}(X_i - \bar{X})^2}\sqrt{\sum_{i=1}^{n}(Y_i - \bar{Y})^2}} \tag{18}$$

where $\bar{X}$ and $\bar{Y}$ are the average values of data X and data Y. The closer the absolute value of r is to 1, the stronger the correlation between the two sets of data. In this section, the two sets of data X and Y are, respectively, the EPAE score and the number of anomalies appearing in the finishing rolling area.

In order to facilitate the data analysis, consider representing the score as follows:

$$\begin{cases} [x], & |x - [x]| < 0.5 \\ [x] + 1, & |x - [x]| \geq 0.5 \end{cases} \quad (19)$$

where x is the EPAE score and $[x]$ is the rounding function. This equation aims to classify data into different categories as much as possible, such as number 1.1, which are classified as 1, since $|1.1 - [1.1]| = |1.1 - 1| < 0.5$, 1.1 is classified as number 1, and so on, 1.6, 1.7 are represented as 2. After the above operations, the same score may correspond to multiple abnormal times, so these abnormal times need to be averaged.

The EPAE score and the number of abnormal occurrences of production stability in the finishing rolling area of a 2250 mm hot strip production line in a certain month are collected and used in Equation (19) to calculate the Pearson correlation between each EPAE score and the number of abnormal occurrences in the finishing rolling area.

From Table 3, it is not difficult to see that the factors of the finishing rolling side guide plate, looper, automatic gauge control (AGC), finishing rolling bending roll, and shifting roll are negatively correlated with the number of abnormalities in the finishing rolling area. In particular, the absolute value of the correlation coefficient between the finishing rolling side guide plate and the finishing rolling bending roll is large, and the significance level p-value is also much less than 0.05. This shows that the higher the EPAE score, the fewer the number of abnormalities and the higher the production stability. Therefore, the EPAE score will be applied subsequently to reflect the production stability.

Table 3. Process accuracy evaluation and finish rolling stability.

Equipment	Correlation Coefficient	p-Value
Side Guide	−0.768	4.087×10^{-5}
Looper	−0.113	0.382
Automatic Gauge Control	−0.458	0.009
Bending Roller	−0.855	6.627×10^{-16}
Shifting Roller	−0.356	0.024

3.2. Construction of Root-Cause-Tracing Algorithm

During the rolling process, if the EPAE score for the looper is observed to be low, a root-cause-tracing algorithm is designed based on the EPAE model to find the reason from material factors, equipment factors, control factors, etc., enabling swift identification of issues after an abnormality occurs. When an abnormality occurs in the looper, since there are many factors involved and their proportions are different, it is necessary to construct a suitable equation set, calculate the weight of each factor, and give the most likely reason for the low looper score.

Most of the previous classification algorithms used existing data as a reference system, selected appropriate classifiers to fully explore the intrinsic relationships between the data, and established prediction functions. When a new sample comes in, the fault location is determined through the previously established function. The root-cause-tracing algorithm proposed in this paper selects old samples similar to a new sample when entering it into the database and combines the two phases to construct a system of equations to find the source of the fault. This method does not use all the previous data, but selects it selectively, so it has the characteristics of being "lazy" [25]. And this root-cause-tracing algorithm not only refers to past experience, but also fully combines the current situation, so can effectively deal with new sudden failures.

Algorithm Construction Technology

(1) Data preprocessing

The steel coil and its corresponding LP_SCOREALL (average score of 6 loopers) is extracted from the original data set, as well as factors related to loopers such as FORCERATE_BODY, FORCERATE_HEAD. Afterwards, missing values and outliers in the data are eliminated or supplemented to improve data quality and facilitate subsequent analysis.

(2) Calculate the average

There are many factors involved in the looper during the hot strip rolling process, and each factor has multiple measured values. Therefore, in order to reduce data redundancy and simplify calculation complexity, the average values of these data are subsequently used as the factor eigenvalues.

$$x = \frac{\sum_{i=1}^{n} s_i}{n} \tag{20}$$

where s is the score corresponding to different aspects of a certain factor, and x is the average value, which is the characteristic value.

(3) Mean deviation

In order to indicate the quality of the sample, it needs to be compared with the standard value, and the deviation between the two $\Delta x = x - x_{std}$ is calculated as the basis for judgment. In the absence of an exact standard value, the looper group with a higher score is identified and its characteristic value is substituted with the empirical standard value.

(4) Data normalization

The measurement units and magnitudes of the corresponding characteristic values of the loopers are different, making the indicators incomparable. Therefore, before data analysis, it is necessary to eliminate the influence of dimensions between eigenvalues. All features are unified into approximately the same numerical range so that indicators of different magnitudes can be weighted and compared. The normalization method is used to linearly map the original feature data to the interval [0, 1].

$$x' = \frac{x - x_{min}}{x_{max} - x_{min}} \tag{21}$$

where x_{max}, x_{min}, respectively, correspond to the maximum value and minimum value of a certain influencing factor of the looper.

(5) Neural Network

In this paper, due to the unclear functional relationship between the characteristic values of each factor of the looper and its score, a back-propagation (BP) neural network is employed [26]. The characteristic values of each factor of the looper are used as inputs, while the looper score is the output; an appropriate activation function is selected to fit the unknown function to facilitate subsequent analysis.

It can be seen from Figure 2 that material factors, equipment factors, and control factors directly affect the parameters of the looper itself: looper angle and looper tension. Therefore, the above three types of factors are used as the input of the first neural network, and the looper angle and looper tension are used as outputs. Then the second neural network is constructed by utilizing the looper angle and looper tension as inputs and the looper score as the output.

By combining the above two neural networks and using the output of the first neural network as the input of the second neural network, the relationship between each factor of the looper and the looper score can be obtained.

(6) Calculate weight

The state of the looper involves many factors. In order to facilitate subsequent analysis, we express the dimensionless eigenvalues and scores as $x_1 \ldots x_n$ and y, respectively. These factors directly act on the state of the looper, that is, the looper angle $angle = f_1(x_1 \ldots x_n)$

and the looper tension $force = f_2(x_1...x_n)$. The status of the looper directly affects the evaluation score of the looper, that is, $y = u(angle, force)$. Therefore, the relationship between the looper score and the eigenvalue can be directly expressed as

$$y = f(x_1...x_n) \tag{22}$$

Then, a one-stage Taylor expansion of f is performed:

$$f(x_1...x_n) = p_1x_1 + p_2x_2 + ... + p_nx_n + o(x_1...x_n) \tag{23}$$

where $o(x_1...x_n)$ is the higher-order term of each eigenvalue. Since each eigenvalue has been dimensionally processed, p_i can represent the weight of each eigenvalue. A larger p_i means the factor has a greater impact on the looper score. In the actual production process, f is a nonlinear function, and it is difficult to explain its specific expression form. Therefore, it is necessary to use existing data and use the BP neural network [27] to fit f.

The dimensionless characteristic deviation and fractional deviation are put into the above formula to obtain

$$\Delta y = f(\Delta x_1 \cdots \Delta x_n) \tag{24}$$

$$f(\Delta x_1 \cdots \Delta x_n) = \sum_{i=1}^{n} p_i \Delta x_i + o(\Delta x_i) \tag{25}$$

In order to fully consider the contingency of the new sample data, it is necessary to select a value for Δy_m that is not much different from the score deviation Δy in the existing database as the reference data, that is, $\Delta y_m = f(\Delta x_{m1}...\Delta x_{mn})$. Since Δy and Δy_m are not much different, the form of each characteristic deviation is basically similar, so it can be used as a reference to establish the following system of equations:

$$\begin{aligned} f(\Delta x_{11}...\Delta x_{1n}) &= \sum_{i=1}^{n} p_i \Delta x_{1i} + o(\Delta x_{1i}) \\ f(\Delta x_{m1}...\Delta x_{1n}) &= \sum_{i=1}^{n} p_i \Delta x_{mi} + o(\Delta x_{mi}) \end{aligned} \tag{26}$$

Since $\Delta x \in [-1, 1]$, $o(\Delta x_{m1}...\Delta x_{mn})$ is a bounded minimum quantity, which can be specified based on the lower limit of the actual data. Think of p_i as the weight of each factor, $0 \leq p_i \leq 1$. At the same time, new samples exert a more significant influence on the results, so their proportion in the solution process should be appropriately increased.

(7) Particle Swarm Optimization Algorithm

Since each eigenvalue has been dimensionally processed, the coefficient p_i in front of each factor can represent the weight of each factor. In this way, we only need to solve each coefficient p_i in the system of equations to determine the contribution of each influencing factor. Since each equation is nonlinear and cannot be directly solved, the equation-solving problem of the above equations is transformed into an optimization problem.

$$\min \sum_{k=1}^{m} |f(\Delta x_{k_1}...\Delta x_{k_n}) - \sum_{i=1}^{n} p_i \Delta x_{ki} + o(\Delta x_{ki})| \tag{27}$$
$$s.t. \quad 0 \leq p_i \leq 1, i = 0, 1...n$$

Then, the particle swarm optimization (PSO) algorithm is used [28] to solve each p_i. Finally, the weight coefficients are sorted to find the final cause.

We end up with Algorithm 1. The idea of the algorithm is as follows: first preprocess the data, turn it into manageable data. Then, use the BP neural network to fit the functional relationship between the various looper factors and the score; afterwards, construct a system of equations and convert it into an optimization problem with constraints, and solve it using PSO. Finally, the root-cause-tracing results are given.

Algorithm 1 Root-cause-tracing algorithm

1: Give the data processing formula: $x = g(s)$ calculate the feature average, $\Delta x = h(x)$ calculate the feature deviation, $\Delta x' = s(\Delta x)$ to perform data normalization. Specify the standard score of the looper $y_{std} = 80$.
2: Based on the database, give the number of data that needs to be processed L.
3: **for** $\lambda = 0 : L$ **do**
4: $\quad$ Loop $\quad x = g(s) \to \Delta x = h(x) \to \Delta x' = s(x), \Delta y = y - y_{std}$.
5: **end for**
6: Take the Δy as the output, $\Delta x'$ as the input, and use the BP neural network to fit the function f.
7: Load new data and get the looper's EPAE score y'. When $y' < y_{std}$, do the following.
8: Search for historical steel coils with scores similar to the new sample.
9: Use new sample data and historical steel coil data to construct a system of equations, and utilize the PSO algorithm to solve the weight parameters.
10: Sort the factors by weight and give the final result.

At present, most steel industries have mature detection systems, and various variables during the hot rolling process can be measured in real time. Therefore, it is only necessary to train the BP neural network using previous data and input the measured fault data to calculate the result. Therefore, the EPAE score of each product can be calculated in real time, and these data can be used for training the BP neural network. Therefore, the root-cause-traceability algorithm can be seamlessly integrated with existing control and monitoring systems in industrial environments without the need for additional equipment. In addition, there is no need to consider the compatibility of different data sources or architectures, as this algorithm only uses the basic data measured by sensors, and even if the data source changes, it does not affect the basic characteristics of the data.

This algorithm can adapt to dynamic production environments: when there are local changes in operating conditions or the equipment configuration in the production environment, such as replacement of some data collection equipment, the neural network only needs to be retrained with new data. If there are significant structural changes, such as changes in the hot rolling process, it is necessary to modify the corresponding EPAE model and retrain the neural network. Due to the fact that each part of the root-cause-tracing algorithm can be designed and trained separately, the low coupling of the algorithm ensures its effectiveness in constantly changing scenarios.

4. Experimental Results and Analysis

Taking the monthly production data of finishing rolling loopers of the 2250 mm hot tandem rolling production line as the experimental data. In fact, we used 19,418 training data, which is the monthly output of the steel plant, each datum is further divided into 21 aspects. Therefore, we firmly consider the root-cause-tracing algorithm can handle large datasets or more complex production scenarios. And when scalability challenges arise, such as the addition of sensors in industrial sites, the dimensionality of measurement data increases. Only slight changes are needed to some parameters of the neural network and PSO, and the basic theory of the algorithm will not change.

Using the relevant factors of the loopers (material factors, equipment factors, control factors) as model inputs, the data were first analyzed by preprocessing operation, after which the average value of each factor was calculated as the feature value. Some groups with better looper scores are selected as standards for comparison, the deviations between the characteristic values of each sample and the standard values are calculated, and a dimensionless operation is performed on the deviations. The relationship between the eigenvalues and the looper EPAE score f is fitted through the BP neural network. Finally, a system of equations is established and solved using the PSO algorithm. The contribution of each factor to the low looper EPAE score is obtained based on the weight. Finally, by sorting each factor according to its contribution, root cause tracing can be achieved.

In this experiment, the factors in Table 4 were selected as the relevant factors of the looper, and they were numbered to facilitate subsequent processing.

Table 4. Looper corresponding factor table.

Serial Number	Looper Corresponding Factors
1	LP_L2FORCEERS
2	LP_MODECE
3	LP_MORETIME
4	LP_MOSTEACC
5	LP_SEFOPER
6	LP_SEOVHOOT
7	LP_SERITIME
8	LP_SESTEERS
9	LP_SESTTIME
10	FORCERATE_HEAD
11	FORCERATE_BODY
12	FORCERATE_TAIL
13	FORCERATE_WHOLE
14	FURNACE_TEM
15	MIDSTEEL_BIG_LEN
16	MIDSTEEL_BIG_MAXVALUE
17	MIDSTEEL_SMALL_LEN
18	MIDSTEEL_SMALL_MAXVALUE
19	WATERBEAM_INFO_LOCATION
20	WATERBEAM_INFO_VALUE
21	WATERBEAM_MAXVALUE

Two BP neural networks are constructed to represent the relationship between incoming material factors, equipment factors, control factors, and looper scores, as shown in Figures 5 and 6. Their parameters are shown in Table 5.

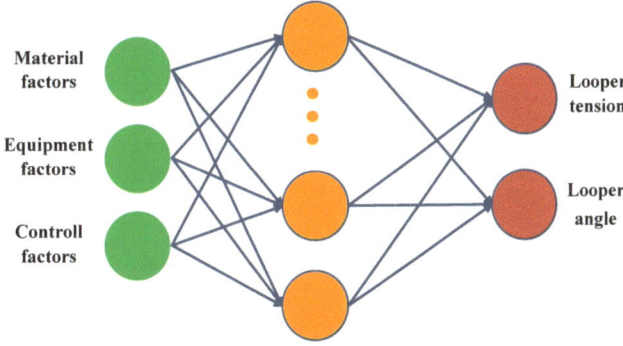

Figure 5. Looper factors and self-parameters.

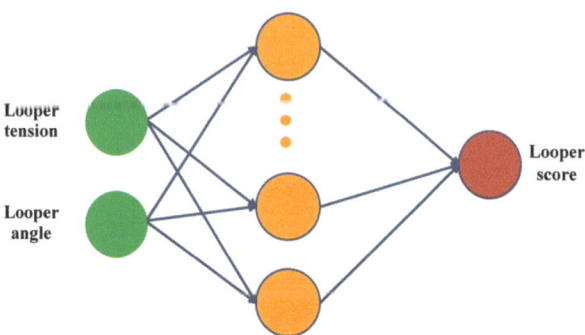

Figure 6. Self-parameters and looper scoring.

Table 5. Neural network parameter settings.

Parameter	Value
Input layer node	21
Middle layer node	7
Output layer node	2
Activation function	Sigmoid function
Error back-propagation	Derivative of sigmoid function
Threshold	0
Loss function	Mean square error function

As an intelligent search algorithm, the particle swarm optimization algorithm has the advantages of fast convergence speed and simple parameters in solving nonlinear problems. The particles in the algorithm adjust their search direction by memorizing the optimal position, as shown in Figure 7.

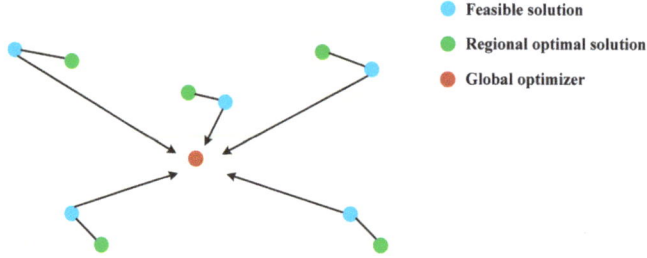

Figure 7. PSO algorithm.

The particle's velocity v_i^d and position x_i^d are updated through the following formula to find the optimal solution to the objective function:

$$v_i^d(k+1) = w \times v_i^d(k) + c_1 \times \text{rand}_1^d \times \left(\text{pBest}_i^d - x_i^d(k)\right) \\ + c_2 \times \text{rand}_2^d \times \left(\text{gBest}_i^d - x_i^d(k)\right) \tag{28}$$

$$x_i^d(k+1) = x_i^d(k) + v_i^d(k+1) \tag{29}$$

where i is the particle number, d is the particle dimension, k is the iterations, w is the weight inertia, c_1 and c_2 are the acceleration coefficients (also called learning factors), $rand_1^d$ and $rand_2^d$ are random numbers on two $[0,1]$, and $pBest_i^d$ and $gBest_i^d$ represent the optimal positions for individuals and groups, respectively. The various parameter settings of the particle swarm algorithm are as shown in Table 6.

Table 6. PSO parameters.

Parameter	Setting Value
ω	0.8
c_1	0.5
c_2	0.5
Upper bound	1
Lower bound	0
Number of particles	50
Number of iterations	1000
Tensor	21

Several groups of question samples are selected with similar looper EPAE scores, and a series of operations is performed on the data of related factors, such as feature extraction, feature deviation calculation, and dimensionality reduction. The results are shown in Figure 8. The characteristic deviation of Figure 8 is processed by Equations (20) and (21) in the root-cause-tracing algorithm. The larger the value, the greater the impact of this factor on the looper failure.

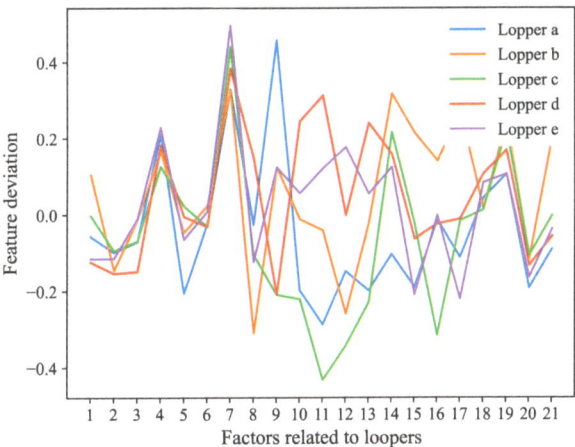

Figure 8. Looper factor characteristics of different steel coils.

Using several similar loop data of EPAE in Figure 8, an equation system is established, like Equation (26), and iteratively solved using the PSO algorithm. After multiple solutions, the results are shown in Table 7 and Figure 9. It can be seen that the results obtained from each solution are roughly similar, and the factor with the highest proportion is also basically the same. Except for a few small changes in factors, the rest are consistent. The higher the proportion, the greater the contribution of this factor to the failure of the looper, and the more likely it is to be the first object for maintenance.

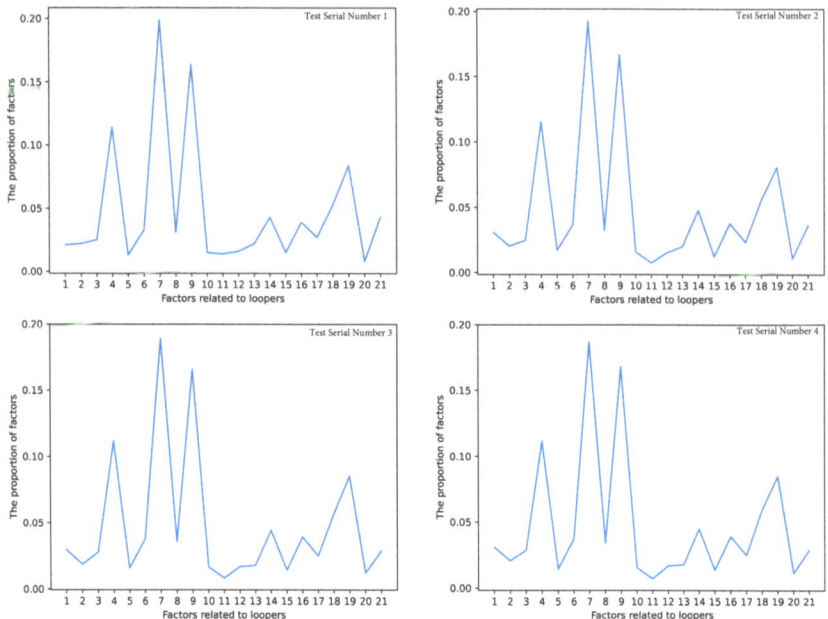

Figure 9. The proportion of each factor under multiple experiments.

Table 7. The iterative process of using PSO to solve the system of equations.

Test Serial Number	Largest Proportion	Second Proportion	Third Proportion
1	LP_SERITIME 0.1926	LP_SESTTIME 0.1670	LP_MOSTEACC 0.1156
2	LP_SERITIME 0.1912	LP_SESTTIME 0.1678	LP_MOSTEACC 0.1144
3	LP_SERITIME 0.1896	LP_SESTTIME 0.1668	LP_MOSTEACC 0.1107
4	LP_SERITIME 0.1870	LP_SESTTIME 0.1681	LP_MOSTEACC 0.1116

The final result are shown in Figure 10. The factors in the figure are sorted according to their contribution and the factors most likely to cause the looper score to be too low are obtained: LP_SERITIME, LP_SESTTIME, LP_MOSTEACC....

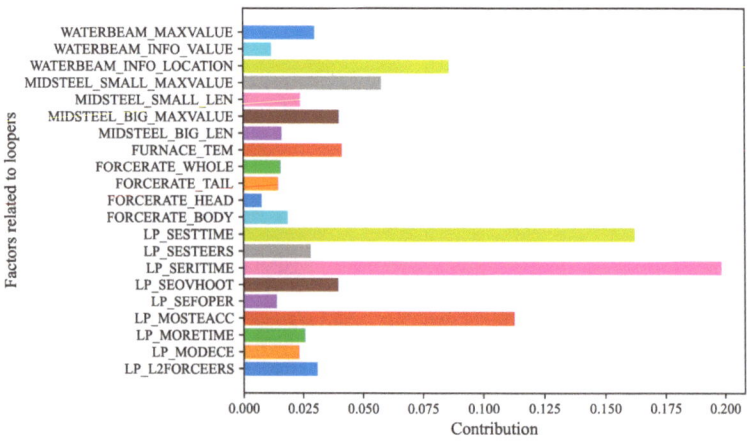

Figure 10. Result of root-cause-tracing algorithm.

It can be seen from Figures 8 and 10 that in Figure 8 the value of LP_SERITIME (loop servo valve adjustment rising time) is the largest, and in Figure 10 the contribution corresponding to LP_SERITIME is also the highest, and the relationship between the other factors is also very similar, so the algorithm can obtain the correct result. It is not difficult to see that the top three factors with the largest contribution are LP_SERITIME, LP_SESTTIME (loop servo valve adjustment steady-state time), and LP_MOSTEACC (rolling mill speed steady-state error). The above factors have the greatest impact on the low EPAE score of the looper, so these aspects should be prioritized for inspection and maintenance.

We use data from different hot rolling production environments and production lines to verify that the algorithm has excellent generalization ability in different manufacturing environments. When the environment changes, the algorithm can still locate the most likely fault problem. At the same time, even when the algorithm deviates from the initial research conditions, PSO can still obtain the optimal solution for weight calculation through its powerful search ability.

5. Discussion and Conclusions

This paper takes the looper equipment in hot rolling as the starting point, and establishes the EPAE model of the looper based on the control accuracy of the three processes of looping, steady state, and dropping during looper operation. Then, the Pearson correlation coefficient is used to measure the degree of correlation between the EPAE model and specific scenarios of production stability, and a root-cause-tracing algorithm is proposed to locate factor faults. Finally, the data from the 2250 production line is used for testing. The experimental results show that the influencing factors analyzed by this algorithm were consistent with the actual fault factors on site.

The EPAE model proposed in this paper has been applied in many production lines. In addition, the algorithm has been tested in other industrial processes or systems outside the hot rolling production line, such as the chemical industry, to find the reasons for the decrease in chemical production, and has received good results. During the application process, the EPAE model and BP neural network were reconstructed based on the chemical industry's own process flow and industrial equipment. The final weight calculation method is consistent with this article.

We have received excellent feedback from the Engineering Research Center, when a fault occurs during the hot rolling process this algorithm can accurately identify the underlying issues. In addition, as production continues, the algorithm requires a fixed amount of time to retrain the network, so the feedback has led the iteration of the algorithm towards performing incremental training based on existing data. And the evaluation indicators mainly rely on expert experience to extract and construct. In the future, it can be expanded to other types of production lines and unified index evaluation standards can be established.

Author Contributions: Conceptualization, F.J.; methodology, F.L. and J.G.; validation, Y.S.; formal analysis, J.L. and Z.F. All authors have read and agreed to the published version of the manuscript.

Funding: This research received no external funding.

Institutional Review Board Statement: Not applicable.

Informed Consent Statement: Not applicable.

Data Availability Statement: The data that support the findings of this study are available upon request from the corresponding author.

Acknowledgments: The authors wish to thank the School of Automation and Electrical Engineering of University of Science and Technology Beijing, and National Engineering Research Center for Advanced Rolling and Intelligent Manufacturing of University of Science and Technology Beijing, for supporting research to continue the research work.

Conflicts of Interest: The authors declare no conflicts of interest.

References

1. Pittner, J.; Simaan, M.A. An initial model for control of a tandem hot metal strip rolling process. *IEEE Trans. Ind. Appl.* **2009**, *46*, 46–53. [CrossRef]
2. Brengelmans, A.; Jones, T.; Tunstall, J. Dynamic simulation of rolling on a six stand hot strip mill. In *IEE Seminar on Tools for Simulation and Modelling*; IET: Stevenage, UK, 2000; pp. 3/1–3/6.
3. Li, X.; He, Y.; Ding, J.; Luan, F.; Zhang, D. Predicting hot-strip finish rolling thickness using stochastic configuration networks. *Inf. Sci.* **2022**, *611*, 677–689. [CrossRef]
4. Song, L.; Xu, D.; Wang, X.; Yang, Q.; Ji, Y. Application of machine learning to predict and diagnose for hot-rolled strip crown. *Int. J. Adv. Manuf. Technol.* **2022**, *120*, 881–890. [CrossRef]
5. Kim, J.; Lee, J.; Hwang, S.M. An analytical model for the prediction of strip temperatures in hot strip rolling. *Int. J. Heat Mass Transf.* **2009**, *52*, 1864–1874. [CrossRef]
6. Liu, Q.; Zhu, Q.; Qin, S.J.; Chai, T. Dynamic concurrent kernel CCA for strip-thickness relevant fault diagnosis of continuous annealing processes. *J. Process Control* **2018**, *67*, 12–22. [CrossRef]
7. Fu, W.; Jiang, X.; Li, B.; Tan, C.; Chen, B.; Chen, X. Rolling bearing fault diagnosis based on 2D time-frequency images and data augmentation technique. *Meas. Sci. Technol.* **2023**, *34*, 045005. [CrossRef]
8. Han, T.; Chao, Z. Fault diagnosis of rolling bearing with uneven data distribution based on continuous wavelet transform and deep convolution generated adversarial network. *J. Braz. Soc. Mech. Sci. Eng.* **2021**, *43*, 425. [CrossRef]
9. Jo, H.N.; Park, B.E.; Ji, Y.; Kim, D.K.; Yang, J.E.; Lee, I.B. Chatter detection and diagnosis in hot strip mill process with a frequency-based chatter index and modified independent component analysis. *IEEE Trans. Ind. Inform.* **2020**, *16*, 7812–7820. [CrossRef]
10. Ding, S.X.; Yin, S.; Peng, K.; Hao, H.; Shen, B. A novel scheme for key performance indicator prediction and diagnosis with application to an industrial hot strip mill. *IEEE Trans. Ind. Inform.* **2012**, *9*, 2239–2247. [CrossRef]
11. Yin, F.C.; Sun, J.; Ma, G.S.; Zhang, D.H. Multivariable decoupling control of hydraulic looper system based on ADAMS-MATLAB Co-simulation. *J. Northeast. Univ. (Nat. Sci.)* **2016**, *37*, 500.
12. Guo, J.; Jia, R.; Su, R.; Zhao, Y. Identification of FIR Systems with Binary-Valued Observations against Data Tampering Attacks. *IEEE Trans. Syst. Man Cybern. Syst.* **2023**, *53*, 5861–5873. [CrossRef]
13. Guo, J.; Wang, X.; Xue, W.; Zhao, Y. System Identification with Binary-Valued Observations Under Data Tampering Attacks. *IEEE Trans. Autom. Control* **2021**, *66*, 3825–3832. [CrossRef]
14. Guo, J.; Diao, J.D. Prediction-based event-triggered identification of quantized input FIR systems with quantized output observations. *Sci. China Inf. Sci.* **2020**, *63*, 112201:1–112201:12. [CrossRef]
15. Choi, I.S.; Rossiter, J.A.; Fleming, P.J. Looper and tension control in hot rolling mills: A survey. *J. Process Control* **2007**, *17*, 509–521. [CrossRef]
16. Militzer, M.; Hawbolt, E.B.; Meadowcroft, T.R. Microstructural model for hot strip rolling of high-strength low-alloy steels. *Metall. Mater. Trans. A* **2000**, *31*, 1247–1259. [CrossRef]
17. Wu, J.; Yan, X. Coupling vibration model for hot rolling mills and its application. *J. Vibroeng.* **2019**, *21*, 1795–1809. [CrossRef]
18. Park, C.J.; Lee, D.M. Input selection technology of neural network and its application for hot strip mill. *Ifac Proc. Vol.* **2005**, *38*, 51–56. [CrossRef]
19. Tan, S.; Liu, J.; Wang, M. Research on the MR-ILQ design method to looper control system in hot strip rolling mills. In Proceedings of the 2010 8th World Congress on Intelligent Control and Automation, Jinan, China, 7–9 July 2010; IEEE: Piscataway, NJ, USA, 2010; pp. 2614–2617.
20. Ji, Y.; Tian, M.; Guo, P.; Hu, X.; Liu, G. Optimization of Looper Control Systems for Hot Strip Mills. *China Mech. Eng.* **2017**, *28*, 410.
21. Saaty, T.L. The analytic hierarchy process in conflict management. *Int. J. Confl. Manag.* **1990**, *1*, 47–68. [CrossRef]
22. Wu, S.; Fu, Y.; Shen, H.; Liu, F. Using ranked weights and Shannon entropy to modify regional sustainable society index. *Sustain. Cities Soc.* **2018**, *41*, 443–448. [CrossRef]
23. Wang, Y.M. Centroid defuzzification and the maximizing set and minimizing set ranking based on alpha level sets. *Comput. Ind. Eng.* **2009**, *57*, 228–236. [CrossRef]
24. Cohen, I.; Huang, Y.; Chen, J.; Benesty, J.; Benesty, J.; Chen, J.; Huang, Y.; Cohen, I. Pearson correlation coefficient. In *Noise Reduction in Speech Processing*; Springer: Berlin/Heidelberg, Germany, 2009; pp. 1–4.
25. Su, C.; Cao, J. Improving lazy decision tree for imbalanced classification by using skew-insensitive criteria. *Appl. Intell.* **2019**, *49*, 1127–1145. [CrossRef]
26. Goh, A.T.C. Back-propagation neural networks for modeling complex systems. *Artif. Intell. Eng.* **1995**, *9*, 143–151. [CrossRef]
27. Li, J.; Cheng, J.H.; Shi, J.Y.; Huang, F. Brief introduction of back propagation (BP) neural network algorithm and its improvement. In *Advances in Computer Science and Information Engineering*; Springer: Berlin/Heidelberg, Germany, 2012; pp. 553–558.
28. Elbes, M.; Alzubi, S.; Kanan, T.; Al-Fuqaha, A.; Hawashin, B. A Survey on Particle Swarm Optimization with Emphasis on Engineering and Network Applications. *Evol. Intell.* **2019**, *12*, 113–129. [CrossRef]

Disclaimer/Publisher's Note: The statements, opinions and data contained in all publications are solely those of the individual author(s) and contributor(s) and not of MDPI and/or the editor(s). MDPI and/or the editor(s) disclaim responsibility for any injury to people or property resulting from any ideas, methods, instructions or products referred to in the content.

Article

Advancements in Data Analysis for the Work-Sampling Method

Borut Buchmeister * and Natasa Vujica Herzog

Faculty of Mechanical Engineering, University of Maribor, Smetanova 17, SI-2000 Maribor, Slovenia; natasa.vujica@um.si
* Correspondence: borut.buchmeister@um.si

Abstract: The work-sampling method makes it possible to gain valuable insights into what is happening in production systems. Work sampling is a process used to estimate the proportion of shift time that workers (or machines) spend on different activities (within productive work or losses). It is estimated based on enough random observations of activities over a selected period. When workplace operations do not have short cycle times or high repetition rates, the use of such a statistical technique is necessary because the labor sampling data can provide information that can be used to set standards. The work-sampling procedure is well standardized, but additional contributions are possible when evaluating the observations. In this paper, we present our contribution to improving the decision-making process based on work-sampling data. We introduce a correlation comparison of the measured hourly shares of all activities in pairs to check whether there are mutual connections or to uncover hidden connections between activities. The results allow for easier decision-making (conclusions) regarding the influence of the selected activities on the triggering of the others. With the additional calculation method, we can uncover behavioral patterns that would have been overlooked with the basic method. This leads to improved efficiency and productivity of the production system.

Keywords: work sampling; observations; analysis; proportions; correlations; interdependence between activities

Citation: Buchmeister, B.; Herzog, N.V. Advancements in Data Analysis for the Work-Sampling Method. *Algorithms* **2024**, *17*, 183. https://doi.org/10.3390/a17050183

Academic Editors: Sheng Du, Zixin Huang, Li Jin and Xiongbo Wan

Received: 31 March 2024
Revised: 23 April 2024
Accepted: 28 April 2024
Published: 29 April 2024

Copyright: © 2024 by the authors. Licensee MDPI, Basel, Switzerland. This article is an open access article distributed under the terms and conditions of the Creative Commons Attribution (CC BY) license (https://creativecommons.org/licenses/by/4.0/).

1. Introduction

Nowadays, the business world is more focused on sales and trade. We are paying less attention to how we work and how to organize and improve production in a high-quality way. It involves a well-thought-out, comprehensive, and systematic coordination of activities, as well as solving all problems that arise to achieve success.

Work-study, as one of the fundamental areas of scientific work organization, provides extensive possibilities for the analysis of any work, as well as the possibility of applying improved working methods and finding ways to determine the necessary times for the completion of the respective work. The processing times of activities can be determined for an existing operation from historical data, work sampling, or time studies [1]. The basic purpose of work-study and time study is to achieve optimal work effects in the performance of work tasks.

The basic requirements for a successful and rationalized business involve controlling and monitoring to reduce delays and time losses in the work process [2]. These delays and time losses are common in the business processes of companies in less developed countries, often to a greater extent when compared to companies in highly industrialized countries; the main reason for this is the relatively low level of work organization. Labor interruptions and downtime are elements that increase production costs and disrupt the production process. Therefore, one of the basic tasks of a work-study is to identify and determine these losses (or unproductive activities) and then use the analysis to separate excused (planned and unplanned) and unexcused work interruptions and time losses and propose measures to eliminate or reduce them to the lowest values. Losses are usually classified into the following:

- Planned losses (business conversations, editing of documentation, preventive maintenance, physiological needs, etc.);
- Unplanned losses (breakdown of working equipment, power outage, waiting for transport, etc.);
- Indiscipline (private absence, private conversations, etc.).

The methods that allow us to measure and analyze the use of time are as follows: the stopwatch time study and the work-sampling method.

Work sampling is a statistical work measurement method in which many observations are made over a period of time on a group of machines, processes, or workers to collect information about the percentage of time spent on specific activities [3].

In this article, we present our original contribution to the data analysis for the work-sampling method. To the usual calculations of percentage time spent, we add a correlation analysis of percentage activities by hours of the work shift to identify potential interdependencies between them pairwise. This can greatly facilitate the adoption of optimal decisions based on the results of the studies conducted, especially in the form of some changes in the process organization to reduce time losses.

We demonstrate the relevance of the research problem with a brief overview of the recent literature in the field of the article.

The scope of application of the work-sampling method in different areas is well covered (in manufacturing, maintenance, product development, construction, garment industry, food industry, logistics, pharmacy, hospitals, etc.). In our analysis, for reasons of relevance, we present some important publications from the last 10 years to emphasize the relevance of the method in question.

Our main focus is on applications in production plants. The work-sampling method is a very useful tool for setting standard times. Garcia et al. proposed a methodology to determine the allowance time based on the heart rate and sampling of a part of a production line consisting of thirteen stations operated by four workers [4]. The result was that the allowance time after the study was higher than before. Similarly, De la Riva et al. conducted an experimental study on work sampling, using a new technology available (heart rate measurement) to allocate the allowance time to a task during the workday [5]. The need for observations represents a considerable cost factor, which is why Martinec et al. introduced self-reporting. They described a self-reported work-sampling approach developed and adapted for production development and the application of the approach in an automotive supplier company [6]. The results provide insight into the engagement of group members at work and how their activity was related to the context, mode, and type of information transaction used.

Work sampling is mainly used as a stand-alone method but can also be used in combination with other methods. This is how Yuan et al. conducted the study, where three different methods were integrated: work sampling, computer simulation, and biomechanical modeling to investigate the physical demands of the job [7]. A work-sampling method was used to quantify the proportion of time spent on specific tasks. Work sampling can also provide key data in ergonomic studies. Dasgupta et al. collected data on the ergonomic strain of workers using the work-sampling method and identified several risk factors in the observed tasks [8]. Similarly, Javernik et al. assessed the workload of workers in collaborative workplaces under different workload conditions [9,10]. The results indicate the need for the individualized treatment of individuals to increase productivity and job satisfaction at the same time.

Work-study is the most important, but not the only, application of work sampling. Skec et al. [11] investigated work sampling in product development. They introduced a work-sampling application for cell phones that can greatly simplify and popularize the use of the method. Grznar et al., on the other hand, reported on the development of a special tool for workplace analysis [12].

In the field of construction, Fischer et al. introduced a hierarchical classification for activity recognition and used a hybrid deep learning model as an alternative to the work-sampling method. Based on the activity recognition results, a discrete event simulation was used to predict the progress of the process [13].

To improve the efficiency of the maintenance department, Dewi et al. analyzed the current workload of technicians and employees using the work-sampling method [14]. The study found that the workload of the maintenance department was so low that a reduction in the number of employees, the creation of more efficient work processes, and an expansion of the workplace were suggested.

Ünal and Güner conducted a work-study using work sampling in the garment industry [15]. They integrated work sampling and fuzzy logic. Since safety and productivity are critical in evaluating performance management in maritime transport and port management, Safa and Craig investigated activity analysis methods and selected work sampling as a suitable method for improvement policy [16].

Lee et al. presented a good overview of the novelties regarding the application of the work-sampling method in construction [17]. Their article contributes to the state of knowledge in construction management through a thorough understanding of the current state-of-the-art activity sampling techniques and research gaps. Their analysis includes a qualitative synthesis of the contributions of the reviewed articles. Mathiassen et al. developed a procedure to evaluate the statistical properties of work-sampling strategies that estimated categorical exposure variables and illustrated the applicability of this procedure to investigate the bias and accuracy of exposure estimates from different sample sizes [18].

Wahid et al. presented a case study on the SME food industry [19]. The results of this study show that work-sampling data can be used as reliable estimates to identify potential bottlenecks and idle times in a factory. Similarly, Rashid and Louis proposed a framework that extends the applicability of event data collection and process models by converting them into DES models for predicting future performance [20].

Examples of work-sampling studies can also be found in the field of hospital care. Wong et al. conducted a work-sampling study in two hospitals [21]. The results make it possible to optimize the workflow with a focus on spending more time on direct patient care. Gupta et al. conducted a work-sampling study with seven participating dentists who were referred to the field and patients who visited the on-site dental center [22]. They concluded that work sampling is a viable method for optimizing healthcare, with a focus on effective use.

The process of work sampling is traditionally carried out manually, which does not exclude more modern approaches with recording devices and automatic activity recognition. Luo et al. improved the work-sampling method and introduced an activity recognition method that accepts surveillance videos as input and generates different and continuous markers for the activity of individual workers in the field of view [23]. Their method can be the basis for effective and objective work sampling.

The remaining sections of the article are organized as follows: Section 2 describes the work-sampling method, the prescribed steps in conducting the observations, and the basic calculations. Section 3 comprehensively describes the factors and causes of production losses (62 factors in total)—as a result of our many years of experience, and as a guide for analysis and decision-making. Section 4 presents the upgraded analysis of the work-sampling results and its advantages. Section 5 provides an example of a work-sampling study in a manufacturing company, which confirms the relevance of upgrading the analysis of the results. Section 6 summarizes the results, presents concluding remarks, and discusses possibilities for future work.

2. Materials and Methods

Work sampling (also called activity sampling) is a statistical method that can be used to solve certain problems in the field of industrial engineering without the need for constant presence or an analytical approach. It is based on the theory of sampling and represents one of the possibilities for the practical application of mathematical statistics in industry. The method is also known in German-speaking countries as the method of observation at random points in time or "Multimomentverfahren". As an example, we identify preselected situations in which the person or object in question may be alone or in a group, using observations at random points in time. On this basis, we determine the expected proportion of this state in the total time with the prescribed accuracy and probability. The work-sampling method was first used by Tippet in the British textile industry in 1934 and described by Stanton [24].

Observations using this method are carried out without a stopwatch so that the analyst walks through all the workplaces belonging to him/her several times a day (e.g., 20 to 30 times) at randomly selected times over a period of two, three, or more weeks. The analyst records the data (a line) on the recording sheet, indicating the type of event, i.e., the activity that he/she notices at the moment of arrival (the recording is, of course, also possible using a computer application on a tablet, laptop, or mobile phone). For semi-automated processes, it is necessary to observe what the worker does and what the machine does. For example, the machine can perform a processing operation while the worker performs a completely different activity (around productive work or losses).

In this way, after recording the cumulative sum of observations of individual activities, a large total number of observations is obtained, which allows us to determine separately the proportion of the workday spent on a particular activity and, thus, actually obtain an objective picture of the structure of the workday at the observed workplaces. This in turn makes it possible to draw appropriate conclusions and make suggestions to improve the situation under investigation [25].

If the results obtained with this method are to be realistic, the following conditions must be met in addition to objective and accurate recordings: enough observations of events and a randomized observation schedule to observe one detail at a time. The time period for the study must be long enough to avoid production peculiarities, seasonal production, etc.

The areas of work and problems to which the work-sampling method can be applied are practically and objectively unlimited, e.g., the analysis of capacity utilization and planning, guidelines for work within a shorter workday, the determination of elements for setting standard times (time allowance coefficient), etc. If we use this method to analyze how to reduce idle times and increase work efficiency, the elements must be placed in such a way that they reveal bottlenecks that depend on the operator himself (e.g., arriving late, leaving work too early, etc.). Some elements can also show us various other organizational shortcomings (e.g., lack of materials, machine breakdowns, indiscipline, etc.). By incorporating the elements of the work-sampling method into a mathematical model, we obtain the results with a certain degree of accuracy. The method does not solve problems but points them out and calculates their probability and frequency [25].

The work-sampling method is characterized by a high degree of activity and economy, which is expressed in the following advantages:

- We can record several workplaces simultaneously and track a relatively large number of activities (time efficiency);
- The time and cost of observations are significantly lower than those of continuous recording with a stopwatch (from 35 to 80%); we obtain the information we need quickly, using fewer resources, and at a lower risk and cost (cost-effectiveness);
- The objectivity of recording the actual situation has an accuracy that is satisfactory in practice; work sampling provides statistically valid data for analyzing work patterns;
- Since the recording technique minimizes the influence of the observed workers on the recording results, the probability of false results is much lower than with continuous recording (less intrusive as it involves periodic observations over a period of time);
- Training analysts for recording is simple, fast, and straightforward; we do not need any special equipment (no timing devices) to carry out recordings;
- It can be applied to various types of work environments (flexibility);
- The study takes longer, minimizing short-term fluctuations;
- The recording can be interrupted or resumed, if necessary, as it does not affect the result.

Of course, this method also has its disadvantages:
- The recording of observations can involve a certain amount of subjectivity, which can lead to inconsistencies in data collection and interpretation;
- Difficulties in recording individual workplaces, especially if they are located further away;
- We cannot capture individual differences between workers as we are observing a group of workers;
- We cannot set standards by sampling work activities;
- It provides an overview of activities without detailed insights into specific tasks or processes;
- It does not capture short-term fluctuations that could be important for identifying inefficiencies or bottlenecks in the process;
- It is practically impossible to ensure adequate accuracy for activities that account for less than 1% of the share, as a very large number of observations (over 150,000) would be required;
- It is very difficult to identify the causes of employee work interruptions and absenteeism, as an understanding of the specific context and work environment is required.

The last one is exactly the area we are mainly contributing to in this article (described in Section 4).

2.1. The Recording Process of the Work-Sampling Method

Before the actual recording, we must study and prepare the necessary steps in detail, which include the following phases [26,27]:

1. Pre-recording preparations: Determining the scope and location of the workplaces, preparing the recording team (a single person can collect 400 to 600 observations per day), informing the workers, making a list of activities, drawing up a plan for random visits to the workplaces (the observation route), and defining the forms—usually recording and collecting sheets. Each analyst draws up the observation schedule randomly and according to the outline of the group of workplaces to be observed (the departure time for observation, the workplace where it starts, and the direction of movement) for each recording day.
2. Recording—collecting observations: preliminary (pilot) recording (usually 3 to 5 days; we check the adequacy of the list of activities and the schedule of random observations; we calculate the proportion of time spent on each activity) and the main (full) recording (we collect the number of observations required according to the most typical or important activity).

With the work-sampling method, a confidence level of 95% and a precision level of 0.05 of the results are completely sufficient, so that the required number of observations is as follows:

$$N = \frac{1.96^2 \cdot (1 - p_i)}{0.05^2 \cdot p_i} = 1537 \cdot \frac{(1 - p_i)}{p_i}, \qquad (1)$$

where

N—denotes the number of observations required,

1.96—number of standard deviations from the mean reflecting the 95% level of confidence,

p_i—proportion of time spent on the major activity (between 0 and 1).

The equation for determining the upper and lower control limits (M_i) for a confidence level of 95% is as follows:

$$M_i = p_i \pm 1.96 \cdot \sqrt{\frac{p_i \cdot (1 - p_i)}{N}}, \qquad (2)$$

2.2. Data Analysis and Calculations

After completing the recording, we calculate the percentage of occurrence of each activity and the accuracy achieved (ε_i) for individual or combined activities, as follows:

$$\varepsilon_i = \pm\, 1.96 \cdot \sqrt{\frac{1 - p_i}{N \cdot p_i}}, \qquad (3)$$

We calculate the results of the activity shares for the entire recording period, by hours of the work shift, days, and shifts [26].

The time allowance factor (TA_f) is calculated according to the following equation:

$$TA_f = \frac{\sum PL}{\sum PW + \sum UL + \sum IN}, \qquad (4)$$

where

PL—number of observations for planned losses,
PW—number of observations for productive work,
UL—number of observations for unplanned losses,
IN—number of observations for indiscipline.

3. Factors and Causes of Losses

When analyzing the level of work organization in manufacturing companies, we first look for the factors that cause overwork and the factors of production. As there are many of them, it is difficult to monitor them all at the same time. We, therefore, group them and carry out a selection of the most influential factors to monitor them. Based on work-sampling studies conducted in manufacturing companies to date, we identified the observed state of the factors or causes of losses (and thus poor capacity utilization), which we categorized into four groups: time losses, material losses, yield losses, and other losses. The following list of factors is part of our article contribution.

The most important factors (16) that cause time losses are as follows:

1—Improper use of personnel, qualifications, and skills of individuals are not matched to the requirements of the jobs;
2—Involvement of workers and officials in the work without prior familiarization with the conditions of the work environment and possible training;
3—Incomplete and inaccurate technical documentation and poorly organized instruction during work;
4—Unsuitable location of workplaces;
5—Irregular operation of workplaces;
6—Unsuitable work equipment;
7—Unstable and insufficiently monitored technological processes;
8—Irrational choice and use of means of transport;
9—Ineffective organization of quality control;
10—Weak organization of preventive, regular, planned corrective maintenance and full restoration of machinery or the general lack of a maintenance system for machinery and equipment;
11—Ineffective functioning of the production control department;
12—Unhealthy relationships between people;
13—Unrealistic time standards;
14—Unfavorable working conditions;
15—Insufficient and improper stimulation to save time;
16—Various unforeseen downtimes, unrealistic operating schedules, irregular power supply, etc.

The most important factors (14) that cause material losses are as follows:

1—Incomplete specification and poor quality of purchased material;
2—Insufficient use of standard materials;

3—Unrealistic material standards;
4—Insufficient and improper stimulation to save materials;
5—Insufficient knowledge of material properties and processing methods;
6—Inadequacy and inaccuracy of machinery and tools;
7—Use of material not fit for purpose, use of better-quality material in the absence of necessary additional processing, and the like;
8—Insufficient interest of workers in product quality;
9—Surplus stocks of materials, raw materials, and the like;
10—Improper and unprofessional handling of materials during placement and manipulation;
11—Improper and unprofessional manipulation of semi-finished and finished products during transport, placement, and packaging;
12—Poorly organized collection, classification, and use of waste materials;
13—Improper use of materials;
14—Ineffectively organized control of materials and semi-finished products.

The most important factors (12) that cause yield losses are as follows:
1—Unprofessional and irresponsible handling of machines, tools, equipment, etc.;
2—Insufficient knowledge of the technical and utilization characteristics of machines, tools, and equipment, as well as incomplete and disorderly maintenance of equipment records;
3—Abnormal use of production equipment;
4—Insufficient maintenance of machines and equipment that are not in use;
5—Indifferent ignoring of minor breakdowns of machines and tools;
6—Incomplete and uneven use of available capacities;
7—Mismatch between component capacities and production program, inappropriate production program, high degree of inconsistency, etc.;
8—Unrealistic operational planning;
9—Inefficient response to production disruptions, weak organization of dispatch service;
10—Inefficient coordination of component production processes;
11—Insufficient insight into production status, poor application of operational records and their use for operational monitoring and analysis of trends in results achieved;
12—Lack of adequate information system and automatic data processing.

The most important factors (20) that cause other losses are as follows:
1—Unsuitable location of factories, departments, workshops, and workplaces and, as a result, harmful crossing of the paths of workpieces and personnel;
2—loss of space due to irrational layout of machines, materials, semi-finished and finished products;
3—Inappropriate layout and maintenance of internal paths;
4—Improper selection and use of means of transport;
5—Disorganization at the workplace;
6—Improper set-up and functioning of the control network;
7—Insufficient lighting at the workplaces;
8—Ineffectiveness of protective measures for persons and property;
9—Weak work discipline;
10—Hesitancy with management bodies in making and implementing decisions;
11—Unfavorable working conditions, humidity, stuffiness, harmful vapors, high temperature, and the like;
12—Unhealthy relations between employees, especially between managers;
13—Poor functioning of the administration (trade unions);
14—Poorly organized meals (wrong timing of hot meals and poor quality of food);
15—High turnover of employees;
16—Lack of a systematic study of the organization and work methods;
17—Lack of instruments regulating inter- and intra-departmental relations;
18—Non-systematic and non-up-to-date monitoring, analysis, and presentation of the results achieved;

19—Insufficiently elaborated planning methodology and weak planning discipline;

20—Lack of a department systematically dealing with problems related to the improvement of production and the business in general.

The company requires consistency (optimization) between the individual factors that control the functions. The discrepancy between certain functions and groups of jobs also causes the occurrence of loss factors and poor utilization of production capacities. Therefore, it is necessary to localize the losses, but it is not possible to quantify them precisely, and therefore we cannot say whether we will first solve the problem of machine maintenance or labor discipline, for example.

4. Upgrade of the Analysis of Work-Sampling Results

We usually report the results of work-sampling study observations in the form of percentages of individual activities (or grouped) by hours, days, and work shifts [27]. We also calculate the achieved accuracy of the results and their control limits [28].

Many unplanned losses can be caused by certain superficially insignificant events, which in turn trigger new events in a chain, leading to extensive time losses. Since the work-sampling method gives us an insight into the activity proportions at the finest level in the workday hours, we can consider using the data from the activity plot by hour and comparing them with each other to identify possible correlations.

The most used measure of the linear relationship between two quantitative variables (two sets of data) is Pearson's correlation coefficient r, which assumes at least one interval type of the two variables analyzed and a linear relationship between the variables. The coefficient can assume values between -1 and 1. Pearson's correlation coefficient answers two questions, namely:

(a)   Is there a linear relationship between the variables at all? and
(b)   How strong is the linear relationship between the variables?

When we examine the existence of a linear relationship, we speak of two types of relationships. A positive correlation exists when the values of the first (x) and second (y) variables are high or low. In this case, the coefficient is positive and close to 1. If one variable changes, the other variable also changes in the same direction. A negative correlation exists if the values of the first (x) variable are high and the values of the second (y) variable are low or vice versa. The coefficient is then negative and close to -1.

To determine the strength of the interdependence between the activities, we use a modified coefficient value scale, which is presented above in Table 1.

Table 1. Strength of interdependence according to the value of the correlation coefficient.

Coefficient Value r	Strength of Interdependence
0.00	None
0.01–0.19	Very weak (negligible)
0.20–0.39	Weak
0.40–0.69	Moderate
0.70–0.89	Strong
0.90–0.99	Very strong
1.00	Perfect (functional)

It should also be emphasized that Pearson's correlation coefficient indicates the relationship between two variables, but not the influence of one variable on another. Therefore, the judgment of the analyst is necessary in accordance with their knowledge of the performance of the observed activities and the possible causes of the correlation.

Therefore, we calculate the correlations between the percentages of all activities by hour and find the correlation coefficient for all possible pairs within an 8 h work shift.

A sample size $n = 8$, values of pairs of variables are as follows: $(x_1, y_1), \ldots, (x_8, y_8)$.

Correlation value equation, adjusted for n = 8 (universal for all studies), is:

$$r = \frac{8 \cdot \Sigma xy - (\Sigma x) \cdot (\Sigma y)}{\sqrt{\left(8 \cdot \Sigma x^2 - (\Sigma x)^2\right) \cdot \left(8 \cdot \Sigma y^2 - (\Sigma y)^2\right)}}, \tag{5}$$

In our methodological development, we use the *t*-test for two independent samples (independent-samples *t*-test, two-tailed) and determine whether there are statistically significant differences in the average value of the two samples. It is a standard method to determine whether the correlation coefficient is statistically significant or not [29].

A 95% confidence interval can be defined as the interval spanning from the 2.5th to the 97.5th percentiles of the resampled *r* values (Figure 1). This corresponds to a significance level of 0.05. The sampling distribution of the studentized Pearson's correlation coefficient follows the Student's *t*-distribution with degrees of freedom (*DOF*) $n - 2$. To determine the critical values for *r*, the following function is applied [29]:

$$r = \frac{t}{\sqrt{n - 2 + t^2}}, \tag{6}$$

Degrees of freedom	Significance level					
	.2	.15	.1	.05	.025	.01
1	3.078	4.165	6.314	12.706	25.452	63.657
2	1.886	2.282	2.920	4.303	6.205	9.925
3	1.638	1.924	2.353	3.182	4.177	5.841
4	1.533	1.778	2.132	2.776	3.495	4.604
5	1.476	1.699	2.015	2.571	3.163	4.032
6	1.440	1.650	1.943	2.447	2.969	3.707
7	1.415	1.617	1.895	2.365	2.841	3.499
8	1.397	1.592	1.860	2.306	2.752	3.355

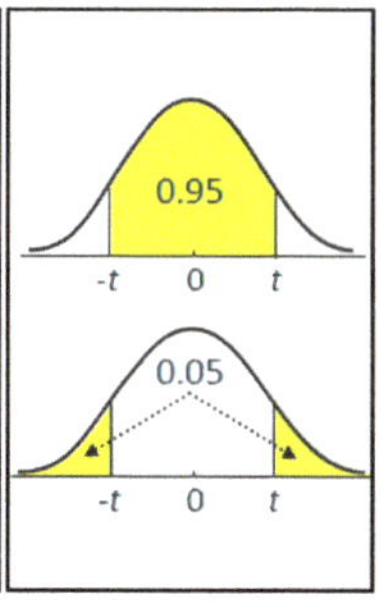

Figure 1. Critical values of *t* for two-tailed tests (part of the table), left [29] and the meaning of confidence interval, right.

In our case, we have the sample size n = 8, and from the *t*-distribution table (Figure 1), we take the value $t_{6, 0.05} = 2.447$, resulting in $r = 0.707$. This is the threshold value for *r*, to decide which pairs of activities should be investigated regarding interdependence.

We consider coefficient values of 0.7 or more (and −0.7 or less) as a threshold for a more detailed investigation or for the search for a logical connection or interdependence between two activities, which gives us the opportunity to find the causes of losses and, consequently, improve the situation. We consider only those pairs where at least one of the activities is from the group of losses and both activities exceed 1% of the hourly share (adequate accuracy limit). The application is demonstrated using a selected real-life example of a study conducted in a company in the metalworking industry.

As already described, the work-sampling method consists of three steps, from the preparation of the recording and its execution to the analysis of the observations and calculations, with a discussion of the results and suggestions for improvement. The steps of the method are shown in Figure 2, with the addition of our original contribution to the method shown in red (in the third step).

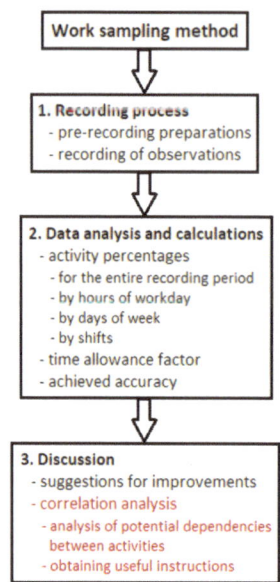

Figure 2. Steps of the work-sampling method with the addition of correlation analysis (in red).

5. Case Study

In the selected medium-sized metalworking company (with make-to-order production), we carried out the necessary observations as part of the work-sampling project. We selected a machining company (turning operations) with 17 workplaces (7 types of machines). The analyst's observation route is shown in Figure 3. Each visit was carried out in a random direction: clockwise or anti-clockwise. Two rounds per hour were possible (only one in the hour in which there was a 30 min break), so that we collected 255 observations in one shift (8 h: $7 \times 2 + 1 = 15$ observations per workplace, 17 workplaces).

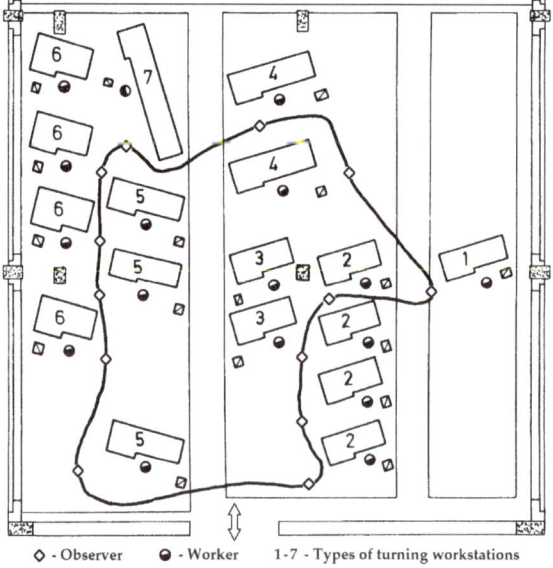

Figure 3. Analyst's observation route in the work-sampling study.

Through pilot recordings, we found that over 4000 observations were necessary and identified 23 operator activities:

During the main recording, 4131 observations were collected. We used the Drigus Multidata recording device shown in Figure 4. We observed labor in two shifts, from Monday to Friday. The results are summarized in Tables 2 and 3. The results for weekdays and shifts are not included.

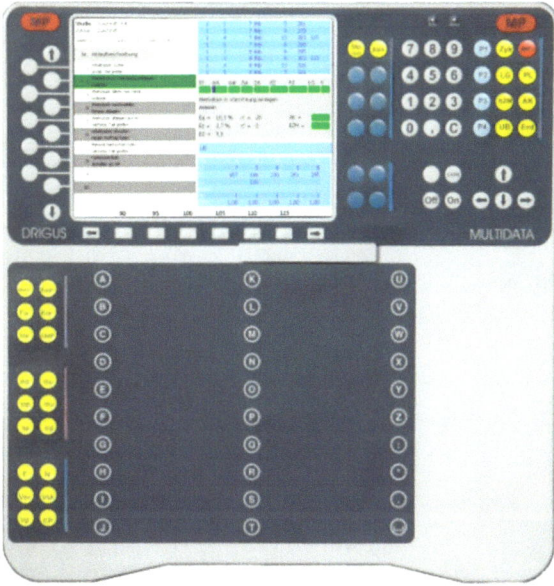

Figure 4. Drigus Multidata recording device.

Table 2. The proportion of the workday spent on each activity.

Activity	Number of Observations	Portion (%)
1. Machining	2129	51.54
2. Clamping/unclamping the workpiece	176	4.26
3. Dimensional control	153	3.70
4. Tool movement in the machining position	19	0.46
5. Clamping/unclamping of the tool	27	0.65
Productive work	2504	60.61
6. Workstation set-up	34	0.82
7. Study of working instructions	49	1.19
8. Conversation about tasks	43	1.04
9. Tool set-up	201	4.87
10. Collecting/returning of tools	51	1.23
11. Cleaning the machine	114	2.76
12. Personal needs (toilet, washing, etc.)	214	5.18
13. Annotation of work results	38	0.92
14. Handover of work	6	0.15
Planned losses	750	18.16
15. Waiting for transport	11	0.27
16. Waiting for documentation	0	0
17. Machine failure	0	0
18. Absence from company	250	6.05
19. Business meeting	37	0.90
20. Power outage	0	0
21. Repair of defects	2	0.05
Unplanned losses	300	7.26
22. Private conversation	377	9.13
23. Private absence from the workplace	200	4.84
Indiscipline	577	13.97
Total	**4131**	**100.00**

Table 3. Activity proportions by workday hours (in %).

Activity	1	2	3	4	5	6	7	8
1. Machining	38.23	63.89	58.33	58.33	63.33	56.85	54.07	21.30
2. Clamping/unclamping the workpiece	11.49	3.33	5.00	4.17	2.78	2.22	3.33	1.85
3. Dimensional control	1.69	3.89	4.44	2.78	5.56	5.37	3.70	1.85
4. Tool movement in the machining position	0.38	0.37	0.74	0.83	0.56	0.56	0.37	0.00
5. Clamping/unclamping of the tool	1.13	0.93	0.37	0.00	0.93	0.56	0.19	0.93
6. Workstation set-up	6.21	0.00	0.19	0.00	0.00	0.00	0.00	0.00
7. Study of working instructions	6.78	0.56	0.74	0.83	0.19	0.00	0.37	0.00
8. Conversation about tasks	2.07	1.48	1.11	0.56	1.85	0.19	0.93	0.00
9. Tool set-up	6.97	4.44	6.67	6.39	5.19	4.81	4.26	0.74
10. Collecting/returning of tools	2.07	0.56	1.30	0.56	0.93	1.11	1.48	1.67
11. Cleaning the machine	0.00	0.00	0.00	0.00	0.00	0.00	1.67	19.44
12. Personal needs (toilet, washing, etc.)	9.79	2.96	2.41	2.22	3.52	10.00	8.15	1.48
13. Annotation of work results	0.00	0.00	0.00	0.56	0.00	0.19	1.67	4.81
14. Handover of work	0.00	0.00	0.00	0.00	0.00	0.19	0.56	0.37
15. Waiting for transport	0.00	0.56	0.74	0.56	0.19	0.19	0.00	0.00
16. Waiting for documentation	0.00	0.00	0.00	0.00	0.00	0.00	0.00	0.00
17. Machine failure	0.00	0.00	0.00	0.00	0.00	0.00	0.00	0.00
18. Absence from company	6.21	6.11	6.11	6.11	6.11	6.11	6.11	5.56
19. Business meeting	5.08	0.00	0.00	0.00	0.00	0.56	0.56	0.74
20. Power outage	0.00	0.00	0.00	0.00	0.00	0.00	0.00	0.00
21. Repair of defects	0.00	0.00	0.00	0.56	0.00	0.00	0.00	0.00
22. Private conversation	1.69	9.44	9.63	14.44	7.59	9.26	10.56	12.04
23. Private absence from the workplace	0.19	1.48	2.22	1.11	1.30	1.85	2.04	27.22
Productive work	**52.92**	**72.41**	**68.89**	**66.11**	**73.15**	**65.56**	**61.67**	**25.93**
Losses	**47.08**	**27.59**	**31.11**	**33.89**	**26.85**	**34.44**	**38.33**	**74.07**

The time allowance factor (TA_f) is calculated according to Equation (4):

$$TA_f = \frac{750}{2504 + 300 + 577} = 0.22$$

The accuracy achieved for the proportion of productive work is ±2.51% and for losses is ±3.86%. The lower and upper limits within which the actual shares of productive work are distributed are 59.1% to 62.1%, and 37.9% to 40.9% for losses.

As already mentioned, the calculation of Pearson's correlations between the activity proportions by workday hours represents a procedural enhancement of the analysis of the results of the work-sampling method. The correlations between all pairs of activities were calculated according to Equation (5) and are shown in Table 4; all values were multiplied by 10 and rounded (we have values between −9 and +9).

Table 4. Correlations between individual activities for the example shown.

A.	1	2	3	4	5	6	7	8	9	10	11	12	13	14	15	16	17	18	19	20	21	22	23
1	\	−1	7	7	−3	−3	−3	3	5	−7	−8	0	−8	−4	5	0	0	7	−4	0	1	1	−8
2		\	−4	0	2	9	9	6	6	5	−3	4	−3	−3	−1	0	0	4	8	0	0	−7	−3
3			\	4	−1	−5	−5	0	1	−4	−5	0	−5	−1	2	0	0	3	−5	0	−2	0	4
4				\	−6	−1	0	1	8	−5	−7	0	−7	−5	6	0	0	6	−2	0	5	1	−7
5					\	4	4	4	−2	3	2	0	0	−2	−3	0	0	−1	5	0	−6	−6	2
6						\	9	5	4	6	−1	5	−2	−2	−3	0	0	3	9	0	−1	−8	−2
7							\	5	4	5	−2	4	−2	−3	−2	0	0	3	9	0	0	−7	−5
8								\	5	0	−5	1	−6	−5	0	0	0	6	4	0	−2	−7	−5
9									\	−1	−8	2	−8	−6	4	0	0	8	2	0	2	−3	−8
10										\	3	4	3	3	−6	0	0	−2	7	0	−4	−5	3
11											\	−3	9	5	−4	0	0	−9	0	0	−1	3	9
12												\	−3	2	−5	0	0	4	5	0	−3	−5	−4
13													\	6	−4	0	0	−9	0	0	0	4	9
14														\	−6	0	0	−4	−1	0	−2	2	4
15															\	0	0	2	−5	0	3	3	−3
16																\	0	0	0	0	0	0	0
17																	\	0	0	0	0	0	0
18																		\	2	0	1	−4	−9
19																			\	0	−2	−8	0
20																				\	0	0	0
21																					\	5	−1
22																						\	3

Note: values are multiplied by 10 and rounded. A—Activity.

Activities whose hourly shares never exceed 1% are not considered in the correlation analysis. Satisfactory accuracy of the result is not guaranteed for these activities, as already described in Section 2 (in the description of the disadvantages of the work-sampling method) and at the end of Section 4. The excluded activities can be found under reference numbers 4, 14, 15, and 21.

Discussion

When analyzing potential dependencies between activities, we must consider pairs that have a value less than −6 or greater than 6, bolded in Table 4. There are 27 such correlations (without excluded activities):

- Machining and collecting/returning of tools (−7)—more processing means less collecting or returning tools.
- Machining and cleaning the machine (−8)—when we are not machining, there is more cleaning of the machines (e.g., in the last hour of the work shift).
- Machining and annotation of work results (−8)—we record the results at the end of the work shift.

- Machining and absence from the company (7)—we cannot confirm the connection (false correlation).
- Machining and private absence from the workplace (−8)—more productive work means less absence and losses (and vice versa).
- Clamping/unclamping the workpiece and workstation set-up (9)—the relationship exists when the batch is started, not later.
- Clamping/unclamping the workpiece and study of working instructions (9)—the comment is the same as the previous one.
- Clamping/unclamping the workpiece and business meeting (8)—we cannot confirm the relationship (false correlation).
- Clamping/unclamping the workpiece and private conversation (−7)—more productive work prevents conversations—due to the distances between the workplaces (and vice versa).
- Workstation set-up and the study of working instructions (9)—there is a logical connection between the activities (we need to familiarize ourselves with the work instructions when setting up the machine).
- Workstation set-up and business meeting (9)—meeting with the aim of perfecting the settings and starting the batch.
- Workstation set-up and private conversation (−8)—when setting up the machine there is less private conversation—because of the distances between workplaces.
- Study of working instructions and business meetings (9)—we cannot confirm the correlation (false correlation).
- Study of working instructions and Private conversation (−7)—good documentation does not encourage the worker to go to another worker for a private conversation.
- Conversation about tasks and Private conversation (−7)—it is obvious that some instruction from the foreman is usually required before starting a new task, which of course precludes the need for a private conversation; the importance of competent managers (useful comment no. **1**).
- Tool set-up and cleaning of the machine (−8)—tool setting is at the start of machining and machine cleaning is usually at the end.
- Tool set-up and annotation of work results (−8)—tool setting is at the start of machining, and the recording of the results is at the end.
- Tool set-up and absence from the company (8)—we cannot confirm the connection (false correlation).
- Tool set-up and private absence from the workplace (−8)—more productive work means less absence (and vice versa).
- Collecting/returning of tools and business meeting (7)—there is a possibility that the worker goes to the tool store and inadvertently attends a short meeting.
- Cleaning the machine and annotation of work results (9)—usual procedure after the job's completion.
- Cleaning the machine and absence from company (−9)—the completion of activities clearly does not encourage absence for other work tasks.
- Cleaning the machine and private absence from the workplace (9)—the completion of a batch of products gives the worker the feeling that he can do some private matters after this; the reason may be the late arrival of a new work assignment or unfavorable working conditions (useful comment no. **2**).
- Annotation of work results and absence from company (−9)—completion of a batch clearly does not encourage absence for other work duties.
- Annotation of work results and private absence from the workplace (9)—completion of a batch with recording the results gives the worker the feeling that he can still do some private matters after this; it is important to check the timeliness of the assignment of a new work order or correct organization of dispatch service (useful comment no. **3**).

- Absence from the company and private absence from the workplace (−9)—it appears that workers do not abuse absence due to other work commitments to attend to personal matters (useful comment no. **4**).
- Business meetings and private conversations (−8)—it seems that private conversations do not continue after meetings, which would lead to additional losses.

We looked at 27 pairs of activities and obtained four useful instructions or hints on the necessary actions that would have been overlooked without this analysis. We can confirm that testing the correlations has given us an additional tool for evaluating the recording data. Even with simple examples, we find certain hints for critical thinking (usually three to five). Sometimes they are correct (there is a link between the activities) and require some changes in the organization of the production process, but it can also be that they are useless.

6. Conclusions

Work sampling offers several benefits in terms of cost efficiency, flexibility, and statistical validity. It is a statistical method for determining the proportion of time workers spend on various defined or identified activities. We observe workers at random times during the work shift and mark what they are doing each time. Work sampling enables rapid analysis, identification, and improvement of work responsibilities, tasks, outstanding competencies, and organizational processes. Its main advantage lies in the study of non-repetitive activities, but it can also be used to develop time standards for repetitive work.

In this article, we present a comprehensive list of the most important loss factors that have emerged from our studies over the last two decades. And the most important thing in this article is that we introduce a pairwise correlation comparison of the measured hourly shares of all activities to examine whether mutual dependencies exist. The results of the work-sampling method are presented in tables, and additional calculations are now made to enable a discussion among the members of the working group about possible shortcomings and the necessary improvements to the processes. With the correlation analysis, we obtain the first signal, where some activities can trigger the occurrence of another activity, which can be without added value or represent a loss. This is an essential contribution to decision-making regarding efficiency improvements. In the example shown, we obtained four useful tips that can contribute to a better organization of processes and higher productivity.

The work-sampling method has two traditional steps: the recording process and data analysis, which includes calculating the activity shares for the entire recording period, by hours of the work shift, by days or by shifts, and the accuracy achieved. We add an upgrade to the data analysis: a correlative comparison of pairs of activities according to their share in the hours of the working day, which can help us to find the causes of the occurrence of losses (causal relationship between activities). This original idea was tested in a case study and led to four further useful suggestions. Applying correlation analysis to work sampling is extremely useful for managers to improve the work performance and productivity of organizations. This work contributes both theoretically (a new idea for data analysis) and empirically (a test case) to labor productivity insights. The procedure requires knowledge of the observed work processes.

Future research will include more sophisticated statistical methods supported by artificial intelligence. Certainly, we can improve the performance of recording by using video recording technology, probably without the use of image processing technology, because it is impossible to determine (automatically) with sufficient reliability what is being done in the workplace. Manual review of video is more time-consuming than direct observation, so the traditional method of manual recording is still acceptable.

Author Contributions: Conceptualization, B.B. and N.V.H.; methodology, B.B.; software, B.B.; validation, B.B. and N.V.H.; formal analysis, B.B.; investigation, N.V.H.; resources, B.B.; data curation, N.V.H.; writing—original draft preparation, B.B.; writing—review and editing, N.V.H.; visualization, B.B.; supervision, N.V.H.; project administration, N.V.H.; funding acquisition, B.B. All authors have read and agreed to the published version of the manuscript.

Funding: This research was funded by ARIS—the Slovenian Research and Innovation Agency, Research Core Funding No. P2-0190 and by the project "Upgrading national research infrastructures—RIUM", which was co-financed by the Republic of Slovenia, the Ministry of Education, Science and Sport, and the European Union from the European Regional Development Fund.

Data Availability Statement: The data and results are original and not manipulated. The archiving and care of the datasets took place at our Laboratory for Production and Operations Management at the Faculty of Mechanical Engineering, University of Maribor.

Acknowledgments: The authors would like to thank A. Polajnar for the useful suggestions in setting up the concept and improving the article.

Conflicts of Interest: The authors declare no conflicts of interest. The funders had no role in the design of the study; in the collection, analyses, or interpretation of data; in the writing of the manuscript; or in the decision to publish the results.

References

1. Tompkins, J.A.; White, J.A.; Bozer, Y.A.; Tanchoco, J.M.A. *Facility Planning*, 4th ed.; John Wiley & Sons: Hoboken, NJ, USA, 2010.
2. Gustaffson, V.; Davidsson, S. *Streamlining the Invisible Value Chain—Reduction of Losses within Administrative Processes: A Case Study*; Linnaeus University, School of Engineering: Växjö, Sweden, 2011.
3. Khanna, R.B. *Production and Operations Management*, 2nd ed.; PHI Learning Private Limited: Delhi, India, 2015.
4. Garcia, K.Y.F.; Rodriguez, J.D.; Leal, J.S.; Reyes-Martinez, R.M.; Prieto, A.W. Determination of allowance time by work sampling and heart rate in manufacturing plant in Juarez Mexico. *J. Eng.* 2019, *2019*, 1316734. [CrossRef]
5. De la Riva, J.; Garcia, A.I.; Reyes, R.M.; Woocay, A. Methodology to determine time allowance by work sampling using heart rate. *Procedia. Manuf.* 2015, *3*, 6490–6497. [CrossRef]
6. Martinec, T.; Skec, S.; Savsek, T.; Perisic, M.M. Work sampling for the production development: A case study of a supplier in European automotive industry. *Adv. Prod. Eng. Manag.* 2017, *12*, 375–387. [CrossRef]
7. Yuan, L.; Buchholz, B.; Punnett, L.; Kriebel, D. An integrated biomechanical modeling approach to the ergonomic evaluation of drywall installation. *Appl. Ergon.* 2016, *53*, 52–63. [CrossRef] [PubMed]
8. Dasgupta, P.S.; Fulmer, S.; Jing, X.-L.; Punnett, L.; Kuhn, S.; Buchholz, B. Assessing the ergonomic exposures for drywall workers. *Int. J. Ind. Ergonom.* 2014, *44*, 307–315. [CrossRef]
9. Javernik, A.; Buchmeister, B.; Ojstersek, R. Impact of cobot parameters on the worker productivity: Optimization challenge. *Adv. Prod. Eng. Manag.* 2022, *17*, 494–504. [CrossRef]
10. Javernik, A.; Buchmeister, B.; Ojstersek, R. The NASA-TLX approach to understand workers workload in human-robot collaboration. *Int. J. Simul. Model* 2023, *22*, 574–585. [CrossRef]
11. Skec, S.; Storga, M.; Ribaric, Z.T. Work sampling of product development activities. *Tech. Gaz.* 2016, *23*, 1547–1554. [CrossRef]
12. Grznar, P.; Gregor, M.; Gola, A.; Nielsen, I.; Mozol, S.; Seliga, V. Quick workplace analysis using simulation. *Int. J. Simul. Model* 2022, *21*, 465–476. [CrossRef]
13. Fischer, A.; Bedrikow, A.B.; Tommelein, I.D.; Nuebel, K.; Fottner, J. From activity recognition to simulation: The impact of granularity on production models in heavy civil engineering. *Algorithms* 2023, *16*, 212. [CrossRef]
14. Dewi, R.S.; Rahman, A.; Astuti, R.D. Workload analysis in a University Maintenance Division. *Ind. Eng. Manag. Syst.* 2019, *18*, 685–691. [CrossRef]
15. Ünal, C.; Güner, M. Job and personnel assessment in the apparel industry using fuzzy logic. *Fibres Text. East. Eur.* 2014, *22*, 17–22.
16. Safa, M.; Craig, B.N. Maritime and port activity analysis tool. In *Advances in Human Aspects of Transportation*; Stanton, N., Landry, S., Di Bucchianico, G., Vallicelli, A., Eds.; Springer: Cham, Switzerland, 2017; Volume 484, pp. 1065–1074. [CrossRef]
17. Lee, T.Y.; Ahmad, F.; Sarijari, M.A. Activity sampling in the construction industry: A review and research agenda. *Int. J. Prod. Perform. Manag.* 2023. Early access. [CrossRef]
18. Mathiassen, S.E.; Jackson, J.A.; Punnett, L. Statistical performance of observational work sampling for assessment of categorical exposure variables: A simulation approach illustrated using PATH data. *Ann. Occup. Hyg.* 2014, *58*, 294–316. [CrossRef]
19. Wahid, Z.; Daud, M.R.C.; Ahmad, K. Study of productivity improvement of manual operations in soya sauce factory. *IIUM Eng. J.* 2020, *21*, 202–211. [CrossRef]
20. Rashid, K.M.; Louis, J. Integrating process mining with discrete-event simulation for dynamic productivity estimation in heavy civil construction operations. *Algorithms* 2022, *15*, 173. [CrossRef]
21. Wong, D.; Feere, A.; Yousefi, V.; Partovi, N.; Dahri, K. How hospital pharmacists spend their time: A work-sampling study. *Can. J. Hosp. Pharm.* 2020, *73*, 272–278. [CrossRef] [PubMed]

22. Gupta, V.; Krishnappa, P.; Goel, P. Optimising time for effective patient care: Work-sampling analysis. *J. Health Manag.* **2023**, *25*, 829–833. [CrossRef]
23. Luo, X.C.; Li, H.; Cao, D.P.; Yu, Y.T.; Yang, X.C.; Huang, T. Towards efficient and objective work sampling: Recognizing workers' activities in site surveillance videos with two-stream convolutional networks. *Automat. Constr.* **2018**, *94*, 360–370. [CrossRef]
24. Stanton, R.G. The work of L. H. C. Tippett. *Ars. Textrina* **1987**, *7*, 179–185.
25. Kirwan, B.; Ainsworth, L.K. *A Guide to Task Analysis*; CRC Press: London, UK, 1992.
26. Barnes, R.M. *Work Sampling*, 7th ed.; Wiley: New York, NY, USA, 1980.
27. Badiru, A.B. *Handbook of Industrial and Systems Engineering*; CRC Press: Boca Raton, FL, USA, 2005.
28. Rao, P.S.R.S. *Sampling Methodologies with Applications*; CRC Press: Boca Raton, FL, USA, 2001.
29. Kendall, M.G.; Stuart, A. *The Advanced Theory of Statistics, Volume 2: Inference and Relationship*, 4th ed.; Griffin: London, UK, 1979.

Disclaimer/Publisher's Note: The statements, opinions and data contained in all publications are solely those of the individual author(s) and contributor(s) and not of MDPI and/or the editor(s). MDPI and/or the editor(s) disclaim responsibility for any injury to people or property resulting from any ideas, methods, instructions or products referred to in the content.

 *algorithms*

Article

A Data-Driven Approach to Discovering Process Choreography

Jaciel David Hernandez-Resendiz [1], Edgar Tello-Leal [2,*] and Marcos Sepúlveda [3]

1. Multidisciplinary Academic Unit Reynosa-Rodhe, Autonomous University of Tamaulipas, Reynosa 88779, Mexico
2. Faculty of Engineering and Science, Autonomous University of Tamaulipas, Victoria 87000, Mexico
3. Department of Computer Science, School of Engineering, Pontificia Universidad Católica de Chile, Santiago 8331150, Chile
* Correspondence: etello@docentes.uat.edu.mx

Abstract: Implementing approaches based on process mining in inter-organizational collaboration environments presents challenges related to the granularity of event logs, the privacy and autonomy of business processes, and the alignment of event data generated in inter-organizational business process (IOBP) execution. Therefore, this paper proposes a complete and modular data-driven approach that implements natural language processing techniques, text similarity, and process mining techniques (discovery and conformance checking) through a set of methods and formal rules that enable analysis of the data contained in the event logs and the intra-organizational process models of the participants in the collaboration, to identify patterns that allow the discovery of the process choreography. The approach enables merging the event logs of the inter-organizational collaboration participants from the identified message interactions, enabling the automatic construction of an IOBP model. The proposed approach was evaluated using four real-life and two artificial event logs. In discovering the choreography process, average values of 0.86, 0.89, and 0.86 were obtained for relationship precision, relation recall, and relationship F-score metrics. In evaluating the quality of the built IOBP models, values of 0.95 and 1.00 were achieved for the precision and recall metrics, respectively. The performance obtained in the different scenarios is encouraging, demonstrating the ability of the approach to discover the process choreography and the construction of business process models in inter-organizational environments.

Keywords: process choreography; IOBP; data-driven; process mining; discovery

Citation: Hernandez-Resendiz, J.D.; Tello-Leal, E.; Sepúlveda, M. A Data-Driven Approach to Discovering Process Choreography. *Algorithms* 2024, 17, 188. https://doi.org/10.3390/a17050188

Academic Editors: Zixin Huang, Li Jin, Xiongbo Wan and Sheng Du

Received: 10 April 2024
Revised: 28 April 2024
Accepted: 28 April 2024
Published: 29 April 2024

Copyright: © 2024 by the authors. Licensee MDPI, Basel, Switzerland. This article is an open access article distributed under the terms and conditions of the Creative Commons Attribution (CC BY) license (https://creativecommons.org/licenses/by/4.0/).

1. Introduction

In collaborative networks, the partners work together to create competitive advantages by defining the activities to be carried out by each organization, the business processes to be executed, the roles to be played, the communication channels, and the definition of interoperability at both the process and system levels in order to achieve common business goals [1–3]; e.g., a supply chain process may involve several organizations [4]. Collaborative networks foster joint problem-solving through resource sharing and the fusion of complementary skills. This collaborative environment enhances organizations' potential to create and acquire knowledge, leading to the innovation of products or services [5]. In this context of collaborative innovation, members of the supply chain plan and implement actions for knowledge sharing and knowledge application to develop new products and services quickly and efficiently, enabling them to maintain and improve their performance in the long term [6]. Furthermore, in Industry 4.0, end-to-end digital integration is required in the supply chain, with a business process design logic that crosses organizational boundaries. These business processes can be defined using the business process model and notion (BPMN) language [7,8], a standard for graphically representing the logic of the business process and its subsequent automation [9], which not only makes the logic more understandable but also makes it easier to integrate the perspective of the control flow, the subprocesses, the data flows (internal or external), and the resources involved in the processes into a BPMN diagram [10].

Data-driven approaches are characterized by decision-making based on the analysis and interpretation of data, rather than observations, allowing decisions and solutions to be supported by facts [11,12]. Process mining techniques are implemented through data-driven approaches, making it possible to discover process patterns within event logs and detect and diagnose differences between observed and modeled behavior [10,13], which helps in decision-making to improve and optimize business processes [14,15]. In this way, approaches based on process mining techniques have been implemented to verify and enhance business processes. These techniques are characterized by supporting discovery, conformance checking, enhancement, and predictive analytic tasks [16–18]. In a discovery approach to the business process model, event data generated by the execution of business processes are analyzed, making it possible to identify the logic and behavior of the process from these event data, known as event logs. Process conformance checking consists of evaluating the alignment of the behavior of the actual business process model against the behavior discovered in the event log (generated by the business process itself), to detect any possible deviations. In the process improvement task, various analyses are carried out, considering all the attributes available in the event log and in the real business process model to detect possible bottlenecks, high time consumption in task execution, deviations, and duplication of the execution of tasks by different resources, among others; making it possible to identify opportunities for improvement in the business process.

In approaches based on process mining techniques that implement tasks such as predictive process monitoring or trace clustering, an event log preprocessing stage is included, in which the input data must be encoded to feed the prediction or inference algorithm. At this stage, an encoding method is typically implemented to transform complex event data into a numerical or representative feature space [19]. One of the most important methods for this purpose is Doc2Vec, based on representation learning, developed in natural language processing (NLP) [20]. This learning uses neural network architecture models to automatically learn distributed vector representations of a concept of interest (for example, an activity or a trace) with high quality. Doc2Vec is an architecture for computing continuous vector representations of words from large datasets with high dimensionality. In the process mining domain, several approaches based on representation learning techniques have been presented to significantly improve the performance of the inference algorithm. In [21], the authors proposed several activity-level models, traces, models, and logs to deal with the high dimensionality of real-life event logs and to generate a distributed representation that can be used in different process mining tasks. In [22], the authors presented a case-level solution that uses word embeddings for business process data to better encode process instances. For their part, ref. [23] expounded an approach for conformance verification based on vector representations of each activity/task present in the model and the event log. Therefore, the vectors generated by Doc2Vec can be used to find similarities between traces, allowing for the quick analysis of large event logs by expressing words in the vector-space model and considering the context when learning through the co-occurrence of activities.

Recent studies have proposed solutions for different process mining tasks applied in intra-organizational business processes [24–27]. However, when process mining solutions are implemented in inter-organizational business processes (IOBP), aspects such as the process's privacy and autonomy; data with different levels of granularity; and event data stored in other sources, formats, and distribution form must be considered. Therefore, managing independently generated event logs requires methodologies and algorithms to process, align, and merge the event logs generated by process-oriented information systems [28]. Importantly, events need to be correlated across organizational boundaries. Then, by implementing process mining techniques, the tasks of discovery, monitoring, compliance, and improvement of IOBPs, which have yet to be studied to date, can be carried out. Furthermore, the analysis can be extended to discover and verify the process choreography, which represents the formalization of interactions through messages from the participants in an inter-organizational collaboration [29].

In this sense, automatic analysis of the historical information recorded from the execution of the business processes of the participating organizations can help to find relationships within the IOBP. The above can be achieved through data-driven and process model-level analysis. At the structured data level, the organizations participating in the IOBP are responsible for selecting and structuring the data from their information systems and consequently choosing the appropriate level of abstraction and the point of view of the data. At the level of process models, the business process flow of the participating organizations is analyzed, in search of patterns that can complement the analysis of structured data, to obtain sufficient information for identifying collaboration patterns between organizations and discovering the IOBP model. Different approaches are available in the state of the art that partially address analyzing and discovering process choreography, focusing on the analysis of the information contained in event logs [30–32], in business process models [33–37], document electronics, and information related to the business process [38].

Therefore, this paper proposes a data-driven methodology supported by semi-automatic methods that enable the discovery of the IOBP model and the process choreography in a collaborative environment. The relationships between the organizations participating in the business process are identified, labeled, and defined using a method based on the Doc2Vec algorithm and by calculating the cosine similarity measure between events to identify possible message-type tasks and their task subtype (send/receive), for which a set of definitions are specified to formalize the relationships, as well as a group of rules for assigning the message task subtype. These criteria are formulated in terms of relationships at the trace level and the event level. Next, each collaboration participant's intra-organizational business process model is determined, marking in the model the tasks previously identified as message-type tasks and their subtype, and defining the relationship between the processes through flow message connectors, which allows building an IOBP, including its process choreography. Subsequently, an inter-organizational event log is generated from the intra-organizational event logs, applying a fusion of traces from the relationships identified by the message-type tasks and their subtype, containing the event data of both traces. Finally, the process choreography and intra- and inter-organizational models are evaluated using the metrics of precision, recall, F-score, and generalization. The proposed approach was evaluated using four event logs derived from real-life IOBPs and two artificial event logs. The results achieved are very acceptable, with an overall performance in the discovery of the process choreography of 0.86 for the *relationship precision* metric, a *relationship recall* of 0.89, and with a measurement *F-score of the relationship* of 0.86, with a performance over 89% in the message-type task identification task. On the other hand, for the average evaluation of the quality level of the IOBP discovered, a *precision* of 0.94 was achieved, with a *recall* value of 0.99, and *generalization* indicator of 0.63, which indicates that the model of the inter-organizational process discovered could reflect more than 94% of the behavior contained in the merged event log.

2. Related Work

In [39], a technique to discover collaboration models from intra-organizational event logs was proposed. The structure of the event log was extended to support interaction data between participants by adding attributes to contain the message name, message identifier, participant role, and type of communication between participants. Interactions between participants are identified through an event data analysis in the event log, determining the correlation between the messages exchanged. Subsequently, the intra-organizational models discovered with the information from the interaction of messages are combined, which enables the generation of an inter-organizational business process model aligned with the BPMN language. Intra-organizational business process models are discovered for each participant in the collaboration by applying algorithms available in the state of the art. Similarly, ref. [40] presented a process mining approach to discover inter-organizational business processes and process choreography from an extended event log. This log requires information about the participants and the messages exchanged between the participants, to discover a model of the inter-organizational process represented by the BPMN language. The extended event log includes information required for the inter-organizational process model and process choreography. For example, the participant attribute identifies the participant that executes the event, and an attribute contains the type of event; in the case of message-type events, the information of the participant who receives the message is required. A fundamental stage in this proposal is extracting all message-type events and the information related to the message: the participant who sends or receives it. With this extra event log, a model of the process with the message interactions between the participants involved in the collaboration is discovered. This model is used to build process choreography and inter-organizational models in conjunction with the intra-organizational process models discovered for each participant. Our proposal takes a different approach from the studies mentioned above. It does not require the extension of the event log or adding information about the messages and resources exchanged between the collaboration participants. Instead, our method is based on a unique set of methods and formal rules. These tools allow for the identification of potential message tasks and the determination of the task's subtype, which in turn defines the message's meaning (send/receive).

On the other hand, ref. [41] proposed a process mining technique to merge intra-organizational event logs and discover an inter-organizational process model represented by a directly-follows graph. This approach is characterized by only using the common elements of an event log: case ID, timestamps, and activity. Furthermore, it is based on the premise that two activities of different organizations occur consecutively with a very short time difference, for which several time thresholds are defined. Therefore, adjacent activities with the minimum time difference should be interconnected and extracted, since they belong to the same trace within an inter-organizational event log, forming the sequence of the activities of the merged event log, ordered by the timestamp value. Each extracted activity pair will be identified in this log by concatenation with the original case IDs. The rest of the events of the same trace (which were not extracted) of each participant are embedded in the trace according to the timestamp value, with which the trace is constructed with all its events. This procedure is executed until no adjacent activities are identified in the event logs of each collaboration participant. In our case, the relationship between message tasks is determined by a cosine similarity measure that ensures that two tasks (from different participants) are close and possibly related. Furthermore, the task's subtype is determined through a set of rules that allow analyzing the context of the message-type task, that is, the antecedent and consequent tasks for both parties of the collaboration.

Differently, ref. [42] presented an approach based on a Petri net extension that supports the management of message attributes and resources exchanged in workflows (called RM_WF_net) to formalize healthcare processes in hospitals, particularly inter-departmental processes. From the formalization, algorithms are applied to discover intra-departmental models and identify collaboration patterns in each intra-departmental model, with which a collaboration model is built. The first algorithm discovers a control-flow structure based on WF-net. Subsequently, the event log is processed to identify messages and resources, which generates a RM_WF_net for each department. On the other hand, ref. [43] presented a process mining approach in an inter-organizational environment for a cloud computing multi-tenancy architecture through declarative models. Through a set of business rules, information related to the processes of systems that run in the cloud is extracted, and distributed data are identified, enabling the building of an event log. This approach makes it possible to represent processes with high variability. The previous proposals differ from our approach since using Petri nets reduces the expressiveness of the discovered model notation and does not support high-level notations compared to a BPMN-based model. In addition, there may be some difficulties in representing complex behaviors in the process logic, for example, in event-based gateways, which does not happen in BPMN-based models.

3. Preliminary Formalization

This section introduces the main foundations of the proposed approach, which formalizes the methodology phases and enables the identification of message-type tasks from direct tasks (previous or subsequent) or non-direct tasks. The above facilitates the marking of message tasks by their subtype (send/receive), making it possible to merge event logs and discover the correlation of messages exchanged in a collaboration.

Definition 1 (Mapping an event to a sentence). *This refers to a sentence of words that represent each event E_j. The sentence of words is generated from the values of the attributes Et_k that makeup E_j, representing the sentence's words.*

Definition 2 (Mapping a trace to a document). *This refers to statements representing each case T_i in the event log L. This document is generated from the values of the Et attributes of each activity $E_j \in T_i$, which represent the document's words (see Definition 1).*

Definition 3 (Incoming ($\bullet\theta$) and Outgoing edges ($\theta\bullet$) for the task θ). *Given a BPMN model $M = (i, o, T, G, E_m)$ and a task $\theta \in T$, its incoming edges $\bullet\theta = \{(c,d) \in E_m \mid d = \theta\}$ and its outgoing edges $\theta\bullet = \{(c,d) \in E_m \mid c = \theta\}$ [24].*

Definition 4 (Direct predecessors of task m). *Given a BPMN model $M = (i, o, T, G, E_m)$ and a task $m \in T$, its set of t-predecessors of task m are all tasks $p \notin G$, such that there is a direct path between p and m; and this path is contained in its set of incoming edges $\bullet m$ (see Definition 3).*

Definition 5 (Direct successors of task m). *Given a BPMN model $M = (i, o, T, G, E_m)$ and an event $m \in T$, its set of t-successors of m are all tasks $s \notin G$ such that there is a direct path between m and s, and this path is contained in the set of outgoing edges $m\bullet$ (see Definition 3).*

Definition 6 (Non-direct predecessors of task m). *Given a BPMN model $M = (i, o, T, G, E_m)$ and a task $m \in T$, the set of its t-non-direct predecessors is the set of tasks $TSK \in T$ such that for each $tsk \in TSK$, there are one or more paths between the tasks i and m that visit the event $tsk \notin G$.*

4. Materials and Methods

This section describes a conceptual representation of the scheme for discovering process choreography in inter-organizational environments. Figure 1 shows, in general terms, the phases and methods that compose the proposed methodology.

4.1. Event Log Processing

Our approach assumes that the event logs do not have empty or missing attributes. Furthermore, our methodology requires at least three common attributes in event logs: case ID, activity name, and timestamp. If additional attributes are available, they can be integrated and processed. However, only the value in the activity name attribute is used when marking and labeling the message-type task.

4.1.1. Method 1: Construction of the Vector Representation Matrix (VRM) of the Cases

For each event log L and L', a VRM and VRM' matrix of dimensions of $m \times n$ is generated, respectively. Where one row (a trace in the event log) of the matrix is a VRM representation of $T \in L$ and VRM' of $T' \in L'$, and this representation is mathematically implemented using the Doc2Vec word embedding technique, storing contextual information, in a low-dimensional vector, of all the attributes of a case (within the event log) that describe each of the events of the event logs L and L'. Next, the value of each attribute is identified to separate it into the words contained. The set of identified words form the vocabulary of the word embedding model, enabling the construction of a Doc2Vec representation, where a trace is treated as a document. The size of each word document is equal to the number of different values within the attributes that describe the event contained in a trace. The VRM and VRM' matrices are generated using the following rules:

- Consider any case $T_i \in L$.
- The mapping of a trace T_i to a D_i document is defined, considering all the values of the attributes et_k of each task $e_j \in T_i$, according to Definition 2.
- Stop-words in each D_i document are identified and removed.
- The remaining words in the D_i document form the T_i document. This procedure is performed for L and L', generating a corpus of D and D' documents.
- The cDoc2Vec model is built using the Doc2Vec method.
- The D and D' corpus create a general vocabulary of words.
- The cDoc2Vec model is trained with the corpus of D and D' documents.
- Then, the VRM and VRM' matrices are built from the representation $VRM_i \leftarrow cDoc2Vec.infer(D_i)$ and $VRM'_j \leftarrow cDoc2Vec.infer(D'_j)$, where the function $cDoc2Vec.infer(D_i)$ and $cDoc2Vec.infer(D'_j)$ allows extracting a mathematical representation of each document D_i and D'_j through $cDoc2Vec$ model inference.

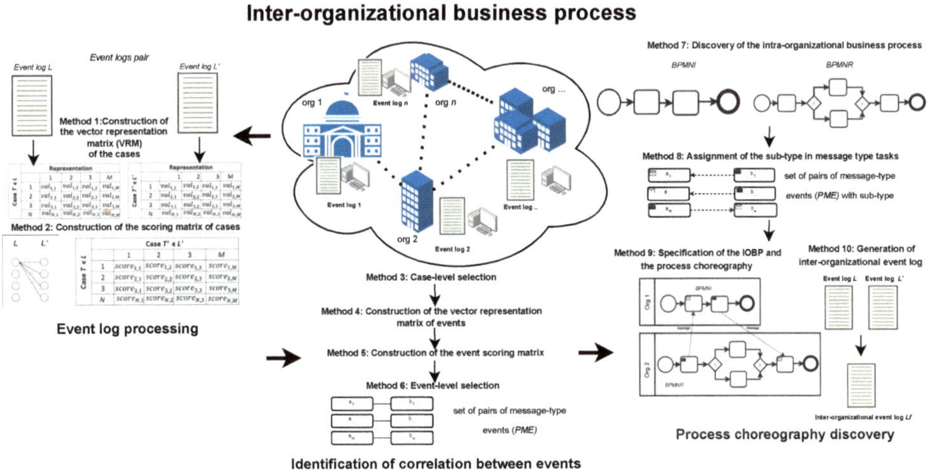

Figure 1. Overview of the proposed data-driven methodology.

4.1.2. Method 2: Construction of the Scoring Matrix of Cases

In this method, for each representation VRM_i contained in VRM, the cosine similarity measure is calculated with all representations contained in VRM'. The value obtained in the measure calculation allows us to know the similarity between vectors representing the traces in an internal product space. Then, a score matrix (SM) is generated with the similarity values between the VRM and VRM' vectors, constructing a matrix of size $|L| * |L'|$.

4.2. Identification of the Correlation between Events

4.2.1. Method 3: Case-Level Selection

The scoring matrix SM is filtered by applying the condition that, for each value $SM_{i,j}$ that exceeds threshold U_t, it must be extracted, generating a set of document pairs D_i and D'_j. For these documents $D_i \leftarrow T_i \in L$ y $D'_j \leftarrow T'_j \in L'$, there is a relationship at the case level, since they share information of the IOBP. The pair of traces of these selected documents are stored in the set $SCP \leftarrow (T_i, T'_j)$.

4.2.2. Method 4: Construction of the Vector Representation Matrix of Events

From the set of case pairs (SCP) selected in method 3, the event attributes that can provide information on the exchange of messages and business documents of the collaborative process are identified. Then, for each event $E_j \in T_i$ and $E'_l \in T'_k$ of each pair of cases $T_i \in L$ and $T'_k \in L'$ contained in SCP, this is mapped as an event-level statement RE_j and RE'_l, according to Definition 1. Their event representation vector is generated through the RE_j and RE'_l statements by inferring the previously trained $eDoc2Vec$ model. This model is trained similarly to the $cDoc2Vec$ model, but using event-level input data. The representations RE_j and RE'_l for each of the pairs of cases $T, T' \in SCP$ are generated by the following rules:

- We consider a pair of cases $T, T' \in SCP$.
- The events contained in $E_j \in T$ and $E'_l \in T'$ are mapped to a statement document $SD_j \leftarrow E_j$ and $SD'_l \leftarrow E_l$, considering all the values of their attributes $Et_k \in E_j$ and $E't_k \in E'_l$, according to Definition 1.
- Stop-words are identified and removed from the SD_j and SD'_l statement documents. The remaining words in SD_j and SD'_l form the final version of these statement documents.
- Finally, the vectors RE_j and RE'_l are generated from the representation $RE_j \leftarrow eDoc2Vec.infer(SD_j)$ and $RE'_l \leftarrow eDoc2Vec.infer(SD'_l)$, where the inference function allows you to extract a mathematical representation of each document SDj and SD'_l, using the previously trained $eDoc2Vec$ model.

4.2.3. Method 5: Construction of the Event Scoring Matrix

For each of the representations RE_j, their similarity with all representations of RE' is measured using the cosine distance metric. The similarity measure values allow the construction of an event-level scoring matrix (ESM), where each row of $ESM_{j,l}$ contains the similarity measure of the representations RE_j and $RE'_{1,2,\ldots,l}$.

4.2.4. Method 6: Event-Level Selection

The event score matrix (ESM) is traversed row-wise for each position within ESM_j to identify the highest similarity value in $ESM_{j,l}$. This similarity value will be selected if it meets the condition of exceeding the threshold U_a. The event pairs E_j and E'_l that satisfy the condition are considered possible message-type events, allowing a vector to be generated that stores all pairs of message-type events (PME). Subsequently, filtering is applied to select the pair of events with the highest similarity value, since the case may arise that an event E_j or E'_l may have more than one relationship with another event that contains similar information and exceeded the threshold U_a. Then, each of the events E_j that is related to the event E'_l with the highest similarity value is added to PME.

4.3. Process Choreography Discovery

4.3.1. Method 7: Discovery of the Intra-Organizational Business Process

In our experiment, considering the event logs L and L' (for the minimum number of participants required in a collaborative process), the BPMN process models of the initiating participant and the receiving participant are generated, denoted as $BPMNI \leftarrow L$ and $BPMNR \leftarrow L'$. This method uses the split-miner algorithm [24] to perform business process discovery. The essential operation of the algorithm is as follows:

- Consider an event log L.
- From the event log L, a directly-follows graph (DFG) is generated. This graph is a component $g = N, E$, where N represents the set of events (nodes) identified in the event log, and the set E represents the edges or paths that connect the set of nodes N.
- With the resulting DFG graph, a process model is generated based on the syntax of the BPMN language.

4.3.2. Method 8: Assignment of the Sub-Type in Message Type Tasks

In the discovered BPMN business process models (intra-organizational level), the message type tasks and the subtype of these tasks are identified. For each pair of events $(a, b) \in PME_i$, where $a \in L$ and $b \in L'$, the message subtype is defined, which can have the value of (*send* or *receive*). This subtype specifies the flow and direction of the message in the interaction between the participants in the collaboration. The assignment of the task subtype for each pair of events $(a, b) \in PME_i$ is performed based on the rules described in Table 1, complying with at least one condition defined in the rules.

Table 1. Rules for marking the subtype of the message-type task.

Description	Graphic Representation
Rule 1: Given the $BPMNI$ and $BPMNR$ models, if the *name* of one of the events in its set of direct *a-predecessors* of the event a (see Definition 4) is a compound of one of the elements included in the set $A = \{$*Get, Preparation, Notice, Need, Generate, Evaluate, Information Request, Approval, Process, Analyze, Make a decision, Acceptance, Validate, Communicate, Transport, Calculate, Demand, Order*$\}$, then the event a will be a message-type task and subtype *send* (*a.subtype = send*), and task b will be a message-type task and subtype *receive* (*b.subtype = receive*).	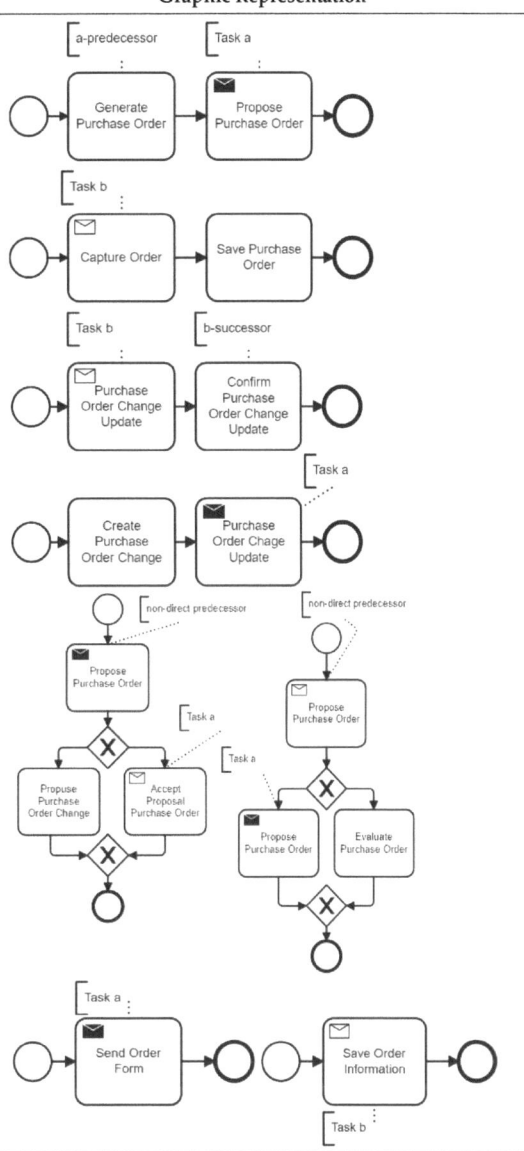
Rule 2: Given the $BPMNI$ and $BPMNR$ models, if the *name* of one of the events in the set of direct *b-successors* of the event b (see Definition 5) is a compound of one of the elements included in the set $C = \{$*Question, Notification, Decision Making, Request, Application, Transfer, Order, Manage, Confirm, Delivery, Safety, Evaluate, Approval*$\}$, then event b will be a message-type task and subtype *receive* (*b.subtype = receive*), and task a will be a message-type task and subtype *send* (*a.subtype = send*).	
Rule 3: Given the $BPMNI$ model, if a non-direct predecessor event to event a is a message-type task and the subtype is to *send* (see Definition 6), then event a will be assigned as a message-type task and subtype *receive* (*a.subtype = receive*). On the other hand, if the non-direct predecessor event to event a is a task of type message and subtype *receive* (see Definition 6), then event a will be assigned as a message task with subtype *send* (*a.subtype = send*). In the case of event b, the same rules are applied using the $BPMNR$ model and event b to assign its task type and subtype.	
Rule 4: Given the models $BPMNI, BPMNR$; the events a and b, if the *name* of the event a is a compound of one of the elements included in the set $S = \{$*Generate, Send, Communicate, Make, Confirm, Set Up, Turn, Order, Report, Transportation*$\}$, then event a will be a message-type task and subtype *send* (*a.subtype = send*), and the task b will be message-type task and subtype *receive* (*b.subtype = receive*).	

Table 1. *Cont.*

Description	Graphic Representation
Rule 5. Given the models $BPMNI$, $BPMNR$; the events a and b, if the *name* of the event a is compound of one of the elements included in the set $R = \{Receive, Accept, Status, Arrival, Notice, Admit\}$, then event a will be a message-type task and subtype *receive* ($a.subtype = receive$), and the task b will be message-type task and subtype *send* ($b.subtype = send$)	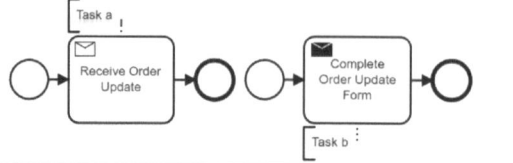

4.3.3. Method 9: Specification of the IOBP and the Process Choreography

The construction of the IOBP model and the process choreography representation are defined using the results (data and models) generated by implementing methods 7 and 8. Therefore, the exchange of messages is specified on the IOBP model based on the data discovered in the previous methods, enabling the process choreography to be visualized through the formalization of the interaction between the participants of the collaboration. The IOBP model and process choreography are built through the following steps:

- Let us consider a pair of BPMN process models from participants $BPMNI = (i, o, T, G, E_m)$ and $BPMNR = (i, o, T, G, E_m)$.
- The set of nodes $T \in BPMNI$ and $T' \in BPMNR$ refers to the set of events contained in the event registers L and L', considering that each node in T and T' has a label with the name of the events in L and L', respectively. This means that $a \subseteq T$ is represented by the events $a \in PME$ and $\subseteq T'$ is represented by the events $b \in PME$.
- The inter-organizational business process (IOBP) is generated by adding the process models $BPMNI$ and $BPMNR$, each model within a *pool* element identified with the *name* of the participant.
- With the set of task event pairs of type message and its subtype (PME), the message flow connection (Mfc) between the subsets of nodes $\subseteq T$ and $\subseteq T'$ is specified. Mfc represents the links that relate message-type tasks (events) between the pools of the IOBP model. Connectors Mfc are added to the $IOBPmodel \leftarrow Mfc$, representing the process choreography that supports the message exchange logic between the process models $BPMNI$ and $BPMNR$.
- The direction of each flow connector Mfc is given by the following conditions (1):

$$Mfc \leftarrow \begin{cases} (a \in PME)x(b \in PME) \mid |a \to b| = 1, & \text{if } a.subtype = send \\ & \text{and } b.subtype = receive, \\ (a \in PME)x(b \in PME) \mid |b \to a| = 1, & \text{if } a.subtype = receive \\ & \text{and } b.subtype = send \end{cases} \quad (1)$$

4.3.4. Method 10: Generation of Inter-Organizational Event Log

The inter-organizational event log is constructed by merging the event logs L and L' and the output data from the previous methods, applying the following procedure.

- Consider the event logs L and L', the set of pairs of the cases $(T, T') \in SCP$, and the set of pairs of the events considered message-type tasks $(a, b) \in PME$.
- A new Lf event log is created, which will contain the values of the merged event log.
- For each pair of cases $(T, T') \in SCP$:
  - In the case of T, the message-type tasks found in case T' are added. Therefore, $T \leftarrow E \in T \cup E' \in T'$ as long as $(a, b) \in PME | E' \in b$.
  - In the case of T', the message-type tasks found in case T are added. Therefore, $T' \leftarrow E' \in T' \cup E \in T$ as long as $(a, b) \in PME | E \in a$.
- Cases T and T' are added to the event log $Lf \leftarrow T$ and $Lf \leftarrow T'$.
- Cases $Tl \in L$ not found in $SCP (Tl \notin SCP)$ are added to the event log $Lf \leftarrow Tl$.

- Cases $Tl' \in L'$ not found in $SCP(Tl' \notin SCP)$ are added to the event log $Lf \leftarrow Tl'$.

The resulting event log Lf (merged) allows you to visualize the IOBP model, including all participants and their interactions. In this log, the event attributes that compound the cases contain information about the interaction through messages from the participants involved in the inter-organizational collaboration.

4.4. Evaluation Metrics

The discovered process choreography is evaluated in a supervised manner, for which a reference inter-organizational process model ($RIOBP$) is required. This model contains the process logic, behavior, and real interaction of the participants of the IOBP. Then, process choreography data are extracted from the $RIOBP$ model, including the message-type tasks, the subtype of each message-type task, and the message exchange sequence (noted as *relevant relationships* previously). Furthermore, in the set PME (see Method 6), the relationships selected by our proposal are searched and counted because they met the condition of exceeding the threshold U_a and with the highest value in the measure of cosine similarity, which we call *found relationships*. Moreover, relations with a cosine similarity value greater than or equal to the threshold U_a are recovered. These relationships are identified as *recovered relationships*. Then, *found relationships* are the subset of *relevant relationships* found by our proposal in the set *recovered relationships*; that is,

$$found\ relationships \subset recovered\ relationships | found\ relationships \in relevant\ relationships \quad (2)$$

Considering the above, we propose the following metrics to evaluate the discovered process choreography:

- **Relationship Precision (RP)** is the proportion of *relevant relationships* encountered out of all *recovered relationships*. This metric evaluates whether the complete process choreography has been discovered ($found\ relationships = |relevant\ relationships \cap recovered\ relationships|$) without adding relations not found in the process choreography of the reference model (*relevant relationships*).

$$RP : \frac{|relevant\ relationships \cap recovered\ relationships|}{recovered\ relationships} \quad (3)$$

- **Relationship Recall (RR)** is the proportion of *found relationships* matching *relevant relationships*. This metric indicates the percentage of the process choreography discovered versus the process choreography of the reference IOBP model *relevant relationships*.

$$RR : \frac{|relevant\ relationships \cap recovered\ relationships|}{relevant\ relationships} \quad (4)$$

- **F-score of the Relationship (FsR)** is the harmonic mean between the RP and RR, which allows us to determine the performance of the proposed approach. This metric indicates the ability of the method to discriminate between relevant and non-relevant relationships.

$$FsR = 2 \times \frac{RP \times RR}{RP + RR} \quad (5)$$

Furthermore, the quality of intra-organizational business process models are evaluated through the metrics *precision*, *recall*, and *generalization*, as defined in [44,45]. These metrics have as input an event log and an intra-organizational business process model, comparing the information available in the event log and the discovered business process model. In our experimentation, it is also required to evaluate the inter-organizational business process model ($IOBP$) built from the merged event log (Lf), for which it is required to implement the following modifications in the process logic of the $IOBP$ model, to represent it as an intra-organizational model, making it possible to determine the quality of the model discovered through the application of the *precision*, *recall*, and *generalization* metrics.

- Let us consider the $IOBP$ model and the collaborative Lf model previously generated.
- In the $IOBP$ model, the following elements contained in the *pools* BPMNI = (i, o, T, G, E_m) and BPMNR = (i', o', T', G', E'_m) are updated:
  1. the initial activity i and i' of the BPMNI and BPMNR models, respectively, are eliminated, and
  2. a unique initial activity I is added, from which the intra-organizational models start, formed as BPMNI = (I, o, T, G, E_m) and BPMNR = (I, o', T', G', E'_m).
- Next, the $IOBP$ models BPMNI = (I, o, T, G, E_m) and BPMNR = (I, o', T', G', E'_m) are updated in the following way:
  1. their final activities o and o' are eliminated, respectively, and
  2. a unique final activity O is added, where the two $IOBP$ models end with the following structure BPMNI = (I, O, T, G, E_m) and BPMNR = (I, O, T', G', E'_m).
- A set of edges or paths $Exor$ is created between the activities/nodes of message type; for each pair of activities/nodes $(a, b) \in PME$, the virtual edges are created according to the following conditions:
  1. if $a.subtype = send$, then a gateway of the XOR ($Gxor \leftarrow gxor$) type is created, and the paths connecting the nodes $Exor \leftarrow (a \rightarrow gxor)$, $Exor \leftarrow (for \rightarrow b)$ and $Exor \leftarrow (for \rightarrow a - successor)$ are added to $Exor$; removing the message flow connector $(a, b) \in IOBP$.
  2. if $b.subtype = send$, then a gateway XOR ($Gxor \leftarrow gxor$) type is created and the paths that connect the nodes $Exor \leftarrow (b \rightarrow gxor)$, $Exor \leftarrow (gxor \rightarrow a)$ and $Exor \leftarrow (gxor \rightarrow b - successor)$ are added to $Exor$, removing the message flow connector $(a, b) \in IOBP$.
- The resulting model is made up of the following components: $IOBPf = (I, O, (T \cup T'), (G \cup G' \cup Gxor), (E_m \cup E'_m \cup Exor))$.

5. Experimentation

5.1. Inter-Organizational Event Logs

The proposed approach was evaluated using the event logs of 4 real-life scenarios and 2 artificial scenarios of IOBPs. Table 2 summarizes the characteristics of each event log corresponding to the scenarios used in our experimentation.

1. **Air quality system**. This scenario was derived from an autonomous air quality monitoring system based on IoT technology. The collaborative process includes the interaction between 3 participants; consult the description at [46] for more details. The first participant, the *IoT Air quality monitor*, includes activities regarding the validation of the monitoring system's sensors, requests for access to the system, and assigning a valid network address for the monitoring system. Furthermore, it manages all activities for data census through sensors, validation, and sending of air pollution data and meteorological factors through a web service and system shutdown information. The second participant, the *System Access Service*, manages system access requests (accepted and rejected), assigns network addresses for the operation to the IoT air quality monitoring system, and registers active clients. This participant establishes communication with each instance of the *IoT Air quality monitor* participant. The third participant's *Repository Management Service* manages each request for data storage in a database located in a cloud service. It also manages the validation activities of the data sent by the participant *IoT Air quality monitor* (with acceptance or rejection options) and inserts these data into the database.
2. **Healthcare**. This scenario is made up of the activities of 4 participants (*Patient, Gynecologist, Laboratory*, and *Hospital*) involved in an IOBP within a healthcare scenario (e-healthcare) [31]. The process begins when the *Patient* participant provides information regarding her health status and waits for a response about her treatment or, if applicable, a request for hospitalization. The participant *Gynecologist* coordinates laboratory blood studies and hospitalization activities with the participant *Laboratory*

and the participant *Hospital*. The collaboration begins when a *Patient* sends information about her illness to the *Gynecologist*. The *Gynecologist* examines the *Patient* and, in parallel, takes blood samples from the *Patient* and sends them to the *Laboratory* for analysis. The *Laboratory* studies the blood samples, generating a report with the study results for the participant *Gynecologist*. Subsequently, the *Gynecologist* decides whether the *Patient* should be prescribed medicine or needs hospitalization, informing the *Patient*. When hospitalization is required, the *Gynecologist* communicates with the hospital to request the patient's admission and sends the clinical analysis results. When the *Hospital* begins its process, the patient's clinical history is created. Then, it decides whether to consider the blood test results sent by the *Gynecologist* or request a new analysis; in either case, the login information is sent to the *Patient*.

3. **Travel Agency**. This collaborative process involves the participants *Customer* and *Travel Agency* [31]. The process begins with the *Travel Agency* proposing a travel offer to the *Customer*. The *Customer* reviews the offer and can request a reservation for the trip. Next, the negotiation is executed to confirm the reservation, the payment of the services, and the generation of a reservation confirmation by the *Travel Agency*. Finally, the *Travel Agency* confirms the reservation number to the *Customer* and sends the electronic tickets.

4. **Purchase order**. The event log contains instances of the execution of the purchase order management process from 2017 to 2018 involving two organizations in the telecommunications industry [47]. The organization *M-Repair* plays the role of customer, and the organization *M-Parts* plays the role of the supplier of electronic components. The collaborative business process has the business goal of reducing component acquisition management time and accelerating the purchasing process in *M-Repair*, electronically automating confirmation decisions by the supplier.

5. **Transfer of goods**. This case study explores the management of multimodal transportation business processes, artificially generated [48]. The global business process involves the processes of the participants *Sender and Buyer* (owner of the goods), *Consigner* (responsible for carrying out the procedure for transporting the goods through two types of transport), *Carrier* (first means of transport), and *Shipper* (second means of transport). The business process begins with the *Sender and Buyer* organization, which generates and sends a merchandise order request to the *Consigner* organization. The request is processed, and a transport contract is generated, which both participants sign. Subsequently, the participant *Consigner* requests the reservation from the participant's *Carrier* and *Shipper*. The participant, *Carrier* and *Shipper*, evaluate the reservation request and return a response to the participant's *Consigner*. When acceptance of reservation requests is received, the *Consigner* receives a notification to prepare the packaging of the merchandise and transmits the merchandise to the *Carrier*. The participant *Carrier* loads the received goods onto a means of transport and generates an invoice for the *Consigner*. Then, payment for the service is processed by the participant *Consigner*. At the end of the merchandise transfer journey, the participant *Carrier* transfers the merchandise to the participant *Shipper*, who is responsible for continuing the transportation of the merchandise. The *Shipper* then generates an invoice corresponding to the service and requests the corresponding payment from the participant *Consigner*, who processes the request. Finally, the *Consigner* manages the fee for the service made with his client *Sender and Buyer* and notifies the data to track the merchandise transfer.

6. **Manufacturing process**. This artificial collaborative business process describes a supply chain management scenario, considering the manufacturing and delivery process of product orders, and involves six business partners [49,50]. First, the *Bulk Buyer* orders a set of products from the *Manufacturer*. The manufacturing of these products requires that different suppliers supply the raw materials. In this scenario, assume that *Supplier A* and *Supplier B* are raw materials suppliers named A and B. Based on the order, the *Manufacturer* calculates the demand for materials A and B (for example,

the fuselage and engines). *Supplier B* can supply raw material B, while material A is sent to *Middleman*. The *Middleman* forwards the order to *Supplier A*, who obtains permission from the authority and coordinates with the participant's *Special Carrier* to deliver material A to the *Manufacturer*. When the delivery process starts, the *Special Carrier* informs the *Manufacturer*, so that he can prepare the pre-processing procedure for material A. When the raw material is received, the *Manufacturer* performs a quality test, and if it is favorable, pre-processes matter A. In the case of matter B, the quality test is carried out by *Supplier B*. When the pre-processing of material A is completed and the test results of material B have been validated, the *Manufacturer* begins manufacturing the product. Additionally, the *Manufacturer* sends status reports to the *Bulk Buyer* before and after production, with a final testing process and product delivery completing the process.

Table 2. Characteristics of the event log of each inter-organizational scenario.

Scenario	Participants	Collaborations	Cases	Events	Unique Events
Air quality system	IoT Air Quality Monitor (IAQM)	2	9180	511,049	24
	Repository Management Service (RMS)		9180	215,651	8
	System Access Service (SAS)		9180	64,260	7
Healthcare	Patient	4	100	250	4
	Laboratory		100	300	3
	Hospital		50	200	5
	Gynecologist		100	700	9
Travel Agency	Travel Agency	1	100	869	5
	Customer		100	607	5
Purchase order	M-Repair	1	100	714	19
	M-Parts		100	686	18
Transfer of goods	Shipper	4	2	24	12
	Sender and Buyer		2	20	10
	Consigner		2	40	20
	Carrier		2	20	10
Manufacturing process	Bulkbuyer	8	5	60	4
	Middleman		5	56	4
	Manufacturer		5	202	20
	Supplier A		5	78	8
	Supplier B		5	19	4
	Special Carrier		5	39	8

5.2. Experiment Results

This section presents a detailed evaluation (for each scenario) of implementing the proposed methodology for discovering process choreography by identifying message-type events. The performance achieved by the implementation of the approach was measured using the metrics *relationship Precision (PR)* (Equation (3)), *relationship Recall (RR)* (Equation (4)), and *F-score of the relationship (FsR)* (Equation (5)). Moreover, a quantitative evaluation of the quality of the intra-organizational and inter-organizational process models discovered by the proposed approach is presented using the *precision*, *Recall*, and *Generalization* metrics.

Table 3 presents the values obtained for each evaluation metric of the process choreography discovered for each inter-organizational scenario. The second column shows the pairs of participants for which a message exchange was identified. Columns 3, 4, and 5 display the metrics *PR*, *RR*, and *FsR* achieved in the evaluation of the discovered choreography. In addition, Table 3 shows the U_t and U_a thresholds defined for each scenario. The sensitivity of each threshold can be interpreted as follows: If the value of the threshold

U_t is close to 0, a greater number of cases from the event log are analyzed to find the message-type events. On the contrary, if the value of U_t is close to 1, the method analyzes fewer cases, reducing the search space. The U_a threshold is highly sensitive, because a change in this parameter's value will impact the values achieved in the RP, RR, and FsR metrics. So, if the threshold U_a is decreased close to 0, this will allow more relevant relationships to be recovered, making the value of the RP metric high. However, this will cause more non-relevant relationships to be recovered, which will harm (reduce) the RR metric. Otherwise, if the U_a threshold is increased close to 1, this can cause the relationships found to be true and relevant relationships. Therefore, the RR metric would increase, while the RP metric would decrease, because some relevant relationships would not be recovered due to a low value in the similarity measure. In our experiment, the value of U_a was assigned by maximizing the FsR metric, in order to recover the greatest number of relevant relationships and the least number of non-relevant relationships, since FsR represents the weighting of the RP and RR metrics.

Table 3. Results of the evaluation of the proposed methods to identify the message-type tasks and their subtype.

Scenario	Collaboration	RP	RR	FsR	Parameters	Time (s)
Air quality system	IAQM-SAS	1	1	1	$U_t \geq 0.5, U_a \geq 0.98$	105,371
	IAQM-RMS	1	1	1	$U_t \geq 0.5, U_a \geq 0.98$	83,419
Healthcare	Patient-Gynecologist	1	1	1	$U_t \geq 0.2, U_a \geq 0.96$	60
	Gynecologist-Laboratory	1	0.5	0.66	$U_t \geq 0.2, U_a \geq 0.50$	46
	Hospital-Gynecologist	0.5	0.5	0.5	$U_t \geq 0.2, U_a \geq 0.96$	57
	Hospital-Patient	-	-	-	$U_t \geq -, U_a \geq -$	21
Travel agency	Customer-Travel agency	1	1	1	$U_t \geq 0.2, U_a \geq 0.89$	158
Purchase order	M-Repair-M-Parts	0.83	1	0.90	$U_t \geq 0.5, U_a \geq 0.9$	203
Transfer of goods	Sender and Buyer-Consigner	0.8	1	0.88	$U_t \geq 0.5, U_a \geq 0.6$	1
	Carrier-Consigner	0.8	0.8	0.8	$U_t \geq 0.5, U_a \geq 0.6$	1
	Consigner-Shipper	0.75	0.75	0.75	$U_t \geq 0.5, U_a \geq 0.6$	1
	Carrier-Shipper	1	1	1	$U_t \geq 0.5, U_a \geq 0.4$	1
Manufacturing process	Bulkbuyer-Manufacturer	1	1	1	$U_t \geq 0.2, U_a \geq 0.9$	1
	Supplier B-Manufacturer	1	1	1	$U_t \geq 0.2, U_a \geq 0.95$	1
	Middleman-Manufacturer	1	1	1	$U_t \geq 0.2, U_a \geq 0.98$	1
	Middleman-Special Carrier	1	1	1	$U_t \geq 0.2, U_a \geq 0.9$	1
	Middleman-Supplier A	1	1	1	$U_t \geq 0.2, U_a \geq 0.9$	1
	Special Carrier-Supplier A	0.28	1	0.43	$U_t \geq 0.2, U_a \geq 0.9$	1
	Supplier A-Manufacturer	1	1	1	$U_t \geq 0.2, U_a \geq 0.98$	2
	Special Carrier-Manufacturer	1	1	1	$U_t \geq 0.2, U_a \geq 0.98$	2

Moreover, the time costs required for the identification of the message tasks were very acceptable. In event logs with a low level of complexity and a low number of cases and events, the approach identified the message-type tasks in approximately 200 s, using the threshold U_t and U_a parameters presented in Table 3. For the collaborations of the Air Quality System scenario, which are characterized by real-life event logs with a high number of cases and events, as well as a medium-high complexity, the algorithm required 105,371 and 83,419 s for collaborations IAQM-SAS and IAQM-RMS, respectively. The time consumed in this scenario encouraged us to continue experimenting with large event logs with greater complexity. The experimentation was carried out on a personal computer with an AMD Ryzen 5 3400G processor, 3700 MHz, 4 cores, with Radeon Vega Graphics, 16 Gb RAM, and 1 Tb SDD with Windows 10 operating system and the Python 3.7 programming language. The time consumed by the approach to the processing of message task identification in the event logs of the Air Quality System scenario could be decreased, and the first action would be focused on improving the processing characteristics of the computing equipment.

Table 4 shows the average value of the metrics *RP*, *RR*, and *FsR* per scenario in the identification of message-type events. These averages are derived from the values achieved for the metrics presented in Table 3. The overall evaluation of this task was 0.86 for the *RP* metric, 0.89 for the *RR* metric, and a *FsR* of 0.86. The results presented are acceptable, indicating that the approach had a performance greater than 89% in the task of finding message-type events in an inter-organizational scenario; that is, it correctly identified (89%) the interaction of messages between the participants, which is the basis for the specification of the process choreography. Furthermore, 86% of the relationships found were genuinely relevant.

Table 4. Average evaluation of the identification of events at the collaboration level.

Scenario	RP	RR	FsR
Air quality system	1	1	1
Healthcare	0.62	0.50	0.54
Travel agency	1	1	1
Purchase order	0.83	1	0.90
Transfer of goods	0.83	0.88	0.83
Manufacturing process	0.91	1	0.92
Average	0.86	0.89	0.86

Table 5 shows the validation of the quality of the intra-organizational process models discovered, which were recovered from the behavior identified in the event logs through implementing the Split-miner algorithm. The level of quality of the recovered intra-organizational process models is of great importance in the proposed approach, since these models are the basis for discovering inter-organizational processes. Table 5 shows the average value of the evaluation metrics per scenario based on the intra-organizational process models discovered in each scenario. For the *precision* metric, a value between 0.85 and 1.00 was obtained, considering the six scenarios. For the *recall* metric, a value of 1.00 was obtained in all the scenarios evaluated. Values of 0.30 and 0.54 were obtained for the *generalization* metric in the scenarios *transfer of goods* and *manufacturing process*; the evaluation for the rest of the scenarios was between 0.79 and 0.96 for this metric. Overall, these results indicate that the intra-organizational models replicated all behavior from event logs and that the models accounted for 5% of behaviors not included in the event logs. However, it is observed that there was a large number of infrequent events, according to the values obtained for the *generalization* metric.

Table 5. Quality assessment of discovered intra-organizational business process models.

Intra-Organizational Business Process	Precision	Recall	Generalization
Air quality system	1	1	0.96
Healthcare	0.98	1	0.87
Travel agency	0.85	1	0.89
Purchase order	1	1	0.79
Transfer of goods	1	1	0.30
Manufacturing process	0.88	1	0.54
Average	0.95	1	0.72

On the other hand, Table 6 presents the evaluation of the quality level of the IOBPs discovered through the metrics of precision, recall, and generalization. In the experiment, 21 organizations participating in 20 peer collaborations were identified, derived from the event logs analyzed. Considering a general evaluation, a value of 0.94 was obtained for the *precision* metric, 0.99 for the *recall* measure, and a value of 0.63 for the *generalization* indicator.

At that level, the results obtained are acceptable and indicate that the inter-organizational process models discovered were capable of reflecting 99% of the behavior found in the merged collaborative event logs. Furthermore, the discovered models only reflected 6% of behaviors not seen in the event logs. However, low values remained for the *generalization* metric, which denotes infrequent activities in the event log. It is essential to mention that this metric is only informative for knowing the conformation of the event log and does not express a performance value for the discovered model. Due to the nature of business processes, it is common for there to be infrequent activities or behaviors in an event log.

Table 6. Quality assessment of discovered IOBP models.

IOBP	Precision	Recall	Generalization
Air quality system	1	0.99	0.86
Healthcare	1	1	0.67
Travel agency	0.80	1	0.93
Purchase order	1	1	0.50
Transfer of goods	1	1	0.35
Manufacturing process	0.85	0.99	0.48
Average	0.94	0.99	0.63

Figure 2 shows a comparison between the reference IOBP model (see Figure 2a) and the IOBP model discovered (see Figure 2b) for the scenario *Travel Agency*. The figure shows that the process logic, tasks, and gateways discovered coincided with the behavior contained in the reference IOBP. The process choreography deployed through the interaction of messages between pools, represented by the message flow connectors, was similar among the reference and discovered models, with the logic of the matching process and the logic and sequence of the process choreography. In the validation of the discovered process choreography, a value of 1.00 was obtained for all metrics (see Table 4), which indicates that the proposed approach could identify all interactions between participants. On the other hand, in the evaluation of the quality of the collaborative model, values of 0.80 and 1.00 were obtained for the precision and recall metrics, respectively, demonstrating that the collaborative model could reproduce most of the behavior found in the merged event log, without adding behaviors not included in the event log (see Table 6).

The process choreography between the participants *Customer* and *Travel agency* in both models (see Figure 2a,b) contained interactions through five message flow connectors, as described below.

1. The participant *Travel agency* sends a message using the task *Make Travel Offer* of the subtype *send* and the participant *Customer* receives the message using the task *Check Travel Offer* of the subtype *receive*. The interaction is represented by a message flow connector named *offer*, deployed as *message_4* in the discovered process model (see Figure 2b).
2. The *Customer* confirms his interest in the travel proposal through the task *Book Travel* of the subtype *send*, which establishes a communication with the participant *Travel agency* using the message connector *Travel* (*message_0*). The message is received by the company *Travel agency* in the task *Book Received* of the subtype *receive*.
3. The next interaction of *Customer* with the *Travel agency* is presented through the message flow connector *Payment* (*message_3*), which links the task *Pay Travel* of the subtype *send* with the *Payment Received* of subtype *receive* contained in the *pool* of the participant *Travel agency*.
4. The participant *Travel agency* confirms the travel reservation through a message sent by the task *Confirm Booking*, which is received with the *Booking Confirmed* of the subtype *receive* from the participant *Customer*.
5. Finally, the participant *Travel agency* sends a business document about the paid order, sending it in the message flow connector *Ticket* (*message_1*) using the task *Order Ticket* of subtype *send* and the task (*Ticket Received* of the subtype *receive*.

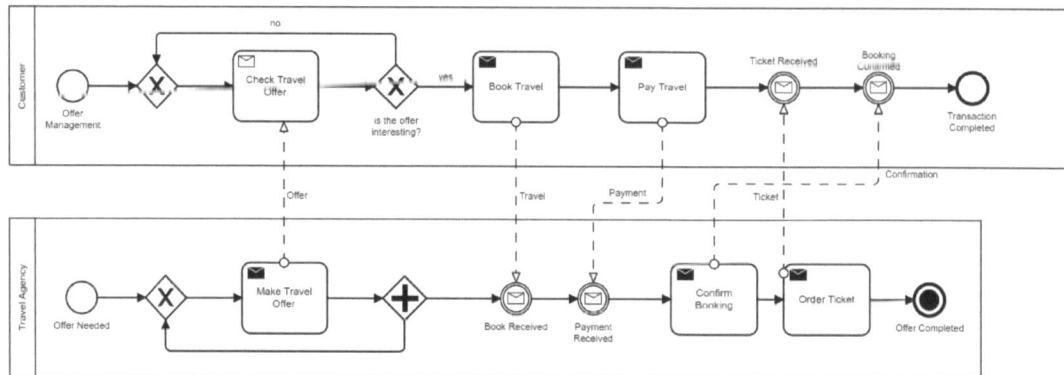

(a) Reference IOBP model.

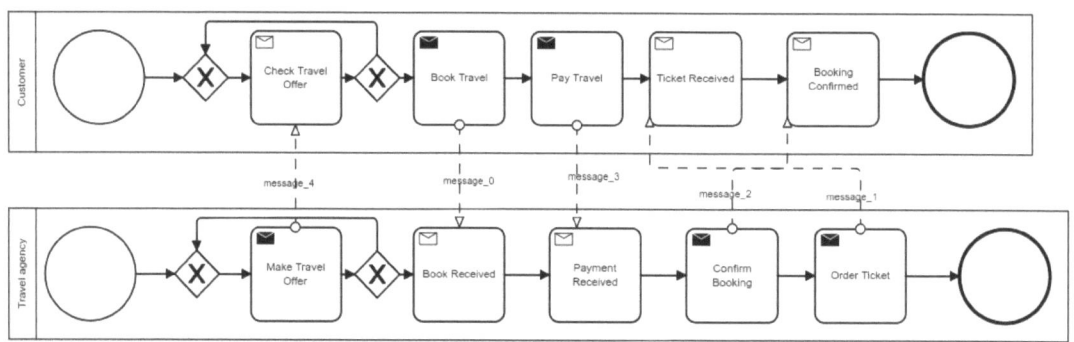

(b) Discovered IOBP model.

Figure 2. Comparison of the reference IOBP/process choreography model versus the discovered IOBP/process choreography model for the *travel agency* scenario.

6. Discussion

The approaches for discovering IOBP models and process choreography presented in [39–41] exhibited a similar objective to our proposal. In [39], the authors described the discovery of an IOBP model and the interaction of messages between the participants using a healthcare scenario, as used in our experimentation. Their experiment obtained values of 0.4 and 1.00 for the fitness and precision metrics, respectively, utilizing an extended version of the event log to identify messages between participants. For their part [40], the authors reported the discovery of an IOBP model using the same Healthcare scenario and an extended event log to manage the message data, reporting independent diagrams for the IOBP model and the choreography process discovered. In our experimentation, the quality assessment of the IOBP model of the healthcare scenario obtained a value of 1.00 for the precision and recall metrics. Furthermore, in the quality assessment of the discovery of the intra-organizational models that made up the IOBP model, values of 0.98 and 1.00 were achieved for the precision and recall, respectively.

On the other hand, ref. [41] obtained results between 0.94 and 1.00 for the precision metric and 0.905 and 1.00 for the recall metric in their discovery of a collaborative model using a classic event log (BPIC 2012) in the process mining domain. In their approach, no additional information is required to determine which tasks can be correlated, applying a technique of adjacent activities, and identifying the minimum execution time between the tasks to assess their link. We presented an experiment with the event log of the Air Quality System scenario, which had characteristics and complexity similar to the BPIC 2012 event log. The results of the identification evaluation of the message task achieved a value of 1 for the precision and recall metrics. In discovering the IOBP model, a precision of 1 and 0.99 for recall was obtained. Our approach demonstrated a high performance on most event logs considered in the experimentation, without including additional information in the event log to identify message-type tasks.

In this way, the proposal to discover the choreography of a process in an inter-organizational collaboration environment is governed by a set of configurable methods. For example, the values of the variables U_t and U_a allow filtering cases with similar information and selecting events that are potentially considered message-type tasks, respectively. The *word embedding* representation used to calculate cosine similarity at the case and event level is highly effective. However, it is limited to the quantity and quality of information within the event logs, to generate a robust model that allows the discovery of the choreography between the participants of an IOBP. Furthermore, the patterns established in Table 1, as well as the models of intra-organizational processes discovered by the Split-miner algorithm, were fundamental elements for identifying the subtype in the message-type tasks, enabling the discovery of the choreography of the process.

According to the results obtained in the evaluation of the discovery of the choreography of the process (see Tables 3 and 4), the following classification can be defined based on the characteristics identified in the experimentation:

- **Complete choreography**. This refers to the fact that the proposed approach can find the complete process choreography in an inter-organizational environment, with the same number and relationships as found in the reference choreography. In conclusion, case-level and event-level representations of the event log only allow the discovery of message-type events.
- **Under-complete choreography**. This refers to an approach that has the ability to find a percentage of the relationships in the choreography of the process. This situation may be because there was insufficient information for the representation obtained from the word embedding model to obtain a high similarity, making it difficult to relate all message-type events.
- **Over-complete choreography**. This refers to the fact that the method finds part of the process's choreography but also recovers irrelevant relationships not found in the reference choreography. This behavior is because the information used to obtain the representation from the event logs is very general. The above issue causes more relationships to be recovered than the existing ones and to meet the condition that the calculated similarity value exceeds the threshold U_a.
- **Partially correct choreography**. This refers to the model identifying a percentage of the process choreography correctly. In addition, with the ability to find partially correct relationships; that is, in a relationship of two identified events (a, b'), an event a or b' is incorrect in the relationship, due to the relationship that is expected to be recovered, according to the reference model, whether (a, c') or (e, b'). The above may be because the identified relationship (a, b') has a higher degree of similarity than the expected relationship (a, c') or (e, b'). This behavior is caused by the fact that the information used to obtain the representation is not sufficiently discriminating to separate the relationships correctly and that the word-embedding model did not correctly learn from the information in the event logs, causing the generation of relationships with high similarity between message-type tasks and other event-types.

In the experimentation carried out, the scenario with the greatest complexity in identifying message-type tasks was *Healthcare*, according to the weighted value of 0.54 in the *FsR* metric. In the *Helthcare* scenario, the process choreographies discovered had the characteristics of a *partially correct choreography* and a *under-complete choreography*. In the *Air Quality System* and *Travel Agency* scenarios, the process choreographies were classified as a *complete choreography*, indicating that the information in the event logs, as well as the patterns defined in the proposed methodology, supported the construction of a process choreography similar to the expected one. Moreover, in the scenarios *Purchase order* and *Manufacturing process*, process choreographies were generated with characteristics of

Complete choreography and *Over-complete choreography*, which indicates that the complete choreography was recovered but relationships that were not part of the choreography were also recovered, as seen in the *RP* metric of 0.83 and 0.91, respectively. Finally, in the *Transfer of goods* scenario, choreographies with characteristics of *over-complete choreography* and *under-complete choreography* were obtained, which were reflected in the *PR* and *RR* metrics, indicating that true relations and relations that were not part of the choreography of the process were recovered.

7. Conclusions

This paper describes a data-driven methodology for discovering inter-organizational business processes (IOBP) and process choreography. The methodology comprises a set of methods and rules that allow information analysis from event logs and intra-organizational models generated by each participant involved in a collaboration. The above enabled the generation of the knowledge necessary for constructing an IOBP model and the interaction between participants through message flow connectors, facilitating the discovery of the process choreography. The results demonstrated the effectiveness of the methods and rules for discovering the choreography of the process, and generating the IOBP models obtained high values in the quality metrics, verifying the ability of the approach to faithfully reproduce the behaviors found in the merged event logs. In summary, we contribute to the process mining domain with formal methods that identify message-type tasks without requiring information to be added to the event log. We provide a set of rules that support defining message task subtypes. Additionally, we contribute a method for merging intra-organizational event logs, which enables the creation of an inter-organizational event log. Finally, three measurement indicators derived from the precision, recall, and f-score metrics are provided to evaluate the quality of the process choreography discovered.

Finally, in future work, the thresholds U_a and U_t will be optimized, since the proposed solution is parametric and the assigned values are individually functional through the analyzed collaboration. Furthermore, we plan to implement a tool that supports the proposed approach as a complement to the ProM process mining framework, as well as incorporating into our tool the Inductive Miner [51] and the Evolutionary Tree Miner [52] procedural algorithms for business process model discovery, which are based on the extraction of process trees from the event log.

Author Contributions: Conceptualization, J.D.H.-R. and E.T.-L.; methodology, J.D.H.-R. and E.T.-L.; software, J.D.H.-R.; validation, J.D.H.-R., E.T.-L. and M.S.; formal analysis, J.D.H.-R., E.T.-L. and M.S.; investigation, J.D.H.-R., E.T.-L. and M.S.; resources, E.T.-L.; data curation, J.D.H.-R.; writing—original draft preparation, J.D.H.-R. and E.T.-L.; writing—review and editing, J.D.H.-R., E.T.-L. and M.S.; visualization, J.D.H.-R.; supervision, E.T.-L. and M.S.; project administration, E.T.-L.; funding acquisition, E.T.-L. All authors have read and agreed to the published version of the manuscript.

Funding: This research was partially funded by Universidad Autónoma de Tamaulipas (México). In addition, this work was supported by the Consejo Nacional de Ciencia y Tecnología (CONACYT) of México under grant number 719519.

Data Availability Statement: The event logs presented in this study are available in the following research papers [31,46–50].

Acknowledgments: The authors are grateful to the Autonomous University of Tamaulipas, Mexico, for supporting this work.

Conflicts of Interest: The authors declare no conflicts of interest.

Abbreviations

The following abbreviations are used in this manuscript:

BPMN	Business process model and notation
VRM	Vector representation matrix
SCP	Set of case pair
ESM	Event score matrix
PME	Pair of message-type events
DFG	Directly-follows graph
IOBP	Inter-organizational business process
RIOBP	Reference inter-organizational business process
RP	Relationship precision
RR	Relationship recall
FsR	F-score of the relationship
IAQM	IoT air quality monitor
RMS	Repository management service
SAS	System access service

References

1. Gutiérrez, B.R.; Quintero, A.M.R.; Parody, L.; López, M.T.G. When business processes meet complex events in logistics: A systematic mapping study. *Comput. Ind.* **2023**, *144*, 103788. [CrossRef]
2. Khan, I.S.; Kauppila, O.; Fatima, N.; Majava, J. Stakeholder interdependencies in a collaborative innovation project. *J. Innov. Entrep.* **2022**, *11*, 38. [CrossRef]
3. Bazan, P.; Estevez, E. Industry 4.0 and business process management: State of the art and new challenges. *Bus. Process. Manag. J.* **2022**, *28*, 62–80. [CrossRef]
4. Rafiei, M.; Van Der Aalst, W.M. An Abstraction-Based Approach for Privacy-Aware Federated Process Mining. *IEEE Access* **2023**, *11*, 33697–33714. [CrossRef]
5. Shi, J.; Jiang, Z.; Liu, Z. Digital Technology Adoption and Collaborative Innovation in Chinese High-Speed Rail Industry: Does Organizational Agility Matter? *IEEE Trans. Eng. Manag.* **2024**, *71*, 4322–4335. [CrossRef]
6. Wang, C.; Hu, Q. Knowledge sharing in supply chain networks: Effects of collaborative innovation activities and capability on innovation performance. *Technovation* **2020**, *94–95*, 102010. [CrossRef]
7. Fernandes, J.; Reis, J.; Melão, N.; Teixeira, L.; Amorim, M. The Role of Industry 4.0 and BPMN in the Arise of Condition-Based and Predictive Maintenance: A Case Study in the Automotive Industry. *Appl. Sci.* **2021**, *11*, 3438. [CrossRef]
8. Ribeiro, V.; Barata, J.; da Cunha, P.R. Modeling Boundary-Spanning Business Processes in Industry 4.0: Incorporating Risk-Based Design. In *Advances in Information Systems Development: Crossing Boundaries between Development and Operations in Information Systems*; Insfran, E., González, F., Abrahão, S., Fernández, M., Barry, C., Lang, M., Linger, H., Schneider, C., Eds.; Springer International Publishing: Cham, Switzerland, 2022; pp. 143–162. [CrossRef]
9. Erasmus, J.; Vanderfeesten, I.; Traganos, K.; Grefen, P. Using business process models for the specification of manufacturing operations. *Comput. Ind.* **2020**, *123*, 103297. [CrossRef]
10. Czvetkó, T.; Kummer, A.; Ruppert, T.; Abonyi, J. Data-driven business process management-based development of Industry 4.0 solutions. *CIRP J. Manuf. Sci. Technol.* **2022**, *36*, 117–132. [CrossRef]
11. Bernabei, M.; Eugeni, M.; Gaudenzi, P.; Costantino, F. Assessment of Smart Transformation in the Manufacturing Process of Aerospace Components Through a Data-Driven Approach. *Glob. J. Flex. Syst. Manag.* **2023**, *24*, 67–86. [CrossRef]
12. Chauhan, A.; Kaur, H.; Mangla, S.K.; Kayikci, Y. Data driven flexible supplier network of selfcare essentials during disruptions in supply chain. In *Annals of Operations Research*; Springer: Berlin/Heidelberg, Germany, 2023; pp. 1–31. [CrossRef]
13. Jans, M.; Laghmouch, M. Process Mining for Detailed Process Analysis. In *Advanced Digital Auditing: Theory and Practice of Auditing Complex Information Systems and Technologies*; Berghout, E., Fijneman, R., Hendriks, L., de Boer, M., Butijn, B.J., Eds.; Springer International Publishing: Cham, Switzerland, 2023; pp. 237–256. [CrossRef]
14. Chapela-Campa, D.; Dumas, M. From process mining to augmented process execution. *Softw. Syst. Model.* **2023**, *22*, 1977–1986. [CrossRef]
15. Camargo, M.; Dumas, M.; González-Rojas, O. Automated discovery of business process simulation models from event logs. *Decis. Support Syst.* **2020**, *134*, 113284. [CrossRef]
16. Van Der Aalst, W. *Process Mining: Data Science in Action*; Springer: Berlin/Heidelberg, Germany, 2016; Volume 2. [CrossRef]
17. Zerbino, P.; Stefanini, A.; Aloini, D. Process science in action: A literature review on process mining in business management. *Technol. Forecast. Soc. Chang.* **2021**, *172*, 121021. [CrossRef]
18. Berti, A.; Schuster, D.; van der Aalst, W.M.P. Abstractions, Scenarios, and Prompt Definitions for Process Mining with LLMs: A Case Study. In *International Conference on Business Process Management*; De Weerdt, J., Pufahl, L., Eds.; Springer Nature: Cham, Switzerland, 2024; pp. 427–439. [CrossRef]

19. Tavares, G.M.; Oyamada, R.S.; Barbon, S.; Ceravolo, P. Trace encoding in process mining: A survey and benchmarking. *Eng. Appl. Artif. Intell.* **2023**, *126*, 107028. [CrossRef]
20. Le, Q.; Mikolov, T. Distributed Representations of Sentences and Documents. In Proceedings of the 31st International Conference on Machine Learning, Bejing, China, 22–24 June 2014; Xing, E.P., Jebara, T., Eds.; Volume 32, pp. 1188–1196.
21. De Koninck, P.; vanden Broucke, S.; De Weerdt, J. act2vec, trace2vec, log2vec, and model2vec: Representation Learning for Business Processes. In *Business Process Management: 16th International Conference, BPM 2018, Sydney, NSW, Australia, 9–14 September 2018*; Weske, M., Montali, M., Weber, I., vom Brocke, J., Eds.; Springer International Publishing: Cham, Switzerland, 2018; pp. 305–321. [CrossRef]
22. Luettgen, S.; Seeliger, A.; Nolle, T.; Mühlhäuser, M. Case2vec: Advances in Representation Learning for Business Processes. In *International Conference on Process Mining*; Leemans, S., Leopold, H., Eds.; Springer International Publishing: Cham, Switzerland, 2021; pp. 162–174. [CrossRef]
23. Peeperkorn, J.; vanden Broucke, S.; De Weerdt, J. Conformance Checking Using Activity and Trace Embeddings. In *Business Process Management Forum: BPM Forum 2020, Seville, Spain, 13–18 September 2020, Proceedings 18*; Fahland, D., Ghidini, C., Becker, J., Dumas, M., Eds.; Springer International Publishing: Cham, Switzerland, 2020; pp. 105–121. [CrossRef]
24. Augusto, A.; Conforti, R.; Dumas, M.; La Rosa, M.; Polyvyanyy, A. Split miner: Automated discovery of accurate and simple business process models from event logs. *Knowl. Inf. Syst.* **2019**, *59*, 251–284. [CrossRef]
25. Augusto, A.; Conforti, R.; Dumas, M.; La Rosa, M.; Maggi, F.M.; Marrella, A.; Mecella, M.; Soo, A. Automated discovery of process models from event logs: Review and benchmark. *IEEE Trans. Knowl. Data Eng.* **2018**, *31*, 686–705. [CrossRef]
26. Dunzer, S.; Stierle, M.; Matzner, M.; Baier, S. Conformance checking: A state-of-the-art literature review. In Proceedings of the 11th International Conference on Subject-Oriented Business Process Management, Seville, Spain, 26–28 June 2019; pp. 1–10. [CrossRef]
27. Cherni, J.; Martinho, R.; Ghannouchi, S.A. Towards Improving Business Processes based on preconfigured KPI target values, Process Mining and Redesign Patterns. *Procedia Comput. Sci.* **2019**, *164*, 279–284. [CrossRef]
28. Dumas, M.; La Rosa, M.; Mendling, J.; Reijers, H.A. *Fundamentals of Business Process Management*; Springer: Berlin/Heidelberg, Germany, 2018. [CrossRef]
29. Ladleif, J.; Weske, M. A legal interpretation of choreography models. In *Business Process Management Workshops: BPM 2019 International Workshops, Vienna, Austria, 1–6 September 2019, Revised Selected Papers 17*; Springer International Publishing: Cham, Switzerland, 2019; pp. 651–663. [CrossRef]
30. Bala, S.; Mendling, J.; Schimak, M.; Queteschiner, P. Case and activity identification for mining process models from middleware. In Proceedings of the IFIP Working Conference on The Practice of Enterprise Modeling, Vienna, Austria, 31 October–2 November 2018; pp. 86–102. [CrossRef]
31. Corradini, F.; Re, B.; Rossi, L.; Tiezzi, F. A Technique for Collaboration Discovery. In *Proceedings of the International Conference on Business Process Modeling, Development and Support, International Conference on Evaluation and Modeling Methods for Systems Analysis and Development*; Springer International Publishing: Cham, Switzerland, 2022; pp. 63–78. [CrossRef]
32. Zeng, Q.; Duan, H.; Liu, C. Top-down process mining from multi-source running logs based on refinement of Petri nets. *IEEE Access* **2020**, *8*, 61355–61369. [CrossRef]
33. Elkoumy, G.; Fahrenkrog-Petersen, S.A.; Dumas, M.; Laud, P.; Pankova, A.; Weidlich, M. Secure Multi-party Computation for Inter-organizational Process Mining. In *Enterprise, Business-Process and Information Systems Modeling*; Springer: Berlin/Heidelberg, Germany, 2020; pp. 166–181. [CrossRef]
34. Corradini, F.; Muzi, C.; Re, B.; Rossi, L.; Tiezzi, F. Animating multiple instances in BPMN collaborations: From formal semantics to tool support. In Proceedings of the International Conference on Business Process Management, Sydney, NSW, Australia, 9–14 September 2018; pp. 83–101. [CrossRef]
35. López-Pintado, O.; Dumas, M.; García-Bañuelos, L.; Weber, I. Interpreted execution of business process models on blockchain. In Proceedings of the 2019 IEEE 23rd International Enterprise Distributed Object Computing Conference (EDOC), Paris, France, 28–31 October 2019; pp. 206–215. [CrossRef]
36. Köpke, J.; Franceschetti, M.; Eder, J. Optimizing data-flow implementations for inter-organizational processes. *Distrib. Parallel Databases* **2019**, *37*, 651–695. [CrossRef]
37. Mo, Q.; Song, W.; Dai, F.; Lin, L.; Li, T. Development of collaborative business processes: A correctness enforcement approach. *IEEE Trans. Serv. Comput.* **2019**, *15*, 752–765. [CrossRef]
38. Klinkmüller, C.; Ponomarev, A.; Tran, A.B.; Weber, I.; Aalst, W.v.d. Mining blockchain processes: Extracting process mining data from blockchain applications. In Proceedings of the International Conference on Business Process Management, Vienna, Austria, 1–6 September 2019; pp. 71–86. [CrossRef]
39. Corradini, F.; Pettinari, S.; Re, B.; Rossi, L.; Tiezzi, F. A technique for discovering BPMN collaboration diagrams. In *Software and Systems Modeling*; Springer: Berlin/Heidelberg, Germany, 2024; pp. 1–21. [CrossRef]
40. Peña, L.; Andrade, D.; Delgado, A.; Calegari, D. An Approach for Discovering Inter-organizational Collaborative Business Processes in BPMN 2.0. In *Process Mining Workshops*; De Smedt, J., Soffer, P., Eds.; Springer Nature: Cham, Switzerland, 2024; pp. 487–498. [CrossRef]
41. Tajima, K.; Du, B.; Narusue, Y.; Saito, S.; Iimura, Y.; Morikawa, H. Step-by-Step Case ID Identification Based on Activity Connection for Cross-Organizational Process Mining. *IEEE Access* **2023**, *11*, 60578–60589. [CrossRef]

42. Liu, C.; Li, H.; Zhang, S.; Cheng, L.; Zeng, Q. Cross-Department Collaborative Healthcare Process Model Discovery From Event Logs. *IEEE Trans. Autom. Sci. Eng.* **2023**, *20*, 2115–2125. [CrossRef]
43. Bernardi, M.L.; Cimitile, M.; Mercaldo, F. Cross-Organisational Process Mining in Cloud Environments. *J. Inf. Knowl. Manag.* **2018**, *17*, 1850014. [CrossRef]
44. Buijs, J. Flexible Evolutionary Algorithms for Mining Structured Process Models. Ph.D. Thesis, Technische Universiteit Eindhoven, Eindhoven, The Netherlands, April 2014. [CrossRef]
45. Janssenswillen, G.; Donders, N.; Jouck, T.; Depaire, B. A comparative study of existing quality measures for process discovery. *Inf. Syst.* **2017**, *71*, 1–15. [CrossRef]
46. Hernandez-Resendiz, J.D.; Tello-Leal, E.; Ramirez-Alcocer, U.M.; Macías-Hernández, B.A. Semi-Automated Approach for Building Event Logs for Process Mining from Relational Database. *Appl. Sci.* **2022**, *12*, 10832. [CrossRef]
47. Hernandez-Resendiz, J.D.; Tello-Leal, E.; Marin-Castro, H.M.; Ramirez-Alcocer, U.M.; Mata-Torres, J.A. Merging Event Logs for Inter-organizational Process Mining. In *New Perspectives on Enterprise Decision-Making Applying Artificial Intelligence Techniques*; Springer: Berlin/Heidelberg, Germany, 2021; pp. 3–26. [CrossRef]
48. Liu, C.; Duan, H.; Qingtian, Z.; Zhou, M.; Lu, F.; Cheng, J. Towards comprehensive support for privacy preservation cross-organization business process mining. *IEEE Trans. Serv. Comput.* **2016**, *12*, 639–653. [CrossRef]
49. Fdhila, W.; Rinderle-Ma, S.; Knuplesch, D.; Reichert, M. Change and Compliance in Collaborative Processes. In Proceedings of the 2015 IEEE International Conference on Services Computing, New York, NY, USA, 27 June–2 July 2015; pp. 162–169. [CrossRef]
50. Borkowski, M.; Fdhila, W.; Nardelli, M.; Rinderle-Ma, S.; Schulte, S. Event-based failure prediction in distributed business processes. *Inf. Syst.* **2019**, *81*, 220–235. [CrossRef]
51. Leemans, S.J.J.; Fahland, D.; van der Aalst, W.M.P. Discovering Block-Structured Process Models from Event Logs Containing Infrequent Behaviour. In *Business Process Management Workshops: BPM 2013 International Workshops, Beijing, China, 26 August 2013, Revised Papers 11*; Lohmann, N., Song, M., Wohed, P., Eds.; Springer International Publishing: Cham, Switzerland, 2014; pp. 66–78. [CrossRef]
52. Buijs, J.C.A.M.; van Dongen, B.F.; van der Aalst, W.M.P. Quality Dimensions in Process Discovery: The Importance of Fitness, Precision, Generalization and Simplicity. *Int. J. Coop. Inf. Syst.* **2014**, *23*, 1440001. [CrossRef]

Disclaimer/Publisher's Note: The statements, opinions and data contained in all publications are solely those of the individual author(s) and contributor(s) and not of MDPI and/or the editor(s). MDPI and/or the editor(s) disclaim responsibility for any injury to people or property resulting from any ideas, methods, instructions or products referred to in the content.

Article

Intelligent Ship Scheduling and Path Planning Method for Maritime Emergency Rescue

Wen Ying [1], Zhaohui Wang [1], Hui Li [1], Sheng Du [2] and Man Zhao [1,*]

[1] School of Computer Science, China University of Geosciences, Wuhan 430074, China
[2] School of Automation, China University of Geosciences, Wuhan 430074, China; dusheng@cug.edu.cn
* Correspondence: zhaoman@cug.edu.cn; Tel.: +86-18627151803

Abstract: Intelligent ship navigation scheduling and planning is of great significance for ensuring the safety of maritime production and life and promoting the development of the marine economy. In this paper, an intelligent ship scheduling and path planning method is proposed for a practical application scenario wherein the emergency rescue center receives rescue messages and dispatches emergency rescue ships to the incident area for rescue. Firstly, the large-scale sailing route of the task ship is pre-planned in the voyage planning stage by using the improved A* algorithm. Secondly, the full-coverage path planning algorithm is used to plan the ship's search route in the regional search stage by updating the ship's navigation route in real time. In order to verify the effectiveness of the proposed algorithm, comparative experiments were carried out with the conventional algorithm in the two operation stages of rushing to the incident sea area and regional search and rescue. The experimental results show that the proposed algorithm can adapt to emergency search and rescue tasks in the complex setting of the sea area and can effectively improve the efficiency of the operation, ensure the safety of the operation process, and provide a more intelligent and efficient solution for the planning of maritime emergency rescue tasks.

Keywords: maritime emergency rescue; intelligent navigation; path planning; A* algorithm; B-spline interpolation; regional search

---

Citation: Ying, W.; Wang, Z.; Li, H.; Du, S.; Zhao, M. Intelligent Ship Scheduling and Path Planning Method for Maritime Emergency Rescue. *Algorithms* **2024**, *17*, 197. https://doi.org/10.3390/a17050197

Academic Editor: Günther Raidl

Received: 1 March 2024
Revised: 26 April 2024
Accepted: 29 April 2024
Published: 8 May 2024

Copyright: © 2024 by the authors. Licensee MDPI, Basel, Switzerland. This article is an open access article distributed under the terms and conditions of the Creative Commons Attribution (CC BY) license (https://creativecommons.org/licenses/by/4.0/).

1. Introduction

Ship navigation scheduling and planning have broad application prospects in maritime emergency rescue, maritime safety governance, maritime shipping control, and other fields [1]. Specifically, in the field of emergency rescue, after receiving the maritime rescue news alert, the search and rescue center needs to immediately dispatch rescue vessels to the incident area and carry out search and rescue operations. However, due to the opaque information and inflexibility of the information of ships, facilities, and operators, there will be inaccurate intelligent scheduling and low efficiency. The application of intelligent ship navigation scheduling and planning can make the search and rescue command center more flexible and allow it to have a more reasonable allocation of search and rescue resources, which is conducive to improving the efficiency of maritime search and rescue operations.

The existing studies on ship navigation scheduling and planning are mainly based on traditional planning algorithms and intelligent bionic path planning algorithms [2]. The traditional planning algorithms mainly include the depth-first search algorithm [3], Dijkstra algorithm [4], A* algorithm [5], and the artificial potential field algorithm [6]. The authors of [7] designed a global path planning algorithm with a mandatory point constraint by integrating an improved A* algorithm and simulated annealing algorithm for the problem of non-point to point global path planning. The authors of [8] improved the hybrid path planning algorithm based on a static environmental potential field and dynamic environmental attraction and repulsion, combined with the typical mariner ship type and proportional differential control, which was suitable for local minimum problems in restricted waters such as narrow waters. The D* algorithm is a dynamic programming algorithm based on the A* algorithm which can adapt to dynamic programming in complex environments and has a good [9,10] effect in real-time planning and scheduling. The intelligent bionic algorithm [11–13] is a kind of random search algorithm that operates by simulating biological evolution or population behavior; it is widely used in path planning. In reference, a static path planning method based on a simulated annealing algorithm is proposed, which uses neighborhood search and probabilistic jumping strategies to find a feasible and optimal observation path. The authors of [14] proposed a dynamic path planning method based on game theory. By establishing a game model and designing a reasonable negotiation mechanism, the problem of resource competition and conflict was solved, and the overall observation efficiency was improved. The ant colony search algorithm does not rely on a lot of prior knowledge; the structure of the algorithm is simple and easy to understand and implement, and it has strong adaptability for optimizing solutions to complex problems. However, the iteration speed of the algorithm [15–17] is slow, and it is easy to fall into local optimum. In reference [18], a particle swarm optimization (PSO) algorithm was proposed, which used the idea of genetic mutation for reference to increase the population diversity of particles and effectively improve the convergence speed of the algorithm. The authors of [19] proposed a path planning with dynamic obstacle avoidance method of the manipulator based on a deep reinforcement learning algorithm soft actor-critic (SAC). A comprehensive reward function of dynamic obstacle avoidance and target approach is designed to avoid the moving obstacle in the environment and make real-time planning. In addition, some studies related to trajectory planning and trajectory analysis have been conducted by using AIS and SOS data. The authors of [20] propose a multi-regime vessel trajectory reconstruction model based on a large AIS dataset. Through the removal of outliers, ship navigational state estimation, and vessel trajectory fitting, the proposed trajectory can eliminate the noise in the raw AIS data quite well. Ref. [21] quantified the operational risk management strategies of shipping companies using AIS data, providing a new research direction regarding AIS in the field of shipping risk management.

The above methods still cannot fully meet the actual needs in ship mission planning for maritime search and rescue. On the one hand, the development of danger is difficult to predict. Although the current maritime SOS alarm system has been widely used, it takes time for the rescue force to rush to the incident area. The vessels and personnel in distress may be affected by environmental and human factors, and when the rescue force arrives, it may not be in the position of the news report. And sometimes the actual situation may be more complex and severe; for example, the hull may have capsized, disintegration and/or drift with the current may have occurred, or some people may have rescued themselves from the initial position, making it necessary to search the surrounding area of the incident. On the other hand, the complexity and uncertainty of the maritime environment bring greater challenges to mission planning, which needs to consider multiple constraints and risk factors, such as weather changes, sea state fluctuations, and obstacle avoidance at sea. In addition, real-time and computational efficiency are also important factors which need to considered to provide a fast response while ensuring the accuracy of planning results.

In order to improve the efficiency and safety of the execution of maritime rescue tasks and to intelligently manage and schedule maritime ships and operating facilities, this paper proposes an intelligent planning method for ship action for the whole process of maritime search and rescue. The algorithm uses the A* algorithm with added constraints for large-scale route pre-planning; then, a complete coverage path planning algorithm (CCPP) [22] is used to search the target area for full coverage. The experimental results show that the intelligent ship scheduling and path planning method proposed in this paper can adapt to search and rescue missions in the complex setting of the sea and provide a more intelligent and efficient solution for the planning of maritime emergency rescue missions. Regarding the structure of this paper, firstly, the intelligent action planning method for maritime emergency rescue is described, including three parts: algorithm principle, experimental strategy, and evaluation index. Section 2 analyzes the experimental data, and Section 3 compares the experimental results of the algorithm with a conventional algorithm, including the ship navigation planning stage and the conventional A* algorithm for comparison. In the region search stage, a differential evolution algorithm is used for comparison experiments. Finally, the experimental results are discussed and analyzed.

2. Intelligent Ship Action Planning Method for Ocean Targets

2.1. Principle of Algorithm

1. A* algorithm [5]

Compared with the traditional Dijkstra algorithm and the best first search algorithm, the A* search algorithm can combine the actual cost from the starting point to the current goal and the total cost from the current goal to the endpoint and has higher planning accuracy and lower computational complexity. The A* algorithm determines the search direction through the evaluation function, expands from the starting point position, calculates the cost value of each surrounding node through the evaluation function, and selects the minimum cost node as the next expansion node. This process is repeated until the goal point is reached and the final path is generated. The cost function is calculated as follows:

$$f(n) = g(n) + h(n) \tag{1}$$

where f(n) represents the evaluation function from the starting point to the target point through any node n; g(n) represents the actual cost from the starting point to node n; and h(n) represents the estimated cost of node n to the target point. The estimated distance of h(n) is calculated by the Euclidean distance, and the formula is as follows:

$$h(n) = \sqrt{(x_2 - x_1)^2 + (y_2 - y_1)^2} \tag{2}$$

where (x_1, y_1) and (x_2, y_2) represent the coordinates of the two nodes n_1 and n_2, respectively.

The process of the A* algorithm described in this paper is shown in Figure 1. The open table, close table, and path table are defined to store the expansion nodes, and the mask is initialized to 0. The optimal node is selected from the open table and stored in the close table, and its successor nodes are put into the open list. The optimal node is selected by repeated operation, and the optimal node is stopped when the target is reached or the open list is empty.

2. CCPP algorithm [22]

Suppose that the region under test is a polygon, where V represents the set of vertices of the region under test with the origin of the regional coordinate system as a reference, and E represents the set of edges formed with vertex elements in V. In the process of ship search path planning, the system first receives the task starting point coordinates (X_0, Y_0) and the endpoint coordinates of the observation area v as inputs, where X^o and Y^o represent the endpoint coordinates of the detection area in the WGS84 coordinate system, respectively. If the feature of the area to be measured is mostly an irregular polygon, the regional coordinate system is set up with the nearest side of the starting coordinate and the normal line of the ship position as the axis, and the full coverage path planning algorithm is used for efficient operation.

The distance L_V between the geometric center of the polygon in the measurement area and all endpoints in the observation area is calculated, and whether the element L_V in $(\overline{X}, \overline{Y})$ is within the maximum range of the hull's omnidirectional sensing device is determined. If the distances of all endpoints are within the range of the device, the range of the omnidirectional sensing device is scheduled to cover the endpoint in the observation area that is farthest from the current position of the ship. If not, the scanning area of the task ship is determined by establishing the regional coordinate system, the hull position point is selected as the starting point, and the navigation direction is clockwise along the edge of the region. The navigation distance is based on the detection range radius of the ship-borne detection equipment to ensure the rational utilization of resources. When an endpoint is completely covered, the direction will be converted, and the conversion Angle formula is as follows:

$$\theta^r = \tan^{-1}\left(\frac{Y_B^r}{|X_B^r - X_A^r|}\right) \quad (3)$$

where θ^r represents the conversion Angle under the regional coordinate system; Y_B^r represents the ordinate of region endpoint B in the regional coordinate system. X_A^r and X_B^r represent the horizontal coordinates of the region endpoints A and B in the regional coordinate system, respectively.

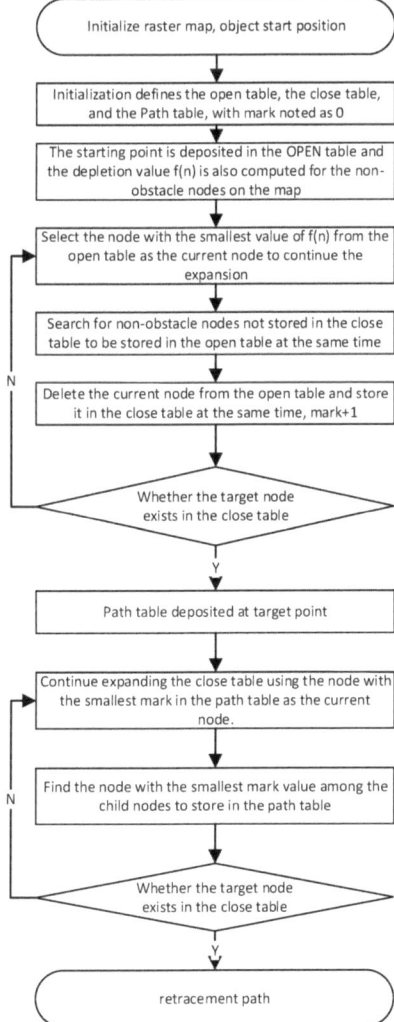

Figure 1. Flowchart of the improved A* algorithm.

2.2. Experimental Strategy

An intelligent ship action planning method for maritime emergency rescue is the impetus that allows for maritime rescue forces to carry out actions. According to the task requirements, an intelligent action planning model algorithm is constructed to plan the sailing route and action steps of maritime rescue vessels, continuously track the ongoing action tasks, and feed back the task execution in real time. As shown in Figure 2, intelligent ship action planning for maritime emergency rescue is mainly divided into two stages: the navigation planning and regional search stages. In the navigation planning stage, according to the pre-planning of the navigation route in the maritime rescue area, it is ensured that the ship can quickly and safely reach the incident area from the starting point. After the ship reaches the incident area, it enters the regional search phase. In the regional search stage, the ship delimits the search area and carries out search route planning according to the reported location of the incident, searches for the target that needs to be rescued along the way, and continues the regional search after the rescue is completed.

In the ship navigation planning stage, the optimal navigation route from the starting point to the emergency rescue area is planned based on the A* algorithm, which takes the longitude and latitude coordinates of the observation area and the longitude and latitude coordinates of the ship's starting point as inputs and combines the ship archives, power duration parameters, sea and land rasterization data, and related constraints. At the same time, a variety of constraints need to be considered, as shown in Table 1. The first is the time constraint, which requires that the start time and duration of the navigation path must meet the time requirements of the mission; the second is the space constraint, which specifies the starting and ending points of the navigation path and requires that the navigation path should only pass through the navigable area and avoid the non-navigable areas such as land and islands. Secondly, the task conflict constraint solves the problem of time window conflict under multi-task processing and determines the execution order according to the priority of the task. Finally, there is the ship performance constraints, including ship sailing speed constraints, ship cruising range constraints, etc.

Table 1. Constraints of navigation route planning.

Categories of Constraints	Constraints	Constraint Meaning
Time constraint	Sailing path start time	The ship's departure time cannot be later than the start time of the mission
	Sailing path duration	The sailing time cannot exceed the mission duration
Spatial constraint	Starting point of the navigation path	The starting point of the A* route planning algorithm
	Sailing path target point	The end point of the A* route planning algorithm
	Navigable area	The planned route can only pass through navigable areas
Task conflict constraint	Task time window	Task time window conflict solution
	Task priority	Tasks considered priorities are executed first
Ship performance constraint	Ship speed constraint	The estimated sailing time refers to the maximum speed and average speed of the ship
	Ship range constraints	The distance of the planned navigation route shall not exceed the maximum sailing mileage of the ship

After the ship arrives at the emergency rescue area, it enters the regional search and rescue route planning stage. It uses the full coverage path planning algorithm to establish the survey area coordinate system with the ship as the reference point, iteratively updates the travel distance and turning Angle, and searches the observation area in an all-directional way. After the rescue operation is completed, the scope of the unsearched area is recalculated, and the full coverage path planning is carried out again until the entire emergency search area has been searched.

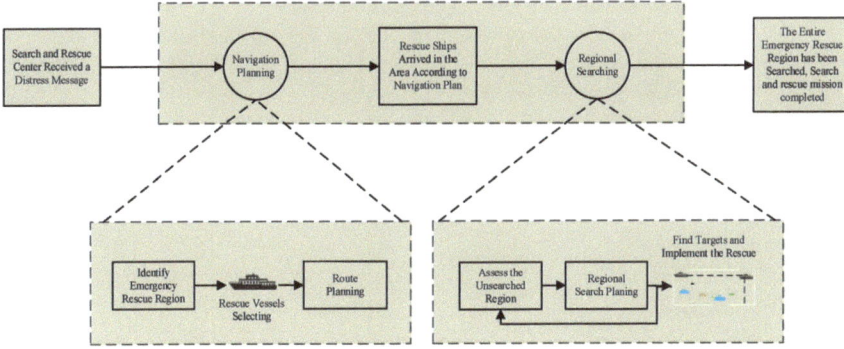

Figure 2. Intelligent planning process for maritime emergency rescue.

2.3. Evaluation Metrics

In order to effectively evaluate the planning effect of the two stages of navigation planning and regional search, the evaluation indicators shown in Table 2 are used. The ship's voyage planning stage involves pre-planning the path from the large scale of space. Therefore, compared with other stages, only the path economic benefit and trip safety are considered, that is, the path length, the number of turns, and the average turning Angle. In the area search stage, it needs to search the area of interest in an all-round way, so it needs to consider the area search coverage rate and task completion rate and other indicators. The ship target observation stage needs to take into account the real-time planning of sensors and the detailed and comprehensive exploration of the area of interest, so it is also the stage with the most considerations in the whole navigation process, which needs to take into account both timeliness and task completion.

Table 2. Evaluation indicators of the algorithm proposed in this article.

Running Stage	Algorithm Name	Evaluation Metrics
Navigation Planning	Regular A* algorithm, algorithm in this paper	Path length, number of turns, average turn Angle
Regional Search	Differential evolution algorithm, algorithm in this paper	Path length, regional coverage rate, point arrival rate, trajectory prediction accuracy

3. Experimental Data

The intelligent planning of the ship's navigation route mainly needs to consider the time and space relationship between the current position of the ship and the position of the area to be observed, as well as the start time of the mission. The planning parameters of the algorithm are shown in Table 3. The current latitude and longitude of the ship is automatically captured through the ship positioning system, and the position coordinates of the observation area and the start time of the task are obtained through the human–computer interaction interface configuration.

Table 3. Table of parameters of intelligent planning algorithm for ship navigation routes.

Types	Parameter Name	Symbol Name	Unit	Precision	Range of Values
Ship's current position	Vessel longitude	*Loncp*	°		$[-180°, 180°]$
	Vessel latitude	*Latcp*	°		$[-90°, 90°]$
Position coordinates of the area to be observed	Longitude 1	*Lonul*	°	10^{-6}	$[-180°, 180°]$
	Latitude 1	*Latul*	°		$[-90°, 90°]$
	Longitude 2	*Lonbr*	°		$[-180°, 180°]$
	Latitude 2	*Latbr*	°		$[-90°, 90°]$
Time	Mission start	*starTime*	ms	1	$[0, 2554372347000]$

The data used for the creation of this paper were sourced from the raster data of sea and land maps provided by Natural Earth [23] This dataset uses the WGS-84 (World Geodetic System 1984) coordinate system, with a total of about 900 million pixels, each pixel representing a spatial area of 500 m × 500 m on the Earth's surface. The rasterized map data are intercepted according to the coordinate values of the starting point and the target point in the exploration mission and inputted into the algorithm to correct the coordinates. A large number of rosters are simplified, and the electronic chart is appropriately trimmed according to the regional scope required by the mission planning, as shown in Figure 3.

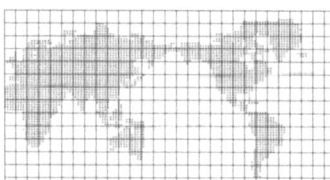
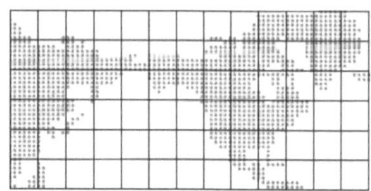

Figure 3. Dataset cropping diagram.

Horizontal and vertical grid lines are used to divide the task area delivery into grid cells of the same size. According to the selected task area, the human–computer interaction simulation platform extracts the sea, land, and water depth information in the task area by traversing and sets the land, islands, and areas with shallow water depth as obstacle areas. After determining the position of the obstacle area, the grid map of the obstacle grid, the free grid (navigable area), and the initial position grid (the initial position of the ship) are established. According to the tiff files of different precision, they are converted into the corresponding rasterized data, as shown in Figure 4.

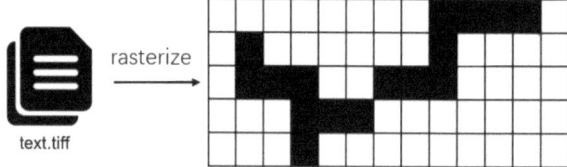

Figure 4. Grid conversion diagram.

4. Experiment and Analysis

4.1. Route Pre-Planning in the Navigation Planning Stage

In order to verify the performance of the route pre-planning model in the ship's voyage planning stage, it was compared with the conventional A*algorithm. Taking Sanya Port of China as the planning starting point, the target maritime rescue position of 109°15.4′ E and 18°12.5′ N was selected, and the experiment was carried out in the period when the weather and sea conditions are relatively stable.

The results are shown in Table 4. The path length of the proposed algorithm is shorter than that of the A* algorithm, which indicates that the navigation route planned by the proposed algorithm can reduce the navigation time and energy consumption and improve the efficiency and economy of navigation. In terms of the number of turns, the proposed algorithm has fewer than the A* algorithm, indicating that the navigation route planned by the algorithm can reduce the difficulty and risk of ship control and improve the stability and safety of navigation. In terms of the average turning Angle, the average turning Angle of the algorithm proposed in this paper is smaller, and the sailing route is smoother. The algorithm has a smaller turning radius and ship inertia, which improves the flexibility and stability of navigation.

Table 4. Experimental results of conventional A * algorithm and algorithm proposed in this paper.

Algorithm	Path Length/Nautical Mails	Number of Turns/Times	Average Turn Angle/(°)
Regular A* algorithm	35.4	6	30.7
Algorithm of this article	29.6	4	29.3

4.2. Search Route Planning for the Regional Search Stage

We conducted another experiment in order to verify the performance of the ship search route planning model in the regional search stage. Taking the rescue location as the starting point, a search and rescue area of 109°13.4′ E~109°19.2′ E, 18°9.9′ N~18°14.3′ N (about 130 square kilometers) was selected, the average speed of the search and rescue ship was set to 11 knots, the visual range was 6 km, and the effective search and rescue time was 30 min. The differential evolution algorithm [24] and the algorithm proposed in this paper were used for comparison experiments, and the experimental results are shown in Table 5. From the perspective of path length, when the regional search task is carried out within the same time limit, the path planned by the proposed algorithm is shorter, and the regional coverage rate is higher, which provides obvious advantages in terms of planning efficiency.

Table 5. Experimental results of differential evolution algorithm and algorithm proposed in this paper.

Algorithm	Path Length/Nautical Mails	Area Coverage/%
Differential evolution algorithm	47.8	82.1
Algorithm of this article	43.2	93.4

4.3. Discussion of Analysis

The core problem of route planning is how to minimize the distance and time from the departure location to the mission location under the influence of external conditions such as weather and obstacles so as to maximize the utilization of resources. According to the location of the incident area and the constraints of each stage of the mission planning, the path is reasonably planned to help to comprehensively reduced consumption and achieve the greatest benefit.

The experimental results show that the performance of the improved A* algorithm presented in this paper is better than that of the traditional algorithm in terms of path length, number of turns, and average turn Angle, indicating that the algorithm is more efficient, economical, safe, and flexible in planning the navigation route and is more suitable for the actual needs of maritime navigation. Compared with the differential evolution algorithm, the full coverage path planning algorithm has a shorter planned path and greater regional coverage rate within the specified time, which provides obvious advantages in terms of path planning efficiency.

5. Conclusions

Aimed at the practical application scenario of an emergency rescue center receiving rescue messages and dispatching emergency rescue vessels to the incident area for rescue, this paper proposes an intelligent ship scheduling and path planning method for the whole process of maritime emergency rescue operation. The work of this paper is summarized below:

- For the task planning stage in the process of maritime emergency rescue, through the improved A* algorithm, taking the longitude and latitude coordinates of the observation area as inputs and considering the ship's own performance, current status, and external environmental constraints, the large-scale navigation route of the search and rescue vessels is planned in advance to meet the needs of the search and rescue vessels to allow them to rush to the incident area quickly and safely. The experimental results show that the proposed algorithm can generate large-scale measurement action

- plans that meet the task requirements. Compared with the traditional A* algorithm, the proposed algorithm can reduce the sailing distance and turning frequency and improve the navigation efficiency and safety.
- For the regional search and rescue stage in the process of maritime emergency rescue, the full coverage path planning algorithm is used to plan the search route with the goal of reaching the full coverage of the search area as soon as possible. By updating the route and Angle of the ship's navigation in real time, the needs of the search and rescue vessels, which need to search the incident area efficiently and without going missing, are met. The experimental results show that compared with the differential evolution algorithm, the proposed algorithm has shorter path plans and greater regional coverage, which provides obvious advantages in terms of path planning efficiency.

In summary, intelligent ship scheduling and path planning for maritime emergency rescue tasks is an effective method which is helpful for improving the efficiency and safety of ships in maritime search and rescue activities. Future research could further optimize and improve this method to ensure it can adapt to more complex maritime environments and mission requirements and provide more intelligent and efficient solutions for the planning of maritime emergency rescue missions.

Author Contributions: Conceptualization, W.Y. and Z.W.; methodology, W.Y. and H.L.; software, W.Y. and S.D.; resources, W.Y.; data curation, M.Z.; writing—original draft preparation, W.Y.; writing—review and editing, Z.W.; supervision, H.L. All authors have read and agreed to the published version of the manuscript.

Funding: This research received no external funding.

Data Availability Statement: The research data is currently unavailable due to privacy or ethical restrictions.

Conflicts of Interest: The authors declare no conflict of interest.

References

1. Na, G.Y. Path planning and optimal network construction of ship maritime logistics under intelligent network. *Ship Sci. Technol.* **2019**, *41*, 211–213.
2. Hejing, W.; Lina, W. Review of Robot Path Planning Algorithms. *J. Guilin Univ. Technol.* **2023**, *43*, 137–147.
3. Wenchao, L.; Hongsen, Y. A Depth-first Search Algorithm Based on PFSP Properties. *Control Decis.* **2009**, *24*, 1203–1208. (In Chinese)
4. Wen-peng, Z.; Run-nan, L.; Cheng-yuan, Z. Taxiing path optimization Based on improved Dijkstra Algorithm. *J. Civ. Aviat. Univ. China* **2022**, *40*, 1–6.
5. Jinyue, Z.; Zhicheng, H.; Gong, Z.; Weijun, W.; Wenlin, Y. Improved A* Algorithm Based on Traffic Constraint and Multivariate Heuristic Function. *Modul. Mach. Tool Autom. Manuf. Technol.* **2021**, *1*, 53–56.
6. Huiwei, C.; Yujie, C.; Fei, F. Research status analysis of unmanned vessel Path Planning based on artificial potential field method. *Sci. Technol. Innov.* **2020**, *17*, 23–25.
7. Hu, J.; Zhu, Q.; Chen, R. Global Path Planning of Intelligent Vehicle with Mandatory Point Constraint. *Automot. Eng.* **2023**, *45*, 350–360.
8. Hongguang, L.; Yong, Y. Path Planning of unmanned vessel Based on Vector data modeling of electronic chart. *Traffic Inf. Saf.* **2019**, *37*, 94–106.
9. Ferguson, D.; Stentz, A. *Field D*: An Interpolation-Based Path Planner and Replanner*; Robotics Research; Springer: Berlin, Heidelberg, 2007; pp. 239–253.
10. Raheem, F.A.; Hameed, U.I. Heuristic D* Algorithm Based on Particle Swarm Optimization for Path Planning of Two-link Robot Arm in Dynamic Environment. *Al-Khwarizmi Eng. J.* **2019**, *15*, 108–123. [CrossRef]
11. Liang, Z.; Li, H.; Wang, Z.; Hu, K.; Zhu, Z. Dynamic multi-objective Evolutionary Algorithm with Adaptive Change Response. *Acta Autom. Sin.* **2023**, *49*, 1688–1706.
12. Leizheng, S.; Dongfang, L. Research on autonomous navigation Planning of unmanned vessel Based on partition evolutionary Genetic Algorithm. *J. Chengdu Inst. Technol.* **2024**, *27*, 47–51.
13. Dalei, S.; Kunling, L.; Xiaoping, C.; Wenhao, Y.; Jiangli, C. Full coverage Path planning of unmanned vessel based on deep reinforcement learning. *Mod. Electron. Technol.* **2022**, *45*, 1–7.
14. Miao, H.; Tian, Y.-C. Dynamic robot path planning using an enhanced simulated annealing approach. *Appl. Math. Comput.* **2013**, *222*, 420–437.

15. Wang, Z.; Lu, H.; Qin, H.; Sui, Y. Autonomous Underwater Vehicle Path Planning Method of Soft Actor–Critic Based on Game Training. *J. Mar. Sci. Eng.* **2022**, *10*, 2018.
16. Cheng, W.; Jia, R.; Yu, Z. Path planning of unmanned vessel based on improved ant colony algorithm. *J. Hainan Univ. (Nat. Sci. Ed.)* **2021**, *39*, 242–250.
17. Guoliang, H.; Yi, Z.; Kun, Z. Global Ship Path Planning Method Based on improved ant colony Algorithm. *Ship Ocean Eng.* **2023**, *52*, 97–101.
18. Songying, Z.; Xingye, C. Global Path Planning Method of intelligent Ship Based on Improved Ant colony. *Mar. Electr. Technol.* **2022**, *42*, 72–76.
19. Chengjun, D.; Xin, W.; Yubo, F. AGV Path Planning Based on Particle Swarm Optimization algorithm. *Sens. Microsyst.* **2020**, *39*, 123–126.
20. Chen, P. Pei, J.; Lu, W.; Li, M. A deep reinforcement learning based method for real-time path planning and dynamic obstacle avoidance. *Neurocomputing* **2022**, *497*, 64–75. [CrossRef]
21. Shuxia, L.; Juncheng, Y. An Improved Full Coverage Path Planning Algorithm. *Comput. Mod.* **2021**, *2*, 100–103+116.
22. Zhang, L.; Meng, Q.; Xiao, Z.; Fu, X. A novel ship trajectory reconstruction approach using AIS data. *Ocean Eng.* **2018**, *159*, 165–174. [CrossRef]
23. Bai, X.; Cheng, L.; Iris, Ç. Data-driven financial and operational risk management: Empirical evidence from the global tramp shipping industry. *Transp. Res. Part E Logist. Transp. Rev.* **2022**, *158*, 102617. [CrossRef]
24. Yan, L.; Xuanyi, B.; Zongran, D. Optimal Design of ship branch Pipe Layout Based on Cooperative Differential Evolution Algorithm. *Shipbuild. China* **2023**, *64*, 194–206.

Disclaimer/Publisher's Note: The statements, opinions and data contained in all publications are solely those of the individual author(s) and contributor(s) and not of MDPI and/or the editor(s). MDPI and/or the editor(s) disclaim responsibility for any injury to people or property resulting from any ideas, methods, instructions or products referred to in the content.

Article

Three-Dimensional Finite Element Modeling of Ultrasonic Vibration-Assisted Milling of the Nomex Honeycomb Structure

Tarik Zarrouk [1,2,*], Mohammed Nouari [2,*], Jamal-Eddine Salhi [3,4], Mohammed Abbadi [5] and Ahmed Abbadi [5]

1. CREHEIO (Centre de Recherche de L'Ecole des Hautes Etudes d'Ingénierie), Oujda 60000, Morocco
2. CNRS, LEM3, IMT, GIP InSIC, Université de Lorraine, F-88100 Saint Dié des Vosges, France
3. Department of Mathematics, Saveetha School of Engineering, SIMATS, Chennai 602105, Tamil Nadu, India; j.salhi@ump.ac.ma
4. Laboratory of Energetics (LE), Faculty of Sciences, Abdelmalek Essaadi University, Tetouan 93000, Morocco
5. Laboratory of Mechanics and Scientific Calculation, National School of Applied Sciences, Oujda 60000, Morocco
* Correspondence: zarrouk.tarik@ump.ac.ma (T.Z.); mohammed.nouari@univ-lorraine.fr (M.N.)

Abstract: Machining of Nomex honeycomb composite (NHC) structures is of critical importance in manufacturing parts to the specifications required in the aerospace industry. However, the special characteristics of the Nomex honeycomb structure, including its composite nature and complex geometry, require a specific machining approach to avoid cutting defects and ensure optimal surface quality. To overcome this problem, this research suggests the adoption of RUM technology, which involves the application of ultrasonic vibrations following the axis of revolution of the UCK cutting tool. To achieve this objective, a three-dimensional finite element numerical model of Nomex honeycomb structure machining is developed with the Abaqus/Explicit software, 2017 version. Based on this model, this research examines the impact of vibration amplitude on the machinability of this kind of structure, including cutting force components, stress and strain distribution, and surface quality as well as the size of the chips. In conclusion, the results highlight that the use of ultrasonic vibrations results in an important reduction in the components of the cutting force by up to 42%, improves the quality of the surface, and decreases the size of the chips.

Keywords: modeling finite elements (EF); NHC core; RUM technology; UCK cutting tool; surface quality; stress and strain distribution; chip size

Citation: Zarrouk, T.; Nouari, M.; Salhi, J.-E.; Abbadi, M.; Abbadi, A. Three-Dimensional Finite Element Modeling of Ultrasonic Vibration-Assisted Milling of the Nomex Honeycomb Structure. *Algorithms* **2024**, *17*, 204. https://doi.org/10.3390/a17050204

Academic Editors: Sheng Du, Zixin Huang, Li Jin and Xiongbo Wan

Received: 8 April 2024
Revised: 7 May 2024
Accepted: 8 May 2024
Published: 10 May 2024

Copyright: © 2024 by the authors. Licensee MDPI, Basel, Switzerland. This article is an open access article distributed under the terms and conditions of the Creative Commons Attribution (CC BY) license (https://creativecommons.org/licenses/by/4.0/).

1. Introduction

The aerospace and aeronautics sectors place significant emphasis on developing solutions that integrate lightweight materials with exceptional performance characteristics, particularly in demanding and extreme environments [1,2]. This pursuit is driven by the need to enhance fuel efficiency, reduce emissions, and improve overall operational efficiency in aircraft and spacecraft applications. Lightweight materials, such as advanced composites including carbon fiber-reinforced polymers and Nomex material, offer substantial weight savings without compromising strength and durability [3,4]. Due to their notable mechanical properties, Nomex honeycomb structures are widely used in these sectors, particularly in the manufacturing of aircraft wings and tails [5,6]. However, shaping these structures presents a challenge due to the geometry of the NHC core and the fragility of the Nomex paper that comprises it [7]. Shaping of the honeycomb structure is usually carried out through conventional processes such as cutting using thin-bladed tools [8]. However, these methods are limited by their efficiency, the presence of significant machining defects, high cutting forces, and rapid tool wear as well as significant dust pollution [9,10]. For this purpose, RUM technology was applied to overcome the problems of conventional cutting of the honeycomb structure. The interest in this new technology is gradually increasing to machine a wide range of conductive and dielectric materials, including titanium and aluminum alloys [11,12]. For example, Xia et al. [13] conducted a study to optimize the dimensions of an ultrasonic disc tool with the aim of evaluating the influence of its geometric properties on its energy density and stiffness. Their results demonstrated a significant correlation between the processing efficiency of the NHC structure and geometric parameters such as cutting angle. The study carried out by Sun et al. [14] shows the benefits of integrating rotary ultrasonic machining (RUM) into the milling process of aluminum honeycomb structures. Their study established that the use of this technology resulted in the reduction of the cutting force, which helped to mitigate the plastic deformation of the walls of the structure. In general, the machining of Nomex honeycomb structures is often carried out using an experimental approach, with direct involvement of the machine tool. In this regard, Ahmad et al. [15] compared the cutting forces generated during the milling of Nomex honeycomb composites (NHCs), using conventional and ultrasonic machining. Their results demonstrated that ultrasonic vibration machining induced a notable reduction in cutting forces. In the same way, Kang et al. [16] carried out a comparative study of the quality machined surface of the Nomex honeycomb structure using rotary ultrasonic milling (RUM) technology and conventional milling. Their findings demonstrated a notable reduction in the formation of defects on surfaces generated by ultrasonic vibration-assisted machining. In this perspective, Xiang et al. [17] proposed the use of a disc milling cutter with vibration conditions combining longitudinal torsion for the machining of Nomex honeycomb composites (NHCs). Their research found that adding torsional vibrations to longitudinal vibrations not only increased the instantaneous cutting speed of the cutting disc but also promoted material breakage. These improvements result in shorter burrs, reduced burr rates, and less tearing. Due to the rapid movement of the cutting tool and the difficulty in accessing the interface between the cutting tool and the structure to be machined, the experimental process fails to adequately follow the cutting process and the formation of shavings. Therefore, numerical modeling presents itself as a valuable tool for monitoring chip formation and analyzing in detail the machinability characteristics of the structure. Nevertheless, the significant lack of numerical work detailing the machining process of Nomex honeycomb structures highlights the growing imperative to conduct research based on numerical simulations in order to better understand and optimize the machining of these particular structures. In this direction, Wojciechowski et al. [18] proposed a comprehensive micro-milling cutting force model, highlighting high accuracy in predicting forces during the cutting operation. Furthermore, Yuan et al. [19] developed an accurate mechanistic model of cutting force specific to micro-end milling, demonstrating the agreement between the developed numerical model and experimental results. This paper presents a 3D numerical model FE for ultrasonic vibration-assisted milling of the Nomex honeycomb core, developed using the commercial software ABAQUS. From this model, various aspects were carefully examined to optimize the machinability of this type of structure. In conclusion, the results highlight that the application of ultrasonic vibration results in a notable decrease in the cutting force components, while improving the machined surface and reducing the chip size.

2. Finite Element Model
2.1. Material Parameters

Experimental research has focused on exploring the milling characteristics of Nomex honeycomb composite (NHC) structures using the THU Ultrasonic 850 machine tool, which was developed by Tsinghua University in China (refer to Figure 1) [20]. This specialized machine tool incorporates ultrasonic vibration technology to enhance machining efficiency and precision when working with composite materials like Nomex honeycomb. By utilizing the THU Ultrasonic 850, researchers can investigate and optimize milling parameters such as feed rate, spindle speed, and vibration amplitude to achieve the desired machining outcomes. This experimental approach not only advances the understanding of NHC machining processes but also contributes to the development of innovative manufacturing techniques for aerospace and other high-performance applications. In order to validate the obtained results of the experiment, a numerical approach using the finite element (FE) method is proposed. In the context of machining simulation, it is essential to precisely establish the geometric characteristics of the part and the cutting tool. This approach is crucial to guarantee the accuracy and reliability of the results, which makes it imperative to carefully define the mechanical properties of the structure as well as the cutting tool. The materials forming the Nomex honeycomb structure are composed of aramid fibers and phenolic resin, recognized for their high mechanical and thermal resistance. The geometric characteristics of the cell are shown in Figure 1.

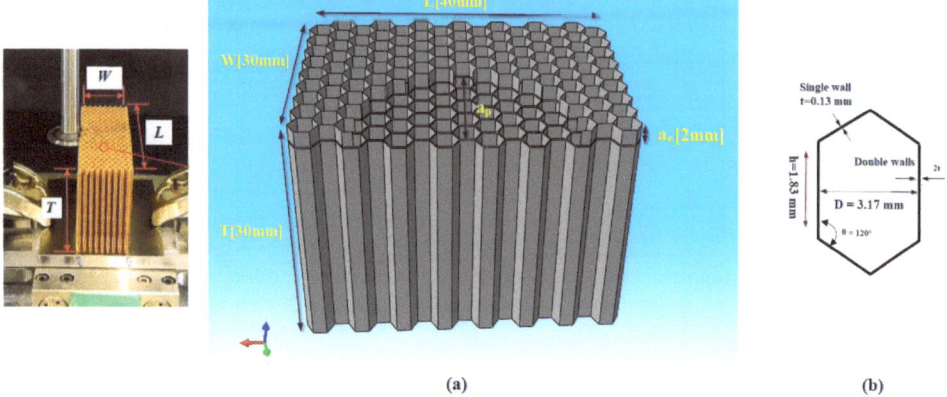

Figure 1. (**a**) Dimensions of the Nomex honeycomb structure (NHC); (**b**) Dimensions of the alveolar cell [21].

In accordance with the experimental methodology, milling was conducted using a specific cutting tool designated as a high-speed steel (HSS-W18Cr4V) ultrasonic circular milling cutter (See Figure 2) [20]. For this purpose, the design of the UCK tool was designed, considering the geometric parameters used throughout the experimental step (See Figure 3).

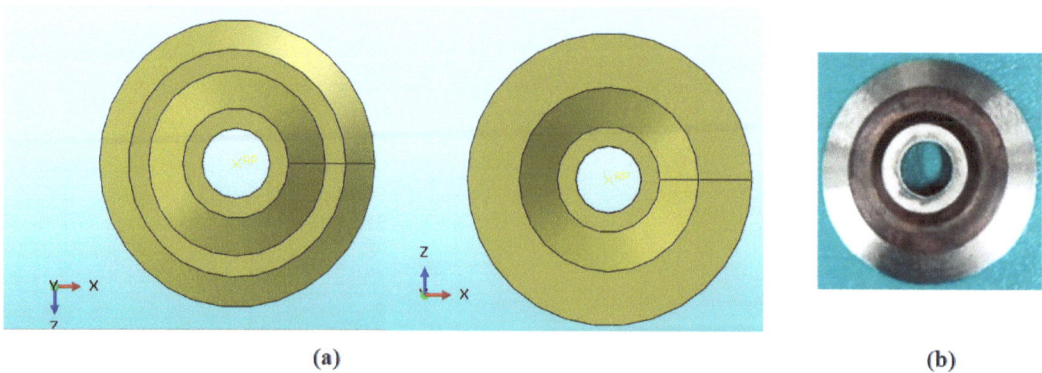

Figure 2. UCK cutting tool: (**a**) UCK used in milling simulation; (**b**) UCK used in the experiment phase.

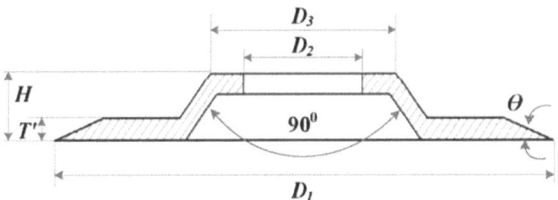

Figure 3. Dimensions of the UCK milling cutter.

2.2. Law of Behavior Applied

Milling of a composite structure requires subjecting the material to significant deformation when in contact with a cutting tool, which results in the creation of chips. Thus, it is essential to determine the constitutive law appropriate to the material constituting the part and the cutting tool in order to be able to carry out effective numerical simulations. In this work, the material constituting the NHC core exhibits isotropic elastoplastic behavior [22,23]. This behavior is made up of two parts: a reversible elastic part and an irreversible plastic part, as described in Equation (1).

$$\varepsilon = \varepsilon^{el} + \varepsilon^{p} \qquad (1)$$

ε is the total stress tensor, and ε^{el} and ε^{p} represent the elastic and plastic strain tensor, respectively.

In general, the elastic behavior of the material is described using Hooke's law, which constitutes a fundamental model of linear elasticity. This law describes a linear relationship between the stress σ and the strain ε of elastic materials according to Equation (2).

$$\{\varepsilon\} = [C]\{\sigma\} \qquad (2)$$

C is the tensor of the reasoner of order 4.

The law, therefore, becomes the following:

$$\begin{pmatrix} \varepsilon_{11} \\ \varepsilon_{22} \\ \varepsilon_{33} \\ \varepsilon_{23} \\ \varepsilon_{31} \\ \varepsilon_{12} \end{pmatrix} = \begin{pmatrix} \frac{1}{E} & -\frac{\vartheta}{E} & -\frac{\vartheta}{E} & 0 & 0 & 0 \\ -\frac{\vartheta}{E} & \frac{1}{E} & -\frac{\vartheta}{E} & 0 & 0 & 0 \\ -\frac{\vartheta}{E} & -\frac{\vartheta}{E} & \frac{1}{E} & 0 & 0 & 0 \\ 0 & 0 & 0 & \frac{1}{G} & 0 & 0 \\ 0 & 0 & 0 & 0 & \frac{1}{G} & 0 \\ 0 & 0 & 0 & 0 & 0 & \frac{1}{G} \end{pmatrix} \begin{pmatrix} \sigma_{11} \\ \sigma_{22} \\ \sigma_{33} \\ \sigma_{23} \\ \sigma_{31} \\ \sigma_{12} \end{pmatrix} \qquad (3)$$

To precisely define the elastic properties of a material, it is essential to determine the Lame coefficients, λ and μ. These coefficients are linked to Young's modulus E and Poisson's ratio ν by Equations (4) and (5).

$$\lambda = \frac{\vartheta E}{(1+\vartheta)(1-2\vartheta)} \qquad (4)$$

$$\mu = \frac{E}{2(1+\vartheta)} \qquad (5)$$

Isotropic elastoplastic behavior has been attributed to Nomex material by several authors [24]. Figure 4 demonstrates the mechanical properties of the Nomex material, highlighting the elastic thresholds and variations in plastic behavior as a function of wall thickness. The principal mechanical characteristics attributed to Nomex material are described in Table 1.

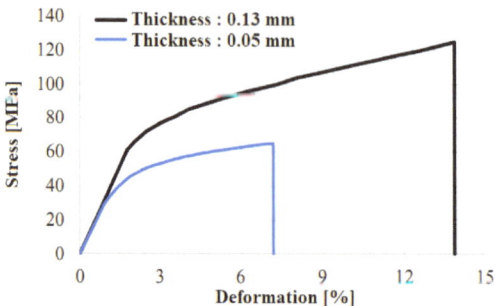

Figure 4. Evolution of the stress and deformation of the Nomex material [22,23].

Table 1. The mechanical properties of Nomex paper [22,23].

Mechanical Properties	
Density [g/cm^3]	1.4
E [MPa]	3400
Poisson's ratio	0.3
Yield strengths for simple wall thickness (MPa)	29
Yield strengths for double wall thickness (MPa)	61

2.3. Chip Separation Criterion

In the machining process, where the material is cut using a suitable cutting tool, defining a failure criterion is of crucial importance to simulate the machining precisely. Failure criteria are usually associated with the intrinsic mechanical and thermal properties of the material. As part of this study, the shear failure criterion is specifically chosen, and its modeling is assigned to the finite element analysis software Abaqus. The process of assessing damage starts with gathering the initial mechanical characteristics, which are detailed in Table 1. Subsequently, the motion of the milling cutter induces a force exerted on the workpiece, where the determination of dynamic normal and shear stresses is carried out through various interfaces. When the rupture coefficient, denoted ω, exceeds a critical threshold of 1 (Equation (6)), it indicates deterioration of the material and the formation of chips.

$$\omega = \sum \frac{\Delta \varepsilon}{\varepsilon^f} \qquad (6)$$

where ω represents the shaping limit value or destruction coefficient, $\Delta \varepsilon$ represents the incremental equivalent plastic strain, and ε^f indicates the total strain at which the material experiences damage.

2.4. Finite Element Modeling

This paper provides a simulation study of the rotary ultrasonic machining (RUM)-assisted cutting process of the NHC core. This simulation is based on a numerical FE model developed with the Abaqus/Explicit software. The cell walls of the Nomex honeycomb structure are composed of two-thirds single-cell walls and one-third double-cell walls. The corresponding thicknesses of single- and double-cell walls are set to 0.13 mm and 0.26 mm, respectively, in the numerical model. In this approach, the meshing of the NHC core walls is achieved using reduced-integration four-node S4R shell elements, as shown in Figure 5a. Throughout the numerical modeling, the UCK tool is supposed to be rigid, which means that it is non-deformable during the milling process. Therefore, the UCK milling cutter is meshed using rigid quadrangular elements with four nodes (R3D4), as presented in Figure 5b.

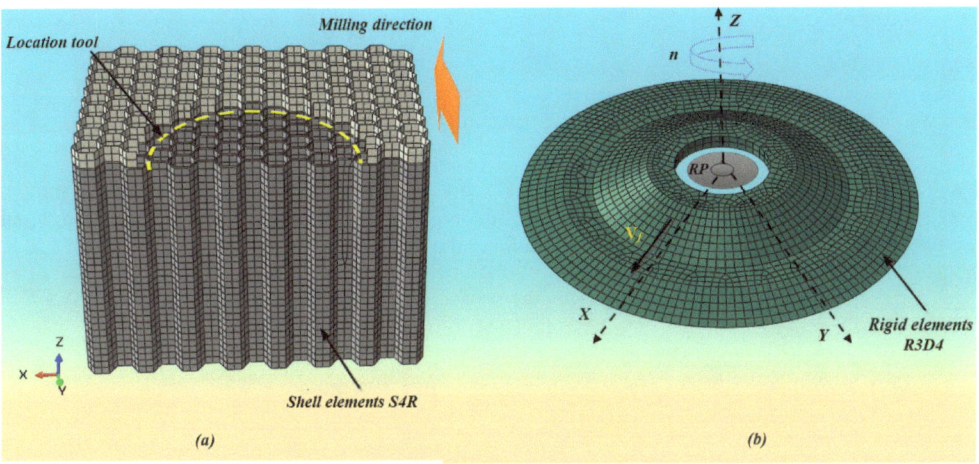

Figure 5. (**a**) Mesh of the part (NHC); (**b**) Mesh of the cutting tool and location of reference point (RP) [21].

Before starting the implementation of the numerical code, it is essential to conduct a preliminary phase aimed at examining the nonlinear parameters that can impact the convergence of the numerical results, in particular the type and size of the mesh. It is important to note that using a fine mesh size can result in a substantial increase in calculation time, particularly in the context of 3D configurations. It is, therefore, essential to find an optimal balance between the size of the mesh and the exactness of the results, while maintaining a reasonable calculation time. As part of the simulation of the machining process, a general contact was used to describe the interaction between the UCK milling cutter and the Nomex honeycomb core. Since the walls of the Nomex honeycomb structure are thin, the contact between it and the cutting tool is considered punctual. For this purpose, the friction coefficient adopted to carry out the numerical simulations is set at 0.1. In order to ensure permanent contact between the milling cutter and the workpiece, an initial integration between the part and the tool was set up, taking into account the geometric particularities of the NHC core and the UCK milling cutter (see Figure 5a). The boundary conditions were adopted according to the experimental process [20] so that the lower surface of the NHC structure remained stationary and incapable of undergoing displacements or rotations. For this purpose, in the numerical modeling, complete fixation is imposed on the bottom surface of the NHC core, preventing any translational movement ($U_x = U_y = U_z = 0$) along the X, Y, and Z axes as well as any rotation around these axes ($U_{Rx} = U_{Ry} = U_{Rz} = 0$), as shown in Figure 6b. The difference between conventional milling and ultrasonic vibration-assisted axial milling is the introduction of ultrasonic vibrations along the Z axis at the end of the milling cutter. The ultrasonic rotary machining (RUM) process represents an approach in mechanical manufacturing that involves the synchronization of three types of motions. These motions include translation of the tool along the axis OY, characterized by the feed rate V_f, rotation of the cutting tool around the axis OZ, expressed by the spindle speed n, and the vibration of the tool along the OZ axis, generating a sinusoidal ultrasonic wave (see Figure 6). To guarantee precise monitoring of the milling simulation process, a reference point denoted RP, was assigned along the axis of revolution of the cutting tool in accordance with the representation in Figure 5b. This point assumes an essential role in assigning cutting parameters and in assessing the cutting forces acting throughout the milling operation. In order to describe the motion of the cutting tool, the following equations are used to define its global coordinates xyz:

$$V_x = V_c \cos\left(\frac{2\pi n\, t}{60}\right) + V_f \quad (7)$$

$$V_y = V_c \sin\left(\frac{2\pi n\, t}{60}\right) \quad (8)$$

$$V_z = A \sin(2\pi f t) \quad (9)$$

In the current article, A denotes the amplitude of ultrasonic vibration; V_c stands for the cutting speed; and f denotes the vibration frequency, which is fixed at 21.26 KHz.

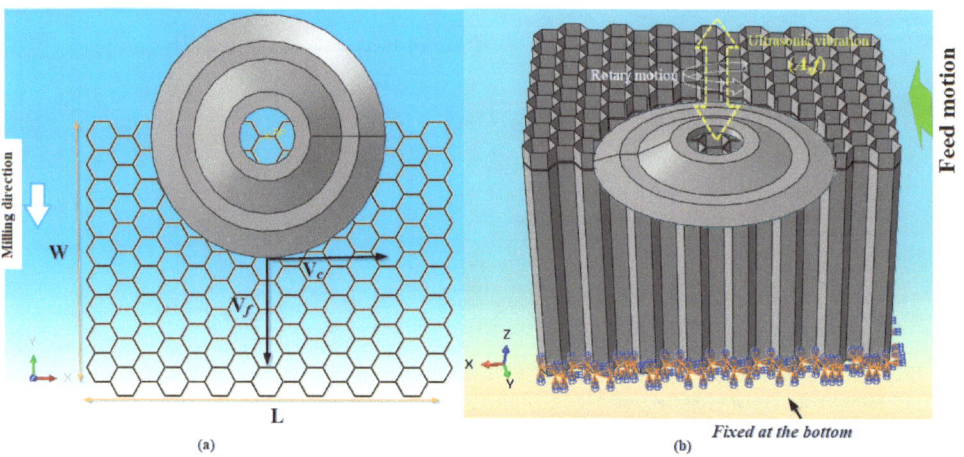

Figure 6. (a) Milling planar representation of the NHC core; (b) Boundary conditions adopted in the numerical modeling [21].

2.5. Components of the Cutting Force

Throughout the experimental stage, the components of the cutting force, denoted by F_y and F_x, are evaluated using the KISTLER-9256C2 dynamometer. The advantage of this technique lies in its ability to determine the average values in both directions using these formulas:

$$F_x = \frac{1}{t_2 - t_1} \int_{t_1}^{t_2} |F_{CX}|\, dt \quad (10)$$

$$F_y = \frac{1}{t_2 - t_1} \int_{t_1}^{t_2} |F_{CY}|\, dt \quad (11)$$

F_x and F_y represent the average values of the cutting force components along the X and Y axes.

3. Results and Discussion

3.1. Mesh Size Study

The choice of mesh size is closely linked to the nature of the underlying mechanic phenomenon and the objectives of the simulation. This mainly results from its direct effectiveness both on the precision of the results and on the time necessary to carry out the calculation. Although the use of a coarse mesh makes it possible to reduce the calculation time, it results in lower precision of the results. On the contrary, using a finer mesh results in an increase in calculation time, but allows for better-quality results. Thus, during each simulation, it is essential to seek the right accommodation between the size of the mesh, the calculation time, and the precision of the obtained results. In this section, our attention was focused on the impact of mesh size on the components of the cutting force when modeling the milling process. To this end, eight simulations were carried out by adjusting the mesh dimensions, varying from 0.2 mm to 0.9 mm. The simulations were carried out with the same cutting conditions, including a feed rate of 3000 mm/min, a spindle speed of 5000 rpm, and an amplitude vibration is 25 µm. The obtained results are shown in Figure 7.

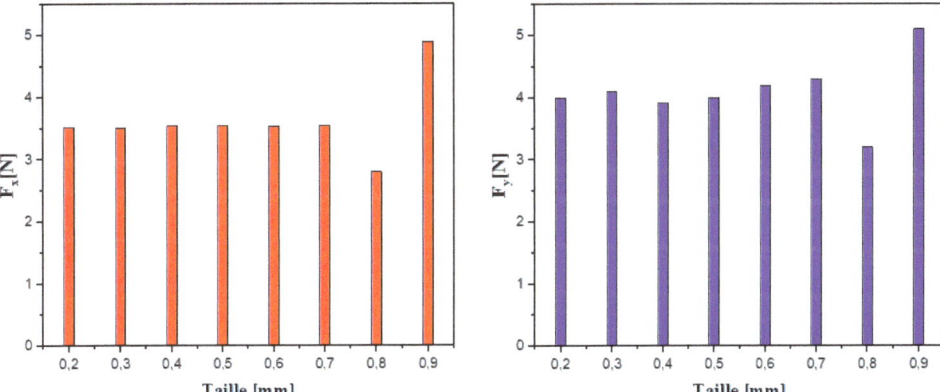

Figure 7. Evolution of the F_x and F_y components as a function of the mesh size.

The convergence range of the mesh is remarkably established between 0.2 mm and 0.6 mm; this observation remains consistent for the two components F_x and F_y. However, the cutting force components recorded a weak decrease between sizes 0.7 mm and 0.8 mm, followed by a sharp increase between sizes 0.8 mm and 0.9 mm. The noticed variation can be credited to the elastic-restoring forces of the NHC core walls. Thus, as soon as the element reaches its breaking point, it is deleted, which results in a loss of contact between the wall of the structure and the milling cutter, leading to a reduction in the F_x and F_y components. Effectively, the force resulting from spring back due to the uncut walls resists the rotation of the tool, thereby increasing the cutting force components. Despite this, small elements have a lower capacity to resist deformation. Therefore, mesh distortion issues manifest themselves more quickly, which can lead to calculation failures. In principle, a mesh size of 0.2 mm seems to provide an ideal compromise between the accuracy of the results and the efficiency of the calculation. However, it was essential to re-evaluate this approach and adapt it to a size of 0.4 mm in order to achieve the best balance between mesh quality and the calculation time. The objective of this adaptation is to guarantee an appropriate resolution of physical phenomena while preventing the deformation of the elements.

3.2. Influence of Cutting Width on Cutting Force Components

A numerical simulation was carried out to verify the validity of the numerical model, evaluating the impact of different cutting widths on the F_x and F_y components when milling the NHC core. This analysis was performed using RUM technology regardless of whether or not ultrasonic vibrations were applied. To carry out this study, four cutting width values were examined, including 4 mm, 6 mm, 8 mm, and 10 mm. Other cutting parameters remained constant throughout the analysis, including a feed rate of 2000 mm/min, a spindle speed of 3000 rpm, and an amplitude vibration is 25 µm. The obtained results are illustrated in Figure 8 [20].

The results of the numerical simulation confirm the experimental tendency noticed for the F_x and F_y components, revealing a significant increase in these components as a function of the cutting width when milling the NHC structure, regardless of whether ultrasonic vibrations are used or not. Increasing the cutting width causes a distension of the contact surface between the milling cutter and the part, which results in an increase in the volume of material removed per unit of time. Similarly, a large cutting width can result in high friction resistance during the machining process, thereby causing an increase in cutting force components. During the process of cutting the Nomex honeycomb structure using rotary ultrasonic machining, it is clear that the use of ultrasonic vibrations results in a remarkable decrease in the F_x and F_y components, with a reduction reaching up to 42%. In this context, the cutting tool undergoes intense rotation and vibrations, which encourage the formation of cracks in the walls of the NHC structure. This eases the penetration of the tool without encountering resistance from the material constituting the NHC structure. Although increasing the cutting width can improve cutting efficiency, it is also linked to an increase in cutting force components, which can lead to other complications such as premature wear of the cutting tool and degradation of the quality of the machined surface. It is important to determine an optimal value of the cutting width in order to reconcile these two characteristics when machining the NHC core. This optimal value aims to maximize the material removal volume while keeping the cutting force components at a satisfactory level. Thus, this approach guarantees acceptable cutting efficiency and robust numerical results.

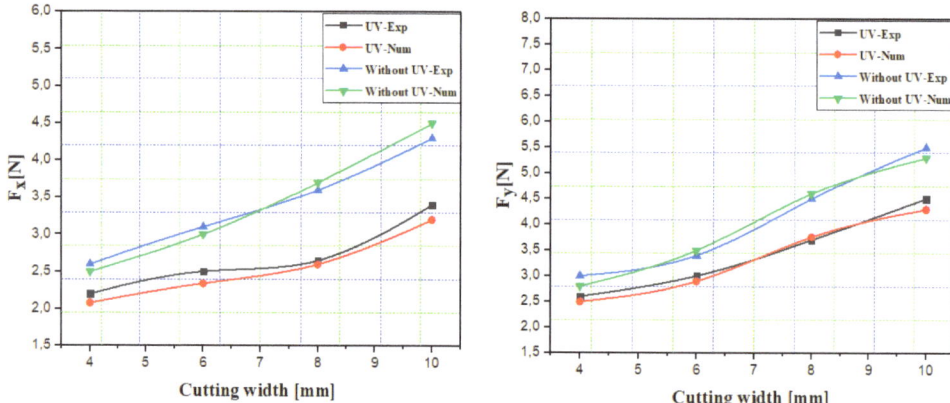

Figure 8. Evolutions of the cutting force components (F_x, F_y).

3.3. Impact of Vibration Amplitude on Machined Surface

The machined surface of the Nomex honeycomb core is essential to building the sandwich structures. Its precise optimization is essential to ensure the robustness and durability of these materials in various industrial applications. Typically, imperfections in the machining of NHC structures come in various forms, including burrs, tears of the walls, and uncut fibers. These defects can appear at different stages of the machining process and have the potential to impact the final quality of the structure. Therefore, in-depth analysis is required to adjust manufacturing parameters and minimize these imperfections. To study the effect of vibration amplitude on the machined surface, numerical simulations were conducted by adjusting the vibration amplitudes to values of 0 µm, 10 µm, and 25 µm. The cutting simulation is carried out under the same cutting conditions, notably a feed rate at 3000 mm/min and a spindle speed at 1000 rpm, which were kept constant throughout the milling simulation. The machining defects generated by the numerical model were spotted by visual inspection with the naked eye and are illustrated in Figure 9.

The main results of this research indicate a gradual enhancement in the quality of the surface with increasing ultrasonic vibration amplitude. This observation highlights a direct relationship between vibration amplitude and surface quality, demonstrating the potential benefits of this technique in machining processes. Furthermore, the numerical results demonstrate that the predominant machining imperfections noticed on the Nomex honeycomb core are wall deformations and tears. Though, the numerical model failed to detect the burrs, characterized by excess material on the cell walls since they were characterized by S4R shell elements without thickness. In fact, at low spindle speeds, the cutting tool cannot apply adequate force to the walls of the NHC core, which increases the risk of elastic deformation of these walls until their rupture. The use of ultrasonic vibrations highlights the notable benefits they bring to the machining. These vibrations reduce contact between the tool and the thin walls of the honeycomb structure, thereby reducing friction and improving heat dissipation during cutting. The interaction of these parameters facilitates the engagement of the milling cutter with the walls of the honeycomb core, which contributes to the reduction of machining defects and the improvement of the fineness of the machined surface. This finding highlights the effectiveness of ultrasonic vibrations in improving the quality of the machined surface, which allows for improved milling techniques.

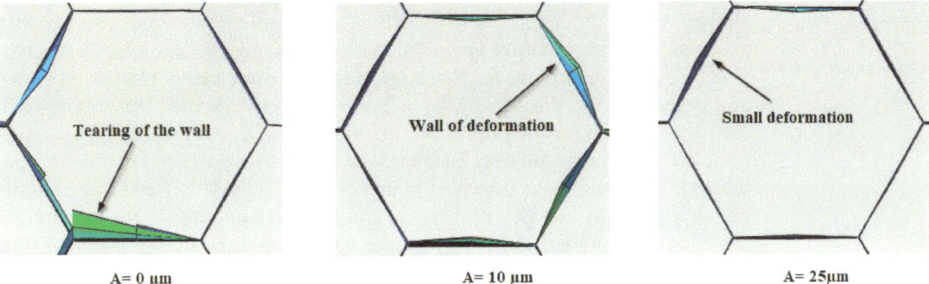

Figure 9. Evolution of the machined surface as a function of the vibration amplitude.

3.4. Analysis of the Distribution of Stresses and Displacements in the Cutting Zone

Studying the stress distribution on the walls of the honeycomb structure of the NHC provides crucial insights into the cutting conditions in the vicinity of the machining zone. This analysis enables a deeper understanding of how ultrasonic vibrations affect the cutting process. By examining the stress patterns, researchers can gain valuable information about how vibrations impact material behavior and chip formation during machining. This enhanced understanding ultimately contributes to optimizing cutting parameters and improving the efficiency and quality of the machining process. This section presents a series of numerical simulations that aim to study the impact of the vibration amplitude on the distribution of stresses and displacements throughout the cutting process of the NHC structure. The vibration amplitudes of the milling cutter were varied at 0 µm, 10 µm, and 25 µm. The simulations are carried out under the cutting parameters, namely a feed rate of 3000 mm/min and a spindle speed of 3000 rpm. The results of these simulations are presented in Figures 10 and 11.

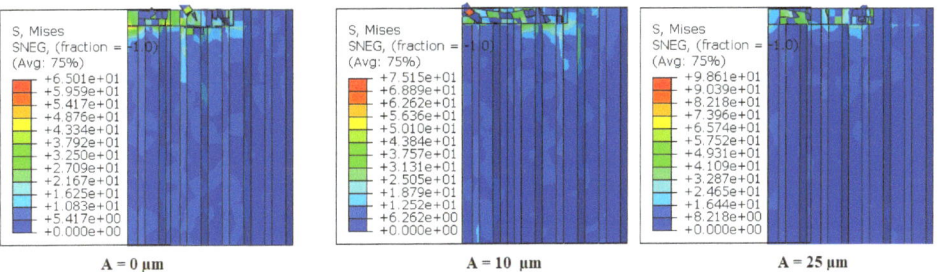

Figure 10. Stress distribution at different vibration amplitudes.

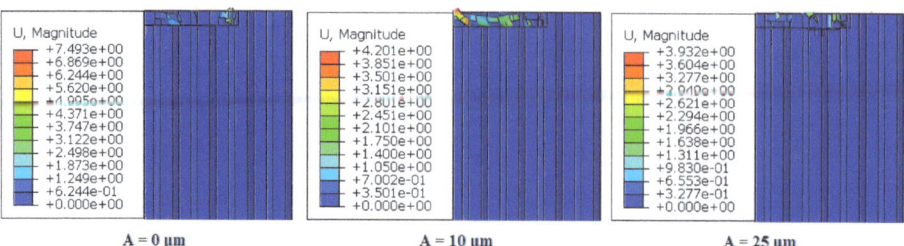

Figure 11. Displacement distribution at different vibration amplitudes.

The study of the stress distribution on the walls of the honeycomb structure of the NHC offers important data on the cutting conditions near the machining zone, which allows a better understanding of the effects of ultrasound vibrations throughout the cutting process. The figures above show the evolution of stresses and displacements of the cell walls for diverse amplitudes. In order to optimize the visual clarity of cell wall stresses and deformations, the representations shown do not include the cutting tool. The rupture occurred under the impact of tall amplitudes, due to the high stresses to reach the established rupture criterion. Elements subjected to stresses below the breaking limit are discernible, while those subjected to higher stresses have suffered fragmentation and are no longer visible. For an amplitude of 0 µm (conventional cut), the extreme stress on the structure is evaluated at 65.01 MPa, which is lower compared to the values observed for amplitudes of 10 µm and 25 µm. Nevertheless, the cell wall displacement is meaningfully higher than that seen throughout the ultrasonic cutting process. Therefore, in the ultrasonic cutting process of the Nomex honeycomb, increasing the ultrasound amplitude results in reaching the ultimate strength of the cut cell wall faster, which allows cutting without significant deformations or major damage. In this context, research carried out on ultrasonic vibration-assisted cutting, both for aluminum honeycomb structures, has reached similar conclusions [14,25]. This study demonstrated that the use of ultrasonic vibrations in the cutting process shows consistent results, demonstrating the efficiency and advantages of this method in various situations.

3.5. The Influence of Vibration Amplitude on the Size of the Chips Generated

This section proposes a series of numerical simulations aimed at analyzing the effect of machining techniques on the size of the chips generated. To do this, two techniques were examined: conventional machining without vibrations (amplitude of 0 µm) and machining assisted by ultrasonic vibrations (amplitude of 15 µm). It is important to note that the numerical simulations are carried out under the same cutting parameters, namely a feed of 3000 mm/min and a spindle speed of 5000 rpm. The results of this study are presented in Figure 12.

The machining of NHC structures involves a complex two-stage process. Initially, the milling cutter engages with the thin walls of the structure, directing them towards the upper part of the tool where the high spindle speed shreds and pushes the material back, forming chips. This dynamic interaction between the material's structural geometry and the cutting tool is significantly influenced by the rapid spindle rotation, showcasing the intricate responsiveness of machining operations to tool movement and speed. The obtained results demonstrate a clear correlation between chip size and vibration amplitude. Increasing the vibration amplitude leads to a noticeable reduction in chip size, attributed to the combined effect of high-intensity vibrations and rapid spindle speed, which minimizes contact between the milling cutter and the NHC core walls. In this regard, the reduced contact facilitated by high-intensity vibrations and rapid spindle speed allows for easier tool penetration, promoting crack propagation and small chip formation. This reduction in chip size not only lowers cutting forces but also improves overall milling quality and efficiency, extending the cutting tool lifespan.

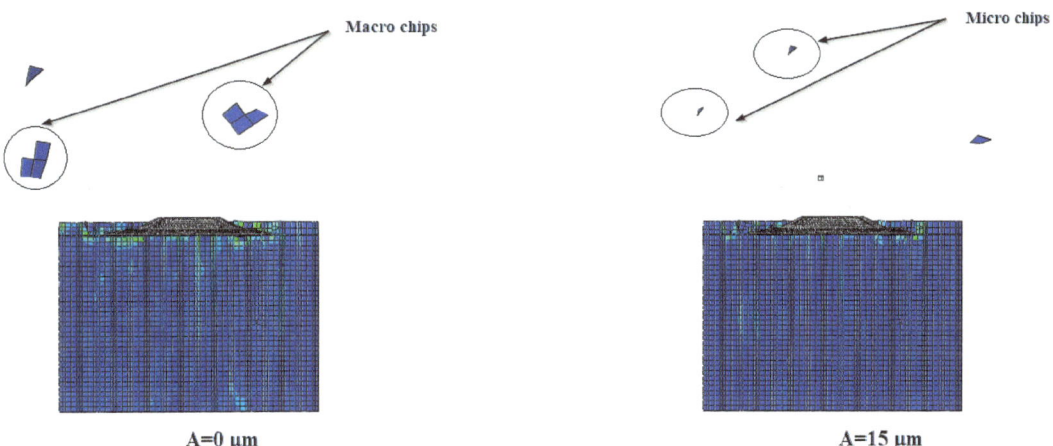

Figure 12. Chip size for different vibration amplitudes.

4. Conclusions

This paper introduces a numerical finite element (FE) model for ultrasonic vibration-assisted milling of Nomex honeycomb structures. Initially, an optimal mesh size was selected to balance CPU calculation time and result accuracy. Simulations were carried out after the validation of the numerical model to analyze the effect of the vibration amplitude on several parameters, notably the quality of the surface, the size of the chips, and the distribution of stresses and displacement in proximity to the cutting zone. Based on this study, the following conclusions can be made:

- The study of the impact of the cutting width on the components of the cutting force is carried out, finding a significant increase in these components with increasing cutting width, both in simulations and in experiments. Our results suggest that the use of ultrasonic vibrations helps to mitigate the negative effects of the F_x and F_y components in both directions. Furthermore, a significant agreement between the results of the numerical model and the experimental data was observed.
- The amplitude of the ultrasonic vibration directly impacts the chip size, leading to a reduction in this one with increasing vibration amplitude.
- The amplitude of the vibration influences the surface quality, leading to an improvement of the latter when the amplitude of the vibrations is increased.
- Applying ultrasonic vibration to the cutting tool induces additional stress in the cutting area of the honeycomb cell wall, accelerating material deterioration while reducing cell wall deformation, facilitating a more efficient milling of the Nomex honeycomb core.
- By continuing this research, it is planned to develop the numerical model by taking into account other parameters in order to detect the burrs that form on the thin walls during the machining process.
- In the industrial context, the optimization of manufacturing processes often requires costly and time-consuming tests to evaluate different configurations. The 3D modeling presented thus offers a considerable advantage in terms of speed, efficiency, and profitability.

Author Contributions: T.Z. performed analyzed and interpreted data and results. M.N. analyzed and interpreted data and was a major contributor to writing the manuscript. J.-E.S. was a major contributor to writing the manuscript. M.A. analyzed and interpreted data and results. A.A. was a major contributor to writing the manuscript. All authors have read and agreed to the published version of the manuscript.

Funding: This research received no external funding.

Data Availability Statement: Data are contained within the article.

Conflicts of Interest: The authors declare no conflicts of interest.

References

1. Zhao, Y.Z.; Yao, S.J.; Xiong, S.W.; Li, B.Y.; Wang, X.Y.; Yang, F.H.; Jia, Y.B.; Wang, L.X.; Wang, H. Preparation of high breakdown strength meta-aramid composite paper reinforced by polyphenylene sulfide superfine fiber. *Polym. Eng. Sci.* **2023**, *63*, 1579–1587. [CrossRef]
2. Ranga, C.; Kumar, A.; Chandel, R. Influence of electrical and thermal ageing on the mineral insulating oil performance for power transformer applications. *Insight-Non-Destr. Test. Cond. Monit.* **2020**, *62*, 222–231. [CrossRef]
3. Li, L.; Song, J.; Lei, Z.; Kang, A.; Wang, Z.; Men, R.; Ma, Y. Effects of ambient humidity and thermal aging on properties of Nomex insulation in mining dry-type transformer. *High Volt.* **2021**, *6*, 71–81. [CrossRef]
4. Wei, X.; Xiong, J.; Wang, J.; Xu, W. New advances in fiber-reinforced composite honeycomb materials. *Sci. China Technol. Sci.* **2020**, *63*, 1348–1370. [CrossRef]
5. Gao, Y.; Chen, X.; Wei, Y. Graded honeycombs with high impact resistance through machine learning-based optimization. *Thin-Walled Struct.* **2023**, *188*, 110794. [CrossRef]
6. Xie, S.; Wang, H.; Jing, K.; Feng, Z. Mechanical properties of Nomex honeycombs filled with tubes of carbon fiber reinforced vinyl ester resin composites. *Thin-Walled Struct.* **2022**, *180*, 109933. [CrossRef]
7. Zarrouk, T.; Nouari, M.; Makich, H. Simulated study of the machinability of the Nomex honeycomb structure. *J. Manuf. Mater. Process.* **2023**, *7*, 28. [CrossRef]
8. Jaafar, M.; Atlati, S.; Makich, H.; Nouari, M.; Moufki, A.; Julliere, B. A 3D FE modeling of machining process of Nomex® honeycomb core: Influence of the cell structure behavior and specific tool geometry. *Procedia Cirp* **2017**, *58*, 505–510. [CrossRef]
9. Dong, Z.; Qin, Y.; Kang, R.; Wang, Y.; Sun, J.; Zhu, X.; Liu, Y. Robust cell wall recognition of laser measured honeycomb cores based on corner type identification. *Opt. Lasers Eng.* **2021**, *136*, 106321. [CrossRef]
10. Jaafar, M.; Makich, H.; Nouari, M. A new criterion to evaluate the machined surface quality of the Nomex® honeycomb materials. *J. Manuf. Process.* **2021**, *69*, 567–582. [CrossRef]
11. Xie, W.; Wang, X.; Liu, E.; Wang, J.; Tang, X.; Li, G.; Zhao, B. Research on cutting force and surface integrity of TC18 titanium alloy by longitudinal ultrasonic vibration assisted milling. *Int. J. Adv. Manuf. Technol.* **2022**, *119*, 4745–4755. [CrossRef]
12. Sun, J.; Kang, R.; Qin, Y.; Wang, Y.; Feng, B.; Dong, Z. Simulated and experimental study on the ultrasonic cutting mechanism of aluminum honeycomb by disc cutter. *Compos. Struct.* **2021**, *275*, 114431. [CrossRef]
13. Xia, Y.; Zhang, J.; Wu, Z.; Feng, P.; Yu, D. Study on the design of cutting disc in ultrasonic assisted machining of honeycomb composites. *IOP Conf. Ser. Mater. Sci. Eng.* **2019**, *611*, 012032. [CrossRef]
14. Sun, J.; Dong, Z.; Wang, X.; Wang, Y.; Qin, Y.; Kang, R. Simulation and experimental study of ultrasonic cutting for aluminum honeycomb by disc cutter. *Ultrasonics* **2020**, *103*, 106102. [CrossRef] [PubMed]
15. Ahmad, S.; Zhang, J.; Feng, P.; Yu, D.; Wu, Z.; Ke, M. Research on design and FE simulations of novel ultrasonic circular saw blade (UCSB) cutting tools for rotary ultrasonic machining of Nomex honeycomb composites. In Proceedings of the 2019 16th International Bhurban Conference on Applied Sciences and Technology (IBCAST), Islamabad, Pakistan, 8–12 January 2019; pp. 113–119.
16. Kang, D.; Zou, P.; Wu, H.; Duan, J.; Wang, W. Study on ultrasonic vibration–assisted cutting of Nomex honeycomb cores. *Int. J. Adv. Manuf. Technol.* **2019**, *104*, 979–992. [CrossRef]
17. Xiang, D.H.; Wu, B.F.; Yao, Y.L.; Liu, Z.Y.; Feng, H.R. Ultrasonic longitudinal-torsional vibration-assisted cutting of Nomex (R) honeycomb-core composites. *Int. J. Adv. Manuf. Technol.* **2019**, *100*, 1521–1530. [CrossRef]
18. Wojciechowski, S.; Matuszak, M.; Powalka, B.; Madajewski, M.; Maruda, R.W.; Krolczyk, G.M. Prediction of cutting forces during micro end milling considering chip thickness accumulation. *Int. J. Mach. Tools Manuf.* **2019**, *147*, 103466. [CrossRef]
19. Yuan, Y.J.; Jing, X.B.; Ehmann, K.F.; Cao, J.; Li, H.Z.; Zhang, D.W. Modeling of cutting forces in micro end-milling. *J. Manuf. Process.* **2018**, *31*, 844–858. [CrossRef]
20. Ahmad, S.; Zhang, J.; Feng, P.; Yu, D.; Wu, Z. Experimental study on rotary ultrasonic machining (RUM) characteristics of Nomex honeycomb composites (NHCs) by circular knife cutting tools. *J. Manuf. Process.* **2020**, *58*, 524–535. [CrossRef]
21. Zarrouk, T.; Nouari, M.; Salhi, J.E.; Benbouaza, A. Numerical Simulation of Rotary Ultrasonic Machining of the Nomex Honeycomb Composite Structure. *Machines* **2024**, *12*, 137. [CrossRef]
22. Foo, C.C.; Chai, G.B.; Seah, L.K. Mechanical properties of Nomex material and Nomex honeycomb structure. *Compos. Struct.* **2007**, *80*, 588–594. [CrossRef]
23. Roy, R.; Park, S.J.; Kweon, J.H.; Choi, J.H. Characterization of Nomex honeycomb core constituent material mechanical properties. *Compos. Struct.* **2014**, *117*, 255–266. [CrossRef]

24. Nasir, M.A.; Khan, Z.; Farooqi, I.; Nauman, S.; Anas, S.; Khalil, S.; Ata, R. Transverse shear behavior of a Nomex core for sandwich panels. *Mech. Compos. Mater.* **2015**, *50*, 733–738. [CrossRef]
25. Arnold, G.; Leiteritz, L.; Zahn, S.; Rohm, H. Ultrasonic cutting of cheese: Composition affects cutting work reduction and energy demand. *Int. Dairy J.* **2009**, *19*, 314–320. [CrossRef]

Disclaimer/Publisher's Note: The statements, opinions and data contained in all publications are solely those of the individual author(s) and contributor(s) and not of MDPI and/or the editor(s). MDPI and/or the editor(s) disclaim responsibility for any injury to people or property resulting from any ideas, methods, instructions or products referred to in the content.

Article

An Interface to Monitor Process Variability Using the Binomial ATTRIVAR SS Control Chart

João Pedro Costa Violante [1], Marcela A. G. Machado [1,*], Amanda dos Santos Mendes [2] and Túlio S. Almeida [1]

[1] Department of Production Engineering, São Paulo State University, Guaratinguetá 05508-070, Brazil; jp.violante@unesp.br (J.P.C.V.); tulio.almeida@unesp.br (T.S.A.)

[2] Department of Administration and Public Administration, Fluminense Federal University, Volta Redonda 27213-145, Brazil; amanda_mendes@id.uff.br

* Correspondence: marcela.freitas@unesp.br

Abstract: Control charts are tools of paramount importance in statistical process control. They are broadly applied in monitoring processes and improving quality, as they allow the detection of special causes of variation with a significant level of accuracy. Furthermore, there are several strategies able to be employed in different contexts, all of which offer their own advantages. Therefore, this study focuses on monitoring the variability in univariate processes through variance using the Binomial version of the ATTRIVAR Same Sample S^2 (B-ATTRIVAR SS S^2) control chart, given that it allows coupling attribute and variable inspections (ATTRIVAR means attribute + variable), i.e., taking advantage of the cost-effectiveness of the former and the wealth of information and greater performance of the latter. Its Binomial version was used for such a purpose, since inspections are made using two attributes, and the Same Sample was used due to being submitted to both the attribute and variable stages of inspection. A computational application was developed in the R language using the Shiny package so as to create an interface to facilitate its application and use in the quality control of the production processes. Its application enables users to input process parameters and generate the B-ATTRIVAR SS control chart for monitoring the process variability with variance. By comparing the data obtained from its application with a simpler code, its performance was validated, given that its results exhibited striking similarity.

Keywords: control chart; ATTRIVAR; variability; variance; application; interface; R; Shiny package

Citation: Violante, J.P.C.; Machado, M.A.G.; Mendes, A.d.S.; Almeida, T.S. An Interface to Monitor Process Variability Using the Binomial ATTRIVAR SS Control Chart. *Algorithms* **2024**, *17*, 216. https://doi.org/10.3390/a17050216

Academic Editors: Zixin Huang, Li Jin, Xiongbo Wan and Sheng Du

Received: 5 April 2024
Revised: 28 April 2024
Accepted: 28 April 2024
Published: 16 May 2024

Copyright: © 2024 by the authors. Licensee MDPI, Basel, Switzerland. This article is an open access article distributed under the terms and conditions of the Creative Commons Attribution (CC BY) license (https://creativecommons.org/licenses/by/4.0/).

1. Introduction

Control charts were initially introduced by [1] and are the primary and most technically sophisticated tools of statistical process control [2]. They are widely employed in process monitoring and serve to detect nonconformities and special causes of variation, thus enabling the early identification of disturbances aimed to minimize negative adverse financial impacts [3].

Among control charts, some utilize variable inspection for monitoring continuous quality characteristics, while others employ attribute inspection, which was initially designed for monitoring non-continuous quality characteristics.

One of which is grounded on the numerical measurements of quality characteristics, and another is based on the attributes defined by [4] as quality characteristics measured in a nominal scale or categorized according to a predetermined scheme of labels. For instance, classifying fruits as being good or rotten, and nails or screws as defective or not defective.

Although the primary purpose of attribute inspection was outlined about 70 years ago, researchers have made contributions by suggesting their use for controlling continuous quality characteristics, and more recent studies have proposed better means for such [5].

There are numerous comparisons between variable and attribute charts in the literature, such as [5–10]. These authors emphasize the superior efficiency and informativeness of variable inspection due to its reliance on measurements, as opposed to a simpler, faster, and cheaper application of attribute inspection.

Several researchers explore the use of attribute inspections for continuous characteristics, such as [8,9,11], in an attempt to continuously seek to improve the efficiency of resource utilization and improve the performance of control charts.

Ergo, what once meant having to use a sample 6.667 times larger in attribute charts to achieve the same level of performance as variable charts [2] now requires a sample less than twice as large using the np_{S^2} proposed by [9].

The strategy of using variable and attribute inspections combined into a single chart had initially been proposed by [12] and is similar to one which was later on called as ATTRIVAR (ATTRIbute + VARiable) by [5]. Thenceforth, these mixed charts combine the advantages of both forms of inspection initially called as such.

A version of [12] consisted in designing the np_x (attribute) and $\overline{X}$ (variable) charts separately and dividing the collected sample into two subsamples. Then, the former was submitted to np_x chart evaluation, and the latter was submitted to $\overline{X}$ chart evaluation if the former had been rejected.

Ref. [7] also proposed a mixed chart without subdividing the sample and used the same sample in both stages of inspection (as in [13,14], and to the proposal herein). Ref. [5] proposed ATTRIVAR-1 chart, which uses the same sample in both stages, in addition to ATTRIVAR-2 chart, which makes use of different samples. In this work, the terminologies SS (same sample) and DS (different sample) refer to these strategies, respectively.

Unlike these proposals, which addressed only mean monitoring, Ref. [10] proposed a mixed chart to monitor variability through variance. The authors coupled the np_{S^2} chart from [9] in the stage of attribute inspection with the S^2 chart in the stage of variable inspection using different samples.

Afterwards, Ref. [15] proposed the Trinomial version of the ATTRIVAR (T-ATTRIVAR) chart aimed at mean monitoring but using three attributes in the first inspection stage instead of two as in other strategies.

Thus, this paper explores the Binomial version of ATTRIVAR Same Sample S^2 (B-ATTRIVAR SS S^2) chart that makes use of the first inspection stage with two attributes ("binomial") using the same sample in both inspection stages ("same sample") to monitor the process variance (S^2).

Although there is a certain number of works on control charts coupling attribute and variable inspections in the literature, research on monitoring the variability of univariate processes through variance, i.e., B-ATTRIVAR SS S^2, is still lacking. The novelty of this study lies in proposing an interface capable of receiving input data from a user thereof, to obtain control limits through simulations and generate a (B-ATTRIVAR SS S^2) chart so as to monitor the variability of a univariate process.

The control chart strategy proposed herein is similar, particularly to those from: Ref. [9], as both make use of attribute inspections to monitor the process variance, Ref. [10], given that the attribute and variable data were also used to monitor process variance, and [15], who proposed the most similar strategy but used it to monitor process mean using three attributes in the first monitoring stage (instead of two as in this study).

Even though in-control process parameters are usually unknown in practice and require estimates using historical data, this paper focuses on monitoring processes where these parameters are known [16].

In addition to advances in statistical process control strategies, an integration of computer interfaces is also crucial to increase the manufacturing system's efficiency. As discussed by [17], the convergence between digital models and physical industrial environments using data is of paramount relevance to smart manufacturing. This is due to the fact that it can provide interaction and information exchange between software, the computational interfaces, and the physical systems of manufacturing processes.

In this context, the application of computational interfaces offers new possibilities for monitoring and controlling industrial processes in real time. Although this work mainly focuses on introducing an interface developed using R and Shiny to monitor process variability, it is also worth mentioning the potential of integrating it with industrial digital systems, such as manufacturing execution systems (MES). Despite not being directly discussed in this study, the role of MES in facilitating quality monitoring and process optimization is also worth being mentioned. The authors of [18] explain that MES can provide a useful platform in quality monitoring, as it allows direct data acquisition and the monitoring of quality parameters' variability. Ref. [19], for instance, explores the possibilities of using control charts to analyze the data stored in MES and provide feedback to the systems aiming to optimize production parameters.

This manuscript is organized as follows: Section 2 describes the B-ATTRIVAR SS S^2 chart and draws a comparison with more usual charts; Section 3 explains how its application was conceived and the manner in which the results have been achieved; Section 4 presents its interface and operation, as well as a validation of its results; and Section 5 draws its conclusion and proposes suggestions for future works.

2. Chart B-ATTRIVAR SS S^2

After sample collection, all n items of the B-ATTRIVAR SS S^2 chart are inspected based on attribute, similarly to the np_{S^2} from [9]. These inspections make use of some device (such as a go/no-go gauge, for example) configured using the discriminant control limits LDL (lower discriminant limit) and UDL (upper discriminant limit). Each item outside these limits is classified as nonconforming. After classifying all items in the sample, Y_D is recorded as the number of rejected items. If $Y_D \geq CL_Y$ (attribute control limit), the process is defined as being out of control. Conversely, it is assessed whether $Y_D < W_Y$ (warning attribute control limit). If so, it is found that the process is in control. If otherwise, the variable inspection process is initiated using the same sample.

The stage of variable inspection is performed similarly to that in the classic S^2 chart described by [2,4], in which quality is measured based on all n items in the sample, and variance S^2 is calculated. If S^2 is outside the acceptance interval defined by LCL (variable lower control limit) and UCL (variable upper control limit), the process is defined as being in control. Otherwise, it is out of control. This entire process is depicted in Figure 1.

It is worth mentioning that it is common to use only the upper control limit to inspect variable S^2, as a process should have the least possible variability, as mentioned by [20], given that this strategy makes the chart more effective at detecting increases in process variance. In such a case, UCL is denoted as CL_{S^2}.

In this paper, both the attribute and variable inspection limits are optimized to achieve acceptable performance values determined by ARL_0 and ARL_1, or by α and β, considering that ARL refers to the average run length or the average number of samples collected until the chart signals for the first time, in addition to the fact that [4]:

$$ARL = \frac{1}{(Probability\ of\ sample\ rejection\ by\ the\ chart)} \quad (1)$$

$$ARL_0 = \frac{1}{\alpha} \quad (2)$$

$$ARL_1 = \frac{1}{(1-\beta)} \quad (3)$$

where α is the probability of type I error, β is the probability of type II error, the index "0" indicates a process in control, and index "1" indicates a process being out of control.

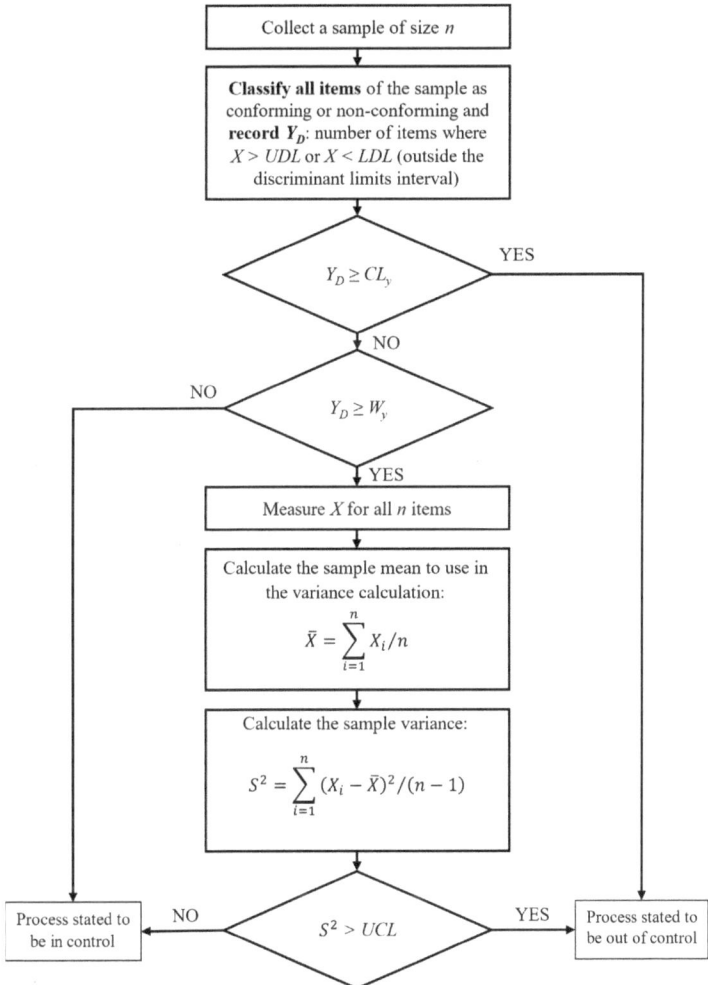

Figure 1. Flowchart of the B-ATTRIVAR SS S^2 Chart.

The performance of the B-ATTRIVAR SS S^2 chart (mixed inspection) was compared to that of S^2 (variable inspection) and np (attribute inspection) charts, as in Table 1, which shows simulated *ARL* values with sample sizes of 5 (n = 5) by varying the standard deviation of simulated samples through λ in each row. The results demonstrate a similar performance of the studied chart to that of the np chart. Nevertheless, it is still worth mentioning its advantages over the np charts, mainly on account of the fact that the quality characteristic measurements required in the stage of variable inspection of the B-ATTRIVAR SS S^2 are capable of providing valuable information to enhance the process analysis and make improvements. Although the performance of the ATTRIVAR proved inferior to that of the S^2 chart, it still offers notable advantage over it, i.e., its operational simplicity [14].

Table 1. Comparison of the performance of charts for monitoring S^2 with $n = 5$.

λ (Lambda)	S^2	ARL np	B ATTRIVAR SS S^2
1.0	367.28	371.71	370.71
1.1	107.93	118.87	120.12
1.2	42.79	50.26	51.54
1.3	21.21	26.72	26.31
1.4	12.32	15.61	15.48
1.5	8.10	10.19	10.22
1.6	5.72	7.18	7.33
1.7	4.33	5.44	5.51
1.8	3.52	4.37	4.34
1.9	2.92	3.54	3.56
2.0	2.51	3.00	3.04

3. Application Development

The application was developed using the RStudio development environment, which is free and offers various packages and functionalities available for installation using a computational programming based on the R language. According to [21], R is ranked among the 10 most popular programming languages used globally and has become a fundamental computational tool for research in various areas, such as statistics, mathematics, physics, chemistry, medicine, among others.

Additionally, the Shiny package was used for interface development, which, according to [21], was launched in 2012 and has continuously gained popularity in developing interactive websites using R language functionalities.

The average run length (ARL) was used for measuring the efficiency or performance of control charts. Ref. [22] considers it as the best-known and most widely used method to measure and analyze control chart performance.

3.1. Inputs and Outputs Definition

Regarding the development of a B-ATTRIVAR SS control chart application aimed to monitor the variability of univariate processes through variance, the code should be capable of generating control limits for the attribute (W_Y and CL_Y) and variable (LCL and UCL, or just CL_{S^2} if $LCL \leq 0$) inspections. Based on these four outputs, the application can effectively perform the primary function of a control chart: either accepting or rejecting samples to classify the process as being in control or out of control.

For such a purpose, the initial necessary inputs would be sample size (n), mean (μ_0), and standard deviation (σ_0) of the process, given that they are essential parameters for the program to perform normal sample simulations.

The user would have to provide the maximum desired probability of a type I error (α_{max}) and the maximum desired probability of a type II error (β_{max}) for a given variation (λ) in standard deviation to obtain the attribute and variable control limits. Thus, α_{max} would define the min ARL_0 and β_{max} for a given λ, which would define the max ARL_1. Then, it would be possible to determine the acceptance intervals, as ARL_0 and ARL_1 are directly related to the control limits.

To start the first stage of monitoring with attribute inspection, The user would have to determine the discriminant limits LDL and UDL, which were also defined as outputs. Thus, these values could be configured using a go/no-go gauge device, for instance. Afterwards, they could conduct inspections and input the number of nonconforming items in each sample into the application to proceed to the next stage.

Furthermore, the user would have to provide the maximum percentage of samples to be submitted to variable inspection ($\%S^2_{max}$) to define the discriminant limits (LDL and UDL).

3.2. Obtaining Control Limits

The process of obtaining control limits was expected to be performed through simulations and trial-and-error iterations. Its logical is that the program makes the first iteration using lower values for the control limits, and it comes to $\%S^2$, α or β in each iteration. Then, the program verifies whether these values are lower than the maximum values established by the user, and it changes the limits and proceeds to the next iteration if otherwise.

To enhance code organization, it was segmented into four sections, namely, A, B, C1, and C2. Each having a beginning and an end, and their own iterations able to calculate and record the results in the form of a matrix.

In section A, it explores the possible combinations of W_Y and CL_Y to derive the smallest discriminant limits (LDL and UDL) satisfying the $\%S^2{}_{max}$ condition:

$$\%S^2{}_{Simulated} = \frac{NV}{TN} \leq \%S^2{}_{max} \qquad (4)$$

where NV is the number of samples, which would be submitted to variable inspection, and TN is the total number of simulated samples.

For such a purpose, it simulates one million samples from a normal distribution based on user-defined parameters (n, μ, and σ) for in-control conditions, and calculates how many would undergo variable inspection, i.e., $W_Y \leq Y_D \leq CL_Y$. Then, it performs the test described in Equation (4). This entire process repeats until the condition is satisfied.

In section B, it accesses each combination of W_Y and CL_Y, but using the values of LDL and UDL for each, and proceeds to obtain the smallest variable control limits (LCL and UCL) meeting the requirement of α_{max}:

$$\frac{1}{ARL_0} \leq \alpha_{max} \qquad (5)$$

For such, it simulates samples under control and submits them to attribute inspections and to variable inspections whenever necessary, until it reaches ten thousand signals. Then, it records the number of simulated samples until each signal's emission, thus allowing it to calculate ARL_0 by computing the arithmetic mean of these ten thousand recorded numbers. Afterwards, it assesses the condition of Equation (5) and repeats this until it is satisfied by incrementing the upper limit and decrementing the lower limit during each iteration, as shown in the Equations (6) and (7). For each combination of W_Y, CL_Y, LDL, and UDL, it assigns the following values to limits by ever incrementing the absolute value of parameter L:

$$LCL = \left[\sigma^2 - L\sigma^2\right] \qquad (6)$$

$$UCL = \left[\sigma^2 + L\sigma^2\right] \qquad (7)$$

Within section C1, it already has recorded the various combinations of W_Y, CL_Y, LDL, UDL, LCL, and UCL, and it assesses whether each of them meets the β_{max} requirement set by the user:

$$1 - \frac{1}{ARL_1} \leq \beta_{max} \qquad (8)$$

For such, it simulates normal samples, albeit out of control, by altering only the standard deviation to $\sigma_1 = \lambda\sigma$ (where λ and σ are defined by the user). These samples undergo the entire B-ATTRIVAR SS S^2 chart flow using the parameters from each obtained combination. Consequently, ARL_1 is calculated for each combination (similarly to ARL_0) and it is tested whether Equation (8) is satisfied. This process is carried out only once for each parameter combination, and it records which combinations can meet this requirement.

In section C2, it accesses combinations meeting the β_{max} requirement and selects the best solution as the one with the lowest calculated β.

Definite results can be seen by the user and are used by the program to perform other steps and ensure the functioning of the control chart itself. The displayed parameters are: n, μ, σ, W_Y, CL_Y, LDL, UDL, $\%S^2$, LCL, UCL, α, λ, and β.

4. Results

Given the objective of developing an interface to enable the utilization of the B-ATTRIVAR SS S^2 chart, it is necessary to initially understand the expected usage dynamics through which the application was conceived.

At first, the application user is expected to input the initial parameters required for obtaining the control limits (as described earlier). Once the program finishes obtaining them, the user should be able to visualize a chart showing horizontal lines representing the control limits and should input the Y_D of their sample, which can be plotted on the chart. If Y_D is between W_Y and CL_Y, something users can verify on the chart, they should input the quality characteristic measurements for all items in the sample. Therefore, the program should calculate and plot sample variance on the chart, and the signal if it somewhat indicates that the process is out of control.

4.1. The Interface

The main layout of its interface was configured as depicted in Figure 2. In the area marked with the number one, there is a sidebar with fields where the user can input values or keep the predefined values in the program (shown in Figure 2). Below this sidebar, in the area marked with the number two, there is the RUN button which the user should click on to execute the code and obtain the results. Adjacent to this, in the area marked with the number three, there are the two tabs of the application, between which the user can switch by clicking on one of them. At the bottom, the area marked with the number four represents where the results of calculations and the chart itself are displayed in the RESULTS AND CHART tab; and the editable table to insert sample data in the INSERT DATA tab.

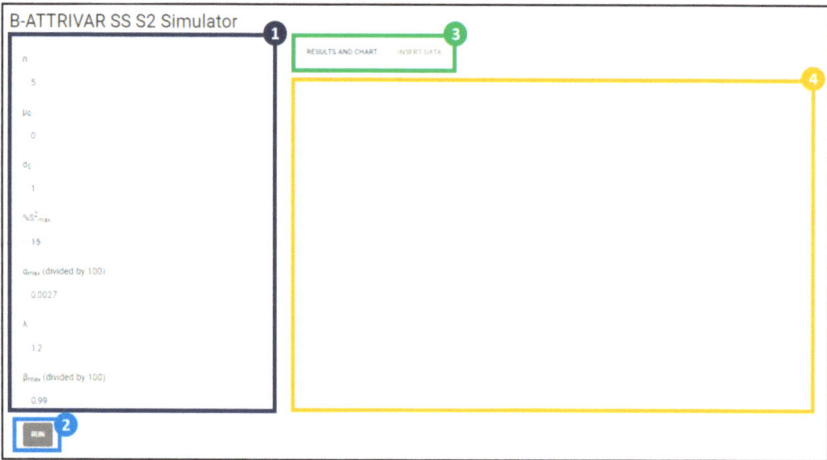

Figure 2. Main layout of the developed interface.

After pressing the RUN button, the end results and the chart are displayed in the RESULTS AND CHART tab, as shown in Figure 3.

Some parameters entered by the user (n, μ_0, σ_0 e λ) are shown below the tab names and above the graph, along with the results found for other parameters through simulations and calculations (W_Y, CL_Y, LDI, LDS, $\%S^2$, LCL, UCL, α, β).

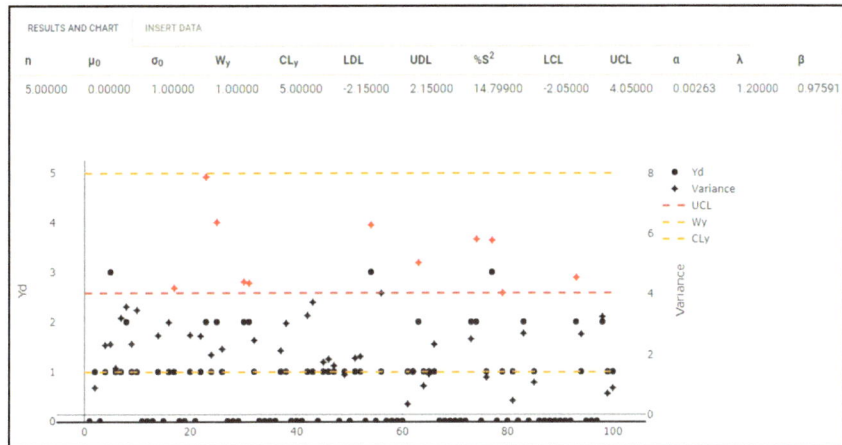

Figure 3. Results and chart displayed in the interface.

4.2. The Chart

Bearing a resemblance to the charts presented by [13–15], Figure 3 shows an x-axis representing the sample number, and two y-axes: one for Y_D on the left side and another for sample variance on the right side.

The chart displays the limits of W_Y and CL_Y on the Y_D axis, and UCL on the variance axis, all represented as dashed lines. The circular points represent the Y_D data series, while the differently shaped points represent the calculated sample variance data series. It is crucial to highlight that the points representing sample variance will be plotted only if $W_y \leq Y_D < CL_y$, due to the fact that samples satisfying $Y_D < W_y$ are accepted and those within $Y_D \geq CL_Y$ are rejected in the B-ATTRIVAR SS chart, and thus do not need to be submitted to variable inspection in both cases.

Points are standardly plotted in black. However, they are shown in red to represent signals (when samples are rejected for instance) to display if they occur in the attribute inspection (circular points) or variable inspection (non-circular points).

The chart is rather dynamic, as any changes in the editable table data lead to automatic adjustments in the plotted points on the chart. Additionally, users can press and hold the mouse button on either of the two abscissa axes to drag them upwards or downwards, thus moving both their labels and associated points. Furthermore, users can zoom in and out by pressing and holding the mouse button over any point in the plot area, then dragging it to form a rectangle defining the area to be zoomed.

4.3. The Editable Table

The data plotted on the chart are from the editable table illustrated in Figure 4 and located in the INSERT DATA tab. It contains some columns dependent on the user-inputted n value, although the first and last columns always represent Y_D and the calculated variance of each sample, respectively, regardless of the inputted n value. Other columns between the first and the last ones are intended for inputting quality characteristic measurements, and thus depend on the sample size (n = 5 in the case of Figure 4, and therefore there are 5 columns for measurements).

All the columns are editable, except for the last one. Although the user can attempt to change its value, the table automatically recalculates it, since the variance values cannot be arbitrary, but are rather calculated from the quality characteristic measurements.

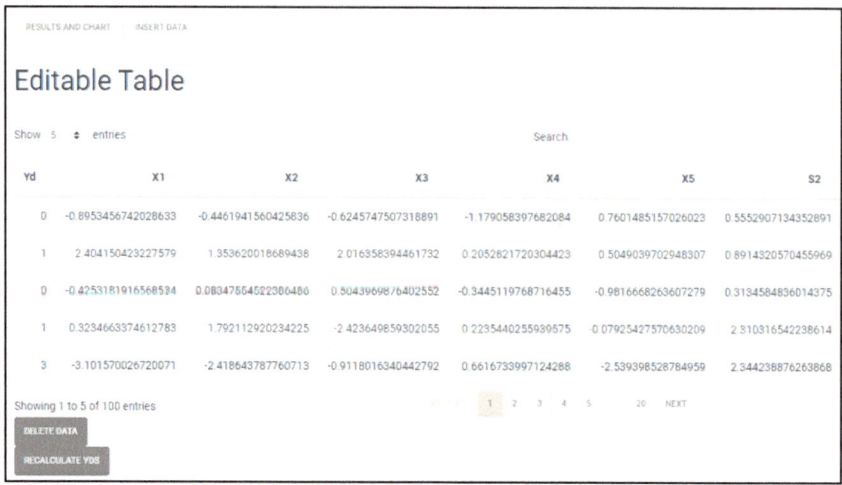

Figure 4. Editable table on the interface.

Before users start monitoring any process, the application offers a preview of its functionality. It generates data for 100 out-of-control samples from a normal distribution, then it submits them to inspections with the definite results of the control limits and plots them on the chart. After clicking on the RUN button at the sidebar, once the results are obtained, the application automatically displays data about the 100 samples in both the table and the chart.

The editable table standardly displays only five rows, but just below the Editable Table title, the number of rows can be changed by clicking on Show 5 entries and altering them to the desired number.

Below the table, there are the DELETE DATA and RECALCULATE Y_Ds buttons. All the values recorded in the table are deleted by pressing the first button, leaving all fields empty for new data input and, consequently, erasing all the plotted points on the chart. The second button recalculates all Y_Ds in the table's first column based on the values of the monitored quality measurements.

Naturally, as previously explained, according to the logic of monitoring a process through an ATTRIVAR chart, the user can start inspections via attribute without conducting any measurements, which is one of the main advantages of this strategy compared to variable control to avoid excessive measurements. These can often be expensive and/or excessively time-consuming; thus, it would be irrelevant to calculate Y_D through measurements.

Moreover, it would also be unreasonable if the user altered any measurement data and if Y_D remained the same, even though the number of nonconforming items might have changed. Furthermore, automatically calculating this column would be inappropriate as well, since it would not allow the user to input Y_D regardless of the measurements, which would contradict the inherent logic of the ATTRIVAR strategy.

Therefore, the Y_D fields are editable so that the user can input the number of nonconforming items for each sample. Additionally, a button is provided for the user to click upon at any time to recalculate all Y_Ds in the table based on the measurements.

4.4. Results Validation

Theoretical calculations of the parameters of this chart have not been identified. Therefore, a simpler code was developed to simulate the ARLs of the B-ATTRIVAR SS S^2 chart aiming to validate the application's results and ensure the consistency of simulations and control limit calculations. Control limits are set in it, and it calculates ARLs for different values of λ.

Hence, to validate the application results, the control limits generated by the application were utilized as input parameters for the code. Subsequently, the results obtained from both methods were compared in terms of $\%S^2$, ARL_0, and ARL_1. The reasons for selecting these parameters are as follows:

- Analyzing whether $\%S^2$ verifies if the chart submits the expected percentage of samples in the stage of variable inspection;
- Analyzing whether ARL_0 verifies if the chart commits to the type I error after the expected number of tested samples is calculated;
- And analyzing whether ARL_1 verifies if the chart detects a signal at the expected speed, or after the expected number of tested samples is calculated.

As shown in Table 2, several scenarios were tested, all being $\mu_0 = 0$ and $\sigma_0 = 1$, and the columns labeled as "reference" correspond to the values obtained through the simpler code.

Table 2. Results comparison and validation ($\mu_0 = 0$, $\sigma_0 = 1$).

n	W_Y	CL_Y	$\%S^2_{max}$	UDL	UCL	$\%S^2$	$\%S^2$ Reference	ARL_0	NMA_0 Reference	ΔARL_0	λ	ARL_1	ARL_1 Reference	ΔARL_1
5	1	3	15%	2.15	4.09	14.81%	14.81%	379.221	368.596	2.88%	1.2	41.9332	41.8994	0.08%
5	1	4	15%	2.15	4.07	14.82%	14.81%	385.416	383.675	0.45%	1.2	42.0345	43.2341	2.77%
5	1	5	15%	2.15	4.07	14.80%	14.80%	392.364	375.318	4.54%	1.2	42.8538	42.4327	0.99%
5	2	4	15%	1.47	4.50	14.74%	14.74%	377.595	362.952	4.03%	1.2	48.7047	49.3499	1.31%
5	2	5	15%	1.47	4.03	14.95%	14.93%	377.669	370.022	2.07%	1.2	43.0950	42.1248	2.30%
5	1	3	10%	2.31	4.06	9.99%	10.01%	374.161	373.848	0.08%	1.2	41.8840	42.1619	0.66%
5	1	4	10%	2.32	4.05	9.75%	9.73%	378.737	371.406	1.97%	1.2	42.7068	42.6622	0.10%
5	1	5	10%	2.32	4.06	9.74%	9.75%	375.552	378.126	0.68%	1.2	43.2554	42.3157	2.22%
5	2	4	10%	1.59	4.12	9.84%	9.84%	376.320	372.540	1.01%	1.2	44.0206	43.6339	0.89%
5	2	5	10%	1.59	4.01	9.96%	9.93%	378.703	367.040	3.18%	1.2	44.0304	43.0009	2.39%
6	1	3	10%	2.38	3.63	9.94%	9.94%	388.136	367.356	5.66%	1.5	6.4295	6.4782	0.75%
6	1	4	10%	2.38	3.63	9.96%	9.93%	386.227	367.750	5.02%	1.5	6.5638	6.5563	0.11%
6	1	5	10%	2.38	3.64	9.97%	9.95%	394.030	376.513	4.65%	1.5	6.6395	6.6466	0.11%
6	1	6	10%	2.38	3.64	9.96%	9.94%	387.306	379.715	2.00%	1.5	6.5732	6.6439	1.06%
6	2	4	10%	1.68	3.74	9.94%	9.98%	377.044	371.606	1.46%	1.5	6.8422	6.7470	1.41%
6	2	5	10%	1.69	3.62	9.70%	9.72%	391.299	377.701	3.60%	1.5	6.8597	7.0055	2.08%
6	2	6	10%	1.69	3.61	9.72%	9.70%	388.899	376.739	3.23%	1.5	6.9539	6.8811	1.06%
6	3	5	10%	1.28	3.89	9.77%	9.79%	383.502	368.495	4.07%	1.5	8.0894	8.1119	0.28%
6	3	6	10%	1.28	3.54	9.94%	9.93%	380.937	365.824	4.13%	1.5	7.1517	7.0933	0.82%

The first five rows on the table represent the execution of simulations with default values set on the application interface, as in Figure 2. In the next five rows, the application was executed only by changing the $\%S^2_{max}$ parameter from 15% to 10%. The next nine rows contained changes not only in $\%S^2_{max}$ but also in n and λ. This approach enables the analysis of whether alterations in one or more parameters affect the validity of its results.

Its results demonstrate a strong consistency with those obtained through the reference code, i.e., $\%S^2$, ARL_0, and ARL_1 show notably similar values. For instance, the largest percentage differences observed in the ΔARL_0 and ΔARL_1 columns were 5.66% and 2.77%, respectively.

4.5. Example

To exemplify how the proposed application functions, the code was run using the default values for inputs (the same values set in the interface fields shown in Figure 3). After having calculated control limits as described in Section 3.2, the application is ready to be used for process monitoring.

In this example, the simulations converged to the following values for control limits: $W_Y = 1$; $CL_Y = 3$; and $UCL = 4.07$.

Although the application was designed with the purpose of allowing the user to start monitoring via the attribute inspections, the following example is a simulation. Therefore, as shown in Table 3, 25 random (out of control) samples of measurements were generated and Y_Ds were calculated from them. For samples where Y_D is between W_Y and CL_Y limits, the variances were calculated (S^2).

Table 3. Example data.

	X_1	X_2	X_3	X_4	X_5	Y_D	S^2
1	−0.068	−1.419	0.512	1.599	−1.242	0	-
2	−2.434	0.416	−0.550	−0.157	2.045	1	2.628
3	−0.595	−2.908	−2.326	−0.192	−0.627	2	1.453
4	0.964	2.562	−0.595	−0.552	0.193	1	1.716
5	−1.033	−0.648	−0.040	−0.714	1.571	0	-
6	−0.604	0.862	1.348	0.560	1.623	0	-
7	0.362	0.478	2.527	2.959	1.228	2	1.399
8	0.250	−3.543	−1.195	0.386	−0.528	1	2.546
9	−0.399	0.227	−0.220	2.194	1.783	1	1.420
10	1.010	−0.340	0.551	−0.488	1.335	0	-
11	1.177	0.091	1.738	−1.572	0.261	0	-
12	−2.305	0.427	−0.083	0.396	−0.686	1	1.279
13	−1.511	2.279	−1.349	−0.571	−0.322	1	2.323
14	−1.945	−0.888	1.219	1.238	1.557	0	-
15	−2.502	−0.879	−1.618	−0.047	1.013	1	1.857
16	0.327	0.213	0.075	−0.544	−2.475	1	1.356
17	1.332	−1.233	−1.886	−2.049	0.597	0	-
18	0.577	−0.307	0.463	0.723	−0.726	0	-
19	0.554	−0.112	2.413	0.950	0.743	1	0.865
20	−0.954	2.335	−1.239	−0.935	−0.466	1	2.168
21	−2.057	−1.459	−1.045	0.483	0.569	0	-
22	−0.364	−1.582	0.092	−0.601	0.154	0	-
23	−3.362	1.516	0.590	−2.660	0.043	2	4.506
24	−1.749	−1.797	0.928	−0.830	−0.913	0	-
25	−2.969	−1.621	−2.386	−1.518	0.492	2	1.719

Figure 5 shows how the interface plots data from Table 3. As aforementioned, the Y_Ds of all samples are plotted as circular points, and S^2 are plotted as non-circular points whenever necessary.

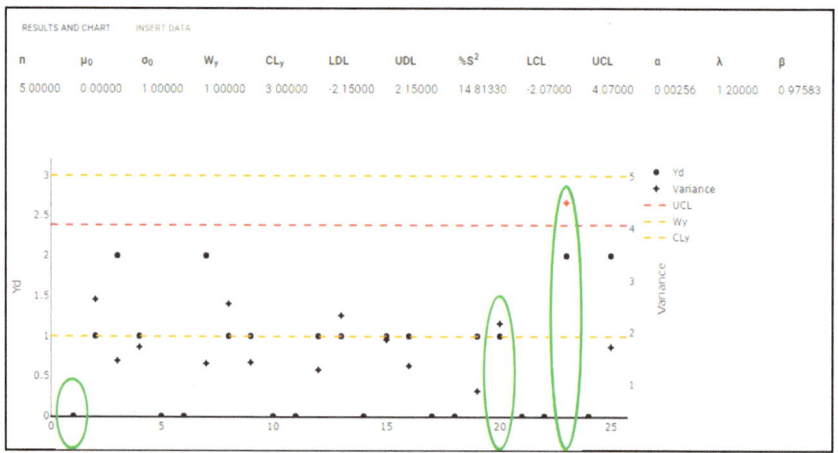

Figure 5. Example chart.

The first sample highlighted in the chart is a case where $Y_D \leq W_Y$ and S^2 does not need to be calculated thereof (as shown in Table 3), thus not being plotted in the chart (as in Figure 5).

The twentieth sample, also highlighted in the chart, is a case where $CL_Y < Y_D \leq W_Y$. Thereby, S^2 is calculated and plotted, since $S^2 \leq UCL$, and the variance is plotted in black in this example.

Similarly, the twenty-third sample, also circled in the chart, is a case where Y_D is also within the range of attribute control limits, and the variance is calculated and plotted. However, $S^2 > UCL$ and the chart signals plotting the variance are in red.

Likewise, in cases where $Y_D > CL_Y$, the chart signals that the process is out of control, and Y_D is plotted in red.

5. Conclusions

In this study, an interface was developed to generate and display control limits for the B-ATTRIVAR SS S^2 chart, enabling the real-time monitoring of process variance. It was achieved through inputting process data and user-defined requirements, and the program uses these data to compute the control limits and render a chart showing them and sample data. Once users have their process data, they can input it and use the control chart to monitor process variability. Although the application has not been tested in actual processes, its results have been validated in this study through comparisons with reference values, thus revealing low percentage deviations.

As an opportunity for improvement and further research, it is imperative to explore methods to reduce its execution time. Due to multiple iterations aimed at generating more precise results, the program might last a significantly long execution time depending on the device on which it is run. One potential approach to face this challenge is leveraging artificial intelligence tailored for optimizing code performance.

Furthermore, investigating the feasibility of adapting the application to integrate it with business and industrial systems, such as manufacturing execution systems (MES), could enhance its versatility and potential for automation across various industrial applications, including real-time production monitoring and control.

Moreover, future research should analyze the influence of variations in input parameters on results, in addition to conducting extensive studies and interface development aimed to consider the application of the proposed control strategy using estimated parameters, thereby extending its applicability. Furthermore, exploring methods for theoretically and mathematically deriving the $ARLs$ and control limits of the proposed strategy would be of significant interest.

Author Contributions: Conceptualization, J.P.C.V. and M.A.G.M.; methodology, A.d.S.M. and T.S.A.; software, J.P.C.V. and A.d.S.M.; validation, M.A.G.M. and T.S.A.; formal analysis, J.P.C.V., M.A.G.M., A.d.S.M. and T.S.A.; investigation, J.P.C.V. and M.A.G.M.; resources, A.d.S.M. and T.S.A.; data curation, J.P.C.V., M.A.G.M., A.d.S.M. and T.S.A.; writing—original draft preparation, J.P.C.V., M.A.G.M., A.d.S.M. and T.S.A.; writing—review and editing, J.P.C.V., M.A.G.M., A.d.S.M. and T.S.A.; visualization, J.P.C.V., M.A.G.M., A.d.S.M. and T.S.A.; supervision, M.A.G.M.; project administration, M.A.G.M.; funding acquisition, M.A.G.M. All authors have read and agreed to the published version of the manuscript.

Funding: This research received no external funding, and the APC was founded by São Paulo State University under process EDITAL PROPG 16/2024.

Data Availability Statement: No new data were created or analyzed in this study. Data sharing is not applicable to this article.

Acknowledgments: Thanks to PIBIC/CNPq-EDITAL 2020 and CNPq process 307945/2019-7.

Conflicts of Interest: The authors declare no conflicts of interest.

References

1. Shewhart, W.A. *Economic Control of Quality of Manufactured Product*, 1st ed.; D. Van Nostrand Company: Nova York, NY, USA, 1931.
2. Montgomery, D.C. *Introduction to Statistical Quality Control*, 6th ed.; John Wiley & Sons: Hoboken, NJ, USA, 2009.
3. Ali, S.; Abbas, Z.; Nazir, H.Z.; Riaz, M.; Zhang, X.; Li, Y. On developing sensitive nonparametric mixed control charts with application to manufacturing industry. *Qual. Reliab. Eng. Int.* **2021**, *37*, 2699–2723. [CrossRef]
4. Aslam, M.; Saghir, A.; Ahmad, L. *Introduction to Statistical Process Control*, 1st ed.; John Wiley & Sons: Hoboken, NJ, USA, 2020.
5. Ho, L.L.; Aparisi, F. Attrivar: Optimized control charts to monitor process mean with lower operational cost. *Int. J. Prod. Econ.* **2016**, *182*, 472–483. [CrossRef]

6. Aparisi, F.; Ho, L.L. M-ATTRIVAR: An attribute-variable chart to monitor multivariate process means. *Qual. Reliab. Eng. Int.* **2018**, *34*, 214–228. [CrossRef]
7. Aslam, M.; Azam, M.; Khan, N.; Jun, C.H. A mixed control chart to monitor the process. *Int. J. Prod. Res.* **2015**, *53*, 4684–4693. [CrossRef]
8. Bezerra, E.L.; Ho, L.L.; Quinino, R.d.C. GS2: An optimized attribute control chart to monitor process variability. *Int. J. Prod. Econ.* **2018**, *195*, 287–295. [CrossRef]
9. Ho, L.L.; Quinino, R.C. An attribute control chart for monitoring the variability of a process. *Int. J. Prod. Econ.* **2013**, *145*, 263–267.
10. Ho, L.L.; Quinino, R.d.C. Combining attribute and variable data to monitor process variability: MIX S 2 control chart. *Int. J. Adv. Manuf. Technol.* **2016**, *87*, 3389–3396. [CrossRef]
11. Wu, Z.; Khoo, M.B.C.; Shu, L.; Jiang, W. An np control chart for monitoring the mean of a variable based on an attribute inspection. *Int. J. Prod. Econ.* **2009**, *121*, 141–147. [CrossRef]
12. Sampaio, E.S.; Ho, L.L.; de Medeiros, P.G. A combined $np_x - \overline{X}$ control chart to monitor the process mean in a two-stage sampling. *Qual. Reliab. Eng. Int.* **2014**, *30*, 1003–1013. [CrossRef]
13. Leoni, R.C.; Costa, A.F.B. The performance of the truncated mixed control chart. *Commun. Stat.-Theory Methods* **2019**, *48*, 4294–4301. [CrossRef]
14. Costa, A.F.B.; Neto, A.F. Monitoring the process mean with an ATTRIVAR chart. *Commun. Stat.-Theory Methods* **2022**, *51*, 4903–4920. [CrossRef]
15. Simões, F.D.; Costa, A.F.B.; Machado, M.A.G. The Trinomial ATTRIVAR control chart. *Int. J. Prod. Econ.* **2020**, *224*, 1–8. [CrossRef]
16. Faraz, A.; Heuchenne, C.; Saniga, E. An exact method for designing Shewhart and S2 control charts to guarantee in-control performance. *Int. J. Prod. Res.* **2018**, *56*, 2570–2584. [CrossRef]
17. Xia, K.; Sacco, C.; Kirkpatrick, M.; Saidy, C.; Nguyen, L.; Kircaliali, A.; Harik, R. A digital twin to train deep reinforcement learning agent for smart manufacturing plants: Environment, interfaces and intelligence. *J. Manuf. Syst.* **2021**, *58*, 210–230. [CrossRef]
18. Gendre, Y.; Waridel, G.; Guyon, M.; Demuth, J.-F.; Guelpa, H.; Humbert, T. Manufacturing execution systems: Examples of performance indicator and operational robustness tools. *Chimia* **2016**, *70*, 616–620. [CrossRef] [PubMed]
19. Li, B.; Chen, R.-S.; Liu, C.-Y. Using intelligent technology and real-time feedback algorithm to improve manufacturing process in IoT semiconductor industry. *J. Supercomput.* **2021**, *77*, 4639–4658. [CrossRef]
20. Aparisi, F.; Mosquera, J.; Epprechet, E.K. Simultaneously guaranteeing the in-control and out-of-control performances of the S2 control chart with estimated variance. *Qual. Reliab. Eng. Int.* **2018**, *34*, 1110–1126. [CrossRef]
21. Giorgi, F.M.; Ceraolo, C.; Mercatelli, D. The R Language: An Engine for Bioinformatics and Data Science. *Life* **2022**, *12*, 648–673. [CrossRef] [PubMed]
22. Chakraborti, S.; Graham, M.A. *Nonparametric Statistical Process Control*, 1st ed.; John Wiley & Sons: Hoboken, NJ, USA, 2019.

Disclaimer/Publisher's Note: The statements, opinions and data contained in all publications are solely those of the individual author(s) and contributor(s) and not of MDPI and/or the editor(s). MDPI and/or the editor(s) disclaim responsibility for any injury to people or property resulting from any ideas, methods, instructions or products referred to in the content.

Article

Data-Driven Load Frequency Control for Multi-Area Power System Based on Switching Method under Cyber Attacks

Guangqiang Tian [1,*] and Fuzhong Wang [2]

1. School of Intelligent Engineering, Huanghe Jiaotong University, Jiaozuo 454950, China
2. School of Electrical Engineering and Automation, Henan Polytechnic University, Jiaozuo 454000, China; wangfzh@hpu.edu.cn
* Correspondence: tectian@zjtu.edu.cn

Abstract: This paper introduces an innovative method for load frequency control (LFC) in multi-area interconnected power systems vulnerable to denial-of-service (DoS) attacks. The system is modeled as a switching system with two subsystems, and an adaptive control algorithm is developed. Initially, a dynamic linear data model is used to model each subsystem. Next, a model-free adaptive control strategy is introduced to maintain frequency stability in the multi-area interconnected power system, even during DoS attacks. A rigorous stability analysis of the power system is performed, and the effectiveness of the proposed approach is demonstrated by applying it to a three-area interconnected power system.

Keywords: load frequency control; switching system; event-triggered; model-free adaptive control

Citation: Tian, G.; Wang, F. Data-Driven Load Frequency Control for Multi-Area Power System Based on Switching Method under Cyber Attacks. *Algorithms* **2024**, *17*, 233. https://doi.org/10.3390/a17060233

Academic Editors: Sheng Du, Zixin Huang, Li Jin and Xiongbo Wan

Received: 28 April 2024
Revised: 23 May 2024
Accepted: 24 May 2024
Published: 27 May 2024

Copyright: © 2024 by the authors. Licensee MDPI, Basel, Switzerland. This article is an open access article distributed under the terms and conditions of the Creative Commons Attribution (CC BY) license (https://creativecommons.org/licenses/by/4.0/).

1. Introduction

The power system, a critical component of national infrastructure, provides stable and reliable electrical energy services to diverse socio-economic sectors. It plays a crucial role in driving modernization and serves as a safeguard for it. The system's stability, quality, and safety significantly impact national energy security, living standards, and sustainable development. Operational disruptions due to unexpected events and uncertainties can cause frequency deviations from the nominal value in the system. Prolonged frequency deviations not only affect user experience and damage system equipment but can also trigger grid collapse, leading to widespread power outages and significant societal losses. Extensive research has focused on improving the reliable and stable operation of power systems through the study of LFC methods. This research aims to identify more effective frequency control strategies to improve the economic and safety aspects of power systems [1].

Recently, the academic community has proposed diverse control strategies for LFC in multi-area power systems, employing various theoretical frameworks. These strategies encompass Model Predictive Control [2,3], Robust Control [4,5], Fuzzy Logic Control [6–8], Sliding Mode Control [9,10], Linear Matrix Inequality (LMI) Control [11,12], Reinforcement Learning [13,14], and other methods. Reference [2] integrates dynamic event-triggered mechanisms and a hybrid H2 performance index to design a robust Model Predictive Control (MPC) strategy for LFC in power systems, capable of effectively handling network attacks and disturbances. Reference [3] introduces a novel dynamic event-based model predictive control strategy designed to enhance the robustness and stability of power system load frequency control in the presence of cyber attacks. Reference [4] designs a robust Proportional-Integral (PI)-type LFC scheme for power systems, taking into account sampling periods and transmission delays in communication networks. Simultaneously, this scheme introduces an Exponential Decay Rate (EDR) as a design parameter. Adjusting the value of EDR can achieve robust performance evaluation regarding parameter uncertainty, load fluctuation, and communication networks. Reference [5] presents a robust LFC strategy for power systems that effectively accounts for transmission delays and varying sampling periods, ensuring improved system stability and performance. Reference [7] presents a sampled memory-event-triggered fuzzy load frequency control method for wind power systems. This approach is specifically designed to address outliers and transmission delays, therefore improving system reliability and performance. Reference [10] introduces a novel sliding model LFC strategy for renewable power systems, addressing time-delay uncertainty, parameter uncertainty, and load disturbances. Subsequently, the sliding mode switching surface and controller are designed based on the standard form. Using the isokinetic convergence law, the system state is directed to reach the switching surface within a finite timeframe, ensuring stable sliding motion on this surface. Reference [11] contributes to power system stability by designing a robust load frequency control (LFC) system capable of coping with inherent time delays by utilizing Linear Matrix Inequalities (LMI). It introduces a novel delay margin estimation technique to ascertain the maximum permissible delay for maintaining system stability, which enhances the control system's robustness compared to traditional methods. Using brain-inspired deep meta-reinforcement learning, reference [13] enhances multi-area grids' load frequency control (LFC). This approach develops a fault-tolerant LFC system that adapts to disturbances and faults, showing superior adaptability and robustness compared to traditional methods.

Multi-area interconnected power systems depend on power communication networks for exchanging information and transmitting control commands across regions. Although power communication networks offer advantages like low cost, they also pose new challenges to modern control systems [15]. Reference [16] introduced an advanced LFC strategy for power systems strategically designed to withstand specific categories of DoS attacks. The strategy employs a time-varying Lyapunov function methodology that adapts to the attack parameters' characteristics, effectively ensuring system stability. Reference [17] explores the application of adaptive dynamic programming-based auxiliary control to a particular class of discrete-time networked systems. Reference [18] explores resilient load frequency control of power systems, addressing random time delays and time-delay attacks. The proposed approach allows practical adjustments for real power systems, balancing accuracy and computational efficiency while considering communication delays. Reference [19] explores the delay-dependent stability of load frequency control under conditions of adjustable computation accuracy and complexity. The researchers propose a novel tuning scheme with adjustable conservatism and computational complexity. Reference [20] focuses on event-triggered load frequency control for power systems, specifically considering limited communication bandwidth. The approach aligns with control performance standards, ensuring stability and efficiency in the presence of communication constraints. The LFC scheme, based on the theory of switched systems in [21], effectively mitigates the DoS attacks' effects in open communication networks. It calculates the maximum duration and frequency of potential attacks the system can endure and devises a load frequency control strategy for mitigating denial-of-service attacks. This strategy utilizes a dual-loop communication channel and PI controller.

Constructing an accurate mathematical model for power systems remains challenging due to their highly nonlinear and uncertain dynamic characteristics. Therefore, designing model-independent load frequency controllers is crucial. Model-free adaptive control, a data-driven algorithm, directly designs and analyzes controllers using input-output data from the controlled system. This approach enables parameter adaptation and structural adjustments for unknown nonlinear control systems and has found applications in various fields [22,23]. Reference [24] introduced a model-free adaptive quasi-sliding mode control algorithm grounded in a data-driven approach. This algorithm effectively handles nonuniformly sampled nonlinear systems, mitigates the impact of external disturbances, and enhances the system's robustness and stability. Additionally, the LFC scheme was developed for power systems in [25], using an event-triggered and data-driven approach. However, to our knowledge, there have been limited discussions on MFAC methods for power systems based on switching systems. In this study, we investigate the model-free adaptive LFC method according to switching systems for multi-area power systems under denial-of-service attacks. We conceptualize the multi-area power system under DoS attacks as a switching system composed of two subsystems. We design a switching model-free adaptive controller (SSMFAC) based on this system and use the Lyapunov theory to demonstrate system stability. Finally, we validate the effectiveness of this approach using a three-area interconnected power system. The main contributions of this paper are summarized as follows:

(1) In this paper, a data-driven load frequency control algorithm based on the switching method is proposed for a multi-area interconnected power system under DoS attack. A switching system model with two subsystems is established to represent the power system under a DoS attack with multi-area interconnection. On this basis, an MFAC algorithm for the switching system is designed.

(2) In this paper, an event-triggered MFAC is developed for the LFC, and the proposed design alleviates the communication and computation burden of the system compared to existing model-free adaptive control (MFAC) methods in the reference [22]. In addition, existing MFAC system stability analyses use the shrinkage mapping technique tool. However, in this paper, stability analysis is given using the Lyapunov theory approach.

2. Problfm Formulation

2.1. Power System Model

Interconnected power systems comprise multiple regions interconnected via tie lines. Frequency variations in one region can affect neighboring regions through propagation. To keep frequency and tie-line power deviations within specified limits, we term the overall output signal of each control system the Area Control Error (ACE):

$$\text{ACE}_i = \beta_i \Delta f_i + \Delta P_{tie-i} \tag{1}$$

where β_i represents the frequency deviation factor, $\beta_i = 1/R_i + D_i$, and D_i denote the generator damping coefficients, and R_i corresponds to the bias coefficient. The linear model representing interconnected power systems was introduced in reference [14]. The dynamic behavior of this model is described by the following equations:

$$\begin{cases} \Delta \dot{f}_i(t) = \frac{1}{M_i}(\Delta P_{mi}(t) - \Delta P_{di}(t) - \Delta P_{tie-i}(t) - D_i \Delta f_i(t)) \\ \Delta \dot{P}_{mi}(t) = \frac{1}{T_{chi}}(\Delta P_{vi}(t) - \Delta P_{mi}(t)) \\ \Delta \dot{P}_{gi}(t) = \frac{1}{T_{gi}}\left(\Delta P_{ci}(t) - \frac{1}{R_i}\Delta f_i(t) - \Delta P_{vi}(t)\right) \\ \Delta \dot{P}_{tie}(t) = 2\pi \sum_{j=1, j \neq i}^{n} T_{ij}(\Delta f_i(t) - \Delta f_j(t)) \end{cases} \tag{2}$$

The relevant parameters and associated signals in the equation are defined as shown in Table 1.

Defining $x_i(t) = \begin{bmatrix} \Delta f_i & \Delta P_{mi} & \Delta P_{gi} & \Delta E_i & \Delta P_{tie-i} \end{bmatrix}^T$, $y_i(t) = ACE_i(t)$, and $u_i(t) = \Delta P_{ci}(t)$ as system inputs, and $\vartheta_i^T(t) = \begin{bmatrix} \Delta P_{di}(t) \sum_{j=1, j \neq i}^{N} T_{ij} \Delta f_j(t) \end{bmatrix}$ as the disturbance vector, the dynamic model (1) can be transformed into the following state-space equation:

$$\begin{cases} \dot{x}(t) = Ax(t) + Bu(t) + F\vartheta(t) \\ y(t) = Cx(t) \end{cases} \tag{3}$$

where

$$x(t) = \begin{bmatrix} x_1(t) & x_2(t) & \dots & x_N(t) \end{bmatrix}^T,$$
$$y(t) = \begin{bmatrix} y_1(t) & y_2(t) & \dots & y_N(t) \end{bmatrix}^T,$$
$$u(t) = \begin{bmatrix} u_1(t) & u_2(t) & \dots & u_N(t) \end{bmatrix}^T,$$
$$\Delta P_d(t) = \begin{bmatrix} \Delta P_{d1}(t) & \Delta P_{d2}(t) & \dots & \Delta P_{dN}(t) \end{bmatrix}^T,$$

$$A = \begin{bmatrix} A_{11} & A_{12} & \cdots & A_{1N} \\ A_{21} & A_{22} & \cdots & A_{2N} \\ \vdots & \vdots & \vdots & \vdots \\ A_{N1} & A_{N2} & \cdots & A_{NN} \end{bmatrix},$$

$$B = \text{diag}\begin{bmatrix} B_1 & B_2 & \cdots & B_N \end{bmatrix},$$

$$C = \text{diag}\begin{bmatrix} C_1 & C_2 & \cdots & C_N \end{bmatrix}$$

$$F = \text{diag}\begin{bmatrix} F_1 & F_2 & \cdots & F_N \end{bmatrix}.$$

The state and matrix representation of the region are as follows:

$$A_{ii} = \begin{bmatrix} -\frac{D_i}{M_i} & \frac{1}{M_i} & 0 & 0 & \frac{-1}{M_i} \\ 0 & \frac{-1}{T_{chi}} & \frac{1}{T_{chi}} & 0 & 0 \\ \frac{-1}{RT_{gi}} & 0 & \frac{-1}{T_{gi}} & 0 & 0 \\ \beta_i & 0 & 0 & 0 & 1 \\ 2\pi \sum_{j=1, j \neq i}^{n} T_{ij} & 0 & 0 & 0 & 0 \end{bmatrix}, A_{ij} = \begin{bmatrix} 0 & 0 & 0 & 0 & 0 \\ 0 & 0 & 0 & 0 & 0 \\ 0 & 0 & 0 & 0 & 0 \\ 0 & 0 & 0 & 0 & 0 \\ -2\pi T_{ij} & 0 & 0 & 0 & 0 \end{bmatrix}$$

$$B_i = \begin{bmatrix} 0 & 0 & \frac{1}{T_{gi}} & 0 & 0 \end{bmatrix}^T, C_i = \begin{bmatrix} 0 & 0 & 0 & 0 & 1 \\ \beta_i & 1 & 0 & 0 & 0 \end{bmatrix} F_i = \begin{bmatrix} \frac{-1}{M_i} & 0 & 0 & 0 & 0 \end{bmatrix}^T,$$

To accurately represent the operational behavior of power systems, this research employs a discretization process on the continuous state-space equation. Given a specific sampling period T, the discrete representation of the power system model is articulated as follows:

$$\begin{cases} x(k+1) = Gx(k) + Hu(k) + W\vartheta(k) \\ y(k) = Cx(k) \end{cases} \quad (4)$$

in the equation, the variable k is formally defined as the discrete-time point used for sampling within the system, and $G = e^{AT}, H = \int_0^T e^{At} B dt, W = \int_0^T e^{At} F dt$, represents unknown matrices.

Table 1. Definition of related signals in region i.

Symbolic	Meaning
Δf_i	Frequency deviation (Hz)
ΔP_{mi}	The amount of mechanical power variation in the generator (pu)
ΔP_{gi}	The governor increases the power (pu)
ΔP_{tie-i}	The governor increases the power (pu)
T_{gi}	Governor time constant (s)
T_{ij}	Synchronous coefficient of tie line (pu/Hz)
T_{ti}	Prime mover time constant (s)
H_i	Equivalent inertia coefficient (pu/s)
ΔP_{Li}	Load disturbance (pu)
D_i	Equivalent damping coefficient (pu/Hz)
R_i	Equivalent damping coefficient (Hz/pu)
β_i	Frequency deviation factor (pu/Hz)
ΔP_{ci}	Control input (pu)

2.2. Modeling of LFC System under DoS Attacks

DoS attacks are common network attacks targeting power systems. These attacks disrupt communication links within the grid, severing information exchange among internal components and obstructing the transmission of sensor measurement data and control commands over network channels. Significantly, DoS attacks do not require prior or extensive familiarity with the physical power system or grid topology. These attacks can be periodic or intermittent. Consequently, DoS attacks are regarded as low-cost, high-impact attack strategies that real-world adversaries can exploit to compromise critical data transmitted across communication networks.

Subsequently, we model DoS attacks using random variables following the Bernoulli distribution:
$$\begin{cases} \Pr\{\alpha(k)=2\} = \mathbb{E}\{\alpha(k)\} = \alpha \\ \Pr\{\alpha(k)=1\} = 1 - \mathbb{E}\{\alpha(k)\} = 1 - \alpha \end{cases} \quad (5)$$

here, we use the Bernoulli distribution to model the distribution of random variables associated with DoS attacks where $\alpha \in (0,1)$, when $\alpha(k) = 2$, indicates that DoS attacks have occurred.

In this context, an on-off signal is introduced as a means to depict two distinct attack scenarios.
$$\alpha(k) = \begin{cases} 1 & u(k) = u(k) \\ 2 & u(k) = u(k-1) \end{cases}$$

In the context of DoS attacks, the hybrid power system in each region can be represented by i switching system $\wp_{\alpha(k)}(\alpha(k) = 1, 2)$:
$$\begin{cases} \bar{x}(k) = \bar{A}\bar{x}(k) + \bar{B}\bar{u}_{\alpha(k)}(k) + \bar{F}\vartheta(k) \\ y(k) = \bar{C}\bar{x}(k) \end{cases} \quad (6)$$

where $\bar{u}_1(k) = u(k), \bar{u}_2(k) = u(k-1), \bar{A} = G, \bar{B} = H, \bar{F} = W$.

Each subsystem can be represented by the following model:
$$\begin{cases} \bar{x}_{\alpha(k)}(k+1) = \bar{A}\bar{x}_{\alpha(k)}(k) + \bar{B}\bar{u}_{\alpha(k)}(k) + \bar{F}\vartheta(k) \\ y_{\alpha(k)}(k) = \bar{C}\bar{x}_{\alpha(k)}(k) \end{cases} \quad (7)$$

2.3. Dynamic Linearization Scheme

From a holistic perspective, considering the impact of governor dead zones and physical limitations, the power system can be characterized as a profoundly intricate nonlinear system. The LFC subsystem model (7) can be redefined as a comprehensive nonlinear function:
$$y(k+1) = f_{\alpha(k)}(y(k), u(k)) \quad (8)$$

In the equation, $f_{\alpha(k)}(\cdot)$ denotes an unknown nonlinear function. Before linearizing the nonlinear power system, we establish the following two assumptions.

Assumption 1. *The partial derivative of $f_{\alpha(k)}(\cdot)$ with respect to the variable $u(k)$ is continuous at any given sampling instant k.*

Assumption 2. *The nonlinear system (8) adheres to the generalized Lipschitz condition, which implies that for all instances of $k > 0$ and $\Delta u(k) \neq 0$, the following condition is met:*
$$|\Delta y(k+1)| \leq b|\Delta u(k)| \quad (9)$$

where $\Delta y(k+1) = y(k+1) - y(k), \Delta u(k) = u(k) - u(k-1), b > 0$ is a constant.

Remark 1. *From a practical standpoint, the two assumptions above on the power system (3) are both reasonable and fulfilled. Assumption 1 is a common restriction for a general nonlinear system and the continuity of $f_{\alpha(k)}(\cdot)$ can be inferred from Equation (3). Assumption 2 restricts the maximum pace at which the system output can vary. If the change in ΔP_{ci} is limited, the change in output energy ACE_i generated by the power system is also limited, from an energy utilization standpoint.*

Theorem 1. *For subsystems (7) meeting Assumptions 1 and 2, under the condition $|\Delta u(k)| \neq 0$, there exists a time-varying model called the parameter pseudo-partial derivative (PPD). This* parameter ensures that the nonlinear power subsystem model is equivalent to the following compact form dynamic linearization (CFDL) data equations:

$$\Delta y(k+1) = \phi_{\alpha(k)}(k)\Delta u(k) \tag{10}$$

The parameter $\phi_{\alpha(k)}(k)$ is defined as time-varying and remains bounded at every instant.

3. Controller Design

Consider the following input performance index:

$$J(u(k)) = |y_d(k+1) - y(k+1)|^2 + \lambda_{\alpha(k)}|u(k) - u(k-1)|^2 \tag{11}$$

where $\lambda_{\alpha(k)} > 0$ represents the weight factor, and $y_d(k+1)$ correlates with the targeted or intended system output.

Substituting Equation (10) into the performance index (11), set the derivative of (11) with respect to $u(k)$ be zero:

$$u(k) = u(k-1) + \frac{\rho_{\alpha(k)}\phi_{\alpha(k)}(k)}{\lambda_{\alpha(k)} + |\phi_{\alpha(k)}(k)|^2}(y_d(k+1) - y(k)) \tag{12}$$

in this context, the symbol $\rho_{\alpha(k)}$ shows the factor of step size, $\rho_{\alpha(k)} \in (0,1]$.

Next, to estimate the parameter $\phi_{\alpha(k)}(k)$, we design the following performance index:

$$J(\phi_{\alpha(k)}(k)) = |\Delta y(k) - \phi_{\alpha(k)}(k)\Delta u(k-1)|^2 + \mu_{\alpha(k)}|\phi_{\alpha(k)}(k) - \hat{\phi}_{\alpha(k)}(k-1)|^2 \tag{13}$$

where $\hat{\phi}_{\alpha(k)}(k)$ represents the estimate of $\phi_{\alpha(k)}(k)$, and $\mu_{\alpha(k)} > 0$ is a weighting coefficient.

Minimizing the performance index (13), we obtain the following PPD estimation algorithm:

$$\hat{\phi}_{\alpha(k)}(k) = \hat{\phi}_{\alpha(k)}(k-1) + \frac{\eta_{\alpha(k)}\Delta u(k-1)}{\mu_{\alpha(k)} + \Delta u^2(k-1)} \times \left(\Delta y(k) - \hat{\phi}_{\alpha(k)}(k-1)\Delta u(k-1)\right) \tag{14}$$

where $\eta_{\alpha(k)}(k)$ denote step size factor.

To broaden the applicability of the PPD estimation algorithm (14), we incorporate the following reset algorithm:

$$\hat{\phi}_{\alpha(k)}(k) = \hat{\phi}_{\alpha(k)}(1) \text{ if } |\hat{\theta}_{\alpha(k)}(k)| \leq \varepsilon \text{ or } \text{sign}\left(\hat{\phi}_{\alpha(k)}(k)\right) \neq \text{sign}\left(\hat{\phi}_{\alpha(k)}(1)\right) \tag{15}$$

where $\varepsilon > 0$ is a small constant.

$$\hat{\phi}_{\alpha(k)}(k) = \hat{\phi}_{\alpha(k)}(k-1) + \frac{\eta_{\alpha(k)}\Delta u(k-1)}{\mu_{\alpha(k)} + \Delta u^2(k-1)} \times \left(\Delta y(k) - \hat{\phi}_{\alpha(k)}(k-1)\Delta u(k-1)\right) \tag{16}$$

$$\hat{\phi}_{\alpha(k)}(k) = \hat{\phi}_{\alpha(k)}(1), \text{ if } |\hat{\phi}_{\alpha(k)}(k)| \leq \varepsilon, \text{ or } \text{sign}\left(\hat{\phi}_{\alpha(k)}(k)\right) \neq \text{sign}\left(\hat{\phi}_{\alpha(k)}(1)\right) \tag{17}$$

$$u(k) = u(k-1) + \frac{\rho_{\alpha(k)}\hat{\phi}_{\alpha(k)}(k)}{\lambda_{\alpha(k)} + |\hat{\phi}_{\alpha(k)}(k)|^2}(y_d(k+1) - y(k)) \tag{18}$$

In this section, we design an event-triggered, data-driven LFC strategy to conserve valuable bandwidth resources. The decision to transmit the most recent sampled data to the corresponding SSMFAC controller will be based on the following triggering conditions:

$$k_{r+1} = k_r + \min_{r_{k_r} \in N^+}\left\{r_{k_r} \mid e(k_r)^T \Omega e(k_r) \geq \delta\right\} \tag{19}$$

where $e(k_r) = y(k_r) - y(k)$ represents the triggering error, k_r is an integer denoting the triggering instant, and δ is the triggering threshold parameter.

Combining algorithms (16)–(18), we obtain the following event-triggered SSMFAC algorithm:

$$\hat{\phi}_{\alpha(k)}(k) \begin{cases} = \hat{\phi}_{\alpha(k)}(k_r - 1) + \frac{\eta_{\alpha(k)} \Delta u(k-1)}{\mu_{\alpha(k)} + \Delta u^2(k-1)} \times \left(\Delta y(k) - \hat{\phi}_{\alpha(k)}(k-1) \Delta u(k-1) \right) & k = k_r \\ = \hat{\phi}_{\alpha(k)}(k_r - 1) & k \in (k_{r-1}, k_r) \end{cases} \quad (20)$$

$$\hat{\phi}_{\alpha(k)}(k) = \hat{\phi}_{\alpha(k)}(1), \text{ if } \left| \hat{\phi}_{\alpha(k)}(k) \right| \leq \varepsilon, \text{ or } \text{sign}\left(\hat{\phi}_{\alpha(k)}(k) \right) \neq \text{sign}\left(\hat{\phi}_{\alpha(k)}(1) \right) \quad (21)$$

$$u(k) = \begin{cases} u(k_r - 1) + \frac{\rho_{\alpha(k)} \hat{\phi}_{\alpha(k)}(k)}{\lambda_{\alpha(k)} + \left| \hat{\phi}_{\alpha(k)}(k) \right|^2} \times (y_d(k+1) - y(k_r)) & k = k_r \\ u(k_r - 1) & k \in (k_{r-1}, k_r) \end{cases} \quad (22)$$

The schematic diagram of SSMFAC is shown in Figure 1.

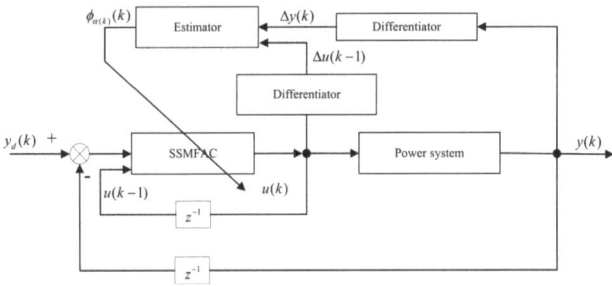

Figure 1. Block diagram of SSMFAC.

4. Convergence Analysis

Theorem 2. *Considering the switched multi-area power system represented by Equation (7), which complies with Assumptions 1 and 2, with respect to $\forall j, l$ and when $j \neq l$, employing the switching system model-free adaptive controller scheme (20)–(22), given positive scalars o_1, o_2, if there exist $\eta_i, \mu_i, \rho_i,$ and λ_i such that:*

$$\aleph = \begin{pmatrix} \Xi_1 & \Xi_2 \\ * & \Xi_3 \end{pmatrix} < 0 \quad (23)$$

where $\Xi_1 = \begin{pmatrix} (1-o_1)Q_i(1-o_1) - Q_i & (1-o_1)Q_i o_2 \\ * & o_2 Q_i o_2 - \Omega \end{pmatrix}$, $\Xi_2 = \text{diag}\{\delta^{\frac{1}{2}}, \delta^{\frac{1}{2}}\}$, $\Xi_3 = \text{diag}\{-I, -I\}$. *The tracking error $e(k)$ of the switched multi-area power system (7) is bounded.*

Proof of Theorem 2. If the conditions of the reset algorithm (17) are met, it becomes clear that the parameter $\hat{\phi}_{\alpha(k)}(k)$ is bounded. Let $\tilde{\phi}_{\alpha(k)}(k) = \hat{\phi}_{\alpha(k)}(k) - \phi_{\alpha(k)}(k)$ represent the PDD estimation error. By subtracting $\phi_{\alpha(k)}(k)$ from both sides of the parameter estimation algorithm (20), we obtain:

$$\tilde{\phi}_{\alpha(k)}(k) = \left(1 - \frac{\eta_{\alpha(k)} \Delta u^2(k-1)}{\mu_{\alpha(k)} + \Delta u^2(k-1)} \right) \tilde{\phi}_{\alpha(k)}(k-1) + \phi_{\alpha(k)}(k-1) - \phi_{\alpha(k)}(k) \quad (24)$$

Obtaining the absolute value of Equation (24), we find:

$$\left| \tilde{\phi}_{\alpha(k)}(k) \right| = \left| \left(1 - \frac{\eta_{\alpha(k)} \Delta u^2(k-1)}{\mu_{\alpha(k)} + \Delta u^2(k-1)} \right) \right| \left| \tilde{\phi}_{\alpha(k)}(k-1) \right| + \left| \phi_{\alpha(k)}(k-1) - \phi_{\alpha(k)}(k) \right| \quad (25)$$

Since $\left|\phi_{\alpha(k)}(k)\right| \leq d_1$ is bounded, there exists $\left|\phi_{\alpha(k)}(k-1) - \phi_{\alpha(k)}(k)\right| \leq 2d_1$ Choosing $\mu_{\alpha(k)} > 0, 0 < \eta_{\alpha(k)} < 1$, we can derive $\eta_{\alpha(k)}\Delta u^2(k-1) < \Delta u^2(k-1) < \mu_{\alpha(k)} + \Delta u^2(k-1)$. Consequently, there must exist γ constant y such that:

$$0 < \gamma < \left(\frac{\eta_{\alpha(k)}\Delta u^2(k-1)}{\mu_{\alpha(k)} + \Delta u^2(k-1)}\right) < 1 \tag{26}$$

Substituting Equation (26) into Equation (25), we obtain:

$$\begin{aligned}\left|\tilde{\phi}_{\alpha(k)}(k)\right| &\leq (1-\gamma)\left|\tilde{\phi}_{\alpha(k)}(k-1)\right| + 2d_1 \\ &\leq (1-\gamma)^2\left|\tilde{\phi}_{\alpha(k)}(k-2)\right| + 2d_1(1-\gamma) + 2d_1 \\ &\leq \cdots \\ &\leq (1-\gamma)^{k-1}\left|\tilde{\phi}_{\alpha(k)}(1)\right| + \frac{2d_1}{\gamma}\end{aligned} \tag{27}$$

Therefore, Equation (27) is bounded, and since $\tilde{\phi}_{\alpha(k)}(k)$ is bounded, $\hat{\phi}_{\alpha(k)}(k)$ is also bounded. The boundedness of tracking error.
We define the system's tracking error as:

$$e(k) = y_d(k) - y(k) \tag{28}$$

By substituting Equations (19) and (13) into Equation (29), we obtain:

$$\begin{aligned}e(k+1) &= y_d(k+1) - y(k+1) \\ &= y_d(k+1) - y(k) - \phi_{\alpha(k)}(k)\Delta u(k) \\ &= e(k) - \frac{\rho_{\alpha(k)}\hat{\phi}_{\alpha(k)}(k)\phi_{\alpha(k)}(k)}{\lambda_{\alpha(k)} + \left|\hat{\phi}_{\alpha(k)}(k)\right|^2}(e(k) - e(k_r)) \\ &= (1 - \Theta(k))e(k) + \Theta(k)e(k_r)\end{aligned} \tag{29}$$

where $\Theta(k) = \frac{\rho_{\alpha(k)}\hat{\phi}_{\alpha(k)}(k)\phi_{\alpha(k)}(k)}{\lambda_{\alpha(k)} + \left|\hat{\phi}_{\alpha(k)}(k)\right|^2}$
Next, consider the following Lyapunov function:

$$V(k) = V_{\alpha(k)}(e(k)) = e^T(k)Q_{\alpha(k)}e(k) \tag{30}$$

For the i th subsystem:

$$V_i(e(k)) = e^T(k)Q_i e(k) \tag{31}$$

Let $\Delta V_i(k+1) = V_i(k+1) - V_i(k)$ to obtain

$$\begin{aligned}\Delta V_i(k+1) &= [(1-\Theta(k))e(k) + \Theta(k)e_r(k)]^T Q_i[(1-\Theta(k))e(k) + \Theta(k)e_r(k)] \\ &\quad - e^T(k)Q_i e(k) \\ &= \ell^T(k)\Lambda\ell(k)\end{aligned} \tag{32}$$

where $\ell(k) = [e(k) e(k_r)], \Lambda = \begin{bmatrix} \nabla_1 & \nabla_2 \\ * & \nabla_3 \end{bmatrix}, \nabla_1 = (1-\Theta(k))Q_i(1-\Theta(k)) - Q_i, \nabla_2 = (1-\Theta(k))Q_i\Theta(k), \nabla_3 = \Theta(k)Q_i\Theta(k)$.
Let $\lambda_{\min} = b^2/4$, using the inequality $a^2 + b^2 \geq 2ab$, we choose $\lambda > \lambda_{\min}$ such that there exists a constant $0 < M < 1$ satisfying:

$$0 < M \leq \frac{\phi_{\alpha(k)}(k)\hat{\phi}_{\alpha(k)}(k)}{\lambda_{\alpha(k)} + \left|\hat{\phi}_{\alpha(k)}(k)\right|^2} \leq \frac{b\left|\hat{\phi}_{\alpha(k)}(k)\right|}{\lambda_{\alpha(k)} + \left|\hat{\phi}_{\alpha(k)}(k)\right|^2} \leq \frac{b}{2\sqrt{\lambda_{\min}}} = 1 \qquad (33)$$

consequently, can have $o_1 < \Theta(k) < o_2$.

Let us consider the event-triggered scheme (19) can have:

$$\Delta V_i(k+1) \leq \ell^T(k)\Lambda\ell(k) + \delta - e(k_r)^T\Omega e(k_r) \qquad (34)$$

By utilizing the Schur complement lemma and combining it with Equation (34), have:

$$\Delta V_i(k+1) \leq \ell^T(k)\aleph(k)\ell(k) < 0 \qquad (35)$$

where $\aleph = \begin{pmatrix} \Xi_1 & \Xi_2 \\ * & \Xi_3 \end{pmatrix}$, $\Xi_1 = \begin{pmatrix} (1-o_1)Q_i(1-o_1) - Q_i & (1-o_1)Q_i o_2 \\ * & o_2 Q_i o_2 - \Omega \end{pmatrix}$, $\Xi_2 = $ diag$\left\{\delta^{\frac{1}{2}}, \delta^{\frac{1}{2}}\right\}$, $\Xi_3 = $ diag$\{-I, -I\}$.

The analysis demonstrates that $V_i(k+1)$ is constrained within a certain range, indicating that the tracking error $e(k)$ is similarly bounded. In summary, the tracking error remains within certain bounds, ensuring stable system behavior.

The output $y(k)$ is bounded because $y_d(k)$ is constant and the tracking error $e(k)$ converges. □

5. Simulation Example

To validate the effectiveness of the proposed load frequency control scheme based on switched systems, this study employs a three-area interconnected power system as the simulation model. The system parameters are derived from data in reference [15] and are provided in Table 2. The total sampling time is denoted by 60 s, with a sampling period of $T = 0.001$ s. Other parameters include $T_{12} = 0.21, T_{13} = 0.24, T_{23} = 0.13$.

Table 2. Simulation parameters for the power system.

Parameters	Area 1	Area 2	Area 3
$D/(\text{pu/Hz})$	1.0	1.5	1.8
$M/(\text{pu}\cdot \text{s})$	10	12	12
$R/(\text{Hz/pu})$	0.05	0.05	0.05
T_t/s	0.30	0.17	0.20
T_g/s	0.37	4	0.35

Assuming a data transmission success rate of $\mathbb{E}\{\alpha(k)\} = 0.6$, the controller parameters are denoted by $\eta_1 = 0.3, \eta_2 = 0.5, \mu_1 = 1.4, \mu_2 = 1.2, \rho_1 = 2.5, \rho_2 = 2.8, \lambda_1 = 1.2, \lambda_2 = 2.7$, $\Omega = 10^{16}, \delta = 0.003$ and the initial responses for the three regions are represented by $u_j(1) = 0, \hat{\phi}_j(1) = 0.3$.

Furthermore, a load disturbance of 0.02 per unit (p.u.) is introduced simultaneously in each region. The system frequency deviation curves, tie-line power variation curves, and system output curves are depicted in Figures 2–4. Notably, after running for a certain duration, the deviations in frequency and variations in tie-line power within each region eventually diminish to zero. The simulation results demonstrate the favorable control performance of the proposed algorithm. Figure 5 shows the switching signals.

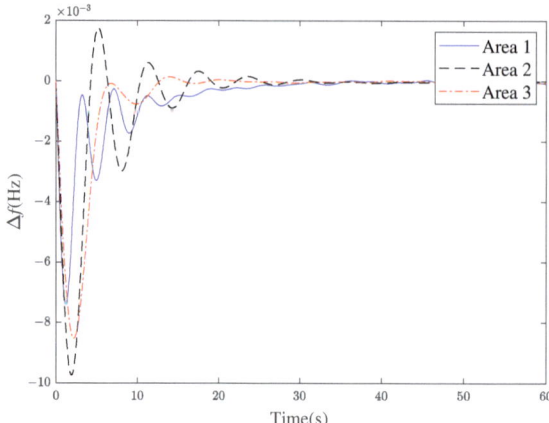

Figure 2. The curve of frequency deviation response.

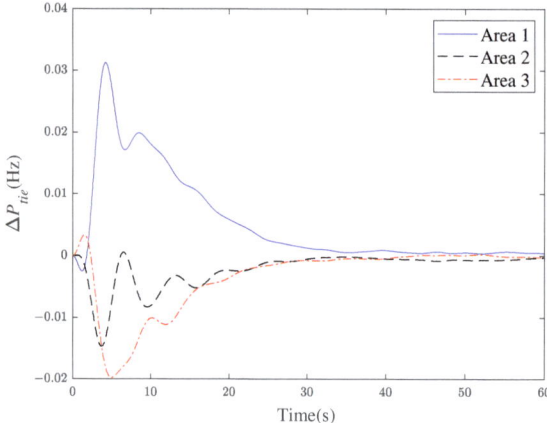

Figure 3. The response curve of change in tie-line power.

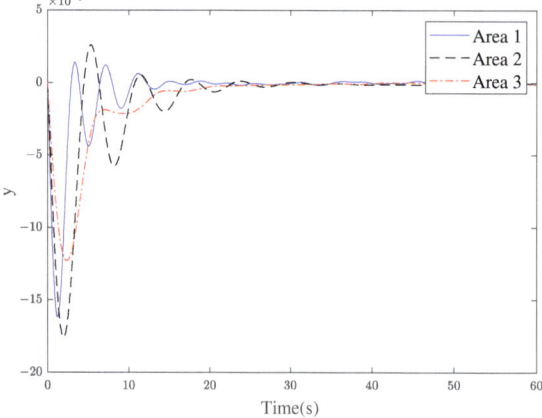

Figure 4. The curve of ACE_i.

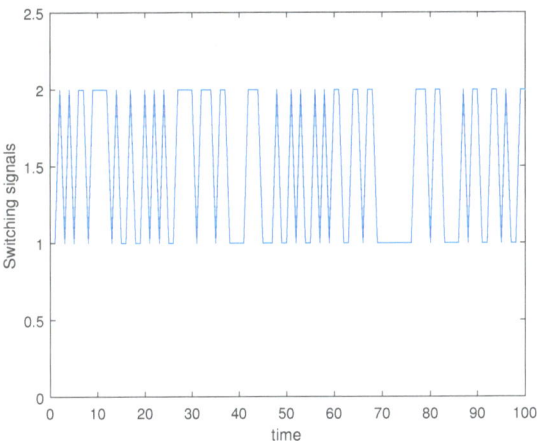

Figure 5. Any 100 switching sequences in the system.

The release times and intervals between sensor outputs are depicted in Figures 6–8, with 255,669, 36,389 and 22,658 trigger occurrences among all sample intervals. Additionally, a comparison was made with the PI control method and frequency curves under the PI and SSMFAC control methods have been plotted in Figure 9. Based on the graph analysis, the SSMFAC control strategy demonstrates superior performance compared to the PI control scheme, showcasing smaller overshoot and faster convergence speed. This observation indicates the effectiveness of the SSMFAC approach in achieving better control system performance.

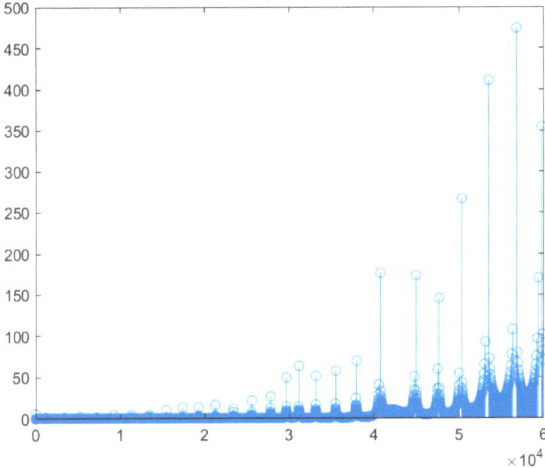

Figure 6. Event triggering intervals in area 1.

Additionally, we utilized the "tic" and "toc" functions in MATLAB to measure the average running time of the two algorithms, which were 1.734 s and 2.2505 s, respectively. The results indicate that the SSMFAC method offers a low computational burden while ensuring control performance. In Table 3, we evaluated the effectiveness of the proposed approach using two performance criteria: the Integral of Absolute Error (IAE) and the Integral of Time multiplied by Absolute Error (ITAE). We compared the results with those obtained from the ETSSMFAC and PI schemes. The results show that the SSMFAC algorithm proposed in this paper performs better.

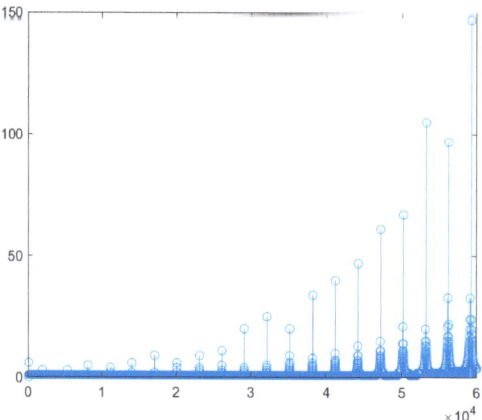

Figure 7. Event triggering intervals in area 2.

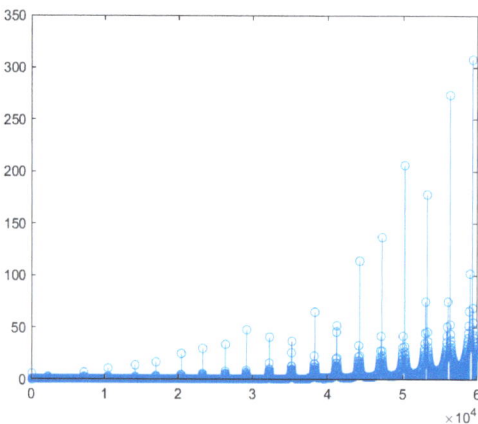

Figure 8. Event triggering intervals in area 3.

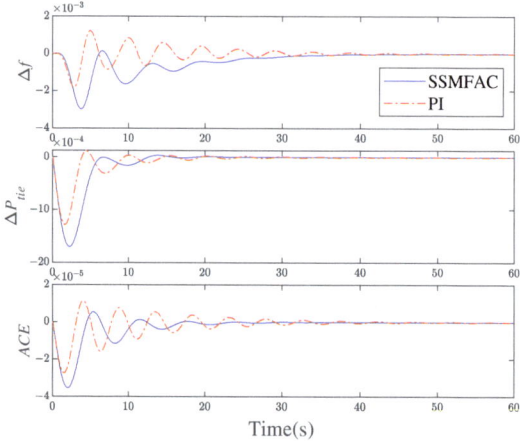

Figure 9. Comparison with PI controller.

Table 3. performance comparison.

Control Program	IAE	ITAE
SSMFAC	0.00014845	0.00078395
ET-SSMFAC	0.00015734	0.00083537
PI	0.00016796	0.0017093

While the event-triggered SSFMAC algorithms (20) and (22) have demonstrated effectiveness in theoretical simulations, it is important to consider practical factors that can influence system control. One such factor is the susceptibility to noise; we have incorporated noise into our simulations to evaluate the robustness of the SSFMAC algorithm under realistic conditions. We modeled noise with mean 0 and variance 0.000000003 as Gaussian white noise added to the input signal.

Figure 10 shows that the system remains stable and performs satisfactorily, but the control accuracy is slightly degraded due to noise. Including noise in the simulations highlights the practical challenges the SSFMAC algorithm faces. While the algorithm remains robust under noisy conditions, additional filtering techniques are necessary to maintain control performance. Future work could focus on developing more advanced noise reduction methods and adaptive filtering techniques to further enhance the control system's robustness.

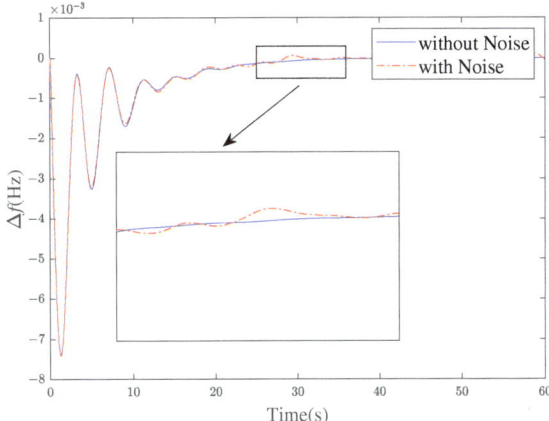

Figure 10. Noise impact on system response.

In the following sections, we replace constant disturbance with variable load disturbance to test whether the proposed algorithm is capable of dealing with the complex working environment. The trajectory of the load power change is shown in Figure 11, and the response curves are drafted in Figure 12. It can be seen that the control scheme designed in this paper still has superior tracking performance, even if the work environment is changeable. Once again, the operating information confirms the effectiveness and practicability of the SSMFAC algorithm.

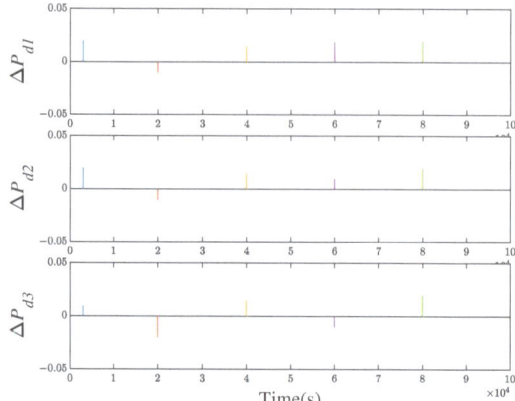

Figure 11. Random load disturbances.

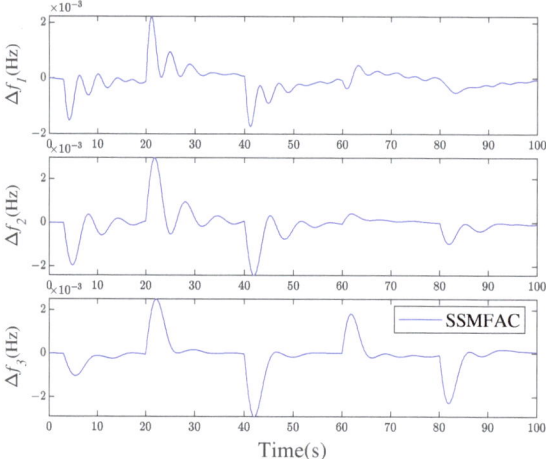

Figure 12. Frequency responses of the LFC scheme.

6. Conclusions

This paper has a new data-driven load frequency control scheme tailored for power systems vulnerable to Denial-of-Service attacks. The method employs an input-output data-driven LFC algorithm, eliminating the need for a precise power system model and thus streamlining controller design. First, the multi-area interconnected power system under DoS attacks is modeled as a switching system consisting of two subsystems. An event-triggered model-free adaptive LFC algorithm is subsequently introduced within the switching system framework to manage load frequency control. The effectiveness of this scheme is demonstrated by applying it to a three-area interconnected power system. Simulation results confirm that the switching-based, model-free adaptive LFC algorithm maintains robust performance even when facing DoS attacks. However, the methodology has certain limitations, including the inherent dependence on data quality, potential computational complexity, and possible stability issues in highly dynamic or noisy environments typically associated with model-free adaptive control approaches.

Author Contributions: Conceptualization, G.T. and F.W.; methodology, G.T. and F.W.; software, G.T. and F.W.; validation, G.T. and F.W.; formal analysis, G.T.; writing—original draft preparation, G.T.; writing—review and editing, G.T. and F.W. All authors have read and agreed to the published version of the manuscript.

Funding: This research received no external funding.

Data Availability Statement: The original contributions presented in the study are included in the article.

Conflicts of Interest: The authors declare no conflict of interest.

References

1. Bevrani, H.L. Robust power system frequency control. In *Robust Power System Frequency Control*; Springer : New York, NY, USA, 2014.
2. Liu, Y.Z.; Chen, Y.; Li, M.T. Dynamic Event-Based Model Predictive Load Frequency Control for Power Systems under Cyber Attacks. *IEEE Trans. Smart Grid* **2021**, *12*, 715–725. [CrossRef]
3. Tang, X.; Li, Y.; Yang, M.; Wu, Y.; Wen, Y. Adaptive Event-Triggered Model Predictive Load Frequency Control for Power Systems. *IEEE Trans. Power Syst.* **2023**, *38*, 4003–4014. [CrossRef]
4. Shangguan, X.C.; Zhang, C.K.; He, Y.; Jin, L.; Jiang, L.; Spencer, J.W.; Wu, M. Robust Load Frequency Control for Power System Considering Transmission Delay and Sampling Period. *IEEE Trans. Ind. Inform.* **2021**, *17*, 5292–5303. [CrossRef]
5. Kim, H.; Zhu, M.H.; Lian, J.M. Distributed Robust Adaptive Frequency Control of Power Systems with Dynamic Loads. *IEEE Trans. Autom. Control* **2020**, *65*, 4887–4894. [CrossRef]
6. Shangguan, X.C.; He, Y.; Zhang, C.K.; Jiang, L.; Wu, M. Adjustable Event-Triggered Load Frequency Control of Power Systems Using Control Performance Standard Based Fuzzy Logic. *IEEE Trans. Fuzzy Syst.* **2022**, *30*, 3297–3311. [CrossRef]
7. Yan, S.; Gu, Z.; Park, J.H.; Xie, X. Sampled Memory-Event-Triggered Fuzzy Load Frequency Control for Wind Power Systems Subject to Outliers and Transmission Delays. *IEEE Trans. Cybern.* **2023**, *53*, 4043–4053. [CrossRef]
8. Li, X.H.; Ye, D. Event-Based Distributed Fuzzy Load Frequency Control for Multiarea Nonlinear Power Systems with Switching Topology. *IEEE Trans. Fuzzy Syst.* **2022**, *30*, 4262–4272. [CrossRef]
9. Qiao, S.; Liu, X.; Liang, Y.; Xiao, G.; Kang, Y.; Ge, S.S. Event-Triggered Sliding Mode Load Frequency Control of Multiarea Power Systems under Periodic Denial-of-Service Attacks. *IEEE Syst. J.* **2023**, *17*, 2803–2814. [CrossRef]
10. Yang, F.; Shao, X.; Muyeen, S.M.; Li, D.; Lin, S.; Fang, C. Disturbance observer based fractional-order integral sliding mode frequency control strategy for interconnected power system. *IEEE Trans. Power Syst.* **2008**, *36*, 5922–5932. [CrossRef]
11. Xiong, L.Y.; Li, H.; Wang, J. LMI based robust load frequency control for time delayed power system via delay margin estimation. *Int. J. Electr. Power Energy Syst.* **2018**, *100*, 91–103. [CrossRef]
12. Ojaghi, P.; Rahmani, M. LMI-Based Robust Predictive Load Frequency Control for Power Systems with Communication Delays. *IEEE Trans. Power Syst.* **2017**, *32*, 4091–4100. [CrossRef]
13. Li, J.W.; Zhou, T.; Cui, H.Y. Brain-Inspired Deep Meta-Reinforcement Learning for Active Coordinated Fault-Tolerant Load Frequency Control of Multi-Area Grids. *IEEE Trans. Autom. Sci. Eng.* **2023**, 1–13. [CrossRef]
14. Yan, Z.M.; Xu, Y. Data-Driven Load Frequency Control for Stochastic Power Systems: A Deep Reinforcement Learning Method with Continuous Action Search. *IEEE Trans. Power Syst.* **2019**, *34*, 1653–1656. [CrossRef]
15. Peng, C.; Li, J.C.; Fei, M.R. Resilient Event-Triggering Load Frequency Control for Multi-Area Power Systems with Energy-Limited DoS Attacks. *IEEE Trans. Power Syst.* **2017**, *32*, 4110–4118. [CrossRef]
16. Hu, S.; Ge, X.; Li, Y.; Chen, X.; Xie, X.; Yue, D. Resilient Load Frequency Control of Multi-Area Power Systems under DoS Attacks. *IEEE Trans. Inf. Forensics Secur.* **2023**, *18*, 936–947. [CrossRef]
17. Wang, X.; Ding, D.; Ge, X.; Dong, H. Neural-Network-Based Control with Dynamic Event-Triggered Mechanisms under DoS Attacks and Applications in Load Frequency Control. *IEEE Trans. Circuits Syst. Regul. Pap.* **2022**, *69*, 5312–5324. [CrossRef]
18. Shangguan, X.C.; He, Y.; Zhang, C.K.; Yao, W.; Zhao, Y.; Jiang, L.; Wu, M. Resilient load frequency control of power systems to compensate random time delays and time-delay attacks. *IEEE Trans. Ind. Electron.* **2022**, *70*, 5115–5128. [CrossRef]
19. Jin, L.; He, Y.; Zhang, C.K.; Jiang, L.; Yao, W.; Wu, M. Delay-dependent stability of load frequency control with adjustable computation accuracy and complexity. *Control Eng. Pract.* **2023**, *135*, 105518. [CrossRef]
20. Shangguan, X.C.; He, Y.; Zhang, C.K.; Jin, L.; Yao, W.; Jiang, L.; Wu, M. Control performance standards-oriented event-triggered load frequency control for power systems under limited communication bandwidth. *IEEE Trans. Control Syst. Technol.* **2021**, *30*, 860–868. [CrossRef]
21. ShangGuan, X.C.; He, Y.; Zhang, C.K.; Jin, L.; Jiang, L.; Wu, M.; Spencer, J.W. Switching system-based load frequency control for multi-area power system resilient to denial-of-service attacks. *Control Eng. Pract.* **2021**, *107*, 104678. [CrossRef]
22. Hou, Z.S.; Chi, R.H.; Gao, H.J. An Overview of Dynamic-Linearization-Based Data-Driven Control and Applications. *IEEE Trans. Ind. Electron.* **2017**, *64*, 4076–4090. [CrossRef]
23. Qi, Y.; Zhao, X.; Huang, J. Data-driven event-triggered control for switched systems based on neural network disturbance compensation. *Neurocomputing* **2022**, *490*, 370–379. [CrossRef]

24. Ye, J.X.; Xie, L.R.; Wang, H.W. Model-Free Adaptive Ouasi Sliding Mode Control for Non-uniformly Sampled Systems. *Electron. Opt. Control* **2023**, *30*, 35–41.
25. Bu, X.; Yu, W.; Cui, L.; Hou, Z.; Chen, Z. Event-Triggered Data-Driven Load Frequency Control for Multiarea Power Systems. *IEEE Trans. Ind. Inform.* **2022**, *18*, 5982–5991. [CrossRef]

Disclaimer/Publisher's Note: The statements, opinions and data contained in all publications are solely those of the individual author(s) and contributor(s) and not of MDPI and/or the editor(s). MDPI and/or the editor(s) disclaim responsibility for any injury to people or property resulting from any ideas, methods, instructions or products referred to in the content.

Article

A Novel Hybrid Crow Search Arithmetic Optimization Algorithm for Solving Weighted Combined Economic Emission Dispatch with Load-Shifting Practice

Bishwajit Dey, Gulshan Sharma * and Pitshou N. Bokoro

Department of Electrical Engineering Technology, University of Johannesburg, Johannesburg 2006, South Africa; bdey@uj.ac.za (B.D.); pitshoub@uj.ac.za (P.N.B.)
* Correspondence: gulshans@uj.ac.za

Abstract: The crow search arithmetic optimization algorithm (CSAOA) method is introduced in this article as a novel hybrid optimization technique. This proposed strategy is a population-based metaheuristic method inspired by crows' food-hiding techniques and merged with a recently created simple yet robust arithmetic optimization algorithm (AOA). The proposed method's performance and superiority over other existing methods is evaluated using six benchmark functions that are unimodal and multimodal in nature, and real-time optimization problems related to power systems, such as the weighted dynamic economic emission dispatch (DEED) problem. A load-shifting mechanism is also implemented, which reduces the system's generation cost even further. An extensive technical study is carried out to compare the weighted DEED to the penalty factor-based DEED and arrive at a superior compromise option. The effects of CO_2, SO_2, and NOx are studied independently to determine their impact on system emissions. In addition, the weights are modified from 0.1 to 0.9, and the effects on generating cost and emission are investigated. Nonparametric statistical analysis asserts that the proposed CSAOA is superior and robust.

Keywords: combined economic emission dispatch (CEED); load shifting; demand side management; crow search algorithm; arithmetic optimization algorithm

Citation: Dey, B.; Sharma, G.; Bokoro, P.N. A Novel Hybrid Crow Search Arithmetic Optimization Algorithm for Solving Weighted Combined Economic Emission Dispatch with Load-Shifting Practice. *Algorithms* **2024**, *17*, 313. https://doi.org/10.3390/a17070313

Academic Editors: Zixin Huang, Li Jin, Xiongbo Wan and Sheng Du

Received: 16 May 2024
Revised: 8 July 2024
Accepted: 9 July 2024
Published: 16 July 2024

Copyright: © 2024 by the authors. Licensee MDPI, Basel, Switzerland. This article is an open access article distributed under the terms and conditions of the Creative Commons Attribution (CC BY) license (https:// creativecommons.org/licenses/by/ 4.0/).

1. Introduction

The generation and use of electrical energy is crucial to modern society. The term economic cost dispatch (ECD) that is associated with the power system, which may minimize the cost of power generating while still satisfying the operating requirements, is a highly essential problem given that thermal power generation is the predominant power generation at present. But, as environmental issues worsen, more people are realizing that we need to consider emissions of dangerous gases such as NO_x, SO_2, and CO_2 in addition to just the generation cost. The cost of producing electricity and the need to reduce emissions are both taken into account by CEED. In common ECD problems, generator cost functions are approximated by quadratic functions. The most frequent form of expressing the CEED issue is as a quadratic function, reflecting the fact that it is a multi-objective optimization problem. Higher order polynomials have been shown to enhance solution methodologies, and studies have indicated that advanced functions can provide an accurate representation of the power generating system's response; however, this will only serve to further exacerbate the issue at hand. To address CEED issues, some scientists use optimization strategies grounded on conventional mathematical modeling. The traditional approach may be used in several power-generating test environments. Benefits include optimality shown mathematically and the absence of problem-specific factors. The conventional method that relies on a coordination equation to tackle the issue of economic emission load dispatch takes into account the limitation of line flow. Using the Min-Max price penalty factor brings about a decrease in the total fuel expense of CEED. Nevertheless, standard mathematical approaches face significant difficulties in resolving these nonlinear issues because of intrinsic nonconvexity and nonlinearity of the existing power generating system and other constraints in the actual production process. Many evolutionary programming and AI-based strategies have been proposed to address CEED issues, including but not limited to the bat algorithm [1], artificial bee colony [2], teaching-and-learning-based optimization [3], cuckoo search [4], flower pollination algorithm [5], firefly algorithm [6], bacterial foraging optimization [7], genetic algorithm [8], differential evolution [9], and particle swarm optimization [10].

1.1. The Literature Review

Authors of [11] exhibit a mathematical model of the mud ring feeding methodology, and its advantages over other current optimization methods are tested using two case studies. A data-driven surrogate-assisted technique is presented in [12] for dealing with high-dimensional large-scale MACEED challenges. This work, outlined in reference [13], presents a hybrid dynamic economic environmental dispatch model that combines an energy storage device, wind turbines, and solar systems, along with thermal power units. The aim of this model is to stabilize the production of renewable energy sources. The authors in [14] propose an advanced algorithm (the knee-guided algorithm (KGA))to simply addresses the EED problem. In this algorithm, the solution is determined using the lowest Manhattan distance technique, which defines the optimal solution. The suggested algorithm aims on finding a solution near the knee point, improving convergence, and delivering the knee solution rather than the entire POF. This approach increases the accessibility of the algorithm's results to policymakers in thermal power plants. Study [15] suggests a hybrid optimization solution for the electrical power systems' multi-objective economic emission dispatch (MOEED) issue. In study [16], researchers provide and execute an adapted iteration of the modified marine predators algorithm (MMPA) to tackle both single- and multi-objective CEED problems. It is recommended that MMPA be used to enhance the efficiency of regular MPA. To forestall the untimely aggregation of knowledge, it incorporates a complete learning strategy in which the best practices of all participants are shared. For reliability-based dynamic economic emission dispatch (DEEDR), the authors of [17] have developed an enhanced NSGA-III (I-NSGA-III). I-NSGA-III incorporates a distinctive crossover operator by using an angle-based connection and normal distribution approach. The authors of article [18] propose a distributed optimization strategy on a hybrid microgrid system to decrease the expenses associated with power generation. The authors of study [19] propose a nondominated sorting genetic algorithm III with three crossover strategies (NSGA-III-TCS) to address the challenges related to combined heat and power dynamic economic emission dispatch (CHPDEED), both with and without forbidden operation zones. In study [20], to handle DEED-PEV, the authors suggest a new NSGA-II (NNSGA-II). In NNSGA-II, the simulated binary crossover operator is swapped out for a Gaussian-based one, and the crossover frequency of each individual is adaptively adjusted depending on its position in the population. In paper [21], the researcher combines demand side management (DSM) and multi-objective dynamic economic and emission dispatch (MODEED) to examine the advantages of DSM on the generation side to minimize economic and emission dispatch problems separately and simultaneously with and without DSM. In paper [22], the competitive swarm optimization (CSO) algorithm, a newly discovered evolutionary method, is used to find the optimal solution for several objectives, including minimizing production costs, carbon emissions, voltage fluctuations, and power losses. The CSO algorithm's efficiency is measured against that of numerous cutting-edge metaheuristics, including GA, PSO, CSA, ABC, and SHADE-SF. The economic emission dispatch problems for combined heat and power production are tackled in article [23] by proposing an improved version of the bare-bone multi-objective particle swarm optimization (IBBMOPSO). In research paper [24], a primal-dual technique is used to replace the bi-level profit-maximizing model with linear single-level optimization. To address an environmental economic dispatch challenge, the authors of article [25] suggest an ordered optimization outline for the MMEG arrangement, which would allow for the energy coordination strategy to be produced in a decentralized fashion. In research article [26], the researchers suggest a cooperative optimization approach for demand side management (DSM)-assisted grid-tied residential microgrid (MG) planning and operation. A combined model of dynamic economic and emission dispatch (DEED) and DSM with the inclusion of renewable energy resources (RERs) is presented by the researcher in study [27]. Research [28] introduces a novel multi-objective evolutionary algorithm dubbed the improved multi-objective exchange market algorithm to solve the MDEEDP when electric vehicles (EVs) are present, when EV drivers exhibit random behavior, and when WP uncertainty exists. A MOEED model that takes solar power variability into account is presented in [29]. Both underestimating and overestimating solar power are modeled, with the latter case incurring additional costs in operation. The authors of article [30] propose a multi-objective optimization technique to address the problem related to economic emission dispatch in integrated energy and heating systems (IEHS). This strategy considers system uncertainties and incorporates multi-energy demand response (MEDR) and carbon capture power plants (CCPPs). The influence of errors in the investigational source of the input/output characteristics of conventional power plants is studied by the authors of [31]. Taking into account LCA and risk cost, research [32] suggests a low-carbon economic schedule for IES. In article [33], the authors develop a crow search optimization algorithm (CSA) based on swarm intelligence to deal with the difficult restricted MEEDP with the modified predictive element of RES. The author of article [34] conducts an analysis to examine how the inclusion of renewable energy sources, an electric vehicle parking lot, and an integrated demand response program affects the economic emission dispatch of a multi-county combined heat and power system. Using a real-world complex three-county test system, researchers employ the strength pareto evolutionary algorithm 2 and the nondominated sorting genetic algorithm-III. In study [35], the authors present an ECSO method, which stands for extended crisscross search optimization. In order to address the combined heat and power economic emission dispatch (CHPEED) issue in a nonlinear and nonconvex area, the authors of research [36] offer a multi-objective multi-criterion decision-making (MCDM) technique with constraint-handling rules tailored to this specific situation. Study [37] introduces a novel method for incorporating loss prediction using artificial neural networks into the dynamic economic emission dispatch model. Economic power dispatch over a whole 24 h period is posed as an optimization issue in [38]. The load dispatch simulation incorporates the modeling of thermal, water resources, and renewable for demand-side management, aiming to create a realistic situation. To tackle the MO-CHPEED problem in a fuzzy environment, a new developed algorithm is developed by [39]—dynamically controlled whale optimization algorithm (DCWOA)—through which problems can be solved like multi-objective nonconvex optimization. The benchmark functions in line with CEC-BC-2017 is outlined in work [40]. The authors' first step involves comparing the original AOA with five enhanced versions of AOA in order to choose the most optimal improved strategy. Subsequently, the authors use simulations to compare the improved method with other intelligent optimization algorithms, therefore confirming its effectiveness. In [41], the three-layer optimization issue is solved using the column-and-constraint generation technique (CCG) and, with this, the best scheduling plan and worst case operating domain are achieved. Paper [42] examines the economic emission dispatch issue for many zones of combined heat and power generation and uses a simulated system to test the efficacy of the method. In [43], researchers optimize the energy costs and then compare the outcomes to choose the best hybrid system. After generating mathematical models for typical benchmark functions, TCSC is deployed at weak locations across many echelons in the proposed work of [44–46] to improve the system voltage profile. The authors' proposal in [47–49] aims to evaluate the impact of photovoltaic (PV) penetration on active power loss, reactive power loss, and enhancement of voltage profile. This is achieved by assessing the location for PV deployment using the voltage collapse proximity index technique. Therefore, an effort is made to analyze the loading characteristic of the

IEEE 14 bus system in conditions of potential voltage collapse, such as when the network is exposed to the use of photovoltaic solar energy sources.

With column headings such as "objective", "optimization algorithm", "system description", and "RES type", Table 1 displays the papers covered in the literature.

Table 1. Analysis of the literature survey.

Objective	Optimization Models Used	System Description	Incorporation of RES	Year	Reference
Dynamic economic load dispatch	Bottlenose dolphin optimizer (BDO)	Twenty-nine functions including seven uni-modal functions	PV, WT	2022	[11]
Minimize operation cost and pollution	Improved mayfly optimization algorithm	Thermal power plant along with PV, WT, and BESS	PV, WT	2022	[13]
Minimize operation cost and pollution	Knee-guided algorithm (KGA)	6, 10, and 11 generating units	NA	2022	[14]
Decreasing the emission of greenhouse gases and the fuel cost	Marine predators algorithm (MMPA)	3, 5, 6, and 26 generating units	NA	2022	[16]
Fuel cost, pollutant emission, and system reliability	NSGA-III (I-NSGA-III)	5, 10, and 30 units	NA	2022	[17]
Minimize the total generation cost in a dynamic economic dispatch problem	Distributed management algorithm for DEDP	6 generating units	NA	2023	[18]
Multi-objective dynamic economic and emission dispatch	Multi-objective particle swarm optimization (MOPSO)	6 generating units with DSM implementation	NA	2018	[21]
Reduction of carbon emissions, in addition to low cost and high efficiency	Competitive swarm optimization (CSO) algorithm	Thermal–solar (TS), thermal–wind (TW), and thermal–wind–solar (TWS)	PV, WT	2022	[22]
Environmental economic dispatch problem	Distributed augmented Lagrangian (ADAL) method	4 multi-micro-energy grid systems	Battery	2022	[25]
Minimization of MG total annual cost and total annual emission	Multi-objective optimization	Residential MG consisting of 1000 smart homes with different DSM participation levels	PV, WT, BESS	2019	[26]
Generation side operational benefits and reduction in environmental pollution level	(NSGA-II) and Monte Carlo simulation (MCS)	DSM-based six thermal generating units, one solar-powered generator, and one wind-powered generator	6 MT, along with 1 PV and WT	PV, WT	[27]
Reducing carbon emissions and improving wind power consumption	Multi-objective optimization	IEEE-30 bus power system and a 6 bus district heating system	WT	2022	[30]
Energy sustainability and climatic benefits	Crow search optimization algorithm (CSA)	Six benchmark test systems with multi-dimensional constraints	PV, WT	2022	[33]
Reduction in cost of economic operation and the pollutant emission	Crisscross search optimization (CSO) algorithm	IEEE-30 bus system, 40 generators system, and hydrothermal generation system	NA	2022	[35]
Reduce the overall generation cost of the system.	CSAJAYA	DSM-implemented two microgrid distribution systems	WT	2023	[50]

1.2. Research Gap and Objective of the Paper

The extensive literature review suggests that combined economic emission dispatch problems have always been an emerging topic for the power system engineers. Researchers have developed various optimization algorithms to solve this problem for decades and some algorithms have proven better than others. The implementation of an economic strategy called demand side management (DSM) is rarely used, but the literature has proven that shifting the loads to lesser priced hours results in a much lower operational cost of a distribution system. This article implements DSM on two dynamic systems and thereafter studies the impact of it on obtaining a balanced and distributed minimal cost and emission on the test structures. An exclusive hybrid CSAOA is provided as the optimization tool of the research study.

1.3. Methodology and Contributions

The aim of the paper is to minimize both cost and emission simultaneously. Cost refers to the fuel cost utilized by the generators in supplying power, and emission refers to the pollutants emitted by the combustion of fossil fuels during the process of producing power. Simultaneous minimization of both cost and emission with proper balance is called combined economic emission dispatch (CEED) and there are 3 ways to evaluate CEED. All generators have maximum and minimum limits within which they operate, and this is called the inequality constraints. The sum of the power outputs of the generators should be exactly equal to the load demand every hour and this is called equality constraint. A proposed hybrid CSAOA is utilized to minimize the cost (ECD) and all the three types of CEED, which are the fitness functions of the work. An economic strategy called DSM is also implemented as a step before CEED to restructure the load demand, which helps in reducing the cost component furthermore. All the mathematical modeling of fitness functions and formation of CSAOA are explained in further sections of the manuscript.

The novel contributions of the work conducted in this article can be listed as follows:

a. A unique hybrid CSAOA is suggested as the optimization technique for this study. Prior to using it to address the DEED issue, the suggested methodology is additionally tested on six multi-dimensional and varied modal benchmark functions.
b. The test system leverages a combination of conventional generating plants and combined heat and power (CHP) plants. This allows for the evaluation of various dispatch strategies, including dynamic economic dispatch, emission dispatch, and weighted economic emission dispatch, contributing to the optimization of power generation based on cost, emissions, or a balance of both.
c. A load-shifting policy called demand side management (DSM) is also considered and all the above-mentioned studies are also conducted in the presence of DSM to highlight its benefits.

The remainder of this paper is set out as follows: in Section 2, we outline the formalization of the issue; in Section 3, we focus on how the suggested hybrid algorithm is used here; the simulation findings are described in Section 4, and this paper is wrapped up in Section 5.

2. Objective Function Formulation

The objective of economic cost dispatch (ECD) is to minimize the cost of electricity generation while ensuring compliance with all relevant fairness and equity requirements. Dynamic economic load dispatch has been implemented to handle changing demand and hourly power schedules.

2.1. Cost Function for DG Units

Fuel costs money. The cost of generating one unit of electricity from a fossil-fuel generator is known as its generation cost. The generating cost function of generating units is represented by a linear quadratic equation. Equation (1) denotes a quadratic equation [50,51].

$$ECD = \sum_{t}^{24} \sum_{j=1}^{n} (a_j P_{j,t}^3 + b_j P_{j,t}^2 + c_j P_{j,t} + d_j) \tag{1}$$

Multiplying the power output (P_j) of the jth DG unit by the associated costs $(a_j, b_j, c_j,$ and $d_j)$ yields the total system cost. Considering that n is the total number of DG units, the overall price is ECD. The total expenditure for a 24 h period is calculated based on an economic dynamic load, where the variable "t" represents the specific number of hours.

2.2. Emission Dispatch for DG Units

While producing power, alternative fossil-fuel generators release harmful emissions into the environment. Toxic gases, such as nitrogen oxides, sulfur, and carbon, are often emitted into the air in the form of thick black smoke. Scheduling power plants to reduce emissions of hazardous gases is known as "emission dispatch" (EMD). By utilizing Equation (2) and having knowledge of the emission coefficients, one can determine the objective function of the emission dispatch. The total emission can be represented as EMD, while emission coefficients can be represented as α_j, β_j, and γ_j [52].

$$EMD = \sum_{t=1}^{24} \sum_{j=1}^{n} \sum_{CO_2 NO_X SO_2} (\alpha_j P_{j,t}^3 + \beta_j P_{j,t}^2 + \gamma_j P_{j,t} + \delta_j) \tag{2}$$

2.3. PPF-Based Combined Economic Emission Dispatch

Fuel cost reduction is the focus of ECD, whereas pollution control is the focus of EMD, with regards to traditional fossil-fuel generators and their impact on the environment. Hence, it is essential to find a mutually acceptable resolution that may effectively achieve the objectives of reducing fuel expenses and mitigating pollution emissions. To combine Equations (1) and (2) into a CEED, we use the price penalty factor (PPF), which is a parameter that incorporates both ECD and EMD in a mixed objective function. This is shown in Equation (3) [50].

$$CEED = \sum_{t}^{24} \sum_{j=1}^{n} \sum_{CO_2 NO_X SO_2} \begin{bmatrix} (a_j P_{j,t}^3 + b_j P_{j,t}^2 + c_j P_{j,t} + d_j) + \\ ppf * (\alpha_j P_{j,t}^3 + \beta_j P_{j,t}^2 + \gamma_j P_{j,t} + \delta) \end{bmatrix} \tag{3}$$

Equation (4) provides the form of price penalty factors (ppf). The jth generator's maximum values are denoted by P_j^{max}.

$$ppf_{j,max,max} = \frac{ECD(P_j^{max})}{EMD(P_j^{max})} \tag{4}$$

2.4. FP-Based Combined Economic Emission Dispatch

Through the given approach, two objective functions that are incompatible are analyzed here that share common choice and control variables, and resolve them by computing their ratio. For instance, (1) represents the economic dispatch equation, while (2) represents the emission function; together, they are referred to as ECD and EMD. Then, by minimizing the ratio of EMD to ECD, a compromise solution may be reached using the FP technique. Equation (5) provides the numerical expression for this [50].

$$FP = \frac{EMD}{ECD} \tag{5}$$

2.5. The Proposed Environment-Constrained Economic Dispatch (ECED)

Both of the aforementioned CEED strategies have as their primary goal the lessening of atmospheric pollution. The system's generating cost increases substantially, surpassing the highest value attained by economic dispatch. Equation (6) shows how to combine two objective functions with distinct aims in order to achieve a better quality compromise solution [50,51]. Whether a system is unimodal or multimodal is determined by (1) and (2). The characteristics of the economic dispatch equation and the emission dispatch equation are given in accordance with this equation.

$$ECED = \mu \left[\frac{ECD - ECD_{min}}{ECD_{max} - ECD_{min}} \right] + (1-\mu) \left[\frac{EMD - EMD_{min}}{EMD_{max} - EMD_{min}} \right] \quad (6)$$

where μ is between 0 and 1, ECD_{min} is the minimum generation cost, EMD_{min} is the minimum amount of pollutants emitted, ECD_{max} is the maximum generation cost, and EMD_{max} is the maximum volume of pollutants released attained by replacing the optimal constraints of EMD_{min} in Equations (1) and (2). The data acquired [51] also suggest the following three procedures and presumptions:

i. Setting $\mu = 0.5$, or providing equal weight to both goal functions, is known to provide the fastest and most effective steps towards obtaining the best compromised solution.

ii. The choice with the largest quality compromise will have a smallest CPI-EPI difference, where the CPI is cost performance index and EPI is emission performance index. The formulae for CPI and EPI are denoted by Formulas (7) and (8).

$$CPI = \left[\frac{ECD - ECD_{min}}{ECD_{max} - ECD_{min}} \right] \times 100\% \quad (7)$$

$$EPI = \left[\frac{EMD - EMD_{min}}{EMD_{max} - EMD_{min}} \right] \times 100\% \quad (8)$$

iii. The generating cost of the higher quality compromise will be closer to ECD_{min}, while the pollution output will be lower than EMD_{min}.

2.6. Equality and Inequality Constraints

The constraints of equality are given in Equation (9), whereas the constraints of inequality are shown in Equation (10) to ensure the values of the DERs are confined.

$$\sum_{j=1}^{n} P_{j,t} = D_t \quad (9)$$

$$P_{j,min} \leq P_j \leq P_{j,max} \quad (10)$$

where D_t is the power demand at the same tth time and $P_{j,t}$ represents the power of the generator.

2.7. Utilization Percentage

Equation (11) may be used to obtain the utilization rate.

$$UP = \frac{\sum_T P_j^t}{24 \times P_j^{max}} \quad (11)$$

The term "UP" is often used to convey the hourly outputs of test systems with a large number of distributed energy resources (DERs) in a manner that is both clear and comprehensible, where G_j^t represents hourly output with respect to time.

2.8. Demand Side Management

The study of microgrid energy management, particularly focusing on economic operation, has been a significant area of research in recent years and is expected to be a major issue in the future. Nevertheless, the economic operation of a microgrid system remains incomplete until the demand side management (DSM) approach is taken into account. The adoption of DSM would reduce costs across the board for the articles discussed in the review of the relevant literature. DSM priorities shift elastic loads on the studied network to cheaper times of day for the grid. Despite the fact that the overall load demand remains the same at the conclusion of the forecast period, which is characteristically a day, there is a substantial decrease in peak demand, resulting in an increase in the load factor. Load shifting, peak clipping, strategic expansion, strategic conversion, variable load shape, and valley filling are just a few of DSM's load-shaping tactics.

Listed below are the specific measures that should be taken while putting DSM into practice:

Step 1: provide the dynamic duration of the time T of the load data in hours.
Step 2: enter the TOU price of energy consumption on the market for T hours.
Step 3: enter the total DSM involvement in % (if elastic loads are not specified).
Step 4: categorize the loads as either elastic or inelastic according to the percentage of engagement in DSM.

For example, when we say x% DSM, it means that x% of the hourly load demand may be adjusted based on elasticity, but the remaining $(100 - x)$ % is not adjustable. Optimal planning is required for elastic load requirements.

Step 5: Calculate the minimum and maximum values, and the total, for the inelastic load. It is important to note that the control variables that need to be optimized have a flexible load prerequisite.

Step 6: apply the optimization approach [52],

$$\text{Minimize } [\text{cost}^t_{grid} \times (load\_elastic^t + load\_inelastic^t)] \tag{12}$$

where

$$0 \leq load\_elastic^t \leq load\_inelastic^{max} \tag{13}$$

$$\text{Total load demand} = \sum_{t=1}^{T} (load\_elastic^t + load\_inelastic^t) \tag{14}$$

Step 7: the total load demand model that has been redesigned incorporating the approach of demand side management (DSM) is determined by summing the load demand in terms of inelastic for each hour with the elastic loads with better optimized values.

3. Optimization Techniques

3.1. Crow Search Algorithm

Crows have a clever strategy for discovering hidden food sources. They observe the movements of their fellow crows and closely monitor other bird populations in the area. Once they are alone, they revisit these locations to conduct further investigations. In addition, when a crow's food is taken by another crow, it becomes more concerned and actively seeks out different locations to avoid having its food stolen again. Furthermore, it utilizes its own specialized knowledge to deter potential intruders. Based on the above, the CSA has been developed by the authors of [53].

The purpose of this metaheuristic is to enable a specific crow to go in the same direction as another crow in order to locate the location of its concealed food supply. This operation should be carried out in such a way that the location of the crow is progressively updated. In addition, the crow is required to migrate to a new area if food is appropriated. According to the theory, there is a d-dimensional environment that contains a great number of crows. Every crow has a memory that recalls the precise location of its hiding place. Every time the iteration is performed, the position of the crow's hiding area is given. When it comes to positions, this is the best one that a crow has ever held. It is said that every crow recalls the place where it had its most memorable experience. It is common for crows to move around the region in search of better food sources. Consider the possibility that in the subsequent iteration, crow "b" wants to go to the site that was identified by crow "a" that came before it. At this point in the process, the first crow makes the decision to follow another crow to the spot where the second crow is hidden. Because of this circumstance, there are two conceivable outcomes.

Case 1: Crow "b" is unaware of the fact that crow "a" is following. Consequently, the first crow "a" will go towards the location where the food of second crow "b" is hidden. In this scenario, the updated location of the first crow "a" is determined by generating a random integer that follows a uniform distribution between 0 and 1, and multiplying it by the flight length of the first crow "a" during the current iteration.

Case 2: Crow "b" is aware that crow "a" is following. In order to safeguard its cache from theft, crow "b" will deceive crow "a" by relocating to a different spot inside the search zone.

In both instances, the following mathematical configurations are possible [53]:

$$M^{a,iter+1} = \begin{cases} M^{a,iter} + rand_a \times fl^a \times (m^{b,iter} - M^{a,iter}), & \text{if } rand_b \geq AP^b \\ a \text{ random position}, & \text{otherwise} \end{cases} \quad (15)$$

where M is the crow's food position. The distance "fl^a" in the above equation represents the direct distance traveled by the ath crow, whereas the random values "$rand_a$" and "$rand_b$" follow a stable distribution between 0 and 1. In both Case 1 and Case 2, there is the possibility of automatic updates being applied to the memory, m.

$$m^{a,iter+1} = \begin{cases} M^{a,iter+1}, & \text{if } f(M^{a,iter+1}) < f(m^{a,iter}) \\ m^{a,iter}, & \text{otherwise} \end{cases} \quad (16)$$

where $f(.)$ is the notation used to refer to the function that is responsible for determining fitness.

"fl" is a value that shows how near the search space is to being reached. AP may discuss crows in terms of their awareness probability. The value of an AP might fluctuate between 0 and 1 when it is used as a probability factor. For the purpose of gaining a better understanding of the current situation, AP may make use of the crow's search approach.

3.2. Arithmetic Optimization Algorithm (AOA)

When used for mathematical calculations, the arithmetic operators [54] imply that the multiplication and divisibility operators are the ones that are most often utilized, yielding diverse values or assessments across different domains, which is important for the investigative search process. However, unlike subtractive and additive operators, the divisive and multiplicative prerequisite aid by swiftly accomplishing the objective owing to their significant dispersion. With the help of these operations, we demonstrate a new function to show how the distributions of different operators are related to one another. Because of this, it is feasible that the optimal solution may be originated by an experimental search, which can be performed through repeated experimentation. Additionally, search controllers based on divisive and multiplicative operators are used to enhance the exploitation phase of the search process by means of improved communication during the optimization phase. The mathematical model for updating the location in AOA is provided below as Equation (17):

$$x_{i,j}(P\_iter+1) = \begin{cases} \text{if } r_1 > MOA \\ \begin{cases} best(x_j) \div (MOP + \epsilon) \times ((UL_j - LL_j) \times \lambda + LL_j), r_2 < 0.5 \\ best(x_j) \times MOP \times ((UL_j - LL_j) \times \lambda + LL_j), & \text{Otherwise} \end{cases} \\ \text{else} \\ \begin{cases} best(x_j) - MOP \times ((UL_j - LL_j) \times \lambda + LL_j), r_3 < 0.5 \\ best(x_j) + MOP \times ((UL_j - LL_j) \times \lambda + LL_j), \text{Otherwise} \end{cases} \end{cases} \quad (17)$$

The control variables' upper and lower limits are denoted by *UL* and *LL*, respectively. As shown in Equations (18) and (19), the *MOA* and *MOP* are adjusted with each iteration of the mathematics optimizer *(MO)*. *P_iter* represents present iteration. $x_{i,j}$ denotes the *j*th position of the *i*th solution at the current iteration, and best (x_j) is the *j*th position in the best obtained solution so far. The tuning parameters *z* and λ are assigned the specific values of 5 and 0.5, correspondingly.

$$MOA(P\_iter) = Min + P\_iter \times \left(\frac{Max - Min}{M\_Iter}\right) \quad (18)$$

$$MOP(P\_iter) = 1 - \frac{P\_iter^{1/z}}{M\_Iter^{1/z}} \quad (19)$$

Max and *Min* are the upper and lower limits of the allowable values for MOA. "*M_iter*" represents the maximum number of iterations. Figure 1 shows the flowchart of AOA.

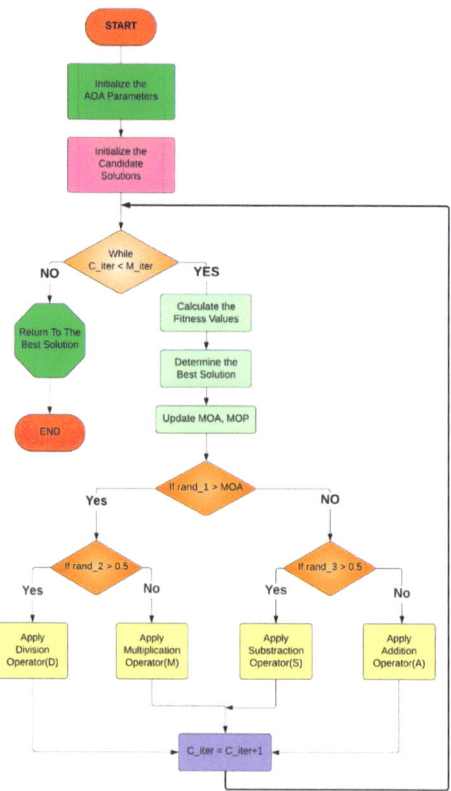

Figure 1. Proposed AOA flow diagram [55].

3.3. Hybrid CSAOA

A prominent algorithm that uses greedy search to continuously increase the fitness function in each iteration has a major impact on the proposed hybrid CSAOA [52,55]. Through the process of substituting the disparity between the upper and lower limits of variables with the optimum solution that is generated from the current iteration of the solution set, Equation (17) of AOA is changed. A representation of the alteration may be seen in Equation (20) below.

$$if\ r_1 > MOA$$
$$x_{i,j}(P\_iter+1) = \begin{cases} best(x_j) \div (MOP+\varepsilon) \times \big((best(x_j))\times rand\times fl + LL_j\big), r_2 < 0.5 \\ best(x_j) \times MOP \times \big((best(x_j))\times rand\times fl + LL_j\big), \quad Otherwise \end{cases}$$
$$else$$
$$x_{i,j}(P\_iter+1) = \begin{cases} best(x_j) - MOP \times \big((best(x_j))\times rand\times fl + LL_j\big), r_3 < 0.5 \\ best(x_j) + MOP \times \big((best(x_j))\times rand\times fl + LL_j\big), Otherwise \end{cases} \qquad (20)$$

The outcome of implementing the projected hybrid CSAOA on several benchmark functions and the subsequent part provides a comprehensive analysis of the findings obtained from this implementation. After that, microgrid systems use the algorithm to execute bilevel DSM for energy management.

3.4. Realization on Benchmark Functions

Metaheuristic algorithms are naturally stochastic, resulting in varying performances across different runs as they strive to find the optimal solution for a given problem. In order to assess the suitability and efficiency of the projected CSAOA algorithm, it is developed and subjected to testing using a predefined set of benchmark functions. In this study, the researchers implement a collection of six benchmark functions utilized by [55] to evaluate the suggested CSAOA approach. The functions F1–F2 are referred to as unimodal functions since they do have just one distinct global optimum instead of a local optimum. These operations determine the efficacy of any multimodal technique in exploiting opportunities. The functions F3-F4 exhibit single global optimum and many local optimal. In order to evaluate the exploratory capabilities of the metaheuristic approach, these functions are of the utmost importance. Additionally, they serve as benchmarks for multimodal optimization. Functions F5 and F6 are the benchmark functions for the fixed dimension multimodal system.

Figure 2 illustrates how well the recommended techniques perform for each of the six functions that serve as benchmarks, which are F1 through F6. A representation of the convergence characteristics of the proposed techniques is shown in Figure 2 for a range of benchmark functions in proportion to the total number of iterations and shows how these characteristics change over time. The convergence characteristics are graphed by calculating the average values of the best solutions from 30 distinct runs in each iteration. The solution that has been proposed demonstrates a mixture of behaviors from a large number of integrated algorithms, which ultimately results in a system performance that is very efficient.

The suggested approach is used to conduct a statistical analysis on the benchmark functions, and the results are provided in Table 2. By virtue of the same algorithm boundaries, the new method has been recommended with better comparison with other techniques, where the total population has been considered as 100 and 300 number of iterations. Table 3 consists of the mean value (F_{mean}), standard deviation (FSD) as given in (21) and (22), and best (F_{best}) and worst (F_{worst}) optimal values obtained over 25 individual runs.

$$F_{mean} = \frac{\sum_{t=1}^{N} f_x}{N} \qquad (21)$$

$$F_{SD} = \sqrt{\frac{\sum_{t=1}^{N}(f_x - F_{mean})^2}{N}} \qquad (22)$$

Let N represent the total number of distinct runs, which in this case is 30.

Based on the statistical data shown in Table 3, it is evident that the suggested CSAOA algorithm demonstrates good performance across various kinds of functions. The uniformity of the various methods may be assessed by generating a boxplot over several iterations, which visually displays the range of ideal values achieved in each iteration. A boxplot displays the highest and lowest values as cross symbols at the top and bottom, respectively. The rectangular box represents the range where 50% of the data are located. It is obvious how the suggested methods prevent users from becoming stuck in local optimums and how the distribution of optimal values acquired over runs may be viewed.

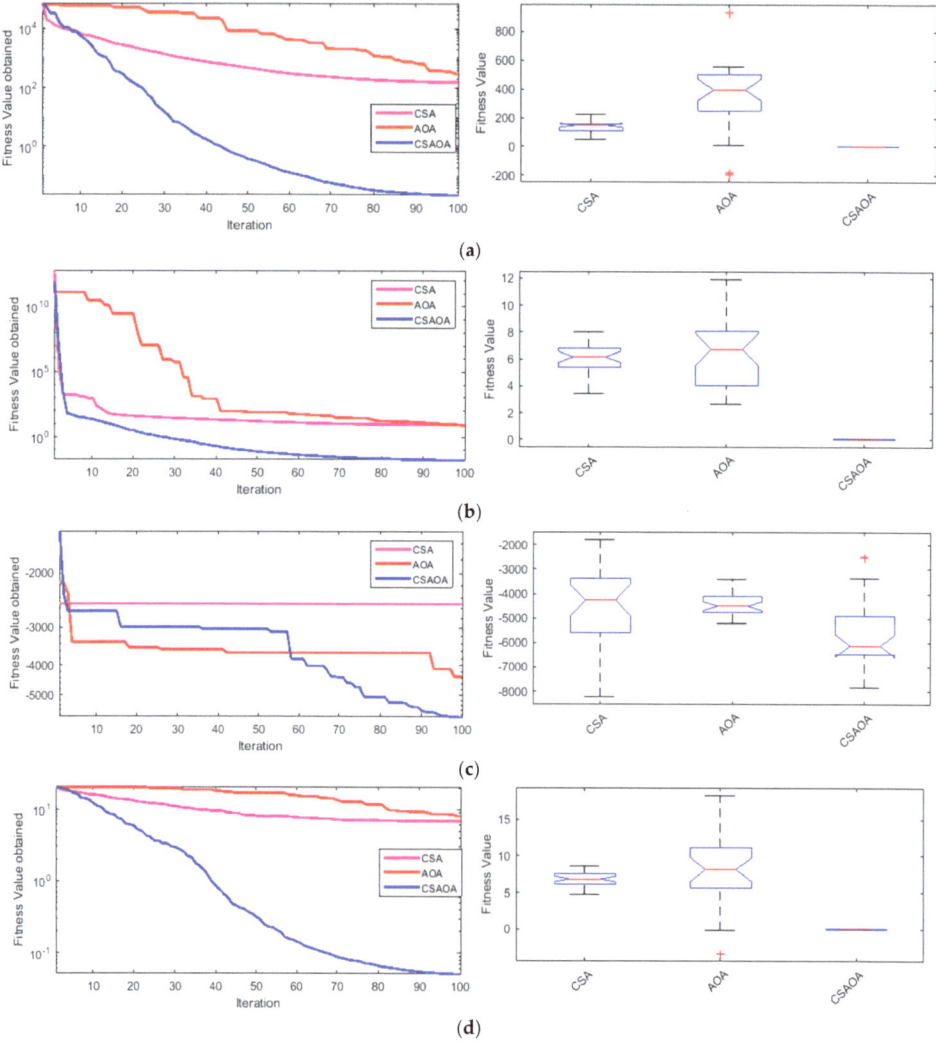

Figure 2. *Cont.*

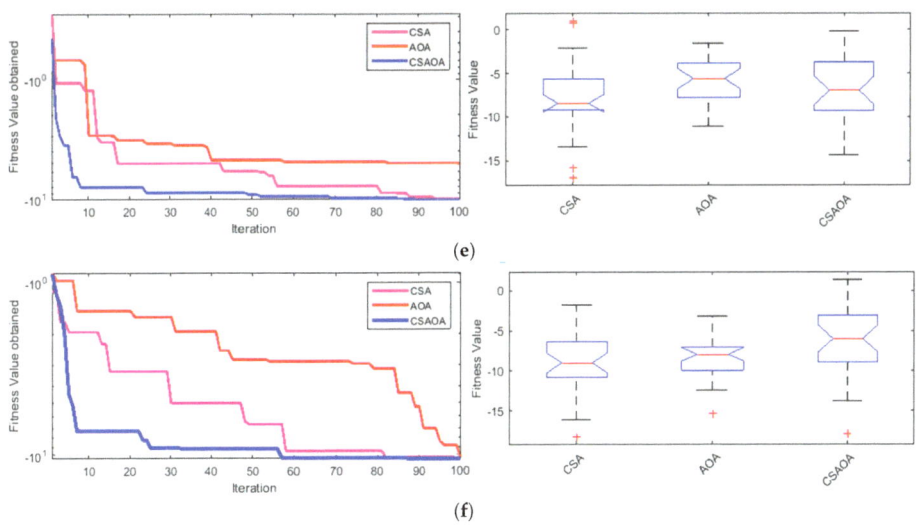

Figure 2. Benchmark function statistical analysis boxplot and cost convergence characteristics (**a**) F1, (**b**) F2, (**c**) F3, (**d**) F4, (**e**) F5, and (**f**) F6 [55].

Table 2. Specifications of the benchmark functions [54].

Function	Dim	Range	f_{min}	
$f_1(x) = \sum_{i=1}^{n} x_i^2$	30	[−100, 100]	0	Unimodal Benchmark Functions
$f_2(x) = \sum_{i=1}^{n} |x_i| + \prod_{i=1}^{n} |x_i|$	30	[−10, 10]	0	
$f_3(x) = \sum_{i=1}^{n} -x_i \sin\left(\sqrt{|x_i|}\right)$	30	[−500, 500]	−418.9829 × 5	
$f_4(x) = -20 \exp\left(-0.2\sqrt{\frac{1}{n}\sum_{i=1}^{n} x_i^2}\right) - \exp\left(\frac{1}{n}\sum_{i=1}^{n} \cos(2\Pi x_i)\right) + 20 + e$	30	[−32, 32]	0	Multimodal Benchmark Functions
$f_5(x) = -\sum_{i=1}^{5} \left[(X - a_i)(X - a_i)^T + c_i\right]^{-1}$	30	[0, 10]	−10.1532	Fixed Dimension Multimodal Benchmark Functions
$f_6(x) = -\sum_{i=1}^{10} \left[(X - a_i)(X - a_i)^T + c_i\right]^{-1}$	30	[0, 10]	−10.5363	

Table 3. Statistical study of benchmark function results using "CSA", "AOA", and "CSAOA".

Function		F1			F2		
Algorithm		CSA	AOA	CSAOA	CSA	AOA	CSAOA
Best	Unimodal benchmark functions	82.18	117.14	0.0096	4.19	3.58	0.01
Worst		332.1716	1061.23	0.14	9.00	14.25	0.07
Mean		150.3337	409.08	0.03	6.02	6.60	0.04
SD		48.6507	246.52	0.02	1.13	2.50	0.01

Table 3. Cont.

Function		F3			F4		
Algorithm		CSA	AOA	CSAOA	CSA	AOA	CSAOA
Best	Multimodal benchmark functions	−7320.13	−5886.74	−7915.45	5.42	4.17	0.01
Worst		−1967.51	−3502.98	−2871.64	9.53	20.55	0.12
Mean		−4414.72	−4454.94	−5513.72	6.76	8.88	0.04
SD		1691.85	536.98	1076.63	0.81	5.46	0.01
Function		F5			F6		
Algorithm		CSA	AOA	CSAOA	CSA	AOA	CSAOA
Best	Fixed-dimension multimodal benchmark functions	−10.14	−9.81	−10.15	−10.53	−10.40	−10.53
Worst		−2.62	−2.37	−2.68	−2.41	−2.32	−2.42
Mean		−7.29	−6.03	−6.41	−8.52	−8.04	−6.23
SD		3.55	2.95	3.79	3.36	2.57	3.83

4. Case Study and Proof of Concept

Two distribution test systems are considered for the evaluation of ECD, EMD, and ECED with and without incorporating DSM strategy. Fossil-fuel generators consider the valve point loading effect, resulting in cost and emission fitness functions that are both nonconvex and nonlinear. The whole of the work conducted in this study is divided into three distinct parts. The first step involves incorporating demand side management (DSM) into the projected load demand model, taking into account the willingness of 40% of consumers to engage in the DSM approach. ECD and EMD are evaluated in the second stage regarding both load demand models, both with and without the DSM strategy being implemented. ECED is evaluated in the third stage to obtain a balanced trade-off result among minimum generation cost and pollutants emitted. An algorithm that was developed recently (AOA) and its variations serve as the optimization tool for this research. The following section provides a detailed discussion of the findings achieved, which are directly related to the issues outlined in Section 2.

4.1. Test System 1

Table 4 shows the operating limits, cost, and emission coefficients of the CHP and fossil fueled units that deliver power to the load demand of distribution test system 1. The hourly load demand data for this test system are gathered from article [19].

Table 4. Conventional and 3 CHP generator cost and emission coefficients.

Power-Only Generators i	1	CHP-Based Generators	1	2	3
a (USD/MW^3)	2.55×10^2	a (USD/MW^3)	1.25×10^3	2.65×10^3	1.57×10^3
b (USD/MW^2)	7.70×10^0	b (USD/MW^2)	3.60×10^1	3.45×10^1	2.00×10^1
c (USD/MW)	1.72×10^{-3}	c (USD/MW)	4.35×10^{-2}	1.04×10^{-1}	7.20×10^{-2}
d (USD)	1.15×10^{-4}	d (USD)	6.00×10^{-1}	2.20×10^0	2.30×10^0
α (tons/MW^2)	4.09×10^{-4}	α (tons/MW^2)	2.70×10^{-2}	2.50×10^{-2}	2.00×10^{-2}
β (tons/MW^2)	−0.0005554	β (tons/MW^2)	1.10×10^{-2}	5.10×10^{-2}	4.00×10^{-2}
γ (tons)	6.49×10^{-4}	γ (tons)	1.65×10^{-3}	2.20×10^{-3}	1.10×10^{-3}
$P_{j,max}$ (MW)	1.35×10^2				
$P_{j,min}$ (MW)	3.50×10^1				

The load model for the first stage has been changed to account for 40% of the loads participating in the DSM approach. During the restructuring, the elastic loads are optimally transferred using the proposed technique. It is determined that a DSM participation level of 40% would result in the total demand, mean demand, peak demand, and load factor computed. Peak demand is lowered by up to 16% when the DSM technique is implemented, according to Table 5. Similarly, a change in the distribution of elastic loads lead to an increase in the load factor, which increases from 0.7489 to 0.8929. Including a DSM approach in the operation of a distribution system can bring various advantages. The total and average demand of the distribution system remains the same both with and without the presence of DSM, which is another important point to take into consideration. Figure 3 depicts the adjusted load model for different levels of DSM participation.

Table 5. Advantages of DSM implementation.

	Without DSM	With DSM
Total Demand (kW)	7171	7171
Mean Demand (kW)	298.7	298.7
Peak Demand (kW)	399	334.62
Reduction in Peak (%)	-	16.14%
Load Factor	0.7489	0.8929

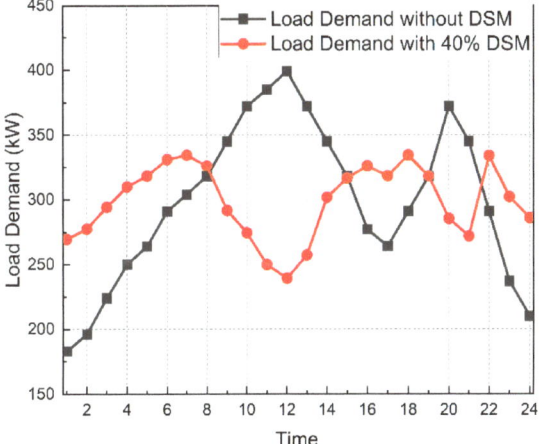

Figure 3. Test system 1 load demand both with and without DSM.

Each fitness function is minimized seriatim using the proposed CSAOA for both the load profiles, and their minimal values obtained are recorded and displayed in Table 3. The results obtained in Table 6 point toward the following inferences:

i. The minimum generation cost is found to be USD 296,744 using CSAOA, which is further reduced to USD 293,098 when DSM integrated load demand is accounted for.
ii. The minimum emission is 54 tons and 31 tons without and with DSM, respectively.
iii. When ECED is assessed to find a trade-off solution between least cost and pollutants (using $\mu = 0.5$), the solution set is found to be (USD 32,4067, 134 tons) which is further improved to (USD 322,365.5, 133 tons) when DSM incorporated load demand model is considered.

Table 6. Fitness function values with proposed CSAOA.

Fitness Function	Without DSM		With DSM	
	Cost (Thousands of USD)	Emission (tons)	Cost (Thousands of USD)	Emission (tons)
ECD	**296.744**	286	**293.098**	287
EMD	359.919	**54**	367.956	**31**
ECED (μ = 0.5)	324.066	134	**322.365**	133

Thereafter, the hourly contributions of the four DERs are analyzed during the minimization of ECD, EMD, and ECED (with μ = 0.5). Figure 4 above shows the hourly output of CHP1, CHP2, CHP3, and G1. The DERs (G1) with less values of cost coefficients are utilized more during ECD minimization and the DERs (CHP1) with less values of emission coefficients are utilized more during EMD minimization. When ECED is minimized giving equal weightage to both cost and emission, a balanced amount of all the DERs is utilized to deliver the power during every hour. Figure 5 represents the percentage utilization of DERs during different fitness functions, as discussed in Figure 4. Only 33% of the total capacity of CHP1 is utilized when ECD is minimized, as the cost coefficients of CHP1 are high, whereas almost 100% of the total capacity of G1 is utilized for the same, as G1 has low-cost coefficients. On the contrary, CHP1 does not emit any harmful toxic pollutants during its operation, whereas fossil-fueled G1 has high emission coefficients. Hence, when EMD is minimized, 90% of CHP1 and only 27% of G1 is utilized. CHP3 is utilized to the maximum extent for all the fitness functions, as it has both low cost and emission coefficients compared with the rest. Table 7 shows the measures of central tendencies when ECED was evaluated for 30 individual trials using CSA, AOA and CSAOA. Hits refer to the number of times the minimum value of ECED was obtained among 30 trials. Lower values of standard deviation indicate the robustness of the algorithm.

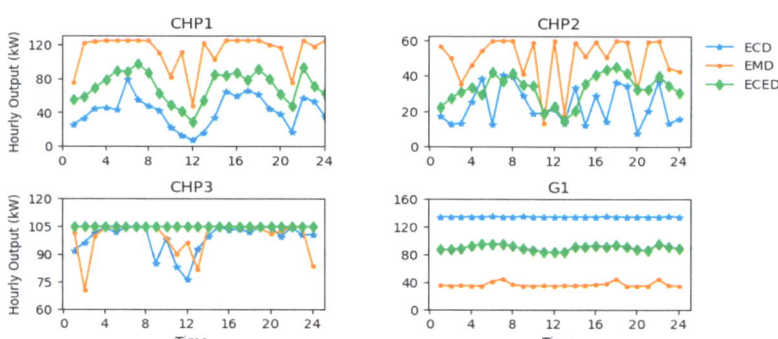

Figure 4. Hourly contribution of the DERs for minimum value of fitness functions.

Table 7. Measure of central tendencies for algorithms when ECED is minimized.

	Best	Worst	Mean	Hits	STD	Time (s)
CSA [S]	0.37458	0.39503	0.380715	21	0.009532	8.0068
AOA [S]	0.37299	0.38851	0.378163	20	0.007441	7.8993
CSAOA [P]	0.37282	0.37662	0.373707	23	0.001635	7.0934

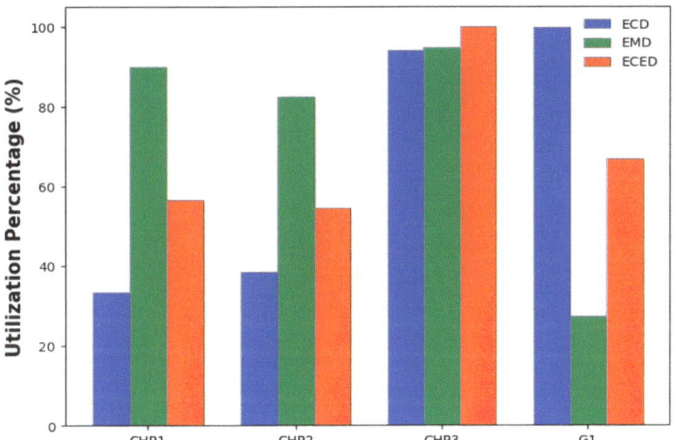

Figure 5. Utilization percentage to measure the depth of usage of individual DERs for various fitness functions.

4.2. Test System 2

Test system 2, which is used to assess the effectiveness described in Section 2, comprises six fossil-fueled generators (FFGs). Tables 8–11 display the DER limitations, associated costs, SO_2, NO_X, and CO_2 emission coefficients, and their corresponding penalty factors, as obtained from reference [40]. The peak load demand is 225 MW. This study aims to evaluate the list of fitness functions described in earlier sections. The arithmetic optimization algorithm (AOA) and the crow search algorithm (CSA) in conjunction with the planned CSAOA are used in order to test the fitness functions. For each of the algorithms, the population size is set at 100, and the fitness function is set at 1000. The codes have been evaluated in MATLAB 2019a environments with a laptop configuration of Intel Core i5 8th generation, 8 GB RAM.

Table 8. Generator power limit and fuel cost factor.

Unit	a_i	b_i	c_i	d_i	$P_{i,\min}$	$P_{i,\max}$
	USD/MW	USD/MW	USD/MW	USD/MW	(MW)	(MW)
P_1	1.00×10^{-1}	9.20×10^{-2}	1.45×10^{-1}	-1.36×10^{-1}	5.00×10^{-1}	2.00×10^{0}
P_2	4.00×10^{-1}	2.50×10^{-2}	2.20×10^{-1}	-3.50×10^{-3}	2.00×10^{-1}	8.00×10^{-1}
P_3	6.00×10^{-1}	7.50×10^{-2}	2.30×10^{-1}	-8.10×10^{-2}	1.50×10^{-1}	5.00×10^{-1}
P_4	2.00×10^{-1}	1.00×10^{-1}	1.35×10^{-1}	-1.45×10^{-2}	1.00×10^{-1}	5.00×10^{-1}
P_5	1.30×10^{-1}	1.20×10^{-1}	1.15×10^{-1}	-9.80×10^{-3}	1.00×10^{-1}	5.00×10^{-1}
P_6	4.00×10^{-1}	8.40×10^{-2}	1.25×10^{-1}	-7.56×10^{-2}	1.20×10^{-1}	4.00×10^{-1}

Table 9. Maximum SO_2 penalty factor and emission coefficient in 6 generator sets.

Unit	Emission Coefficients of SO_2				Penalty Factor of SO_2
	α_{SO2}	β_{SO2}	γ_{SO2}	δ_{SO2}	h_s
	tons/kW	tons/kW	tons/kW	tons/kW	tons/kW
1	5.0000×10^{-4}	1.5000×10^{-1}	1.7000×10^{1}	-9.0000×10^{1}	1.0852×10^{0}
2	1.4000×10^{-3}	5.5000×10^{-2}	1.2000×10^{1}	-3.0500×10^{1}	1.0616×10^{0}

Table 9. *Cont.*

Unit	Emission Coefficients of SO$_2$				Penalty Factor of SO$_2$
	α_{SO2}	β_{SO2}	γ_{SO2}	δ_{SO2}	h_s
	tons/kW	tons/kW	tons/kW	tons/kW	tons/kW
3	1.0000×10^{-3}	3.5000×10^{-2}	1.0000×10^1	-8.0000×10^1	2.1051×10^0
4	2.0000×10^{-3}	7.0000×10^{-2}	2.3500×10^1	-3.4500×10^1	5.9760×10^{-1}
5	1.3000×10^{-3}	1.2000×10^{-1}	2.1500×10^1	-1.9750×10^1	6.7720×10^{-1}
6	2.1000×10^{-3}	8.0000×10^{-2}	2.2500×10^1	-2.5600×10^1	6.1920×10^{-1}

Table 10. Maximum NO$_x$ penalty factor and emission coefficient in 6 generator sets.

Unit	Emission Coefficients of NO$_x$				Penalty Factor of NO$_x$
	α_{NOX}	β_{NOX}	γ_{NOX}	δ_{NOX}	h_n
	tons/kW	tons/kW	tons/kW	tons/kW	tons/kW
1	1.2000×10^{-3}	5.2000×10^{-2}	1.8500×10^1	-2.6000×10^1	9.4070×10^{-1}
2	4.0000×10^{-4}	4.5000×10^{-2}	1.2000×10^1	-3.5000×10^1	1.4962×10^0
3	1.6000×10^{-3}	5.0000×10^{-2}	1.3000×10^1	-1.5000×10^1	1.3870×10^0
4	1.2000×10^{-3}	7.0000×10^{-2}	1.7500×10^1	-7.4000×10^1	8.3080×10^{-1}
5	3.0000×10^{-4}	4.0000×10^{-2}	8.5000×10^0	-8.9000×10^1	2.1705×10^0
6	1.4000×10^{-3}	2.4000×10^{-2}	1.5500×10^1	-7.5000×10^1	1.0930×10^0

Table 11. Maximum CO$_2$ penalty factor and emission coefficient in 6 generator sets.

Unit	Emission Coefficients of CO$_2$				Penalty Factor of CO$_2$
	α_{CO2}	β_{CO2}	γ_{CO2}	δ_{CO2}	h_c
	tons/kW	tons/kW	tons/kW	tons/kW	tons/kW
1	1.5000×10^{-3}	9.2000×10^{-2}	1.4000×10^1	-16.00	7.8230×10^{-1}
2	1.4000×10^{-3}	2.5000×10^{-2}	1.2500×10^1	-93.50	1.1895×10^0
3	1.6000×10^{-3}	5.5000×10^{-2}	1.3500×10^1	-85.00	1.4356×10^0
4	1.2000×10^{-3}	1.0000×10^{-2}	1.3500×10^1	-24.50	1.1333×10^0
5	2.3000×10^{-3}	4.0000×10^{-2}	2.1000×10^1	-59.00	7.4560×10^{-1}
6	1.4000×10^{-3}	8.0000×10^{-2}	2.2000×10^1	-70.00	7.1580×10^{-1}

Along with the integration of the demand side management (DSM) technique, as outlined in Section 2, utilizing AOA, the test system's expected load demand is adjusted. Figure 6 displays the recently reorganized load requirement of the system. DSM offers a significant advantage, resulting in a 12.46% reduction in peak load, from 225 MW to 207 MW, and an increase in the load factor from 0.8291 to 0.8996. The statistical data are additionally documented in Table 12. It is significant to note that in both the pre- and post-DSM scenarios, at the end of the day, total and average load are the same.

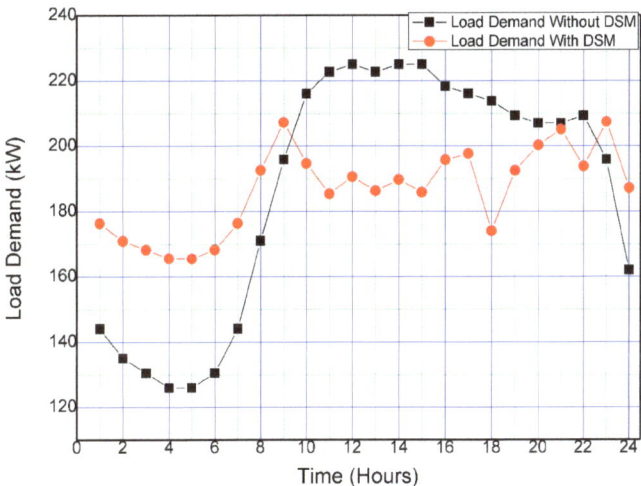

Figure 6. Load–demand curve with and without DSM.

Table 12. Beneficial effects of DSM applications.

	Without DSM	**With 40% DSM**
Peak Load Demand (MW)	225	207.385
Ave. Load Demand (MW)	186.56	186.56
Total Load Demand (MW)	4477.5	4477.4990
Load Factor	0.8291	0.8996
Reduction in Peak (%)	Reference	7.829%

The description of results as displayed in Table 13 (the outcome of implementing CSAOA on all the equations mentioned in Section 2) is as follows:

(a) Cost (ECD) minimization performed on test system 2. The minimum generation cost of the system is found to be USD 76,085 without DSM, which further reduces to USD 74,774 with DSM, respectively. Figures 7 and 8 illustrate, respectively, the hourly production of distributed energy resources (DERs) in the graphical representation, when the cost of generating is USD 76,085 and USD 74,774. On comparing Figures 6–8, the hourly load pattern can be easily traced, meaning that the total load demands every hour are fulfilled by the DERs.

(b) Emission (EMD) minimization is performed on test system 2. The minimum emissions of the plant could be reduced to 236 tons ultimately when DSM is implemented, and the load demand is restructured.

(c) CEED is performed as per the PPF method and FP method. With the PPF method, the cost and emission combination is USD 314,678, 256 tons and, with the FP method, the cost and emission combination is found to be USD 90,775, 249 tons. These values produce much more improved outcomes when the load demand is reorganized utilizing the DSM approach. It can be clearly seen that the FP method of CEED is a better option for obtaining a minimum cost and emission combination compared with PPF-based CEED.

(d) Weighted combined economic emissions dispatch with equal weightage to both cost and emissions function is found to be the best measure of CEED, with a minimum value of USD 78,304 and 246 tons for cost and emissions, respectively. These values, as mentioned above, reduce further for the DSM-based load demand model to USD 78,064 and 243 tons. The hourly output of DERs is shown in Figures 9 and 10, where the weighted ECED is used as the fitness function. Both the cost and emission functions are given equal weights. Similarly, Figures 11 and 12 display the hourly output of DERs when PPF-based CEED is considered as the fitness function.

(e) Thereafter, the minimization of CO_2, SO_2, and NO_x are individually considered as EMD fitness functions and are minimized one at a time. When CO_2 is individually minimized to 75 tons, the values of SO_2 and NO_x are 93 tons and 77 tons, which add to an amount of 246 tons of total emission value. Similarly, SO_2 and NO_x are minimized individually, and all the results are mentioned in Table 14. The values of CO_2, SO_2, and NO_x when the total emission is minimized is also shown in Table 14. Figure 13a–d are the pie-chart representations of Table 14, which highlights the shares of individual emission components as a part of the total emission. The average share of SO_2, CO_2, and NO_x are 37%, 33%, and 30%, respectively.

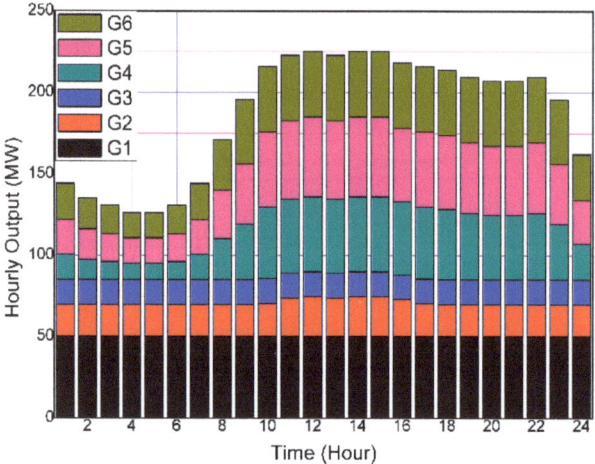

Figure 7. ECD hourly output without DSM.

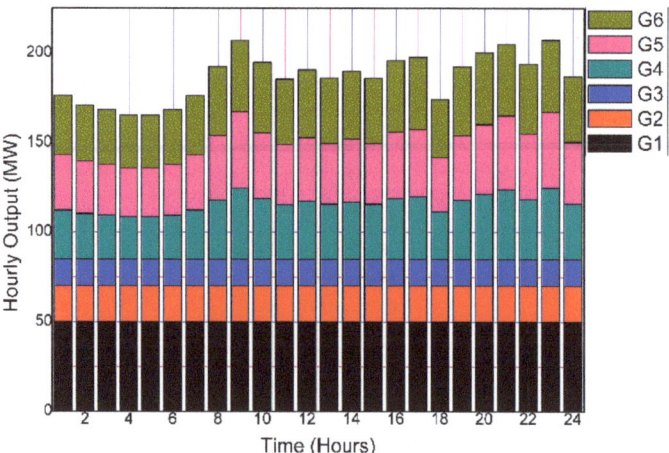

Figure 8. ECD hourly output with DSM.

Table 13. Outcomes of various fitness functions when evaluated using CSAOA.

	Cost and Emission Profiles	Without DSM	With DSM
ECD	Cost minimization (thousands of USD)	76.085	74.774
EMD	Emission minimization (tons)	240	236
CEED (PPF)	Cost (thousands of USD)	314.678	310.264
	Emission (tons)	256	254
CEED (FP)	Cost (thousands of USD)	90.775	92.192
	Emission (tons)	249	244
ECED ($\mu = 0.5$)	Cost (thousands of USD)	78.304	78.064
	Emission (tons)	246	243

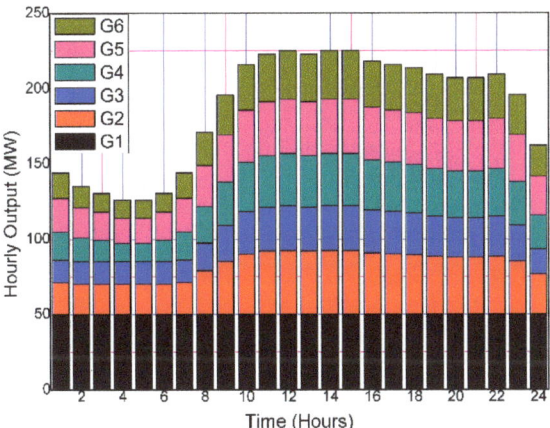

Figure 9. ECED hourly output without DSM.

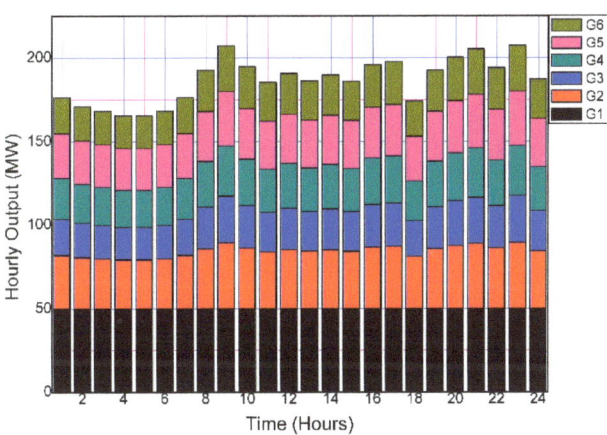

Figure 10. ECED hourly output with DSM.

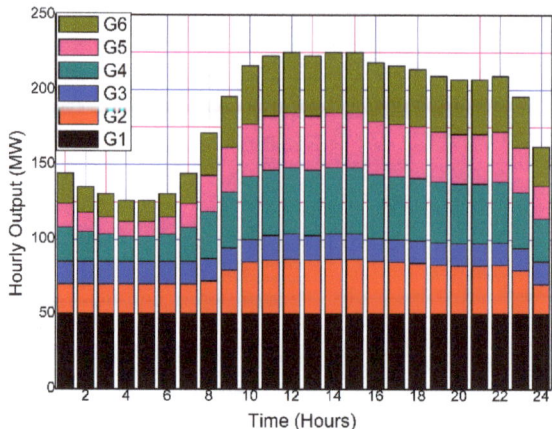

Figure 11. Hourly output of CEED without DSM.

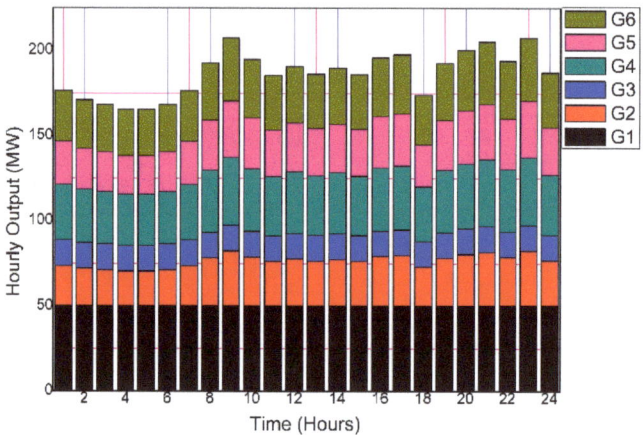

Figure 12. Hourly output of CEED with DSM.

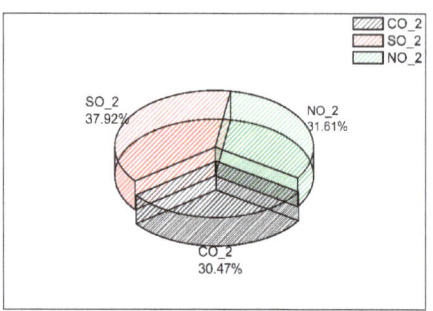 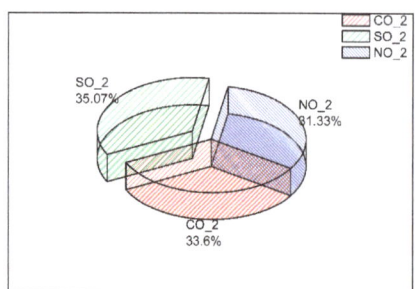

(**a**) Emission Content while minimizing Value of CO_2 only (**b**) Emission Content while minimizing Value of SO_2 only

Figure 13. *Cont.*

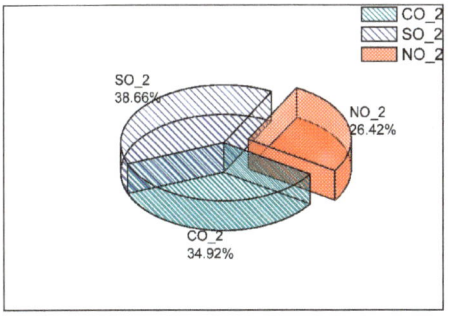 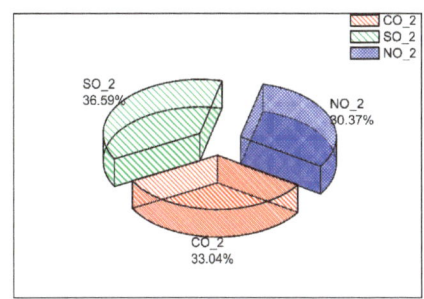

(**c**) Emission Content while minimizing Value of NO₂ only (**d**) Overall Emission Minimization

Figure 13. Emission contents minimization.

Table 14. Emission minimization (tons).

	CO₂ Minimum	SO₂ Minimum	NO$_x$ Minimum	Minimum Emission
CO₂	75	80	88	78
SO₂	93	84	97	86
NO$_x$	77	75	66	71
Overall	246	240	252	236

Both 2D and 3D curves are plotted for cost and emission values of test system 2, with different weightage values ranging from 0.1 and 0.9, and the same is displayed in Figures 14 and 15. The 3D graph shows the coordinates of a balanced compromised solution between cost (USD 78,060) and emission (243 tons), which is obtained when $\mu = 0.5$. μ is represented using the word "mu" in the figure.

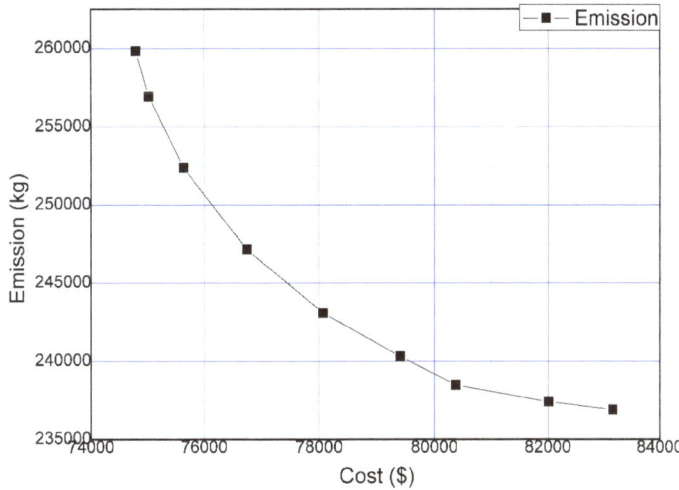

Figure 14. Cost vs. emission curve for different weightage values while evaluating ECED.

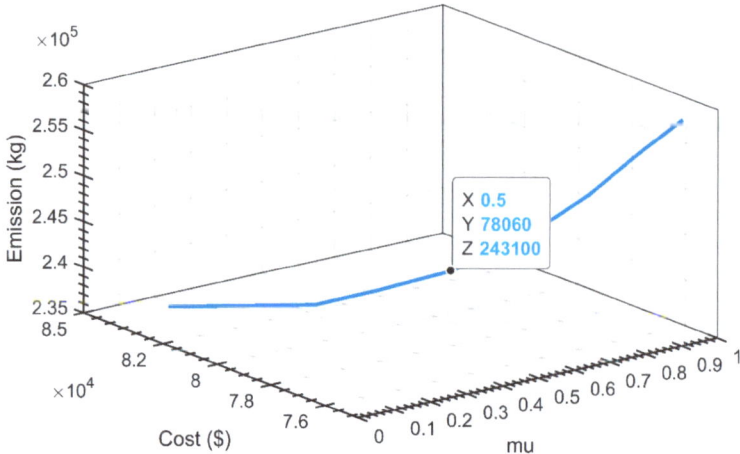

Figure 15. Three-dimensional plot for cost and emission of test system 2 with μ ranging from 0.1 to 0.9.

Measures of central tendencies are evaluated and displayed in Table 15 to statistically analyze the performance of the proposed CSAOA with CSA and AOA. The economic load dispatch equation is minimized in 30 individual trials using all the three algorithms and thereafter the minimum cost, maximum cost, and total number of times the minimum cost is yielded by each algorithm is recorded.

Table 15. Statistical analysis of generation costs for test system 2 after 30 trials.

	Minimum Attained Cost (USD)	Maximum Attained Cost (USD)	Average Attained Cost (USD)	Standard Deviations	Hits to Minimum Cost	Execution Time (s)
CSA	74,792	74,829	74,806.80	18.4361	18	5.06
AOA	74,775	74,822	74,789.10	21.9063	21	4.05
CSAOA	74,774	74,782	74,775.60	3.2547	24	3.20

The suggested CSAOA has a greater level of robustness, as shown by the smallest value of the standard deviation and the maximum hits. Figure 16 shows the boxplot that is drawn using the data mentioned in Table 15. The cost convergence characteristics in Figure 17 show the change in generation cost with the change in iterations for various algorithms. A sensitivity assessment is also operated to comment on the effects of change in tuning parameters fl, and z. fl is changed from 1.5, 2 and 2.5 for z ranging between 1, 5, and 9, as shown in Table 16. The generation cost remains unchanged, whereas the effect of change in tuning parameters is only shown in the execution time.

Table 16. Sensitivity analysis for tuning parameters of CSAOA.

Scenario	fl	z	Cost with DSM (USD)	Execution Time (s)
1	1.5	1	74,774.7027	4.8003
2	2	5	74,774.6995	4.8003
3	2.5	9	74,774.6984	4.8003
4	1.5	1	74,774.7054	3.2005
5	2	5	74,774.6986	3.2005

Table 16. *Cont.*

Scenario	fl	z	Cost with DSM (USD)	Execution Time (s)
6	2.5	9	74,774.6987	3.2005
7	1.5	1	74,774.7075	9.6006
8	2	5	74,774.9023	9.6006
9	2.5	9	74,774.6983	9.6006

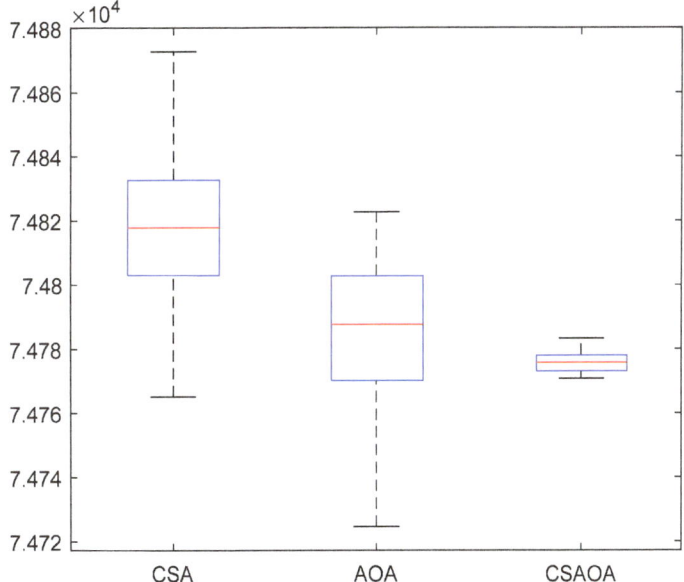

Figure 16. Boxplot of generation costs using various algorithms.

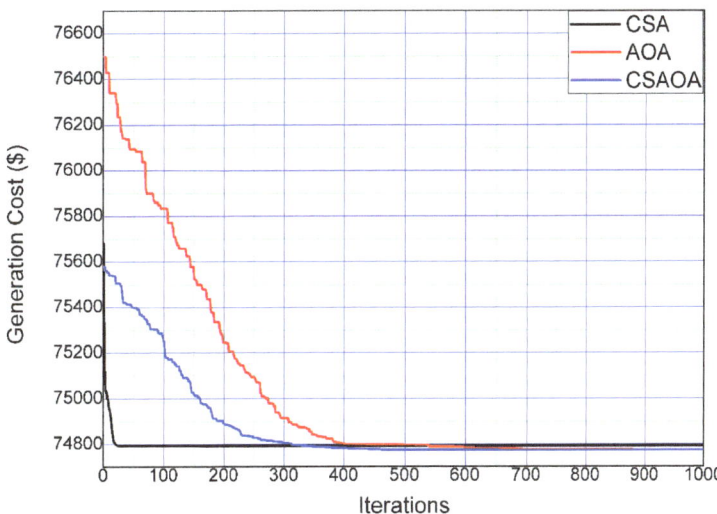

Figure 17. Convergence curve characteristics for the change of generation cost per iteration using various algorithms.

5. Conclusions

The purpose of this article was to build a unique hybrid CSAOA as an optimization tool, which was then applied to address CEED issues after the same was realized on six benchmark functions. CSAOA exhibited good exploration and exploitation capabilities and maintained an adaptive balance between both. Proposed CSAOA also showcased a better convergence rate compared with other existing well-known optimization techniques. Sensitivity analysis performed on CSAOA claimed that it was least affected by change in tuning parameters. The generating cost of the system was reduced from USD 76,085 to USD 74,774 because of DSM initiatives. In addition to this, it improved the load factor of the system and reduced the peak demand from 223 MW to 207 MW. Weighted DEED proved to be a better and economic compromised solution compared with penalty factor-based DEED. Among the limitations used in this paper, voltage profile improvement and transmission loss minimization could have been incorporated, along with the reduction of cost and emissions for both the test systems. Also, DSM implementation requires a set of hourly electricity market prices that is usually available while solving microgrid energy management problem. In this case, since it was not available for the subject test systems, the same had to be collected from the literature.

As an opportunity of forthcoming research, the robustness of the recommended algorithm can be implemented on complex distribution systems such as a microgrid, wherein the effect of battery energy storage systems, renewable energy sources, etc., can be analyzed.

Author Contributions: Conceptualization, B.D. and G.S.; methodology, B.D.; software, B.D.; validation, B.D., G.S., and P.N.B.; formal analysis, G.S.; investigation, G.S.; resources, G.S.; data curation, G.S.; writing—original draft preparation, B.D.; writing—review and editing, G.S. and P.N.B.; visualization, B.D. and G.S.; supervision, P.N.B.; project administration, G.S. and P.N.B.; funding acquisition, G.S. and P.N.B. All authors have read and agreed to the published version of the manuscript.

Funding: This research received no external funding.

Data Availability Statement: The raw data supporting the conclusions of this article will be made available by the authors on request.

Acknowledgments: The authors are grateful to the esteemed reviewers for their valuable insights that helped in raising the standard of the manuscript. The authors are also grateful to Srikant Misra, Assistant Professor, GIET University, Gunupur, Odisha, India for his selfless and generous contribution in preparing the revised manuscript. The authors would also like to thank the University of Johannesburg for its support.

Conflicts of Interest: The authors declare that they have no conflicts of interest.

Abbreviations

a, b, c, d	Cost coefficients
j	Index of generator
$\alpha, \beta, \gamma, \delta$	Emission coefficients
P_j	Power of the generator
n	Index for number of generators
CO_2, NO_X, SO_2	Emissive pollutant components
ppf	Price penalty factor
P_j^{max}	Maximum values of power of the jth generator
$ppf_{j,max,max}$	Form of price penalty factor during maximum cost and maximum pollution
FP	Fractional programming
μ	Constant lies between 0 to 1
ECD_{min}	Minimum cost
ECD_{max}	Maximum cost
EMD_{min}	Minimum emission

EMD_{max}	Maximum emission
CPI	Cost performance index
EPI	Emission performance Index
D_t	Load demand
t	Index for time
UP	Utilization percentage
G_j^t	Hourly output
$\cos t_{grid}^t$	Grid cost
$load\_elastic$	Elastic load
$load\_inelastic$	Inelastic load
$iter/max\_iter$	Iteration/maximum iteration
fl	Flight length
$rand$	Random
AP	Awareness probability
m	Memory
UL	Upper limit
LL	Lower limit
MOA	Mathematics optimizer accelerator
MOP	Mathematics optimizer probability
P_{iter}	Present iteration
x	Solution set
z, λ	Tuning parameter
M_iter	Maximum iteration
ε	Small integer number
F_{mean}	Mean value
F_{worst}	Worst value
f_x	Bench mark function
N	Total number of distinct runs
PV	Photo voltaic
WT	Wind turbine

References

1. Ramesh, B.; Mohan, V.C.J.; Reddy, V.V. Application of BAT algorithm for combined economic load and emission dispatch. *J. Electr. Eng.* **2013**, *13*, 6.
2. Karakonstantis, I.; Vlachos, A. Ant colony optimization for continuous domains applied to emission and economic dispatch problems. *J. Inf. Optim. Sci.* **2015**, *36*, 23–42. [CrossRef]
3. Roy, P.K.; Bhui, S. Multi-objective quasi-oppositional teaching learning based optimization for economic emission load dispatch problem. *Int. J. Electr. Power Energy Syst.* **2013**, *53*, 937–948. [CrossRef]
4. Chandrasekaran, K.; Simon, S.P. Wind-thermal integrated power system scheduling problem using Cuckoo search algorithm. *Int. J. Oper. Res. Inf. Syst. (IJORIS)* **2014**, *5*, 81–109. [CrossRef]
5. Abdelaziz, A.; Ali, E.; Elazim, S.A. Flower pollination algorithm to solve combined economic and emission dispatch problems. *Eng. Sci. Technol. Int. J.* **2016**, *19*, 980–990. [CrossRef]
6. Apostolopoulos, T.; Vlachos, A. Application of the firefly algorithm for solving the economic emissions load dispatch problem. *Int. J. Comb.* **2011**, *2011*, 523806. [CrossRef]
7. Hota, P.; Barisal, A.; Chakrabarti, R. Economic emission load dispatch through fuzzy based bacterial foraging algorithm. *Int. J. Electr. Power Energy Syst.* **2010**, *32*, 794–803. [CrossRef]
8. Song, Y.; Wang, G.; Wang, P.; Johns, A. Environmental/economic dispatch using fuzzy logic controlled genetic algorithms. *IEE Proc.-Gener. Transm. Distrib.* **1997**, *144*, 377–382. [CrossRef]
9. El Ela, A.A.; Abido, M.; Spea, S. Differential evolution algorithm for emission constrained economic power dispatch problem. *Electr. Power Syst. Res.* **2010**, *80*, 1286–1292. [CrossRef]
10. Kumar, A.; Dhanushkodi, K.; Kumar, J.; Paul, C. Particle swarm optimization solution to emission and economic dispatch problem. In Proceedings of the TENCON 2003, Conference on Convergent Technologies for Asia-Pacific Region, Bangalore, India, 5–17 October 2003; IEEE: Piscataway, NJ, USA, 2003; Volume 1, pp. 435–439.
11. Srivastava, A.; Das, D.K. A bottlenose dolphin optimizer: An application to solve dynamic emission economic dispatch problem in the microgrid. *Knowl.-Based Syst.* **2022**, *243*, 108455. [CrossRef]
12. Lin, C.; Liang, H.; Pang, A. A fast data-driven optimization method of multi-area combined economic emission dispatch. *Appl. Energy* **2023**, *337*, 120884. [CrossRef]

13. Li, L.-L.; Lou, J.-L.; Tseng, M.-L.; Lim, M.K.; Tan, R.R. A hybrid dynamic economic environmental dispatch model for balancing operating costs and pollutant emissions in renewable energy: A novel improved mayfly algorithm. *Expert Syst. Appl.* **2022**, *203*, 117411. [CrossRef]
14. Yu, X.; Duan, Y.; Luo, W. A knee guided algorithm to solve multi-objective economic emission dispatch problem. *Energy* **2022**, *259*, 124876. [CrossRef]
15. Sutar, M.; Jadhav, H. A modified artificial bee colony algorithm based on a non-dominated sorting genetic approach for combined economic-emission load dispatch problem. *Appl. Soft Comput.* **2023**, *144*, 110433. [CrossRef]
16. Hassan, M.H.; Yousri, D.; Kamel, S.; Rahmann, C. A modified Marine predators algorithm for solving single-and multi-objective combined economic emission dispatch problems. *Comput. Ind. Eng.* **2022**, *164*, 107906. [CrossRef]
17. Wu, P.; Zou, D.; Yu, N.; Zhang, G.; Kong, L. An improved NSGA-III for the dynamic economic emission dispatch considering reliability. *Energy Rep.* **2022**, *8*, 14304–14317. [CrossRef]
18. Duan, Y.; Zhao, Y.; Hu, J. An initialization-free distributed algorithm for dynamic economic dispatch problems in microgrid: Modeling, optimization and analysis. *Sustain. Energy Grids Netw.* **2023**, *34*, 101004. [CrossRef]
19. Li, D.; Yang, C.; Zou, D. A nondominated sorting genetic algorithm III with three crossover strategies for the combined heat and power dynamic economic emission dispatch with or without prohibited operating zones. *Eng. Appl. Artif. Intell.* **2023**, *123*, 106443. [CrossRef]
20. Zou, D.; Li, S.; Xuan, K.; Ouyang, H. A NSGA-II variant for the dynamic economic emission dispatch considering plug-in electric vehicles. *Comput. Ind. Eng.* **2022**, *173*, 108717. [CrossRef]
21. Lokeshgupta, B.; Sivasubramani, S. Multi-objective dynamic economic and emission dispatch with demand side management. *Int. J. Electr. Power Energy Syst.* **2018**, *97*, 334–343. [CrossRef]
22. Mohapatra, P. Combined economic emission dispatch in hybrid power systems using competitive swarm optimization. *J. King Saud Univ.-Comput. Inf. Sci.* **2022**, *34*, 8955–8971. [CrossRef]
23. Xiong, G.; Shuai, M.; Hu, X. Combined heat and power economic emission dispatch using improved bare-bone multi-objective particle swarm optimization. *Energy* **2022**, *244*, 123108. [CrossRef]
24. Shin, H.; Kim, W. Comparison of the centralized and decentralized environmentally constrained economic dispatch methods of coal-fired generators: A case study for South Korea. *Energy* **2023**, *275*, 127364. [CrossRef]
25. Zhou, X.; Ma, Z.; Zou, S.; Zhang, J. Consensus-based distributed economic dispatch for Multi Micro Energy Grid systems under coupled carbon emissions. *Appl. Energy* **2022**, *324*, 119641. [CrossRef]
26. Bhamidi, L.; Sivasubramani, S. Optimal planning and operational strategy of a residential microgrid with demand side management. *IEEE Syst. J.* **2019**, *14*, 2624–2632. [CrossRef]
27. Lokeshgupta, B.; Sivasubramani, S. Dynamic economic and emission dispatch with renewable energy integration under uncertainties and demand-side management. *Electr. Eng.* **2022**, *104*, 2237–2248. [CrossRef]
28. Nourianfar, H.; Abdi, H. Economic emission dispatch considering electric vehicles and wind power using enhanced multi-objective exchange market algorithm. *J. Clean. Prod.* **2023**, *415*, 137805. [CrossRef]
29. Lv, D.; Xiong, G.; Fu, X. Economic emission dispatch of power systems considering solar uncertainty with extended multi-objective differential evolution. *Expert Syst. Appl.* **2023**, *227*, 120298. [CrossRef]
30. Yang, D.; Xu, Y.; Liu, X.; Jiang, C.; Nie, F.; Ran, Z. Economic-emission dispatch problem in integrated electricity and heat system considering multi-energy demand response and carbon capture Technologies. *Energy* **2022**, *253*, 124153. [CrossRef]
31. Carrillo-Galvez, A.; Flores-Bazán, F.; Parra, E.L. Effect of models uncertainties on the emission constrained economic dispatch. A prediction interval-based approach. *Appl. Energy* **2022**, *317*, 119070.
32. Wu, M.; Xu, J.; Li, Y.; Zeng, L.; Shi, Z.; Liu, Y.; Wen, M.; Li, C. Low carbon economic dispatch of integrated energy systems considering life cycle assessment and risk cost. *Int. J. Electr. Power Energy Syst.* **2023**, *153*, 109287. [CrossRef]
33. Ahmed, I.; Rehan, M.; Basit, A.; Malik, S.H.; Alvi, U.-E.; Hong, K.-S. Multi-area economic emission dispatch for large-scale multi-fueled power plants contemplating inter-connected grid tie-lines power flow limitations. *Energy* **2022**, *261*, 125178. [CrossRef]
34. Basu, M. Multi-county combined heat and power dynamic economic emission dispatch incorporating electric vehicle parking lot. *Energy* **2023**, *275*, 127523. [CrossRef]
35. Tang, X.; Li, Z.; Xu, X.; Zeng, Z.; Jiang, T.; Fang, W.; Meng, A. Multi-objective economic emission dispatch based on an extended crisscross search optimization algorithm. *Energy* **2022**, *244*, 122715. [CrossRef]
36. Lai, W.; Zheng, X.; Song, Q.; Hu, F.; Tao, Q.; Chen, H. Multi-objective membrane search algorithm: A new solution for economic emission dispatch. *Appl. Energy* **2022**, *326*, 119969. [CrossRef]
37. Sundaram, A. Multiobjective multi verse optimization algorithm to solve dynamic economic emission dispatch problem with transmission loss prediction by an artificial neural network. *Appl. Soft Comput.* **2022**, *124*, 109021. [CrossRef]
38. Zhang, L.; Guo, Q.; Liu, M.; Yang, N.; Gao, R.; Sobhani, B. Optimal dispatch of dynamic power and heat considering load management, water pump system, and renewable resources by grasshopper optimization algorithm. *J. Energy Storage* **2023**, *57*, 106166. [CrossRef]
39. Jadoun, V.K.; Prashanth, G.R.; Joshi, S.S.; Narayanan, K.; Malik, H.; Márquez, F.P.G. Optimal fuzzy based economic emission dispatch of combined heat and power units using dynamically controlled Whale Optimization Algorithm. *Appl. Energy* **2022**, *315*, 119033. [CrossRef]

40. Hao, W.-K.; Wang, J.-S.; Li, X.-D.; Song, H.-M.; Bao, Y.-Y. Probability distribution arithmetic optimization algorithm based on variable order penalty functions to solve combined economic emission dispatch problem. *Appl. Energy* **2022**, *316*, 119061. [CrossRef]
41. Wang, H.; Fang, Y.; Zhang, X.; Dong, Z.; Yu, X. Robust dispatching of integrated energy system considering economic operation domain and low carbon emission. *Energy Rep.* **2022**, *8*, 252–264. [CrossRef]
42. Sharifian, Y.; Abdi, H. Solving multi-zone combined heat and power economic emission dispatch problem considering wind uncertainty by applying grasshopper optimization algorithm. *Sustain. Energy Technol. Assess* **2022**, *53*, 102512. [CrossRef]
43. Chaurasia, R.; Gairola, S.; Pal, Y. Technical, economic, and environmental performance comparison analysis of a hybrid renewable energy system based on power dispatch strategies. *Sustain. Energy Technol. Assess* **2022**, *53*, 102787. [CrossRef]
44. Vigya; Raj, S.; Shiva, C.K.; Vedik, B.; Mahapatra, S.; Mukherjee, V. A novel chaotic chimp sine cosine algorithm Part-I: For solving optimization problem. *Chaos Solitons Fractals* **2023**, *173*, 113672. [CrossRef]
45. Raj, S.; Mahapatra, S.; Babu, R.; Verma, S. Hybrid intelligence strategy for techno-economic reactive power dispatch approach to ensure system security. *Chaos Solitons Fractals* **2023**, *170*, 113363. [CrossRef]
46. Mahapatra, S.; Raj, S. A novel meta-heuristic approach for optimal RPP using series compensated FACTS controller. *Intell. Syst. Appl.* **2023**, *18*, 200220.
47. Raj, S.; Bhattacharyya, B. Weak bus determination and real power loss minimization using Grey wolf optimization. In Proceedings of the 2016 IEEE 6th International Conference on Power Systems (ICPS), New Delhi, India, 4–6 March 2016; IEEE: Piscataway, NJ, USA, 2016; pp. 1–4.
48. Raj, S.; Bhattacharyya, B. Optimal placement of TCSC and SVC for reactive power planning using Whale optimization algorithm. *Swarm Evol. Comput.* **2018**, *40*, 131–143. [CrossRef]
49. Dehedkar, S.N.; Raj, S. Determination of optimal location and Implementation of Solar Photovoltaic system using ETAP. In Proceedings of the 2022 IEEE 2nd International Symposium on Sustainable Energy, Signal Processing and Cyber Security (iSSSC), Gunupur, India, 15–17 December 2022; IEEE: Piscataway, NJ, USA, 2022; pp. 1–4.
50. Dey, B.; Raj, S.; Babu, R.; Chhualsingh, T. An approach to attain a balanced trade-off solution for dynamic economic emission dispatch problem on a microgrid system. *Int. J. Syst. Assur. Eng. Manag.* **2023**, *14*, 1300–1311. [CrossRef]
51. Rajasomashekar, S.; Aravindhababu, P. Biogeography based optimization technique for best compromise solution of economic emission dispatch. *Swarm Evol. Comput.* **2012**, *7*, 47–57. [CrossRef]
52. Basak, S.; Bhattacharyya, B. Optimal scheduling in demand-side management based grid-connected microgrid system by hybrid optimization approach considering diverse wind profiles. *ISA Trans.* **2023**, *139*, 357–375. [CrossRef]
53. Askarzadeh, A. A novel metaheuristic method for solving constrained engineering optimization problems: Crow search algorithm. *Comput. Struct.* **2016**, *169*, 1–12. [CrossRef]
54. Abualigah, L.; Diabat, A.; Mirjalili, S.; Abd Elaziz, M.; Gandomi, A.H. The arithmetic optimization algorithm. *Comput. Methods Appl. Mech. Eng.* **2021**, *376*, 113609. [CrossRef]
55. Dey, B.; Misra, S.; Chhualsingh, T.; Sahoo, A.K.; Singh, A.R. A hybrid metaheuristic approach to solve grid centric cleaner economic energy management of microgrid systems. *J. Clean. Prod.* **2024**, *448*, 141311. [CrossRef]

Disclaimer/Publisher's Note: The statements, opinions and data contained in all publications are solely those of the individual author(s) and contributor(s) and not of MDPI and/or the editor(s). MDPI and/or the editor(s) disclaim responsibility for any injury to people or property resulting from any ideas, methods, instructions or products referred to in the content.

Article

Adaptive Sliding-Mode Controller for a Zeta Converter to Provide High-Frequency Transients in Battery Applications

Andrés Tobón [1], Carlos Andrés Ramos-Paja [2,*], Martha Lucía Orozco-Gutiérrez [3], Andrés Julián Saavedra-Montes [2] and Sergio Ignacio Serna-Garcés [1]

[1] Departamento de Electrónica y Telecomunicaciones, Instituto Tecnológico Metropolitano, Medellín 050013, Colombia; andrestobon@itm.edu.co (A.T.); sergioserna@itm.edu.co (S.I.S.-G.)
[2] Facultad de Minas, Universidad Nacional de Colombia, Medellín 050041, Colombia; ajsaaved@unal.edu.co
[3] Escuela de Ingeniería Eléctrica y Electrónica, Universidad del Valle, Cali 760042, Colombia; martha.orozco@correounivalle.edu.co
* Correspondence: caramosp@unal.edu.co; Tel.: +57-317-635-8204

Abstract: Hybrid energy storage systems significantly impact the renewable energy sector due to their role in enhancing grid stability and managing its variability. However, implementing these systems requires advanced control strategies to ensure correct operation. This paper presents an algorithm for designing the power and control stages of a hybrid energy storage system formed by a battery, a supercapacitor, and a bidirectional Zeta converter. The control stage involves an adaptive sliding-mode controller co-designed with the power circuit parameters. The design algorithm ensures battery protection against high-frequency transients that reduce lifespan, and provides compatibility with low-cost microcontrollers. Moreover, the continuous output current of the Zeta converter does not introduce current harmonics to the battery, the microgrid, or the load. The proposed solution is validated through an application example using PSIM electrical simulation software (version 2024.0), demonstrating superior performance in comparison with a classical cascade PI structure.

Keywords: hybrid energy storage system; adaptive sliding-mode controller; battery degradation; supercapacitor; Zeta converter

Citation: Tobón, A.; Ramos-Paja, C.A.; Orozco-Gutiérrez, M.L.; Saavedra-Montes, A.J.; Serna-Garcés, S.I. Adaptive Sliding-Mode Controller for a Zeta Converter to Provide High-Frequency Transients in Battery Applications. *Algorithms* **2024**, *17*, 319. https://doi.org/10.3390/a17070319

Academic Editors: Sheng Du, Zixin Huang, Li Jin and Xiongbo Wan

Received: 17 June 2024
Revised: 5 July 2024
Accepted: 8 July 2024
Published: 21 July 2024

Copyright: © 2024 by the authors. Licensee MDPI, Basel, Switzerland. This article is an open access article distributed under the terms and conditions of the Creative Commons Attribution (CC BY) license (https://creativecommons.org/licenses/by/4.0/).

1. Introduction

Current industrial processes are crucial in pursuing high efficiency, reliability, and adaptability [1,2]. Harnessing the power of data and optimization algorithms is imperative, as they are the key to improving the system's control, which is needed to stay competitive in the evolving industrial landscape. Artificial intelligence (AI) algorithms and data-driven optimization models for intelligent manufacturing processes have been used to improve production efficiency, reduce costs, and improve the quality of manufacturing services [3,4]. The use of optimization algorithms to obtain profitable, productive, controllable, safe, and sustainable processes is presented in [5,6]. In particular, Ref. [5] reviews multi-objective algorithms for energy production, supply chains, and chemical industries.

Meanwhile, in Ref. [6], genetic algorithms (GAs) and artificial neural networks (ANNs) are used to define the objective function of the optimization algorithms applied in the metallurgical industry. In addition, Ref. [7] highlights algorithms for data-based industrial process prediction, namely time series and factor-based predictions. That work tests different prediction techniques in multiple steel plant processes.

Energy transition has forced industries to focus on critical processes such as managing electrical energy storage systems (ESSs). Multiple works have focused on ESS characterization, including the description of their components, control strategies, applications, and technologies for high-power systems [8–10], as well as their use in multi-source power systems [11], their techno-economic assessment when integrated with renewable energy [12], and the implementation of battery management systems (BMSs) [13]. These systems are fundamental in electrical vehicles (EVs) and microgrids (MGs) based on renewable energy. For example, for EVs under heavy-duty conditions, Ref. [14] evaluates different energy storage system topologies, and Ref. [15] presents a comparison study of semi-active ESS topologies for EVs. Ref. [16] provides a critical review of devices with high energy density and high power density used in electrical transportation; meanwhile, Ref. [17] reports a review of standards and challenges of ESSs for EVs. Moreover, Ref. [18] implements several control schemes tested on EVs with a real driving cycle. Similarly, Ref. [19] presents a systematic review of ESS control techniques for grid-connected and standalone systems based on artificial intelligence. In contrast, Ref. [20] discusses the importance of ESSs in MGs with renewable energy sources.

Among energy storage systems, hybrid ESSs (HESSs) are relevant since the joint operation of complementary energy sources, i.e., sources with high energy density and sources with high power density, guarantees improved power quality, increased energy efficiency, and better dynamic response. Ref. [10] presents examples of HESS installations that improve grid stability and power quality with frequency regulation. A detailed review of HESS benefits is reported in Ref. [20], where the contributions of HESS to MGs are highlighted. For example, HESSs contribute to power quality, offering the MG the ability to provide clean and stable power with a constant power flow, as well as a wave-pure and noise-free sinusoidal within the acceptable frequency and voltage limits. Similarly, Ref. [21] evaluates the capabilities of HESSs to mitigate fluctuations and uncertainty of renewable energy. ESSs with high power density, like supercapacitors or flywheels [21,22], can support loads that demand fast power peaks, while ESSs with high energy density, like batteries [21,23], can provide sustained power for a long time (hours or days).

Different topologies exist for implementing HESSs depending on the converters action; those systems are denominated as passive, semi-active, or fully active. In a passive HESS, any source is managed using a converter, while in semi-active HESS, converters manage some of the sources. For example, the battery pack is regularly connected to the DC bus, while a DC/DC converter manages the supercapacitor [24,25]. Finally, in a fully active HESS, each source is managed by a dedicated converter. Some reviews on topologies for HESS have been published in the last few years. According to the analysis reported in [26], multi-input, multi-port, coupled-inductor, switched-capacitor, and z-source/quasi-z-source converter are suitable for a HESS formed by a battery and a supercapacitor. Those topologies provide bidirectional power flow in EVs, DC MGs, and renewable energy applications. Ref. [16] reports a broad analysis of passive, semi-active, and fully active topologies for HESSs formed by a battery and a supercapacitor. That article highlights the strengths, weaknesses, and opportunities associated with each HESS setup. Ref. [27] also reviews the state of the art on HESS topologies, including reconfigurable topologies at the cell and module levels. Similarly, four semi-active HESSs are discussed in Ref. [15], which are based on supercapacitors and batteries.

Many works on HESSs with semi-active and fully active configurations have been recently published. In Refs. [28,29], a PV system with a fully active HESS, formed by a battery, a supercapacitor (SC), and a bidirectional buck-boost converter, is tested with several algorithms, namely classical PI, an ANN, and Model Predictive Control (MPC). In that work, the mathematical model of the controllers is presented, but the implementation of the algorithms is not discussed. In Ref. [30], the combined control between an optimization algorithm and a neural network is applied to a bidirectional DC-DC converter of an EV; the authors state that algorithms enhanced performance and reduced computation time compared with other methods; however, the implementation is not discussed. In Ref. [31], a fully active HESS formed by a PV array, a battery, and a supercapacitor is presented. The control algorithms for each converter are classical PI structures, and the references for the controllers of both the battery and the supercapacitor converters are based on a power management strategy, in which the missing power on the load is first compensated with the battery and later with the supercapacitor. A structure similar to that reported in [31] is proposed in [25], but there is a fuel cell instead of a PV array. In that work, a fuzzy logic algorithm of 36 rules controls an energy management unit (EMU), which distributes the power among sources and sets the references for the centralized algorithm that controls all HESS converters.

Table 1 summarizes the characteristics of some works published in recent years with HESSs similar to the solution proposed in this manuscript. The review shows that HESSs are based on SCs and batteries, fully active topologies, and buck-boost converters. Control algorithms are diverse, but the classical PI structure is the most common solution. However, some works adopt control schemes based on intelligent algorithms (ANN, Recalling-Enhanced Recurrent Neural Network—RERNN), optimization algorithms (Sand Cat Swarm Optimization—SCSO, MPC), and non-linear algorithms (Supertwisting Sliding Mode Controller—SSMC). Nevertheless, none of the analyzed references implement the HESS with a Zeta converter managing the storage devices; only one reference controls the system with sliding-mode control, but it does not protect the battery from fast current transients.

Table 1. Characteristics of some works on HESS.

Ref.	Storage Device	HESS Type	Control's Algorithm	Converter	Comments
[30]	SC-baterry	Fully active	SCSO-RERNN	Buck-boost	EV application
[29]	SC-battery	Fully active	PI (battery), MPC (SC)	BC not specified	MG with PV
[28]	SC-battery	Fully active	ANN	Buck-boost	References' generation with ANN
[31]	SC-battery	Fully active	PI	Buck-boost	PI tunning with LMI-PSO-GA.
[25]	SC-battery	Fully active	SSMC	Buck-boost	References' generation with fuzzy logic
[18]	SC-battery	SC Semi-active	PI	Boost	EV application

This manuscript introduces a unique HESS system with a semi-active topology. In this system, the SC is managed by a bidirectional converter, and the battery is directly connected to the DC bus (see Figure 1). The main feature of this setup is the use of a bidirectional Zeta converter and a sliding-mode controller (SMC). The Zeta converter has two key features; it works with any conversion relations and it has a continuous output current. In this way, the Zeta converter can connect any SC with any battery, and it prevents currents with high derivatives in the battery, decreasing its degradation. Furthermore, the SMC has several advantages when used with switching converters. First, its output is a binary signal, which fits perfectly with the converter control input, avoiding the implementation of a Pulse-Width Modulator (PWM); second, the SMC is a non-linear technique that is able to ensure global stability; third, the SMC is robust to variations in the system parameters; and finally, the SMC is integrated into a co-design process of the plant/controller, which is another contribution of this paper. The SMC algorithm proposed in this manuscript ensures three essential conditions:

- Stable DC/DC converter operation.
- Reduced harmonics in the battery current.
- Safe SC voltage regulation.

In summary, the device proposed in this manuscript is a semi-active HESS. Its purpose is to help the battery to deliver fast current transients to the load without altering the power management or the bus control system. Hence, the device's installation and operation are transparent to the microgrid.

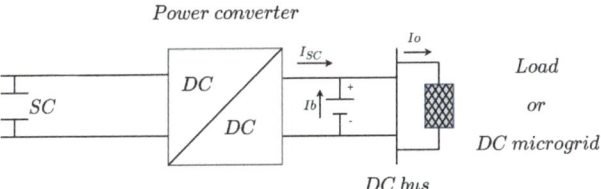

Figure 1. Structure of the hybrid energy storage system.

This manuscript is organized into five more sections: Section 2 presents the modeling of the power circuit, where the switched model, average model, stability conditions, and current/voltage ripple are discussed. In addition, Section 3 shows the design and analysis of the SMC, where the switching function is defined, the global stability is demonstrated, the closed-loop dynamic is designed, and the switching frequency limitation is imposed. The design process of the converter and the controller is presented in Section 4, where the algorithms for the selection of passive components and the implementation of the SMC law are illustrated; this section also includes the design of the high-pass filter used to avoid high-frequency current harmonics in the battery. The algorithms for the adaptive SMC's digital implementation and the PSIM simulations are discussed in Section 5, where the digital implementation reduces the computational burden on a low-cost microcontroller. Finally, the conclusions close the manuscript.

In summary, the contributions of this paper are:

- Definition of the algorithms for designing the power stage and the adaptive SMC.
- Providing a battery current without high-frequency transients.
- Algorithms for implementing the adaptive SMC on low-cost microcontrollers with low computation burden.

2. Power Circuit Modeling

The proposed solution considers the parallel connection of a bidirectional Zeta converter with the battery to be supported; the electrical scheme of this solution is depicted in Figure 2. This circuit describes the electrical structure of the bidirectional Zeta converter, which is formed by two capacitors (C_1 and C_2), two inductors (L_1 and L_2), and two MOSFETs. In addition, the proposed solution requires a fast controller with a wide operation range because the Zeta converter must be stable for capacitor voltages lower, equal to, or higher than the battery voltage; also, it must support positive, negative, and null current conditions. Therefore, the proposed solution includes the design of an adaptive sliding-mode controller (adaptive SMC) to ensure the correct operation of the system. The adaptive SMC requires two voltage sensors, one for the capacitor C_2 voltage (v_{C_2}) and another for the battery voltage (v_b). It also requires three current sensors, one for the L_1 current (i_{L_1}), another for the L_2 current (i_{L_2}), and a final one for the load/microgrid current (i_o) that is served by the battery.

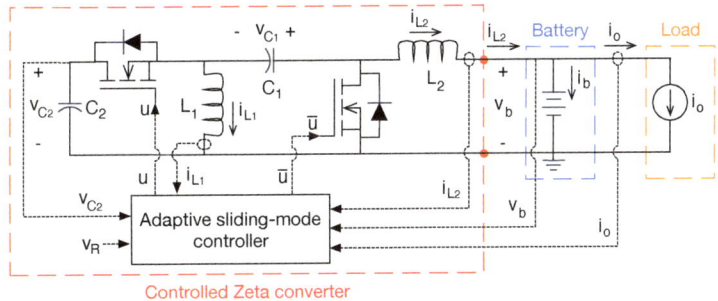

Figure 2. Zeta power system designed to support battery transients.

The design of the adaptive SMC requires a control-oriented model of the power system. Such a model is obtained by writing the differential equations of the inductor currents and capacitor voltages for each possible state of the control signal, i.e., $u = 1$ and $u = 0$, following the classical method based on charge and volt-second balances reported in [32]. For the first condition ($u = 1$), the differential equations are given in Equations (1)–(4).

$$\frac{di_{L1}}{dt} = \frac{v_{C2}}{L_1} \tag{1}$$

$$\frac{di_{L2}}{dt} = \frac{v_{C1} + v_{C2} - v_b}{L_2} \tag{2}$$

$$\frac{dv_{C1}}{dt} = -\frac{i_{L2}}{C_1} \tag{3}$$

$$\frac{dv_{C2}}{dt} = -\frac{i_{L1} + i_{L2}}{C_2} \tag{4}$$

Similarly, for the second condition ($u = 0$), the differential equations are given in Equations (5)–(8).

$$\frac{di_{L1}}{dt} = -\frac{v_{C1}}{L_1} \tag{5}$$

$$\frac{di_{L2}}{dt} = -\frac{v_b}{L_2} \tag{6}$$

$$\frac{dv_{C1}}{dt} = \frac{i_{L1}}{C_1} \tag{7}$$

$$\frac{dv_{C2}}{dt} = 0 \tag{8}$$

The previous two sets of equations must be mixed into a single set of non-linear differential equations, thus forming the switched model of the power system given in Equations (9)–(12). In such a model, u is the control signal of the MOSFETs, and $\bar{u} = 1 - u$ is the complementary control signal.

$$\frac{di_{L1}}{dt} = \frac{v_{C2} \cdot u - v_{C1} \cdot \bar{u}}{L_1} \tag{9}$$

$$\frac{di_{L2}}{dt} = \frac{(v_{C1} + v_{C2}) \cdot u - v_b}{L_2} \tag{10}$$

$$\frac{dv_{C1}}{dt} = \frac{-i_{L2} \cdot u + i_{L1} \cdot \bar{u}}{C_1} \tag{11}$$

$$\frac{dv_{C2}}{dt} = -\frac{(i_{L1} + i_{L2}) \cdot u}{C_2} \tag{12}$$

The switched model can be averaged within the switching period to generate the averaged model, which is useful for analyzing the main dynamic behavior of the power system; this modeling strategy is documented in [32]. Taking into account that the duty cycle d corresponds to the average value of the control signal u, as given in Equation (13), the averaged model of the power system is obtained as reported in Equations (14)–(17), where $d' = 1 - d$ is the complementary duty cycle and T_{sw} is the switching period.

$$d = \frac{1}{T_{sw}} \cdot \int_0^{T_{sw}} u \, dt \tag{13}$$

$$\frac{di_{L1}}{dt} = \frac{v_{C2} \cdot d - v_{C1} \cdot d'}{L_1} \tag{14}$$

$$\frac{di_{L2}}{dt} = \frac{(v_{C1} + v_{C2}) \cdot d - v_b}{L_2} \tag{15}$$

$$\frac{dv_{C1}}{dt} = \frac{-i_{L2} \cdot d + i_{L1} \cdot d'}{C_1} \tag{16}$$

$$\frac{dv_{C2}}{dt} = -\frac{(i_{L1} + i_{L2}) \cdot d}{C_2} \tag{17}$$

Finally, the steady-state conditions of the power system are obtained from the averaged model by considering the derivatives equal to zero, as described in [32]:

$$v_{C1} = v_b \tag{18}$$

$$v_{C2} = \frac{1-d}{d} \cdot v_b \tag{19}$$

$$i_{L1} = \frac{d}{1-d} \cdot i_{L2} \tag{20}$$

Another important analysis concerns the current and voltage ripples in the power system. Then, the magnitude of the ripples on the inductor currents i_{L1} and i_{L2} is calculated from Equations (5) and (6) following the method reported in [32]:

$$\Delta i_{L1} = \frac{v_b \cdot d' \cdot T_{sw}}{2 \cdot L_1} \tag{21}$$

$$\Delta i_{L2} = \frac{v_b \cdot d' \cdot T_{sw}}{2 \cdot L_2} \tag{22}$$

The magnitude of the voltage ripple in the C_2 capacitor must be calculated from the charge stored and extracted from the capacitor during a switching period. Figure 3 shows the C_2 voltage and current ripple waveforms, where current i_{C2} is obtained from Equation (12). The charge stored in C_2 when i_{C2} is positive is equal to the charge extracted when i_{C2} is negative due to the charge balance principle, and it is equal to $\Delta Q_{C2} = d \cdot T_{sw} \cdot \Delta i_{C2}/4$. Such a charge is also related to the voltage change in C_2 as $\Delta Q_{C2} = C_2 \cdot \Delta v_{C2}$, where Δv_{C2} is the voltage ripple at C_2. Moreover, since both i_{L1} and i_{L2} are in phase, as observed in Equations (1), (2), (5) and (6), the ripple magnitude in the C_2 current is $\Delta i_{C2} = \Delta i_{L1} + \Delta i_{L2}$. Finally, the magnitude of the voltage ripple in the C_2 capacitor is given as follows:

$$\Delta v_{C2} = \frac{d \cdot (\Delta i_{L1} + \Delta i_{L2}) \cdot T_{sw}}{4 \cdot C_2} = \frac{d \cdot d' \cdot v_b \cdot T_{sw}^2}{8 \cdot C_2} \cdot \left(\frac{1}{L_1} + \frac{1}{L_2}\right) \tag{23}$$

In addition, Figure 3 also shows that the peak value of the current ripple occurs when the voltage ripple is equal to zero; similarly, the peak value of the voltage ripple occurs when the current ripple is equal to zero. This condition will be important in the analysis of the switching frequency reported in Section 3.5.

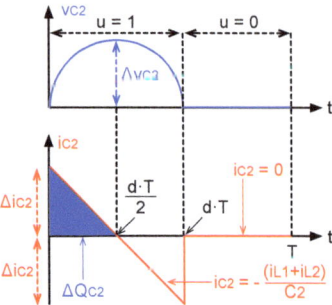

Figure 3. C_2 voltage and current ripple waveforms.

3. Design and Analysis of the Sliding-Mode Controller

The sliding-mode controller must be designed to ensure the following conditions:

- Stable operation of the Zeta converter, which requires the stable relation between i_{L1} and i_{L2} currents given in Equation (20).
- Regulate the output current of the Zeta converter (i_{L2}) to provide the high-frequency components of the load current (i_o), and at the same time, regulate the C_2 voltage to avoid a deep discharge or a dangerous overcharge.

The first condition is ensured by introducing the first part of the switching function Ψ given in Equation (24), which corresponds to relation (20). The second condition is achieved by introducing the second part of Ψ. The i_R value is provided by a high-pass filter, which is discussed in Sections 4.2 and 4.4; the deviation of the C_2 voltage from the safe value v_R is also introduced in this second part, where the value of the k_v gain will be discussed in Section 3.4. Finally, the sliding surface Φ forces the switching function to slide around zero to impose a null error; this is formalized in Equation (25).

$$\Psi = \underbrace{[k_c \cdot i_{L2} - i_{L1}]}_{\text{First part}} + \underbrace{[i_R + k_v \cdot (v_R - v_{C2}) - i_{L2}]}_{\text{Second part}} \quad \text{where} \quad k_c = \frac{d}{d'} \tag{24}$$

$$\Phi = \{\Psi = 0\} \tag{25}$$

The feasibility of designing an SMC based on the previous surface must be confirmed using the transversality, reachability, and equivalent control analyses discussed in [33]; the following subsections report the results of those analyses.

3.1. Transversality Analysis

The transversality condition evaluates the controller's capability to modify the power system's behavior. Such an evaluation is focused on verifying the presence of the control variable u in the derivative of the switching function, which defines the trajectory of the SMC. The formalization of this test is the following:

$$\frac{d}{du}\left(\frac{d\Psi}{dt}\right) \neq 0 \tag{26}$$

Therefore, the time derivative of the switching function (24) is calculated:

$$\frac{d\Psi}{dt} = (k_c - 1) \cdot \left[\frac{(v_{C1} + v_{C2}) \cdot u - v_b}{L_2}\right] - \left[\frac{v_{C2} \cdot u - v_{C1} \cdot \bar{u}}{L_1}\right] \ldots$$
$$+ \frac{di_R}{dt} - k_v \cdot \left[\frac{-(i_{L1} + i_{L2}) \cdot u}{C_2}\right] \tag{27}$$

Then, evaluating the transversality value using the previous derivative leads to the following equation:

$$\frac{d}{du}\left(\frac{d\Psi}{dt}\right) = (v_{C1} + v_{C2}) \cdot \left(\frac{2 \cdot d - 1}{1 - d} \cdot \frac{1}{L_2} - \frac{1}{L_1}\right) + k_v \cdot \frac{i_{L1} + i_{L2}}{C_2} \quad (28)$$

Finally, the design of the parameters of both the Zeta converter and SMC must fulfill the transversality condition (26) using Equation (28); this evaluation is presented in Section 4.3.

3.2. Reachability Analysis

The reachability conditions evaluate the capability of the controller to reach the sliding surface. The analysis is the following:

- Operating under the surface ($\Psi < 0$) requires a positive switching function derivative $\left(\frac{d\Psi}{dt} > 0\right)$ to reach the surface ($\Psi = 0$).
- Operating above the surface ($\Psi > 0$) requires a negative switching function derivative $\left(\frac{d\Psi}{dt} < 0\right)$ to reach the surface ($\Psi = 0$).

The previous analyses are formalized with the following inequalities:

$$\lim_{\Psi \to 0^-} \frac{d\Psi}{dt} > 0 \ \wedge \ \lim_{\Psi \to 0^+} \frac{d\Psi}{dt} < 0 \quad (29)$$

The evaluation of those general reachability conditions depends on the value of the transversality condition (28); a positive value of Equation (28) indicates a direct relation between the control signal u and derivative $\frac{d\Psi}{dt}$, i.e., a positive change on u produces a positive derivative $\left(\frac{d\Psi}{dt} > 0\right)$, and a negative change on u produces a negative derivative $\left(\frac{d\Psi}{dt} < 0\right)$. Instead, a negative value of Equation (28) indicates an inverse relation between u and $\frac{d\Psi}{dt}$, i.e., a positive change on u produces a negative derivative $\left(\frac{d\Psi}{dt} < 0\right)$, and a negative change on u produces a positive derivative $\left(\frac{d\Psi}{dt} > 0\right)$.

Then, for a positive transversality value (28), the general reachability conditions (29) become:

$$\lim_{\Psi \to 0^-} \frac{d\Psi}{dt}\bigg|_{u=1} > 0 \ \wedge \ \lim_{\Psi \to 0^+} \frac{d\Psi}{dt}\bigg|_{u=0} < 0 \quad (30)$$

Evaluating the previous inequalities with the switching function derivative (27) leads to the stability conditions given in inequalities (31) and (32). Those dynamic limitations on $\frac{di_R}{dt}$ must be fulfilled to ensure the reachability of the desired surface in the case of a positive transversality value.

$$\frac{di_R}{dt} > -v_{C2} \cdot \left(\frac{2 \cdot d - 1}{1 - d} \cdot \frac{1}{L_2} - \frac{1}{L_1}\right) - k_v \cdot \left(\frac{i_{L1} + i_{L2}}{C_2}\right) \quad (31)$$

$$\frac{di_R}{dt} < v_b \cdot \left(\frac{2 \cdot d - 1}{1 - d} \cdot \frac{1}{L_2} - \frac{1}{L_1}\right) \quad (32)$$

Instead, for a negative transversality value (28), the reachability conditions are given in Equation (33). Evaluating those inequalities produces the stability conditions given in (34) and (35).

$$\lim_{\Psi \to 0^-} \left.\frac{d\Psi}{dt}\right|_{u=0} > 0 \quad \wedge \quad \lim_{\Psi \to 0^+} \left.\frac{d\Psi}{dt}\right|_{u=1} < 0 \tag{33}$$

$$\frac{di_R}{dt} > v_b \cdot \left(\frac{2 \cdot d - 1}{1 - d} \cdot \frac{1}{L_2} - \frac{1}{L_1}\right) \tag{34}$$

$$\frac{di_R}{dt} < -v_{C2} \cdot \left(\frac{2 \cdot d - 1}{1 - d} \cdot \frac{1}{L_2} - \frac{1}{L_1}\right) - k_v \cdot \left(\frac{i_{L1} + i_{L2}}{C_2}\right) \tag{35}$$

Finally, the reachability conditions impose a dynamic restriction on the positive and negative changes for i_R. Thus, the power system and controller must be designed to achieve the required dynamic response with a stable behavior. This analysis is illustrated in Section 4.3 using an application example.

3.3. Equivalent Control

The equivalent control condition evaluates the average value u_{eq} of the control signal u, which must be constrained by the binary values of u, thus $(0,1)$. In the context of power converters, the average value of u is equal to the duty cycle (13); hence, this equivalent control condition evaluates the non-saturation of the duty cycle:

$$0 < u_{eq} = d < 1 \tag{36}$$

This analysis is performed inside the sliding surface $\left(\Psi = 0 \wedge \frac{d\Psi}{dt} = 0\right)$. Therefore, it ensures that the system remains inside the surface. Replacing the switching function derivative (27) in $\frac{d\Psi}{dt} = 0$, and switching u by u_{eq}, leads to the following equivalent control value:

$$u_{eq} = \frac{v_b \cdot \left(\frac{2 \cdot d - 1}{1 - d} \cdot \frac{1}{L_2} - \frac{1}{L_1}\right) - \frac{di_R}{dt}}{(v_{C1} + v_{C2}) \cdot \left(\frac{2 \cdot d - 1}{1 - d} \cdot \frac{1}{L_2} - \frac{1}{L_1}\right) + k_v \cdot \left(\frac{i_{L1} + i_{L2}}{C_2}\right)} \tag{37}$$

Finally, replacing the equivalent value (37) in inequality (36) produces the same dynamic restrictions on i_R obtained from the reachability conditions. Therefore, as demonstrated by Sira-Ramirez in [34], fulfilling both the transversality and reachability conditions ensures that the equivalent control condition is also fulfilled; hence, the duty cycle of the converter will not be saturated.

3.4. Closed-Loop Dynamics

The next step in the design of the adaptive SMC is calculating the switching function parameter k_v. Such a design is performed considering a stable operation of the SMC (25); thus, $\Psi = 0$ implies $k_c \cdot i_{L2} = i_{L1}$ and $i_{L2} = i_R + k_v \cdot (v_R - v_{C2})$, where $k_c = \frac{d}{d'}$. Since the SMC generates the control signal u, the C_2 voltage can be described using the averaged model given in Equation (17), which results in the following Equation:

$$\frac{dv_{C2}}{dt} = -\frac{k_c}{C_2} \cdot i_{L2} \tag{38}$$

Taking into account that i_R is the output of a high-pass filter acting on the load current, the load transients always end with $i_R = 0$. Therefore, the dynamic behavior of the C_2 voltage is described by the following Equation since $i_{L2} = k_v \cdot (v_R - v_{C2})$ for $i_R = 0$:

$$\frac{dv_{C2}}{dt} = -\frac{k_c}{C_2} \cdot k_v \cdot (v_R - v_{C2}) \tag{39}$$

Transforming the previous expression to the Laplace domain leads to Equation (40), which describes the closed-loop dynamic behavior of the power system. Since the closed-loop exhibits a first-order dynamic, the settling time of C_2 voltage is given by $t_{s,C2} = 3.9 \cdot \tau_{CL}$ as reported in [35]. Therefore, the k_v parameter is calculated in terms of the desired settling time using Equation (41), which shows two characteristics; k_v is an adaptive value with negative sign, which is important information to finish both the transversality and reachability analyses.

$$\frac{v_{C2}}{v_R} = \frac{1}{\tau_{CL} \cdot s + 1} \quad \text{where} \quad \tau_{CL} = -\frac{C_2}{k_c \cdot k_v} \tag{40}$$

$$k_v = -\frac{3.9 \cdot C_2}{k_c \cdot t_{s,C2}} \tag{41}$$

3.5. Switching Frequency

The main problem of theoretical SMC is the infinite switching frequency required for the implementation. A classical solution to this problem is to introduce a hysteresis band $[-\Delta\Psi, +\Delta\Psi]$ around the sliding surface ($\Psi = 0$) to limit the switching frequency:

$$-\Delta\Psi < \Psi < +\Delta\Psi \tag{42}$$

In that way, since the closed-loop operation imposes $\Psi = 0$, the hysteresis band produces the switching function ripple reported in Equation (43). The ripple magnitudes Δi_{L1} and Δi_{L2} were reported in Equations (21) and (22), respectively, and the ripple magnitude Δv_{C2} was reported in Equation (23). Finally, the SMC ensures that i_{L2} follows the reference i_R provided by the high-pass filter. Hence, the subtraction between those two signals is $i_R - i_{L2} = -\Delta i_{L2}$.

$$\Delta\Psi = [k_c \cdot \Delta i_{L2} - \Delta i_{L1}] + [-\Delta i_{L2} + k_v \cdot \Delta v_{C2}] \tag{43}$$

In steady-state operation, $k_c \cdot i_{L2} = i_{L1}$, as given in Equation (20), where $k_c = \frac{d}{d'}$; thus, $i_{L2} = i_R + k_v \cdot (v_R - v_{C2})$. Therefore, the term $[k_c \cdot \Delta i_{L2} - \Delta i_{L1}]$ of Equation (43) is equal to zero. Moreover, the analysis reported in Figure 3 shows that the peak value of i_{L2} occurs when the ripple in v_{C2} is equal to zero; similarly, the peak value of v_{C2} occurs when the ripple in i_{L2} is equal to zero. Therefore, the peak value of the term $[-\Delta i_{L2} + k_v \cdot \Delta v_{C2}]$ of Equation (43) occurs at the peak value of i_{L2} or at the peak value of $k_v \cdot \Delta v_{C2}$, depending on which component has the highest magnitude. This condition is formalized with the following equation for the ripple magnitude of the switching function:

$$\Delta\Psi = \max(|\Delta i_{L2}|, |k_v \cdot \Delta v_{C2}|) \tag{44}$$

Finally, Equation (44) is used to design the hysteresis band $[-\Delta\Psi, +\Delta\Psi]$ in agreement with the maximum switching frequency F_{sw} supported by the MOSFETs used to construct the Zeta converter.

4. Design Procedure and Application Example

This section illustrates the design of both the power stage and the SMC to ensure the desired operation of the battery-supporting system. The first characteristic concerns the battery voltage, which is selected as 48 V due to the wide use of such a voltage level in DC loads and microgrids. The second characteristic is the C_2 nominal voltage, which is selected as 48 V to require a nominal duty cycle near 50%; however, any other value can be selected. Concerning the load transients, this example considers fast current changes up to 70 A/ms with magnitudes of 2 A, where the battery will be protected for frequencies higher than 500 Hz; again, any other values can be used depending on the load and battery characteristics. In addition, the maximum deviation of the C_2 voltage must be limited to 3% for 100 ms, thus avoiding a large discharge or overcharge of the capacitor. Finally, the maximum switching frequency is selected as 120 kHz, which is a conservative value for commercial applications. Table 2 summarizes the previous characteristics.

Table 2. Characteristics of the application example.

Description	Variable	Value
Battery voltage	v_b	48 V
Nominal C_2 voltage	v_R	48 V
Maximum deviation of C_2 voltage	MO_{C2}	3%
Settling time of C_2 voltage	$t_{s,C2}$	100 ms
Maximum derivative in the load current	$\max\left(\left\|\frac{di_o}{dt}\right\|\right)$	70 A/ms
Maximum load transient magnitude	Δi_o	2 A
Maximum safe frequency for the battery	F_{safe}	500 Hz
Maximum switching frequency	F_{sw}	120 kHz

4.1. Inductor Design

Taking into account that i_{L2} (output current of the Zeta converter) provides the high-frequency components of the load current i_o, the maximum derivative of i_{L2} must be enough to supply the maximum derivative of i_o:

$$\max\left(\left|\frac{di_{L2}}{dt}\right|\right) > \max\left(\left|\frac{di_o}{dt}\right|\right) \tag{45}$$

Replacing the derivative magnitude of i_{L2} given in (6) into (45) leads to the following limit for L_2:

$$L_2 < \frac{v_b}{\max\left(\left|\frac{di_o}{dt}\right|\right)} \tag{46}$$

Using the values given in Table 2 in inequality (46) produces $L_2 < 685.71$ µH. However, with such a limit value, the MOSFETs will not switch states during the load transient; hence, to improve the dynamic behavior of the converter, L_2 is selected as half of the limit value, which enables the MOSFETs to produce at least two commutations during a current transient. Then, adjusting to a commercial value, $L_2 = 330$ µH. Finally, L_1 is set equal to L_2 to balance the current ripple injected into the C_1 capacitor; hence, $L_1 = 330$ µH.

4.2. Capacitors and High-Pass Filter Design

The reference current i_R in the switching function (24) is generated by a high-pass filter G_{hp} processing the load current i_o. Equation (47) describes the first-order high-pass filter considered in this solution.

$$i_R = G_{hp} \cdot i_o \quad \text{where} \quad G_{hp} = \frac{s}{s + 2 \cdot \pi \cdot F_{safe}} \tag{47}$$

The most extreme transient corresponds to a step current $i_o = \frac{\Delta i_o}{s}$, which produces the following time-domain waveform obtained from the inverse Laplace transformation of Equation (47):

$$i_R = \Delta i_o \cdot e^{-2 \cdot \pi \cdot F_{safe} \cdot t} \tag{48}$$

The charge extracted from C_2 during a positive load transient (increment in i_o) is obtained by integrating the previous time-domain waveform:

$$Q_{C2} = \int_0^\infty \Delta i_o \cdot e^{-2\cdot\pi\cdot F_{safe}\cdot t}\, dt = -\frac{\Delta i_o}{2\cdot\pi\cdot F_{safe}} \tag{49}$$

During a positive load transient, the v_{C2} voltage is decreased and the voltage deviation is negative, which produces the following charge extraction from C_2:

$$Q_{C2} = -C_2 \cdot (v_R \cdot MO_{C2}) \tag{50}$$

Finally, C_2 capacitance is obtained by relating Equations (49) and (50), as follows:

$$C_2 = \frac{\Delta i_o}{2\cdot\pi\cdot F_{safe}\cdot(v_R\cdot MO_{C2})} \tag{51}$$

The design of C_1 is performed to provide a balance with the energy stored in C_2, which is equal to $E_{C_2} = (C_2\cdot v_R^2)/2$. Taking into account that the energy stored in C_1 is $E_{C_1} = (C_1\cdot v_{C1}^2)/2$, the condition for C_1 to achieve $E_{C_1} = E_{C_2}$ is calculated using Equations (18) and (19), as follows:

$$C_1 = C_2 \cdot \left(\frac{v_R}{v_b}\right)^2 \tag{52}$$

Evaluating Equation (51) with the values given in Table 2 produces a capacitance equal to 442.1 µF, which, adjusted to a commercial value, results in $C_2 = 470$ µF. Similarly, evaluating Equation (52) produces the commercial value $C_1 = 470$ µF.

4.3. Verification of the SMC Stability

The next step is to evaluate the SMC's stability, which requires verifying the transversality and reachability conditions. Evaluating the transversality value given in Equation (28) using the characteristics of Table 2 and the parameters previously calculated produces the average value $\frac{d}{du}\left(\frac{d\Psi}{dt}\right) = -2.9\times 10^5 \neq 0$, which confirms the transversality condition (26).

Taking into account that the transversality value is negative, the reachability conditions that must be evaluated are inequalities (34) and (35). Evaluating those inequalities with the characteristics of Table 2 and the parameters previously calculated leads to the restrictions -145 A/ms $< \frac{di_R}{dt} < 145$ A/ms. Since the reference signal i_R is generated by a high-pass filter processing the load current i_o, as discussed in Section 4.2, the maximum derivative of i_R is the same as that of i_o: $\max\left(\left|\frac{di_R}{dt}\right|\right) = \max\left(\left|\frac{di_o}{dt}\right|\right) = 70$ A/ms. Therefore, the previous calculations confirm that the reachability conditions (33) are fulfilled. It must be noted that, in case of a positive transversality value, inequalities (31) and (32) must be evaluated.

In conclusion, the proposed design of both the power stage and SMC ensures a stable operation of the system, which guarantees the desired support for the battery.

4.4. SMC Control Law

Since the transversality value is negative, the reachability conditions are defined in (33), which also defines the control law. The reachability condition $\lim_{\Psi\to 0^-}\frac{d\Psi}{dt}\big|_{u=0} > 0$ requires that $u = 0$ when $\Psi < 0$, and the reachability condition $\lim_{\Psi\to 0^+}\frac{d\Psi}{dt}\big|_{u=1} < 0$ requires that $u = 1$ when $\Psi > 0$. However, the hysteresis band $[-\Delta\Psi, +\Delta\Psi]$ introduced in Section 3.5 modifies the limits of Ψ to produce changes on u, which defines the final control law, as follows:

$$u = \begin{cases} \text{if } \Psi \leq -\Delta\Psi \to u = 0 \wedge \bar{u} = 1 \\ \text{if } \Psi \geq +\Delta\Psi \to u = 1 \wedge \bar{u} = 0 \end{cases} \tag{53}$$

Evaluating Equation (44) using the characteristics of Table 2, and the parameters previously calculated, leads to $\Delta\Psi = 0.3$ A.

4.5. Summary of the Design and Control Processes

The summary of the design process for the parameters of both the power stage and SMC is synthesized in Algorithm 1. Such a process starts with the design of inductor L_2 to fulfill the maximum load current derivative. To ensure at least two switching periods within the transient, a constant $k_L \leq 1/2$ is used to fulfill inequality (46), where smaller k_L produces higher number of periods per transient, but very small L_2 values will require very small $\Delta\Psi$ limits, which could introduce implementation problems due to circuit sensitivity. Therefore, k_L must be selected to ensure that $\Delta\Psi$ magnitude enables the correct operation of the comparators used to implement the control law (53). Next, L_1 is set equal to L_1 to provide a balance in the current ripple of both inductors.

The capacitor C_2 is designed to limit the voltage deviation up to MO_{C2}, and C_1 is designed to balance the energy stored in both capacitors. Then, the steady-state values of both the current ($k_{c,ss}$) and voltage ($k_{v,ss}$) constants are calculated from the nominal values of the application, and both constants are used to calculate the hysteresis band value $\Delta\Psi$. Finally, depending on the application, the high-pass filter is parameterized in agreement with the safe frequency range defined for the battery transients.

Algorithm 1 Design of both the power stage and SMC parameters

Require: $v_b, v_R, MO_{C2}, t_{s,C2}, \max\left(\left|\frac{di_o}{dt}\right|\right), \Delta i_o, F_{safe}, F_{sw}$

1: $L_2 \leftarrow$ near commercial value of $\left\{k_L \cdot \frac{v_b}{\max\left(\left|\frac{di_o}{dt}\right|\right)}\right\}$ where $k_L \leq \frac{1}{2}$

2: $L_1 \leftarrow L_2$

3: $C_2 \leftarrow$ near commercial value of $\left\{\frac{\Delta i_o}{2 \cdot \pi \cdot F_{safe} \cdot (v_R \cdot MO_{C2})}\right\}$

4: $C_1 \leftarrow$ near commercial value of $\left\{C_2 \cdot \left(\frac{v_R}{v_b}\right)^2\right\}$

5: $k_{c,ss} \leftarrow \left\{\frac{v_b}{v_R}\right\}$

6: $k_{v,ss} \leftarrow \left\{-\frac{3.9 \cdot C_2}{k_{c,ss} \cdot t_{s,C2}}\right\}$

7: $\Delta\Psi \leftarrow \{\max(|\Delta i_{L2}|, |k_{v,ss} \cdot \Delta v_{C2}|)\}$ calculating Δi_{L2} from (22) and Δv_{C2} from (23)

8: $G_{hp} \leftarrow \left\{\frac{s}{s + 2 \cdot \pi \cdot F_{safe}}\right\}$

9: **return** $L_1, L_2, C_1, C_2, \Delta\Psi, G_{hp}$

Implementing the adaptive controller requires processing, in an infinite loop, a series of calculations based on measurements and fixed parameters. Such a control process is synthesized in Algorithm 2. The algorithm requires the desired reference for the voltage in C_2 and the value of the two inductor currents, both the battery and C_2 voltages, and the load current. The next step is to detect the high-frequency transients on the load current using the high-pass filter. Then, both the current (k_c) and voltage (k_v) gains are adapted for the actual operation condition, and with those values, the switching function Ψ for the operation conditions is calculated.

Using the values of Ψ and $\Delta\Psi$, the control law of the SMC (53) is executed, which produces the binary values for controlling the MOSFETs (u and $\overline{u}$). Finally, the loop starts again by measuring the physical variables.

Algorithm 2 Control process

Require: v_R
1: **loop**
2:     measure $i_o, v_{C2}, v_b, i_{L1}, i_{L2}$
3:     $i_R \leftarrow \{G_{hp} \cdot i_o\}$ ▷ Filter the load current to detect the fast transients
4:     $k_c \leftarrow \{\frac{v_b}{v_{C2}}\}$ ▷ Calculate the adaptive current gain
5:     $k_v \leftarrow \{-\frac{3.9 \cdot C_2}{k_c \cdot t_{s,C2}}\}$ ▷ Calculate the adaptive voltage gain
6:     $\Psi \leftarrow \{i_R + k_v \cdot (v_R - v_{C2}) + (k_c - 1) \cdot i_{L2} - i_{L1}\}$ ▷ Calculate Ψ
7:     **if** $\Psi \leq -\Delta\Psi$ **then**   ▷ Apply the control law
8:         $u \leftarrow 0$
9:         $\bar{u} \leftarrow 1$
10:     **else if** $\Psi \geq +\Delta\Psi$ **then**
11:         $u \leftarrow 1$
12:         $\bar{u} \leftarrow 0$
13:     **else**
14:         $u \wedge \bar{u}$ do not change
15:     **end if**
16:     **return** $u, \bar{u}$ ▷ u and $\bar{u}$ are provided to the MOSFETs
17: **end loop**

Table 3 summarizes the circuital parameters calculated for this application example. This table also presents the energy stored in the elements of the Zeta converter needed to support the high-frequency transients of the load current. The table shows that the energy stored in the capacitors C_1 and C_2 is very small. In the case of L_2, since i_{L2} is defined by the high-pass filter given in (47), the steady-state value of i_{L2} is 0 A, and from Equation (20), it is obtained that the steady-state value of i_{L1} is also 0 A; thus, the inductors do not store energy in the steady state, and they operate only as energy buffers during the transient conditions. Therefore, the total energy stored in the Zeta converter is 0.30 mWh or 0.006 mAh.

Table 3. Circuital parameters of the application example.

Parameter	Value	Nominal Condition	Energy Stored
L_1	330 µH	0 A	0 Wh, 0 Ah
L_2	330 µH	0 A	0 Wh, 0 Ah
C_1	470 µF	48 V	0.15 mWh, 0.003 mAh
C_2	470 µF	48 V	0.15 mWh, 0.003 mAh
$\Delta\Psi$	0.3 A	-	-

It must be highlighted that the design of the proposed supporting device (formed by both the Zeta converter and SMC) does not depend on the battery capacity; instead, it only depends on the load transients that must be supported. The battery capacity is related to the load or microgrid operation cycle, which has a low-frequency profile. In contrast, the supporting device capacity only depends on the system's high-frequency transients.

5. Implementation of the Adaptive SMC and Detailed Circuital Simulations

The power system described in Figure 2 was implemented in the power electronics simulator PSIM using the electrical parameters calculated in the previous section. The adaptive sliding-mode controller can be implemented following Algorithm 2 with analog or digital circuits. The following subsections discuss both implementations.

5.1. Analog Implementation of the Adaptive SMC

The implementation of the control algorithm, using analog circuits, is presented in Figure 4. Such a circuit considers the implementation of the high-pass filter using operational amplifiers, as discussed in [36]. Similarly, addition, subtraction, and multiplication by a constant value can be easily implemented with operational amplifiers, as reported in [36]. The multiplication and division operations can be implemented using analog integrated circuits like the AD734 described in [37]. Therefore, the calculation of the adaptive parameters k_c and k_v, the calculation of the i_R signal, and the calculation of the switching function Ψ are easily implemented with analog circuits.

Concerning the control law, the logical operations in Algorithm 2 can be implemented using two comparators and an S-R Flip-Flop, as depicted in Figure 4. When $\Psi \geq +\Delta\Psi$, the signal $Set = 1$ activates the Set input of the Flip-Flop, which imposes $u = 1$ and $\bar{u} = 0$; similarly, when $\Psi < -\Delta\Psi$, the signal $Reset = 1$ activates the $Reset$ input of the Flip-Flop, which imposes $u = 0$ and $\bar{u} = 1$. Finally, Figure 4 shows a diagram of those control signals.

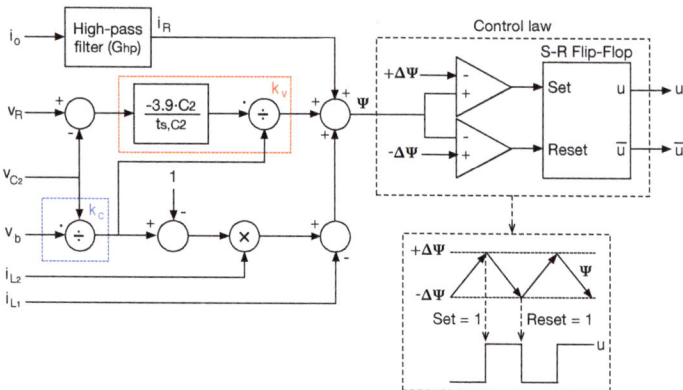

Figure 4. Analog implementation of the control algorithm.

The first simulation of this analog implementation, reported in Figure 5, evaluates the compensation of a load transient from steady state to battery charge with the maximum current derivative $\left|\frac{di_o}{dt}\right| = 70$ A/ms. Figure 5a shows two fast current transients between 0 A and 2 A, and in both cases, the Zeta converter provides the fast current component, while the battery exhibits a slow change in the current, thus fulfilling the desired behavior of the system. In addition, the C_2 voltage is constrained to the MO_{C2} limit for such a transient condition, which validates the design of the converter components. Moreover, since $v_b = v_R$, then the average value of k_c is near 1 and the stability condition of the inductor currents is $i_{L1} = i_{L2}$, which is confirmed in the simulation. It is observed that the switching function Ψ is permanently trapped inside the hysteresis band $[-\Delta\Psi, +\Delta\Psi]$; thus, the SMC is always inside the sliding mode, which ensures the global stability. Finally, the switching frequency is always below the maximum design limit of 120 kHz.

Figure 5b presents a zoom of the previous simulation, which confirms that the Zeta converter provides the current transient, while the battery current changes with the frequency limit defined by the high-pass filter. In addition, the zoom of the inductor currents confirms the relation imposed by the first part of the switching function and confirms both currents' stable behavior. Finally, the zoom of the switching function Ψ shows the frequency reduction at the perturbation instant, which is caused by the fast change in the load current, where the SMC can impose three switching periods during the transient time.

Figure 6 reports a second simulation, which evaluates the compensation of a load transient from steady state to battery discharge with the same maximum current derivative. Figure 6a shows the correct behavior of both the Zeta converter and battery currents, while C_2 voltage and the inductor currents are regulated as expected. As in the previous case, the switching function is constrained to the hysteresis band, ensuring global stability. In this case, Figure 6b shows a zoom for the second transient (from -2 A to 0 A), where the steady-state values of the Zeta current and the battery current are different. After the transient is finished, the Zeta current becomes zero since the supporting device is designed only to provide fast current transients. Therefore, the Zeta converter provides the step-up fast transient from 0 A to 2 A needed to reach the final current of both the battery and the load (0 A). As in the previous case, the waveforms of Figure 6b confirm the stability of the proposed solution and the correct limitation of the switching frequency.

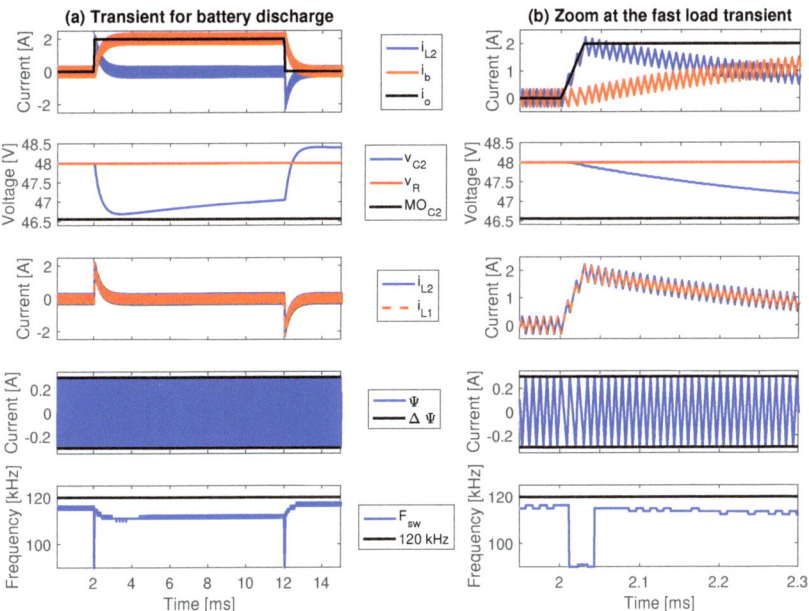

Figure 5. Fast load transient to battery discharge.

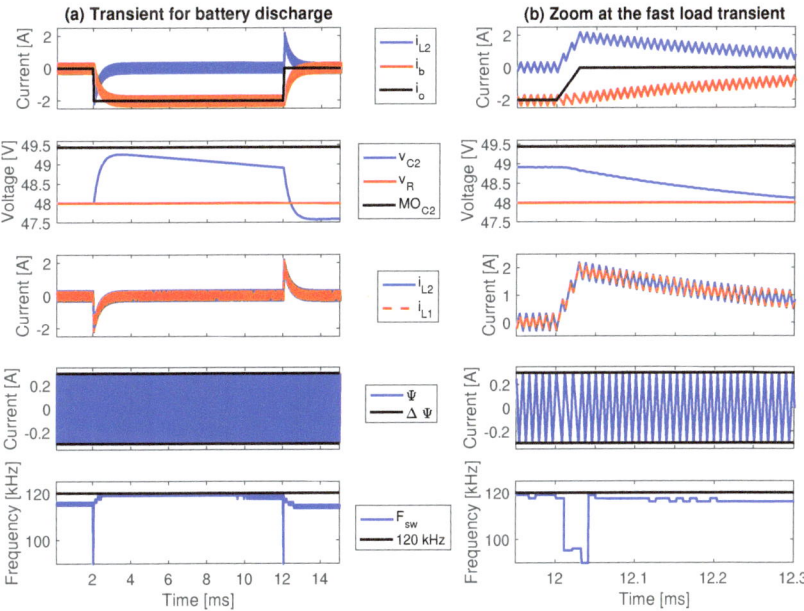

Figure 6. Fast load transient to battery charge.

The next simulation, reported in Figure 7a, evaluates the performance of the proposed solution to a sequence of load transients. In this case, the load current changes from 0 A to 14 A with transients of 2 A. As expected, the Zeta converter provides the fast current transients, returning to 0 A for the steady-state condition. Therefore, despite the consistent increment in the battery current, the supporting device (Zeta converter) always provides the same behavior, which prevents the battery from suffering the fast current transients imposed by the load. Since the consecutive transients occur in intervals of 2 ms, which is much shorter than the settling time ($t_{s,C2} = 100$ ms), the voltage of C_2 capacitor is reduced up to 40 V, but the SMC always operates inside the sliding surface, thus ensuring global stability and demonstrating the adaptability and robustness to changes on the operation conditions.

Figure 7b presents the fourth simulation, which evaluates the settling time of the C_2 voltage. In this test, a single load current perturbation is applied to charge the battery with a load current equal to -2 A. The simulation confirms that C_2 voltage is below the designed deviation MO_{C2} for that perturbation, and the voltage compensation is achieved in the designed settling time (100 ms). Therefore, both discharging (positive load transients) and charging (negative load transients) times are predictable and equal to the designed settling time. This satisfactory performance confirms that the switching function operates as expected, thus ensuring the capability of providing or absorbing load current transients to protect the battery.

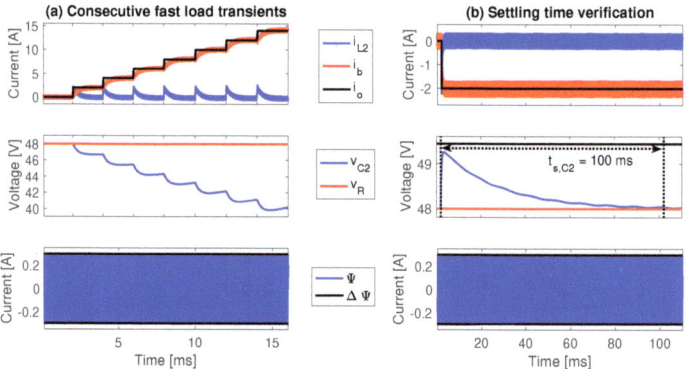

Figure 7. Consecutive perturbations and settling time.

5.2. Digital Implementation of the Adaptive SMC

The proposed SMC can be implemented in a digital microprocessor by coding Algorithm 2 in any supported language. However, such an approach will impose high requirements on the Analog-to-Digital Converters (ADCs) needed to measure the two inductor currents, both the battery and C_2 voltages, and the load current. Since Algorithm 2 produces the control signals u and $\overline{u}$, the time resolution for the rising and falling of u (and $\overline{u}$) impacts the accuracy of the SMC implementation. Therefore, adopting an acquisition time between 80 and 100 times smaller than the switching period is common, thus providing a resolution for the control signal between 1% and 1.25% of the period. Using such a traditional approach, the implementation of Algorithm 2, for the application characteristics reported in Table 2, will require ADCs with sampling frequencies between 9.6 MSPS (9.6×10^6 samples per second) and 12 MSPS, which are very high.

Therefore, this section proposes a modified formulation of the practical sliding surface (42) to reduce the ADC sampling frequency. This new formulation represents the high-frequency signal i_{L1} of Ψ (24) as a function of the other terms, which results in the following representation of the practical sliding surface $-\Delta\Psi < \Psi < +\Delta\Psi$:

$$\Psi_{L1,Set} < i_{L1} < \Psi_{L1,Reset} \tag{54}$$
$$\Psi_{L1,Reset} = i_R + k_v \cdot (v_R - v_{C2}) + (k_c - 1) \cdot i_{L2} + \Delta\Psi \tag{55}$$
$$\Psi_{L1,Set} = i_R + k_v \cdot (v_R - v_{C2}) + (k_c - 1) \cdot i_{L2} - \Delta\Psi \tag{56}$$

Then, using the new Ψ formulation given in (54)–(56), we also obtain a new formulation for the control law (53), as follows:

$$u = \begin{cases} \text{if } i_{L1} \geq \Psi_{L1,Reset} \rightarrow u = 0 \wedge \bar{u} = 1 \\ \text{if } i_{L1} \leq \Psi_{L1,Set} \rightarrow u = 1 \wedge \bar{u} = 0 \end{cases} \tag{57}$$

Then, two processes are needed. The first one calculates the limits $\Psi_{L1,Set}$ and $\Psi_{L1,Reset}$, and the second one uses those limits to calculate the MOSFET signals with Equation (57). Considering that the calculation of $\Psi_{L1,Set}$ and $\Psi_{L1,Reset}$ requires the measurement of multiple analog signals, this process imposes the requirements in the ADC frequency. Instead, the calculations of u and $\bar{u}$ only require simple comparisons; hence, this section proposes using a microcontroller able to perform both processes. For example, the F28379D Microcontroller reported in [38] has multiple ADC channels, has Digital-to-Analog Converters (DACs), and has a Comparator Subsystem (CMPSS). The CMPSS is based on two analog comparators, which have the negative inputs of the comparators connected to two DAC channels, and the positive inputs of the comparators are connected to a single pin of the F28379D. Therefore, two threads can be designed to run with different sampling periods inside the microcontroller, using the CMPSS to perform the analog comparisons of the new control law given in (57).

The first thread (Thread 1) calculates the comparator inputs $\Psi_{L1,Set}$ and $\Psi_{L1,Reset}$. Since such a comparison is used in each switching period, the values of $\Psi_{L1,Set}$ and $\Psi_{L1,Reset}$ must be updated at least twice in each period; thus, the sampling frequency must be at minimum double the maximum switching frequency. From Table 2, it is observed that the application example imposes a maximum switching frequency of 120 kHz, and introducing a safety factor of 10%, the sampling frequency needed is 264 kSPS (0.264 MSPS), hence reducing the sampling frequency to 2.2% of the requirement imposed by the traditional digital implementation. Figure 8 illustrates the digital implementation of the control algorithm, where Thread 1 delivers the limits $\Psi_{L1,Set}$ and $\Psi_{L1,Reset}$ to the CMPSS.

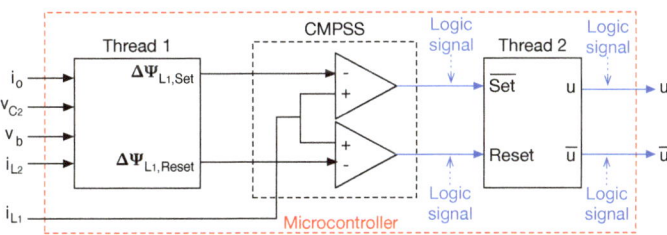

Figure 8. Digital implementation of the control algorithm.

Figure 8 shows that i_{L1} is introduced in the CMPSS; hence, an ADC channel is not needed for i_{L1}. Since the external input of the CMPSS (i_{L1}) is connected to the positive inputs of the comparators, the lower comparator correctly produces the reset signal (*Reset*). In contrast, the upper comparator produces an inverted version of the set signal ($\overline{Set} = 1 - Set$). The outputs of the CMPSS are logic signals, which is the main advantage of the structure given in Figure 8, since those logic signals can be captured by the second thread (Thread 2) at the full speed of the microprocessor (200 MHz); hence, the capture frequency is not limited by the conversion time of the ADC. Similarly, the control signal of the MOSFETs (u and $\bar{u}$) are logic signals; therefore, executing Thread 2 at 10 MHz or

12 MHz will provide a resolution between 1% and 1.25% of the switching period for both the rising and falling times of u (and $\overline{u}$). In fact, executing Thread 2 at the full speed of the F28379D Microprocessor (200 MHz) could improve the resolution of u (and $\overline{u}$) to 0.06% of the switching period.

Algorithm 3 reports the pseudocode for Thread 1, which calculates the comparator inputs $\Psi_{L1,Set}$ and $\Psi_{L1,Reset}$. This algorithm considers the discrete implementation of the high-pass filter given in Equation (58), which is obtained from the analog high-pass filter previously reported in Equation (47) by performing the Tustin transformation $\left(s = [2/T_{adq}] \cdot [z-1]/[z+1]\right)$ discussed in [39], and subsequently applying the inverse Z-transformation to obtain the difference equation representation of $i_{R(k)}$. In such an expression, T_{adq} is the ADC sampling time. Therefore, Thread 1 can be executed at 264 kHz for the application example, which ensures an ADC frequency of 264 kSPS ($T_{adq} = 3.8$ µs). The calculations of $\Psi_{L1,Set}$ and $\Psi_{L1,Reset}$ show that those values are continuous; hence, those signals must be provided to the CMPSS using two DAC channels. The F28379D Microcontroller has DAC channels with minimum conversion times equal to 2 µs; hence, $T_{adq} = 3.8$ µs can be fulfilled by the on-board DAC. Finally, the values of i_R and i_o are stored for the next iteration of the algorithm.

$$i_{R(k)} = \frac{i_{o(k)} - i_{o(k-1)} - \left(\pi \cdot F_{safe} \cdot T_{adq} - 1\right) \cdot i_{R(k-1)}}{\pi \cdot F_{safe} \cdot T_{adq} + 1} \tag{58}$$

Algorithm 3 Thread 1: calculation of the comparator inputs ($\Psi_{L1,Set}$ and $\Psi_{L1,Reset}$)

Require: $v_R, F_{safe}, \Delta\Psi, T_{adq}$
1: **loop**
2:      **measure** $i_{o(k)}, v_{C2(k)}, v_{b(k)}, i_{L2(k)}$
3:      $i_{R(k)} \leftarrow \left\{\frac{i_{o(k)} - i_{o(k-1)} - (\pi \cdot F_{safe} \cdot T_{adq} - 1) \cdot i_{R(k-1)}}{\pi \cdot F_{safe} \cdot T_{adq} + 1}\right\}$ ▷ High-Pass filter
4:      $k_{c(k)} \leftarrow \left\{\frac{v_{b(k)}}{v_{C2(k)}}\right\}$ ▷ Calculate the adaptive current gain
5:      $k_{v(k)} \leftarrow \left\{-\frac{3.9 \cdot C_2}{k_{c(k)} \cdot t_{s,C2}}\right\}$ ▷ Calculate the adaptive voltage gain
6:      $\Psi_{L1,Reset(k)} \leftarrow \left\{i_{R(k)} + k_{v(k)} \cdot \left(v_R - v_{C2(k)}\right) + \left(k_{c(k)} - 1\right) \cdot i_{L2(k)} + \Delta\Psi\right\}$
7:      $\Psi_{L1,Set(k)} \leftarrow \left\{i_{R(k)} + k_{v(k)} \cdot \left(v_R - v_{C2(k)}\right) + \left(k_{c(k)} - 1\right) \cdot i_{L2(k)} - \Delta\Psi\right\}$
8:      $i_{R(k-1)} \leftarrow i_{R(k)}$ ▷ Store $i_{R(k)}$ value
9:      $i_{o(k-1)} \leftarrow i_{o(k)}$ ▷ Store $i_{o(k)}$ value
10:      **return** $\Psi_{L1,Set(k)}, \Psi_{L1,Reset(k)}$ ▷ Signals for the comparators of the CMPSS
11: **end loop**

Algorithm 4 reports the pseudocode for Thread 2, which produces the control signals for the MOSFETs (u and $\overline{u}$); hence, it must be executed between 80 and 100 times the maximum switching frequency. For the application example, 10 MHz was selected. Thread 2 starts by capturing the output signals of the CMPSS ($Reset$ and $\overline{Set}$); then, Thread 2 detects if a rising edge on the $Reset$ signal has been produced by the CMPSS. To take into account that the set Set signal produced by the CMPSS is inverted ($\overline{Set} = 1 - Set$), Thread 2 detects if a falling edge on the $\overline{Set}$ signal has been produced. Then, the algorithm changes the MOSFET signals u and $\overline{u}$ following the new formulation of the control law previously obtained in Equation (57); if no rising edge on $Reset$ or falling edge on $\overline{Set}$ occurs, then u and $\overline{u}$ are not changed. The last steps of the algorithm store the states of $Reset$, $\overline{Set}$, u, and $\overline{u}$ for the next iteration. Figure 9 summarizes the digital implementation, where the processes of both threads are synthesized. In addition, the connection of both threads with the analog CMPSS module is illustrated, which occurs inside the microprocessor to generate the MOSFET control signals. Finally, the figure also illustrates the signal processing of the modified control law adopted for this digital implementation.

Algorithm 4 Thread 2: control signal generator (u and $\overline{u}$)

1: **loop**
2:     **Logic inputs** $\overline{Set}_{(k)}$, $Reset_{(k)}$
3:     **if** $\left(Reset_{(k)} = 1\right)$ & $\left(Reset_{(k-1)} = 0\right)$ **then**   ▷ Detect rising edge in $Reset$
4:         $u_{(k)} \leftarrow 0$
5:         $\overline{u}_{(k)} \leftarrow 1$
6:     **else if** $\left(\overline{Set}_{(k)} = 0\right)$ & $\left(\overline{Set}_{(k-1)} = 1\right)$ **then**   ▷ Detect falling edge in $\overline{Set}$
7:         $u_{(k)} \leftarrow 1$
8:         $\overline{u}_{(k)} \leftarrow 0$
9:     **else**
10:         $u_{(k)} \leftarrow u_{(k-1)}$ ▷ $u_{(k)}$ does not change
11:         $\overline{u}_{(k)} \leftarrow \overline{u}_{(k-1)}$ ▷ $\overline{u}_{(k)}$ does not change
12:     **end if**
13:     $\overline{Set}_{(k-1)} \leftarrow \overline{Set}_{(k)}$ ▷ Store $\overline{Set}_{(k)}$ value
14:     $Reset_{(k-1)} \leftarrow Reset_{(k)}$ ▷ Store $Reset_{(k)}$ value
15:     $u_{(k)} \leftarrow u_{(k-1)}$ ▷ Store $u_{(k)}$ value
16:     $\overline{u}_{(k)} \leftarrow \overline{u}_{(k-1)}$ ▷ Store $\overline{u}_{(k)}$ value
17:     **return** $u_{(k)}, \overline{u}_{(k)}$ ▷ $u_{(k)}$ and $\overline{u}_{(k)}$ are provided to the MOSFETs
18: **end loop**

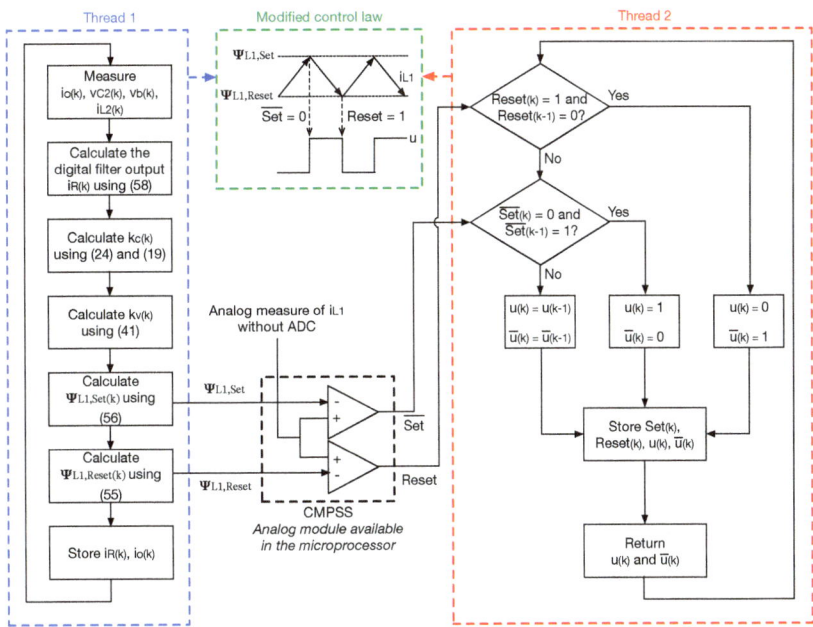

Figure 9. Flowchart of the digital implementation.

The digital implementation of the SMC reported in Figure 9 was performed in the power electronics simulator PSIM, as follows. Thread 1 and Thread 2 algorithms were implemented using a C-code block for each thread, and the CMPSS was implemented using two comparators. Thread 1 was executed with a sampling frequency equal to 264 kHz (sampling time equal to 3.8 µs), while Thread 2 was executed with a sampling frequency equal to 10 MHz (sampling time equal to 0.1 µs).

The simulation of this digital implementation, reported in Figure 10, evaluates the compensation of a load transient from steady state to battery charge with the maximum current derivative $\left|\frac{di_o}{dt}\right| = 70$ A/ms; hence, it reproduces the conditions considered for the simulation of the analog implementation reported in Figure 5. The new simulation results of Figure 10a show two fast current transients between 0 A and 2 A, where the Zeta converter provides the fast current components, as expected. The stable condition $i_{L1} = i_{L2}$ is also confirmed in this simulation, where i_{L1} is constrained by $\Psi_{L1,Set}$ and $\Psi_{L1,Reset}$, thus ensuring the global stability of the SMC, as given in inequality (54). In addition, the C_2 voltage is constrained to the MO_{C2} limit, demonstrating that the SMC's digital implementation provides the same performance of the analog implementation. Finally, the switching frequency is always below the maximum design limit (120 kHz), thus requiring the same MOSFETs used for the analog implementation of the SMC.

Figure 10b shows a zoom of this simulation, which confirms that the Zeta converter provides the high-frequency component of the load current transient. The zoom also shows the detail of $\Psi_{L1,Set}$ and $\Psi_{L1,Reset}$, where the discretization caused by the sampling frequency of Thread 1 (264 kSPS) is observed. This simulation also shows the correct operation of the modified formulation of the sliding surface given in inequality (54), and it reports both the *Set* and *Reset* signals generated by the CMPSS, where $Set = 1 - \overline{Set}$. Finally, the control signal u generated by Thread 2 is also presented, which agrees with the modified control law.

In summary, the simulations of both the analog and digital implementations of the SMC confirm the correct operation of the power system and the adaptive SMC for any operation condition. Therefore, the proposed solution can supply the current transients imposed by the load, thus forcing the battery to supply only low-frequency components. In addition, it was demonstrated that both analog and digital implementations of the adaptive SMC exhibit equivalent performances; hence, the one more suitable for the particular application can be adopted.

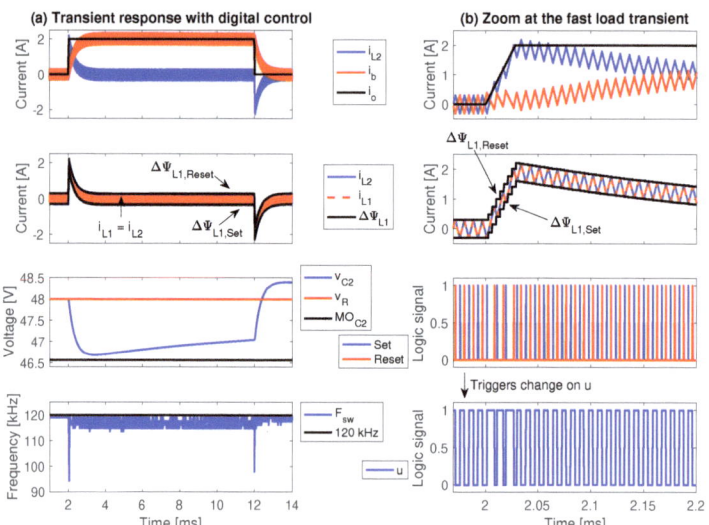

Figure 10. Response of the digital implementation to fast load transients.

5.3. Comparison with a Classical Controller

This subsection presents the design of a cascade structure based on PI controllers to provide a comparison with a classical solution. The first step is to obtain the small-signal model of the power stage as $\dot{\mathbf{X}} = \mathbf{A_m} \times \mathbf{X} + \mathbf{B_m} \times \mathbf{U_x}$, where $\mathbf{X} = [i_{L1}\ i_{L2}\ v_{C1}\ v_{C2}]^T$ is the state vector, $\mathbf{U_x} = [d\ v_b]^T$ is the input vector, $\mathbf{A_m}$ is the state Jacobian and $\mathbf{B_m}$ is the input Jacobian. This process is performed by deriving the differential equations given in (14)–(17), as described in [40], obtaining the following Jacobian matrices:

$$\mathbf{A_m} = \begin{bmatrix} 0 & 0 & -\frac{1-d}{L_1} & \frac{d}{L_1} \\ 0 & 0 & \frac{d}{L_2} & \frac{d}{L_2} \\ \frac{1-d}{C_1} & -\frac{d}{C_1} & 0 & 0 \\ -\frac{d}{C_2} & -\frac{d}{C_2} & 0 & 0 \end{bmatrix} \wedge \mathbf{B_m} = \begin{bmatrix} \frac{v_{C1}+v_{C2}}{L_1} & 0 \\ \frac{v_{C1}+v_{C2}}{L_2} & -\frac{1}{L_2} \\ -\frac{i_{L1}+i_{L2}}{C_1} & 0 \\ -\frac{i_{L1}+i_{L2}}{C_2} & 0 \end{bmatrix}$$ (59)

The output of the small-signal model is calculated from $\mathbf{Y} = \mathbf{C_m} \times \mathbf{X} + \mathbf{D_m} \times \mathbf{U_x}$, where $\mathbf{C_m}$ and $\mathbf{D_m}$ relate the output with the states and the inputs, respectively. The output of the small-signal model is $\mathbf{Y} = [i_{L2}]$ because i_{L2} must be regulated to follow the i_R value provided by the high-pass filter; hence, $\mathbf{C_m} = [0\ 1\ 0\ 0]$ and $\mathbf{D_m} = [0\ 0]$.

The steady-state values of d, i_{L1}, i_{L2}, v_{C1} and v_{C2} are calculated from Equations (18)–(20) and replaced into Jacobians (59), and such a numerical small-signal model is introduced into the sisotool function of Matlab to design a PI controller; in [40], such a design is implemented using the classical root-locus technique. The design of that PI controller considers a damping ratio equal to 0.707 and a closed-loop bandwidth equal to $F_{sw}/10$, which are standard criteria for linearized models; the resulting controller was $G_{PI,c} = \frac{0.1616 \cdot (s+4.125 \times 10^4)}{s}$. Finally, this G_{PI_c} controller processes the error between i_R and i_{L2} to produce the duty cycle of an additional PWM circuit used to generate the MOSFET signals; Figure 11 shows the structure of this inner current loop.

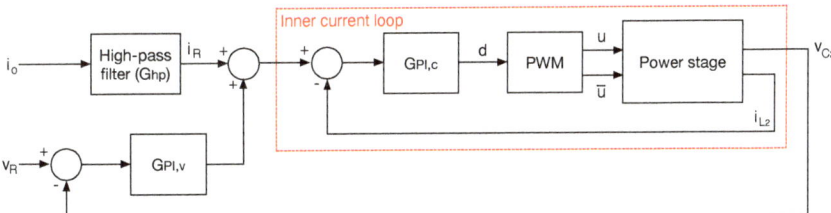

Figure 11. Cascade PI structure.

The v_{C2} voltage is also regulated with a PI controller named $G_{PI,v}$. Such a second PI controller processes the error between v_{C2} and the reference v_R to produce the additional changes on i_{L2} needed to regulate v_{C2} with the desired settling time. This cascade controller requires a closed-loop model of the inner current loop. Equation (17) describes the dynamic behavior of v_{C2} with respect to the inductor currents, where the inner current loop guarantees the current relation given in Equation (20); hence, the resulting closed-loop model is given in both time domain (60) and Laplace domain (61).

$$\frac{dv_{C2}}{dt} = -\frac{d}{1-d} \cdot \frac{i_{L2}}{C_2}$$ (60)

$$\frac{v_{C2}}{i_{L2}} = -\frac{d}{1-d} \cdot \frac{1}{C_2 \cdot s}$$ (61)

The design of the voltage PI controller ($G_{PI,v}$) was performed using Equation (61) for a unitary damping ratio to avoid any voltage oscillation and to request a slow current profile to the battery, thus avoiding high-frequency transients. In addition, the controller was designed to impose the desired settling time $t_{s,C2} = 100$ ms, which results in the controller $G_{PI,v} = \frac{-0.055 \cdot (s+29.412)}{s}$ designed with the sisotool function of Matlab.

The control structure of Figure 11 was implemented in PSIM, and the performances of both the classical solution (cascade PI structure) and proposed SMC were contrasted. Figure 12 shows the circuital simulation of both solutions, where the proposed SMC (right side) imposes the desired low-frequency behavior $i_{LP} = i_o - i_R$ on the battery current; instead, the cascade PI structure (left side) introduces an undesired high-frequency transient to the battery current. This undesired behavior is caused by the tracking error of $G_{PI,c}$ observed in i_{L2} for the cascade PI structure, which is the result of the bandwidth limitation introduced in the linearization process; moreover, i_{L2} also exhibits an overshoot caused by the change on the operation point. Instead, the proposed SMC forces i_{L2} to track i_R with null error, thus ensuring the desired low-frequency behavior of the battery current.

Figure 12 also presents, in the bottom waveforms, the behavior of v_{C2} for both controllers. The v_{C2} waveform imposed by the proposed SMC has the desired MO_{C2} and $t_{s,C2}$ without any overshoot, thus requesting a low-frequency current in the battery in order to restore the energy in C_2. Instead, the $G_{PI,v}$ controller from the cascade PI structure, despite being designed with a unitary damping ratio, cannot avoid the voltage overshoot. In addition, $G_{PI,v}$ imposes a higher derivative, thus requiring faster changes to the battery current, which is an undesired battery condition.

The analog implementation of the cascade PI structure requires two adders, two PI controllers formed by two integrators, two gains and two adders, and a PWM circuit formed by a comparator, a triangular waveform generator and an adder. The analog implementation of the proposed SMC, depicted in Figure 4, requires four adders, two dividers, a multiplier, and a gain; the SMC control circuit is formed by two comparators and an S-R flip-flop. Therefore, the proposed SMC requires integrated circuits for multiplication and division operations, while the cascade PI structure requires analog integrators. Thus, the analog implementation complexity of both controllers is similar. The digital implementation of the cascade PI structure also requires two threads, one for the inner current loop and another for the voltage loop. In addition, a complementary PWM peripheral must be used to produce both control signals. Hence, it has a complexity similar to the digital implementation of the proposed SMC reported in Figure 8.

In conclusion, the proposed SMC performs better than a classical solution based on cascade PI controllers. This performance is observed in the tracking efficiency that ensures $i_{L2} = i_R$, which imposes the desired low-frequency performance in the battery. Finally, the implementation complexity of both solutions is similar since both control solutions can be implemented using a few integrated circuits.

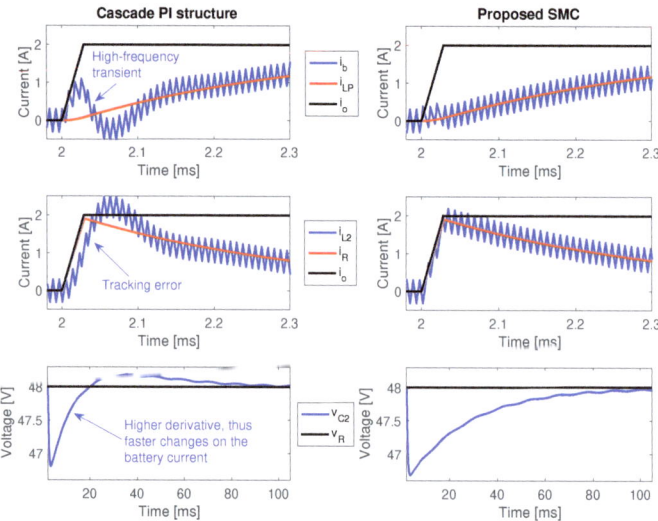

Figure 12. Comparison with a cascade PI structure.

6. Conclusions

This paper presented an algorithm for designing both the power and control stages of a HESS based on a bidirectional Zeta converter, a battery, and a capacitor. The designed adaptive sliding-mode controller, which can be implemented on a low-cost platform, guarantees a safe battery current, which prevents distortion of the DC bus voltage waveform and avoids high-frequency transients that could reduce the battery's lifespan. Moreover, the implementation of the adaptive sliding-mode controller is presented in detail using analog and digital circuits. An application example, where the battery was both charged and discharged, confirmed that during fast current transients, the Zeta converter provided the fast current components, while the battery responded with slow current derivatives. In addition, the switching function remained within the hysteresis band, ensuring the global stability of the adaptive sliding-mode controller. Finally, a comparison with a classical cascade PI structure demonstrated that the proposed adaptive controller provided superior performance, as evidenced by the tracking efficiency, which ensures that the inductor current matches the reference current, thus imposing the desired low-frequency performance on the battery.

Author Contributions: Conceptualization, A.T., C.A.R.-P., M.L.O.-G., A.J.S.-M. and S.I.S.-G.; Methodology, A.T., C.A.R.-P., M.L.O.-G., A.J.S.-M. and S.I.S.-G.; Formal analysis, A.T., C.A.R.-P., M.L.O.-G., A.J.S.-M. and S.I.S.-G.; Investigation, A.T., C.A.R.-P., M.L.O.-G., A.J.S.-M. and S.I.S.-G.; Writing—review & editing, A.T., C.A.R.-P., M.L.O.-G., A.J.S.-M. and S.I.S.-G. All authors have read and agreed to the published version of the manuscript.

Funding: This research was funded by Instituto Tecnológico Metropolitano, Universidad Nacional de Colombia, Universidad del Valle, and Minciencias—Ministerio de Ciencia Tecnología e Innovación of Colombia under project "Estrategias de dimensionamiento, planeación y gestión inteligente de energía a partir de la integración y la optimización de las fuentes no convencionales, los sistemas de almacenamiento y cargas eléctricas, que permitan la generación de soluciones energéticas confiables para los territorios urbanos y rurales de Colombia", with Minciencias code 71148, inside the research program RC80740-178-2021, Hermes code 46771, and Sicop code CI21154.

Data Availability Statement: Data are contained within the article.

Conflicts of Interest: The authors declare no conflicts of interest.

References

1. Sun, Y.N.; Zhuang, Z.L.; Xu, H.W.; Qin, W.; Feng, M.J. Data-driven modeling and analysis based on complex network for multimode recognition of industrial processes. *J. Manuf. Syst.* **2022**, *62*, 915–924. [CrossRef]
2. Van De Berg, D.; Savage, T.; Petsagkourakis, P.; Zhang, D.; Shah, N.; Del Rio-Chanona, E.A. Data-driven optimization for process systems engineering applications. *Chem. Eng. Sci.* **2022**, *248*, 117135. [CrossRef]
3. Liu, S.; Cheng, H. Manufacturing Process Optimization in the Process Industry. *Int. J. Inf. Technol. Web Eng.* **2024**, *19*, 1–20. [CrossRef]
4. Ghahramani, M.; Qiao, Y.; Zhou, M.C.; O'Hagan, A.; Sweeney, J. AI-based modeling and data-driven evaluation for smart manufacturing processes. *IEEE/CAA J. Autom. Sin.* **2020**, *7*, 1026–1037. [CrossRef]
5. Cerda-Flores, S.C.; Rojas-Punzo, A.A.; Nápoles-Rivera, F. Applications of Multi-Objective Optimization to Industrial Processes: A Literature Review. *Processes* **2022**, *10*, 133. [CrossRef]
6. Dey, S.; Gupta, N.; Pathak, S.; Kela, D.H.; Datta, S. Data-Driven Design Optimization for Industrial Products. In *Optimization in Industry*; Datta, S., Davim, J.P., Eds.; Series Title: Management and Industrial Engineering; Springer International Publishing: Cham, Switzerland, 2019; pp. 253–267. [CrossRef]
7. Zhao, J.; Wang, W.; Sheng, C. *Data-Driven Prediction for Industrial Processes and Their Applications*; Information Fusion and Data Science; Springer International Publishing: Cham, Switzerland, 2018. [CrossRef]
8. Aghmadi, A.; Mohammed, O.A. Energy Storage Systems: Technologies and High-Power Applications. *Batteries* **2024**, *10*, 141. [CrossRef]
9. Abo-Khalil, A.G.; Sobhy, A.; Abdelkareem, M.A.; Olabi, A. Advancements and challenges in hybrid energy storage systems: Components, control strategies, and future directions. *Int. J. Thermofluids* **2023**, *20*, 100477. [CrossRef]
10. Leon, J.I.; Dominguez, E.; Wu, L.; Marquez Alcaide, A.; Reyes, M.; Liu, J. Hybrid Energy Storage Systems: Concepts, Advantages, and Applications. *IEEE Ind. Electron. Mag.* **2021**, *15*, 74–88. [CrossRef]
11. Salah, O.; Shamayleh, A.; Mukhopadhyay, S. Energy Management of a Multi-Source Power System. *Algorithms* **2021**, *14*, 206. [CrossRef]
12. Emrani, A.; Berrada, A. A comprehensive review on techno-economic assessment of hybrid energy storage systems integrated with renewable energy. *J. Energy Storage* **2024**, *84*, 111010. [CrossRef]

13. Monhof, M.; Beverungen, D.; Klör, B.; Bräuer, S. Extending Battery Management Systems for Making Informed Decisions on Battery Reuse. In *New Horizons in Design Science: Broadening the Research Agenda*; Donnellan, B., Helfert, M., Kenneally, J., VanderMeer, D., Rothenberger, M., Winter, R., Eds.; Series Title: Lecture Notes in Computer Science; Springer International Publishing: Cham, Switzerland, 2015; Volume 9073, pp. 447–454. [CrossRef]
14. Lei, H.; Li, K.; Chong, B. A Review of Hybrid Energy Storage System for Heavy-Duty Electric Vehicle. *Transp. Res. Procedia* **2023**, *70*, 234–240. [CrossRef]
15. Song, Z.; Hofmann, H.; Li, J.; Han, X.; Zhang, X.; Ouyang, M. A comparison study of different semi-active hybrid energy storage system topologies for electric vehicles. *J. Power Sources* **2015**, *274*, 400–411. [CrossRef]
16. Lencwe, M.J.; Chowdhury, S.P.D.; Olwal, T.O. Hybrid energy storage system topology approaches for use in transport vehicles: A review. *Energy Sci. Eng.* **2022**, *10*, 1449–1477. [CrossRef]
17. Hasan, M.K.; Mahmud, M.; Ahasan Habib, A.; Motakabber, S.; Islam, S. Review of electric vehicle energy storage and management system: Standards, issues, and challenges. *J. Energy Storage* **2021**, *41*, 102940. [CrossRef]
18. Castaings, A.; Lhomme, W.; Trigui, R.; Bouscayrol, A. Practical control schemes of a battery/supercapacitor system for electric vehicle. *IET Electr. Syst. Transp.* **2016**, *6*, 20–26. [CrossRef]
19. Shyni, R.; Kowsalya, M. HESS-based microgrid control techniques empowered by artificial intelligence: A systematic review of grid-connected and standalone systems. *J. Energy Storage* **2024**, *84*, 111012. [CrossRef]
20. Atawi, I.E.; Al-Shetwi, A.Q.; Magableh, A.M.; Albalawi, O.H. Recent Advances in Hybrid Energy Storage System Integrated Renewable Power Generation: Configuration, Control, Applications, and Future Directions. *Batteries* **2022**, *9*, 29. [CrossRef]
21. Wang, W.; Yuan, B.; Sun, Q.; Wennersten, R. Application of energy storage in integrated energy systems—A solution to fluctuation and uncertainty of renewable energy. *J. Energy Storage* **2022**, *52*, 104812. [CrossRef]
22. Barelli, L.; Cardelli, E.; Pelosi, D.; Ciupageanu, D.A.; Ottaviano, P.A.; Longo, M.; Zaninelli, D. Energy from the Waves: Integration of a HESS to a Wave Energy Converter in a DC Bus Electrical Architecture to Enhance Grid Power Quality. *Energies* **2021**, *15*, 10. [CrossRef]
23. Moreno, H.; Schaum, A. Low-Order Electrochemical State Estimation for Li-Ion Batteries. *Algorithms* **2023**, *16*, 73. [CrossRef]
24. Liu, S.; Ling, R.; Feng, F. Equalization strategy for fast energy regulation of supercapacitor in hybrid energy storage system. *J. Energy Storage* **2023**, *65*, 107318. [CrossRef]
25. Rahman, A.U.; Zehra, S.S.; Ahmad, I.; Armghan, H. Fuzzy supertwisting sliding mode-based energy management and control of hybrid energy storage system in electric vehicle considering fuel economy. *J. Energy Storage* **2021**, *37*, 102468. [CrossRef]
26. Lencwe, M.J.; Olwal, T.O.; Chowdhury, S.D.; Sibanyoni, M. Nonsolitary two-way DC-to-DC converters for hybrid battery and supercapacitor energy storage systems: A comprehensive survey. *Energy Rep.* **2024**, *11*, 2737–2767. [CrossRef]
27. Zimmermann, T.; Keil, P.; Hofmann, M.; Horsche, M.F.; Pichlmaier, S.; Jossen, A. Review of system topologies for hybrid electrical energy storage systems. *J. Energy Storage* **2016**, *8*, 78–90. [CrossRef]
28. Ramu, S.K.; Vairavasundaram, I.; Palaniyappan, B.; Bragadeshwaran, A.; Aljafari, B. Enhanced energy management of DC microgrid: Artificial neural networks-driven hybrid energy storage system with integration of bidirectional DC-DC converter. *J. Energy Storage* **2024**, *88*, 111562. [CrossRef]
29. Moghadam, M.; Ghaffarzadeh, N. Suppressing solar PV output fluctuations by designing an efficient hybrid energy storage system controller. *Unconv. Resour.* **2024**, *4*, 100077. [CrossRef]
30. Srinivasan, C.; Sheeba Joice, C. Energy management of hybrid energy storage system in electric vehicle based on hybrid SCSO-RERNN approach. *J. Energy Storage* **2024**, *78*, 109733. [CrossRef]
31. Guentri, H.; Allaoui, T.; Mekki, M.; Denai, M. Power management and control of a photovoltaic system with hybrid battery-supercapacitor energy storage based on heuristics methods. *J. Energy Storage* **2021**, *39*, 102578. [CrossRef]
32. Erickson, R.W.; Maksimović, D. *Fundamentals of Power Electronics*; Springer International Publishing: Cham, Switzerland, 2020. [CrossRef]
33. Perruquetti, W.; Barbot, J.P. *Sliding Mode Control in Engineering*; Marcel Dekker: New York, NY, USA, 2002; Volume 11.
34. Sira-Ramirez, H. Sliding motions in bilinear switched networks. *IEEE Trans. Circuits Syst.* **1987**, *34*, 919–933. [CrossRef]
35. Ogata, K. *Modern Control Engineering*, 5th ed.; eTextbook; Pearson: London, UK, 2021.
36. Clayton, G.B.; Winder, S. *Operational Amplifiers*; Elsevier: Amsterdam, The Netherlands, 2003.
37. Devices, A. *10 MHz, Four-Quadrant Multiplier/Divider AD734*; Datasheet; Analog Device, Inc.: Norwood, MA, USA, 2011.
38. Instruments, T. *TMS320F2837xD Dual-Core Real-Time Microcontrollers*; Datasheet; Texas Instruments, Inc.: Dallas, TX, USA, 2024.
39. Paarmann, L.D. *Design and Analysis of Analog Filters: A Signal Processing Perspective*; Springer Science & Business Media: Berlin/Heidelberg, Germany, 2001; Volume 617.
40. Petrone, G.; Ramos-Paja, C.A.; Spagnuolo, G. *Photovoltaic Sources Modeling*, 1st ed.; Wiley: Hoboken, NJ, USA, 2017. [CrossRef]

Disclaimer/Publisher's Note: The statements, opinions and data contained in all publications are solely those of the individual author(s) and contributor(s) and not of MDPI and/or the editor(s). MDPI and/or the editor(s) disclaim responsibility for any injury to people or property resulting from any ideas, methods, instructions or products referred to in the content.

Article

Novelty in Intelligent Controlled Oscillations in Smart Structures

Amalia Moutsopoulou [1], Markos Petousis [1,*], Georgios E. Stavroulakis [2], Anastasios Pouliezos [2] and Nectarios Vidakis [1]

[1] Department of Mechanical Engineering, Hellenic Mediterranean University Estavromenos Heraklion Crete, 71410 Iraklio, Greece; amalia@hmu.gr (A.M.); vidakis@hmu.gr (N.V.)
[2] Department of Production Engineering and Management, Technical University of Crete, Kounoupidianna, 73100 Chania, Greece; gestavr@dpem.tuc.gr (G.E.S.); tasos@dpem.tuc.gr (A.P.)
* Correspondence: markospetousis@hmu.gr; Tel.: +30-2810-379227

Abstract: Structural control techniques can be used to protect engineering structures. By computing instantaneous control forces based on the input from the observed reactions and adhering to a strong control strategy, intelligent control in structural engineering can be achieved. In this study, we employed intelligent piezoelectric patches to reduce vibrations in structures. The actuators and sensors were implemented using piezoelectric patches. We reduced structural oscillations by employing sophisticated intelligent control methods. Examples of such control methods include H-infinity and H_2. An advantage of this study is that the results are presented for both static and dynamic loading, as well as for the frequency domain. Oscillation suppression must be achieved over the entire frequency range. In this study, advanced programming was used to solve this problem and complete oscillation suppression was achieved. This study explored in detail the methods and control strategies that can be used to address the problem of oscillations. These techniques have been thoroughly described and analyzed, offering valuable insights into their effective applications. The ability to reduce oscillations has significant implications for applications that extend to various structures and systems such as airplanes, metal bridges, and large metallic structures.

Keywords: vibration; intelligent control; piezoelectric structures; H_2 criterion; $H_{\text{-infinity}}$ criterion

Citation: Moutsopoulou, A.; Petousis, M.; Stavroulakis, G.E.; Pouliezos, A.; Vidakis, N. Novelty in Intelligent Controlled Oscillations in Smart Structures. *Algorithms* 2024, 17, 505. https://doi.org/10.3390/a17110505

Academic Editors: Sheng Du, Zixin Huang, Li Jin and Xiongbo Wan

Received: 23 September 2024
Revised: 24 October 2024
Accepted: 25 October 2024
Published: 4 November 2024

Copyright: © 2024 by the authors. Licensee MDPI, Basel, Switzerland. This article is an open access article distributed under the terms and conditions of the Creative Commons Attribution (CC BY) license (https://creativecommons.org/licenses/by/4.0/).

1. Introduction

In this study, a smart engineering structure was used for vibration suppression. Vibration suppression in smart structures involves the use of advanced materials and technologies to control and reduce unwanted vibrations for various engineering applications [1–8]. Smart structures integrate actuators, sensors, and control algorithms to adapt to varying conditions and improve performance. The following are the key aspects of vibration suppression in smart structures. Smart materials play a crucial role in the suppression of vibrations. Piezoelectric materials are a common type of smart material. When these materials are subjected to mechanical stress, they generate electric charge [2–7]. They are capable of serving as actuators as well as sensors, converting mechanical vibrations into electrical signals and vice versa.

Several researchers have used piezoelectric smart structures to suppress vibration [7–13]. Smart structures utilize piezoelectric actuators and sensors. Piezoelectric actuators have revolutionized smart engineering structures by providing precise, responsive, and efficient control mechanisms [14–17]. Their applications across various fields, from aerospace and civil engineering to robotics and optics, demonstrate their versatility and effectiveness. Despite some challenges related to material limitations and costs, ongoing research and technological advancements have been poised to overcome these hurdles, paving the way for broader adoption and new innovations in smart engineering structures. The application of piezoelectric materials as actuators in intelligent engineering structures is a rapidly growing field driven by the unique properties of piezoelectric materials and their ability to perform precise and responsive control functions [18–22]. An in-depth analysis of this subject shows that piezoelectric actuators leverage direct and inverse piezoelectric effects, converting electrical energy into mechanical motion, and vice versa. This enables them to function as both sensors and actuators. Piezoelectric actuators can be very small and lightweight, which is beneficial for applications where weight and space are critical, such as in aerospace and medical devices [23–27].

In this study, piezoelectric materials were used as actuators and sensors. We employed co-localized actuator pairs implanted in laminated composite beams (piezoceramic PZT G-1195N, with a Young's modulus Ep of 6.3×10^{10} N/m^2) composed of graphite/epoxy, glass/epoxy, and metallic (aluminum) beams. Advanced materials and systems, termed as smart piezoelectric structures, utilize the distinctive characteristics of piezoelectric materials to provide intelligent, adaptive, and frequent self-monitoring capabilities. Piezoelectricity denotes the capacity of a material to generate an electrical charge when subjected to mechanical stress. However, these materials may be distorted when an electric field is applied. The use of smart materials is a key component of vibration suppression in smart structures. Piezoelectric materials are among the most commonly used smart materials. These materials possess a distinctive capability to generate an electric charge when subjected to mechanical stress [6–11]. This property enables them to function as actuators and sensors capable of converting mechanical vibrations into electrical signals, and vice versa.

Numerous researchers have explored the use of piezoelectric smart structures for suppressing vibrations [7–17,28]. The integration of piezoelectric actuators and sensors into smart structures has been transformative, offering precise, responsive, and efficient control mechanisms, which have significantly advanced the capabilities of smart engineering structures [14–20,28].

This work can make an important contribution to engineers who want to apply new smart materials with appropriate control techniques that can contribute to the reduction in oscillations [6,7,29–31]. In the field of both civil and mechanical engineering, an important problem is the reduction in oscillations created by dynamic loads, such as earthquakes and wind. The methods and control techniques used were described in detail in [32]. This work has important applications because the problem of reducing oscillations is a common problem for both civil and mechanical engineers [32]. These applications can be used in airplanes, metal bridges, and large metal structures. Structures are stressed by dynamic loads such as wind and earthquake loading [32]. This paper outlines and explains the various methods and control techniques used to address this issue. This research is highly relevant because it addresses the shared challenge of oscillation. The applications of the outlined methods are broad, potentially benefiting areas such as airplane design, metal bridges, and large metal structures, all of which are subjected to dynamic stresses from wind and seismic activity. The development of effective strategies to control these vibrations is essential for the stability and durability of these structures.

When materials are subjected to an electric field, they can experience distortion, a phenomenon that holds significance for engineers working on the development and application of advanced smart materials. By employing appropriate control techniques, these smart materials can play a vital role in minimizing oscillations, which is a crucial concern in various engineering fields. This issue is especially relevant for both civil and mechanical engineers, who frequently grapple with the challenge of reducing vibrations caused by dynamic forces such as earthquakes and wind.

These structures are often exposed to dynamic loading conditions, including those imposed by wind and seismic activity, which can induce vibrations that compromise their stability and integrity. Therefore, it is essential to develop and implement effective control techniques for reducing vibration. The findings of this study could lead to advancements in the design and maintenance of structures that are more resilient to dynamic stresses, ultimately enhancing their safety, performance, and longevity. This study plays a crucial role in advancing the reduction in oscillations, which is an area of significant concern in engineering. This research begins with a comprehensive modeling process utilizing the finite element method as the foundational approach. The equations used for this modeling are meticulously detailed, specifically in Equations (1)–(10), providing a thorough understanding of the application of the finite element method in this context.

Subsequently, this study introduces equations pertinent to control theory, which is an essential aspect of managing and reducing oscillations. A key focus is placed on the derivation of the transfer function, which is fundamental in control theory to understand how systems respond to various inputs. This derivation is presented in detail to ensure clarity in the development and application of the transfer function.

The analysis within the study was multifaceted, employing both state–space domain and frequency domain analyses. The state–space domain analysis is elaborated upon through Equations (10) to (14), offering insights into the system's behavior in the time domain representation. Additionally, frequency domain analysis is thoroughly explored in Equations (15)–(33), providing an in-depth examination of how the system responds to different frequencies. By combining these analytical approaches, this study offers a comprehensive strategy to address and mitigate oscillations in various engineering applications.

2. Motion Formula of the Smart Structure

The beam formula for both mechanical and electrical loads is calculated by [7,17–19,28,33]:

$$EI\frac{\partial^4 y(t,x)}{\partial x^4} + \rho b A b\frac{\partial^2 y(t,x)}{\partial t^2} = f_m(t,x) + f_e(t,x) \quad (1)$$

E is Young's modulus, I is the moment of inertia, p is density, A is area, f_e is the electrical force, and f_m is the disturbance (mechanical force) [33].

Figures 1 and 2 depict a smart beam incorporating an embedded piezoelectric actuator that produces a mechanical load in the form of a force when subjected to an electrical current [6,7]. Figure 1 shows a smart beam with embedded actuators.

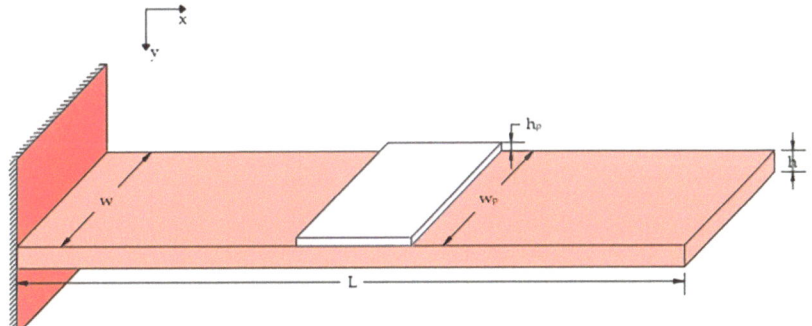

Figure 1. Piezoelectric patch attached to a beam.

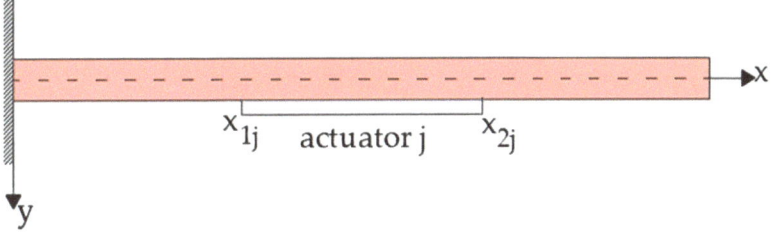

Figure 2. One pair of actuator patches.

Figure 2 shows the actuator integrated into the beam. This figure shows the ends of the actuator used in further equations, which are very important for the electrical matrices of our system. All modeling is based on Equation (1) [33]; from the solution of this equation, the results are given in the time domain. The results without control are given by applying the differential, whereas the results with control are given after the application of the infinity control.

To determine the electric force generated by the piezoelectric actuator $f_e(t,x)$, the following equation was used:

$$f_e(t,x) = \frac{\partial^2 M_{px}(t,x)}{\partial x^2} \qquad (2)$$

where M_{px} is the piezoelectric actuator's bending moment.

Where Pzt (piezoelectric patch) placed on the beam is indicated by the step function H. The bending moment M_{px} is given by

$$M_{px}(t,x) = C_0 e_{pe}(t)\left[H(x-x_{1j}) - H(x-x_{2j})\right]u_j(t) \qquad (3)$$

This equation is derived from the theory of piezoelectric materials, where [16,17]

$$C_0 = EI \cdot K_f \qquad (4)$$

$$K_f = \frac{12 E E_p h h_p \left(2h + h_p\right)}{16 E^2 h^4 + E E_p \left(32 h^3 h_p + 24 h^2 h_p^2 + 8 h h_p^3\right) + E_p^2 h_p^4} \qquad (5)$$

The piezoelectric patch mechanical tension $e_{pe}(t)$ is derived by

$$e_{pe}(t) = \frac{d_{31}}{h_p} u_j(t) \qquad (6)$$

The constant d_{31} combines the electric intensity $e_{pe}(t)$ with the electric voltage $u_j(t)$, which is generated in an actuator j (Figure 2). Where d_{31} is the piezoelectric constant d31 = 280×10^{-12} m/V (Table 1).

Table 1. Smart beam specifications (graphite/epoxy T300/976).

Specifications of the Beam	Value
L stands for length	1.40 m
W stands for the width	0.07 m
h is height	0.02 m
ρ represents the density	1700 kg/m^3
E is the Young's modulus	1.8×10^{11} N/m^2
Pzt thickness is bs and ba	0.003 m
d31 is the electrical conductivity	280×10^{-12} m/V

Thus, Function (3) can be expressed as a flexural moment as follows:

$$M_{px}(t,x) = C_p\left[H(x-x_{1j}) - H(x-x_{2j})\right]u_j(t) \qquad (7)$$

where

$$C_p = EIK_f \frac{d_{31}}{h_p}$$

The electric force is obtained as follows using Equations (2) and (3):

$$f_e(t,x) = C_p u_{aj}(t)[\delta'(x - x1j) - \delta'(x - x2j)] \qquad (8)$$

The following function, which depicts the smart beam's response to the dynamic (electrical) force generated by the piezoelectric patch and the lateral dynamic disturbance, was derived using Equations (1) and (8):

$$EI\frac{\partial^4 y(t,x)}{\partial x^4} + \rho b A b \frac{\partial^2 y(t,x)}{\partial t^2} = q_0(t) + C_p u_j(t)[\delta'(x - x_{1j}) - \delta'(x - x_{2j})] \qquad (9)$$

In the case of j-equivalent piezoelectrics (Figure 3), Equation (9) becomes

$$EI\frac{\partial^4 y(t,x)}{\partial x^4} + \rho b A b \frac{\partial^2 y(t,x)}{\partial t^2} = q_0(t) + C_p u_j(t)\sum_{i=1}^{j}[\delta'(x - r_{1j}) - \delta'(x - x_{2j})]$$

where $\delta'(x)$ is the derivative of the Dirac function with respect to its independent variable.

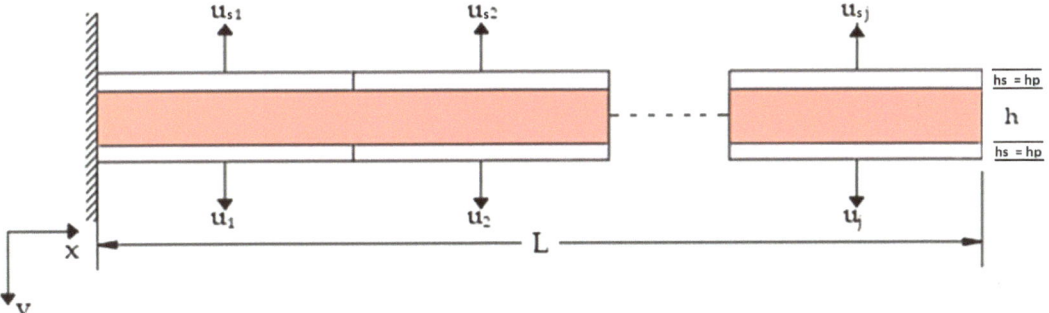

Figure 3. An intelligent beam that incorporates piezoelectric actuators and sensors.

From the solution of the partial differential equations of the beam, we pass to the finite element method, which transforms the system of the beam into a system of ordinary differential equations. The solution of the finite elements converges with the solution of the partial differential equation by increasing the number of elements. In the next chapter, the tables of the damping stiffness mass matrices and electrical matrix used for the modeling, as calculated by the authors, are used [1,33,34].

2.1. Modelling

In this work, the Eyler–Bernoulli beam equation (Equation (1)) is used, by integrating this equation and using a Hermite multivariable, the local matrices are derived for the mass, stiffness, and damping electric charge matrices of the structure. Assembling is then performed on the global stiffness model. A reference related to the finite element method is given [1,33]. In our analysis, we use two degrees of freedom in the finite element method—the transport deflection ψ and the rotation. In addition, we use two different disturbances, one static and one dynamic.

The goal of this study was to reduce oscillations using intricate control techniques and piezoelectric materials. In particular, the locations of piezoelectric actuators were defined. Figure 4 shows the actuators positioned at each of the four points (labels 1, 2, 3, and 4) along the beam. The dynamical description of the system is given by [1,35]

$$M\ddot{q}(t) + D\dot{q}(t) + Kq(t) = fm(t) + fe(t) \qquad (10)$$

where fe represents the results of the electromechanical coupling affecting the global control force vector, D is the viscous damping matrix, K is the global stiffness matrix, and M is the global mass matrix. fm is the mechanical vector of the global external loading and fe is the electrical vector. The independent variable is a vector q(t) composed of transversal deflections ψ_i and rotations w_i, or

$$q(t) = \begin{bmatrix} w_1 \\ \psi_1 \\ \vdots \\ w_n \\ \psi_n \end{bmatrix} \quad (11)$$

where n denotes the finite element number employed in the analysis [7]. As is common practice, we switch the representation to a state–space control form [9–15].

$$\begin{aligned} x(t) &= \begin{bmatrix} q(t) \\ \dot{q}(t) \end{bmatrix} \\ &= \begin{bmatrix} 0_{2n \times n} \\ M^{-1}(f_m(t) + f_e(t)) \end{bmatrix} + \begin{bmatrix} \dot{q}(t) \\ -M^{-1}D\dot{q}(t) - M^{-1}Kq(t) \end{bmatrix} \\ &= \begin{bmatrix} 0_{2n \times n} \\ M^{-1}(f_m + f_e)(t) \end{bmatrix} + \begin{bmatrix} 0_{2n \times 2n} & I_{2n \times 2n} \\ -M^{-1}K & -M^{-1}D \end{bmatrix} \begin{bmatrix} q(t) \\ \dot{q}(t) \end{bmatrix} \\ &= \begin{bmatrix} 0_{2n \times n} \\ M^{-1}f_m(t) \end{bmatrix} + \begin{bmatrix} 0_{2n \times n} \\ M^{-1}f_e(t) \end{bmatrix} + \begin{bmatrix} 0_{2n \times 2n} & I_{2n \times 2n} \\ -M^{-1}K & -M^{-1}D \end{bmatrix} \begin{bmatrix} q(t) \\ \dot{q}(t) \end{bmatrix} \end{aligned} \quad (12)$$

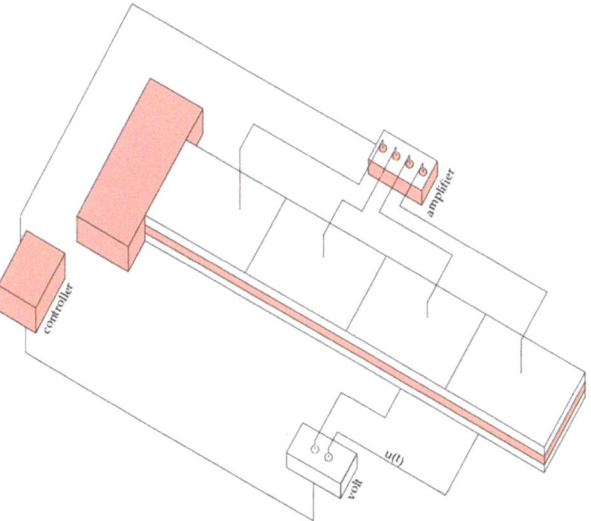

Figure 4. The actuators were positioned over the entire smart structure.

Additionally, the value $f_e(t)$ is denoted as where the unit's piezoelectric force (of size $2n \times n$) is when it is placed on the proper actuator.

$$Fe(t) = \begin{bmatrix} 0 & 0 & 0 & 0 \\ cp & -cp & 0 & 0 \\ 0 & 0 & 0 & 0 \\ 0 & cp & -cp & 0 \\ 0 & 0 & 0 & 0 \\ 0 & 0 & cp & -cp \\ 0 & 0 & 0 & 0 \\ 0 & 0 & 0 & cp \end{bmatrix} \quad (13)$$

where u denotes the actuator voltage. The disturbance vector is denoted as d(t) = f_m(t). Then,

$$\begin{aligned}\dot{x}(t) &= \begin{bmatrix} 0_{2n \times 2n} & I_{2n \times 2n} \\ -M^{-1}K & -M^{-1}D \end{bmatrix} x(t) + \begin{bmatrix} 0_{2n \times n} \\ M^{-1}F_e^* \end{bmatrix} u(t) + \begin{bmatrix} 0_{2n \times 2n} \\ M^{-1} \end{bmatrix} d(t) \\ &= Ax(t) + Bu(t) + Gd(t) \\ &= Ax(t) + [B G] \begin{bmatrix} u(t) \\ d(t) \end{bmatrix} \\ &= Ax(t) + \widetilde{B}\widetilde{u}(t), \end{aligned}$$
(14)

The output function (displacement measured alone) can be used to enhance this result.

$$y(t) = [x1(t)\ x3(t) \ldots xn - 1(t)]T = C\ x(t)$$

where

$$C = [1\ 0\ 0\ \ldots 0; -1\ 0\ 1\ 0\ \ldots 0; 0\ 0\ -1\ 0\ 1\ \ldots 0; 0\ 0\ 0\ 0\ -1\ 0\ 1\ \ldots 0]$$

The ability to convert mechanical stress into strain, and vice versa, is a feature of the piezoelectric effect. The reduction in oscillations attained in this study is based on this. Actuator pairs co-localized with piezoceramics (PZT G-1195) were employed in our simulation for laminated composite beams made of graphite/epoxy, aluminum, and glass/epoxy (Figure 5). Table 1 lists the specifications of the smart beams.

Figure 5. Smart structure.

2.2. Connection to the Issue of Beam Control

The given problem involves taking the disturbance (d) and measurement noise (n) as inputs and producing displacement measurements (y) and controller voltages (u) as the outputs. The provided structural diagrams and equations were employed to simulate this particular issue involving a beam and were implemented using MATLAB v. 5.0. In the frequency domain, the objective is to determine the optimal transfer function N. To achieve this, it is beneficial to derive the input-output relationships for the initial model [16,21].

$$\begin{bmatrix} u \\ e \end{bmatrix} = F(s) \begin{bmatrix} d \\ n \end{bmatrix} \Rightarrow z = F(s)w$$

as illustrated in Figure 5.

In Figure 6, K(s) is the controller, d is the disturbance, e is the error, n is the noise, u is the control voltage, and x is the state vector.

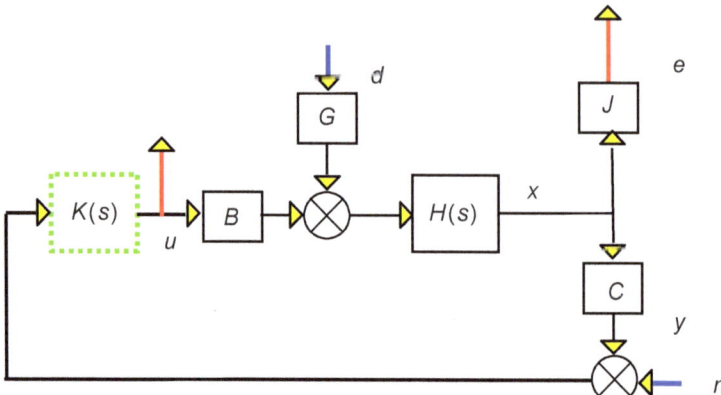

Figure 6. Beam with noise output, error, disturbance input, and controller.

Where the beam is explained by [31]

$$\dot{x}(t) = Ax(t) + [B\ G]\begin{bmatrix} u(t) \\ d(t) \end{bmatrix}$$

In the frequency domain, the transfer function H(s) is

$$H(s) = (sI - A)^{-1} \qquad (15)$$

J is used to select the states that we aim to control, which may differ from y. In most studies, J is

$$J = \begin{bmatrix} 1 & 0 & 0 & 0 & 0 & 0 & 0 & 0 & 0 & 0 & 0 & 0 & 0 & 0 & 0 \\ 0 & 0 & 1 & 0 & 0 & 0 & 0 & 0 & 0 & 0 & 0 & 0 & 0 & 0 & 0 \\ 0 & 0 & 0 & 0 & 1 & 0 & 0 & 0 & 0 & 0 & 0 & 0 & 0 & 0 & 0 \\ 0 & 0 & 0 & 0 & 0 & 0 & 1 & 0 & 0 & 0 & 0 & 0 & 0 & 0 & 0 \end{bmatrix} \qquad (16)$$

We commenced by gradually re-performing Figure 6.

It is clear from Figure 7 that the disruption to the inaccuracy in the transfer function is

$$T_{de} = J \cdot (I - HBKC)^{-1} H \cdot G \qquad (17)$$

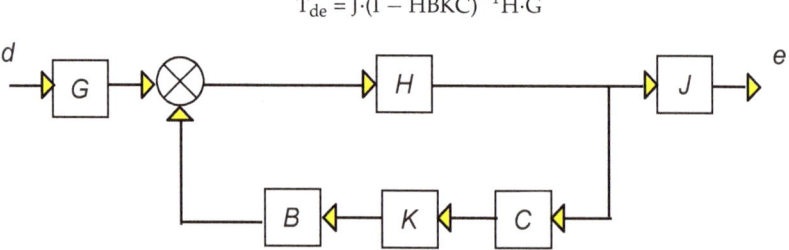

Figure 7. Block diagram disturbance and errors.

Equation (17) is a frequency domain equation, and an attempt was made to derive the transfer function Tde that relates the external disturbance to the error.

It is evident from Figure 8 that the noise-to-error transfer function is

$$T_{ne} = J \cdot (I - HBKC)^{-1} HBK \qquad (18)$$

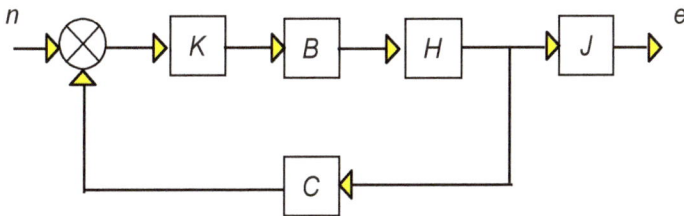

Figure 8. Noise and errors in block diagram form.

Figure 9 illustrates the disturbance for controlling the transfer function:

$$T_{du} = (I - KCHB)^{-1}KCH \cdot G \tag{19}$$

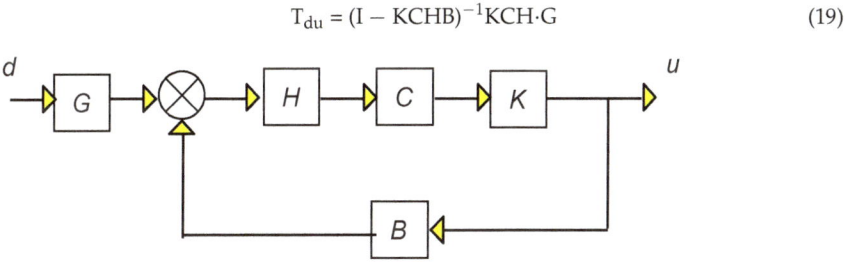

Figure 9. Disturbance and control voltages presented in a block diagram form.

Figure 10 shows that the noise-to-control transfer function is

$$T_{nu} = (I - KCHB)^{-1}K \tag{20}$$

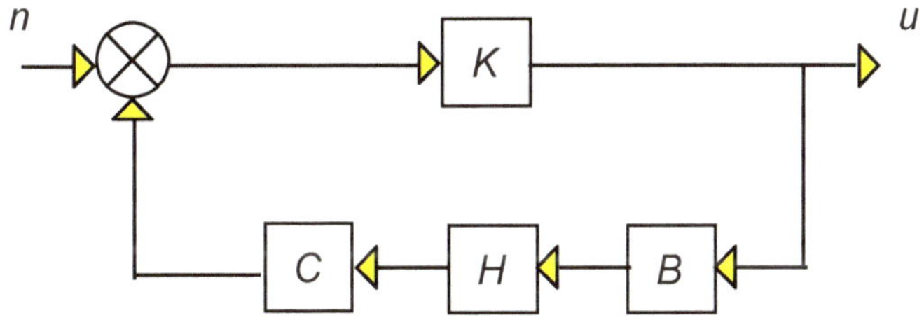

Figure 10. Noise and control voltages presented in a block diagram form.

When we combine these, we obtain

$$e = J \cdot (I - HBKC)^{-1} H \cdot Gd + J \cdot (I - HBKC)^{-1} HBKn \tag{21}$$

$$u = (I - KCHB)^{-1} KCH \cdot Gd + (I - KCHB)^{-1} Kn \tag{22}$$

or

$$\begin{bmatrix} u \\ e \end{bmatrix} = \begin{bmatrix} (I - KCHB)^{-1}KCHG & (I - KCHB)^{-1}K \\ J(I - HBKC)^{-1}HG & J(I - HBKC)^{-1}HBK \end{bmatrix} \begin{bmatrix} d \\ n \end{bmatrix} \tag{23}$$

$$\begin{bmatrix} u \\ e \end{bmatrix} = \begin{bmatrix} F_{du} & F_{nu} \\ F_{de} & F_{ne} \end{bmatrix} \begin{bmatrix} d \\ n \end{bmatrix} \Rightarrow z = F(s)w \tag{24}$$

We proceeded by making the necessary weighting adjustments and redesigning Figure 6 to fit our particular issue.

Next, we created a new version of Figure 11, restructuring it into a two-port diagram. This new diagram should be formatted in a manner similar to that depicted in Figure 6.

This comparison will help us better understand the differences and similarities between the two representations.

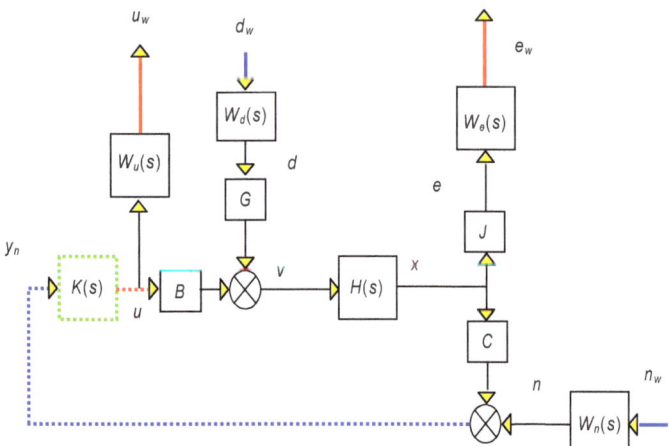

Figure 11. A block diagram showing the beam scenario's weights.

In Figure 12, x and v are auxiliary signals.

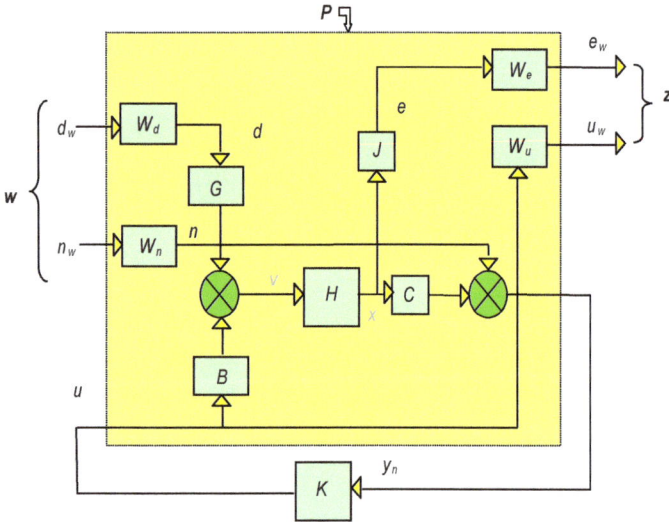

Figure 12. Diagram with two ports for the beam issue.

We were investigating why

$$Q_{zw}(s) = P_{zw}(s) + P_{zu}(s)K(s)\,(I - P_{yu}(s)K(s))^{-1}P_{yw}(s) \tag{25}$$

such that

$$z = Q_{zw}w = F(P, K)w \tag{26}$$

We then attempted to identify P(s). The necessary transfers carried out were

$$ew = WeJx = WeJHv = WeJH(GWddw + Bu) = WeJHGWddw + WeJHBu \tag{27}$$

$$u_w = W_u u \qquad (28)$$

$$y_n = Cx + W_n n_w = CHv + W_n n_w = CH(GW_d d_w + Bu) + W_n n_w = CHGW_d d_w + CHBu + W_n n_w \qquad (29)$$

Combining all these results in

$$\begin{bmatrix} u_w \\ e_w \\ y_n \end{bmatrix} = \begin{bmatrix} 0 & 0 & W_u \\ W_e JHGW_d & 0 & W_e JHB \\ CHGW_d & W_n & CHB \end{bmatrix} \begin{bmatrix} d_w \\ n_w \\ u \end{bmatrix} \qquad (30)$$

or

$$\begin{bmatrix} z \\ y_n \end{bmatrix} = \begin{bmatrix} P_{zw} & P_{zu} \\ P_{yw} & P_{yu} \end{bmatrix} \begin{bmatrix} w \\ u \end{bmatrix} \qquad (31)$$

where

$$P_{zw} = \begin{bmatrix} 0 & 0 \\ W_e JHGW_d & 0 \end{bmatrix}, \; P_{zu} = \begin{bmatrix} W_u \\ W_e JHB \end{bmatrix}, \; P_{yw} = \begin{bmatrix} CHGW_d & W_n \end{bmatrix}, \; P_{yu} = CHB \qquad (32)$$

However, further steps are required to obtain Q_{ij}. To do sp, we used Equation (18), noting that

$$d = W_d d_w, \; n = W_n n_w, \; e_w = W_e e, \; u_w = W_u u$$

Hence,

$$\begin{bmatrix} u \\ e \end{bmatrix} = \begin{bmatrix} W_u^{-1} u_w \\ W_e^{-1} e_w \end{bmatrix} = F(s) \begin{bmatrix} d \\ n \end{bmatrix} = F(s) \begin{bmatrix} W_d d_w \\ W_n n_w \end{bmatrix} \Rightarrow$$

$$\begin{bmatrix} u_w \\ e_w \end{bmatrix} = \begin{bmatrix} W_u & \\ & W_e \end{bmatrix} F(s) \begin{bmatrix} W_d & \\ & W_n \end{bmatrix} \begin{bmatrix} d_w \\ n_w \end{bmatrix}$$

or

$$\begin{bmatrix} u_w \\ e_w \end{bmatrix} = \begin{bmatrix} W_u(I - KCHB)^{-1} KCHGW_d & W_u(I - KCHB)^{-1} KW_n \\ W_e J(I - HBKC)^{-1} HGW_d & W_e J(I - HBKC)^{-1} HBKW_n \end{bmatrix} \begin{bmatrix} d_w \\ n_w \end{bmatrix}$$

Thus, the matrices in

$$z = Q_{zw} w \text{ or } \begin{bmatrix} u \\ e \end{bmatrix} = \begin{bmatrix} Q_{11} & Q_{12} \\ Q_{21} & Q_{22} \end{bmatrix} \begin{bmatrix} d \\ n \end{bmatrix}$$

From the natural partitioning to express P in state–space,

$$P(s) = \begin{bmatrix} A & B_1 & B_2 \\ C_1 & D_{11} & D_{12} \\ C_2 & D_{21} & D_{22} \end{bmatrix} = \begin{bmatrix} P_{zw}(s) & P_{zu}(s) \\ P_{yw}(s) & P_{yu}(s) \end{bmatrix} \qquad (33)$$

(where the shortened format is used), and K's corresponding form is

$$K(s) = \begin{bmatrix} A_K & B_K \\ C_K & D_K \end{bmatrix}$$

Equation (29) describes the equations

$$\dot{x}(t) = Ax(t) + \begin{bmatrix} B_1 & B_2 \end{bmatrix} \begin{bmatrix} w(t) \\ u(t) \end{bmatrix}$$

$$\begin{bmatrix} z(t) \\ y(t) \end{bmatrix} = \begin{bmatrix} C_1 \\ C_2 \end{bmatrix} x(t) + \begin{bmatrix} D_{11} & D_{12} \\ D_{21} & D_{22} \end{bmatrix} \begin{bmatrix} w(t) \\ u(t) \end{bmatrix}$$

and

$$\dot{x}_K(t) = A_K x_K(t) + B_K y(t)$$

$$u(t) = CK \times K(t) + DKy(t)$$

3. Results

3.1. H_2 Norm

In the control theory, the H_2 norm or H_2 performance is used to evaluate the performance of a system [6,7,25–27,29,30]. Significantly, it quantifies a system's ability to reduce noise and disturbances by measuring its energy in response to white noise. The H_2 norm of the system is defined by taking the square root of the sum of the squares of the impulse responses. The total system power response to a unit impulse input can be represented by the H_2 norm. It is an indicator of the amount of energy from the input signals that are attenuated or amplified across all frequency intervals by the system. In principle, a lower H_2-norm indicates higher disturbance rejection and noise attenuation capacity. Minimizing the H_2 norm is often a goal in the control system design, particularly in optimal control frameworks. The use of the H_2 criterion for controllers that perform well under different operational circumstances is widespread in practice because it combines performance with robustness [16–21,28].

Controller design in control systems aims to reduce the H_2 norm, particularly in optimal control frameworks. Because it strikes a good balance between robustness and performance, the H_2 standard is a popular choice for controller design that must operate effectively across various operating conditions [16–21,28]. In summary, the H_2 norm of control theory is useful for building systems that work well on average, even with noise and disturbances. Engineers can then reduce the H_2 norm to develop controllers that enhance the overall robustness and energy efficiency of a system [1,6,7,25–27,29–31,35,36].

3.2. H-Infinity Norm

The H∞ (H-infinity) norm is crucial in control theory, particularly when designing robust controls to assess and ensure system performance in worst-case scenarios [11,35,36]. The highest gain that the system can gain from its input to its output at all frequencies is indicated by the H∞ norm. This denotes the amount of noise or disturbance that can be amplified by the system in the worst-case scenario. A lower H∞ norm will practically result in a more robust system because it is unlikely to cause significant damage, even during worst-case situations. Therefore, it is necessary to minimize this norm when designing control systems for robust performance. The H∞ control structure aims to design controllers with good performance despite uncertainties and worst-case disruptions. Systems that require dependability and safety, such as those in aerospace, are where they matter the most [16–21,28].

It is possible to compute the H∞ norm for state–space representations. Describe a system in which $y = Cx$ and $\dot{x} = Ax + Bu$. Solving the algebraic Riccati equation (ARE) for any given PPP matrix and verifying whether the closed-loop system is stable will yield the H∞ norm. The H_2 norm is not equal to H∞ because it calculates the entire energy response of the system to the white noise inputs. The H∞ norm considers the worst-case scenario, whereas H_2 provides an assessment of performance averaged over time. Therefore, the H∞ norm is more appropriate when a high degree of robustness is required [2,11,35,36].

In summary, the H∞ norm plays the most important role in the robust control theory by demonstrating the highest possible amplification of disturbances by a system. Designing controllers that minimize the H∞ norm allows control engineers to guarantee robust stability even under extreme difficulties. The results are then presented in the following format: in the first case, a sinusoidal loading amplitude of 12N was applied, followed by constant loading. The result is a comparison of control H_2 with H∞. Structures apply the H_2 norm or H_2 performance as a measure of performance, as used in control theory. In particular, it measures the power of the system output due to white noise inputs to show how effectively the system can dampen noise and interference.

3.3. H-Infinity and H_2 Norms Comparison

The H_2 norm is dissimilar to the $H\infty$ norm, which is defined as the peak value of the system gain at all frequencies. The H_2 norm averages the energy measure and the $H\infty$ norm concentrates on the maximum response. Depending on the design requirements, control engineers may choose to minimize either H_2 or the $H\infty$ norm.

In practice, the H_2 norm is beneficial for systems where disturbances and noise are random processes with known statistical characteristics. It is especially useful in cases where the ability of an antenna to work in a frequency range is more important than its ability to work at a precise frequency.

The $H\infty$ norm is another form of the norm and is defined as the maximum gain of the system at any frequency. It estimates the phase margin to account for the maximum possible amplification of the disturbances or noise by the system. For a fair comparison, it was necessary to arrange the results to show that a lower $H\infty$ norm better reflects the robustness of the system because the system is less influenced by worst-case disturbances.

One part of the code for H-infinity controller (Figure 13) is

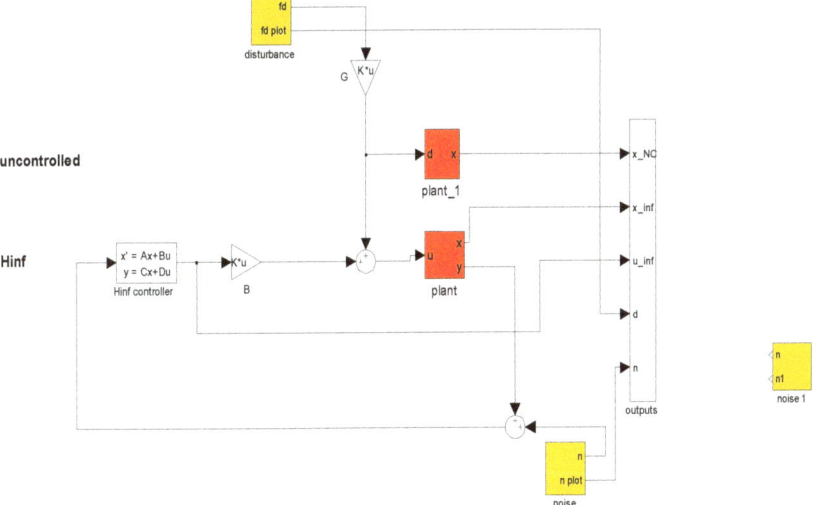

Figure 13. Nominal performance in Simulink, where Wd, Wn, Wu, and We are the whets of our system for disturbances (d) noise (n), control vector (u), and error (e); x is the state vector and y is the output; in the displacement the rotation and the control vector (u), K is our control (H-infinity or H_2). In the results, we take the diagram for the open loop (without control) with H-infinity and the H_2 controller.

```
AT = A0;
BT = [Bm0 zeros(2*nd, nd/2) Be0];
CT = [J; C0];
DT = [zeros(nd, nd) zeros(nd, nd/2) zeros(nd, nd/2); zeros(nd/2, nd) eye(nd/2) zeros(nd/2, nd/2)]
qbeam2 = ss(AT, BT, CT, DT);
szk = size(Kinf.a, 1);
[Kinf, Scl12, gam12] = hinfsyn(qbeam2, nmeas, ncont)
save Kinf.mat Kinf
return
% full weight
systemnames = ' beam0 y sd se su Wu We Wn Wd';
inputvar = '[ n(4); d(8); u(4) ]';
```

```
outputvar = '[ We; Wu; y+Wn]';
input_to_sd = '[Wd]';
input_to_su = '[u]';
input_to_se = '[beam0]';
input_to_beam0 = '[ sd+su ]';
input_to_y = '[ beam0 ]';
input_to_Wd = '[ d ]';
input_to_Wn = '[ n ]';
input_to_We = '[ se ]';
input_to_Wu = '[ u ]';
return
Kinf
```

3.4. Mathematical Modeling Results

Figures 14 and 15 compare the rotations and translations of the nodes in the smart architectures with and without control, respectively. This analysis highlights the significant impact of the control system. Without control, the nodes exhibited substantial rotational movement, indicating a lack of stability and an increased susceptibility to oscillations. Conversely, the rotations were markedly reduced with the control system in place, demonstrating the effectiveness of the system in enhancing stability and minimizing unwanted movements. This comparison underscores the critical role of the control mechanism in retaining the structural integrity and performance of the smart structures.

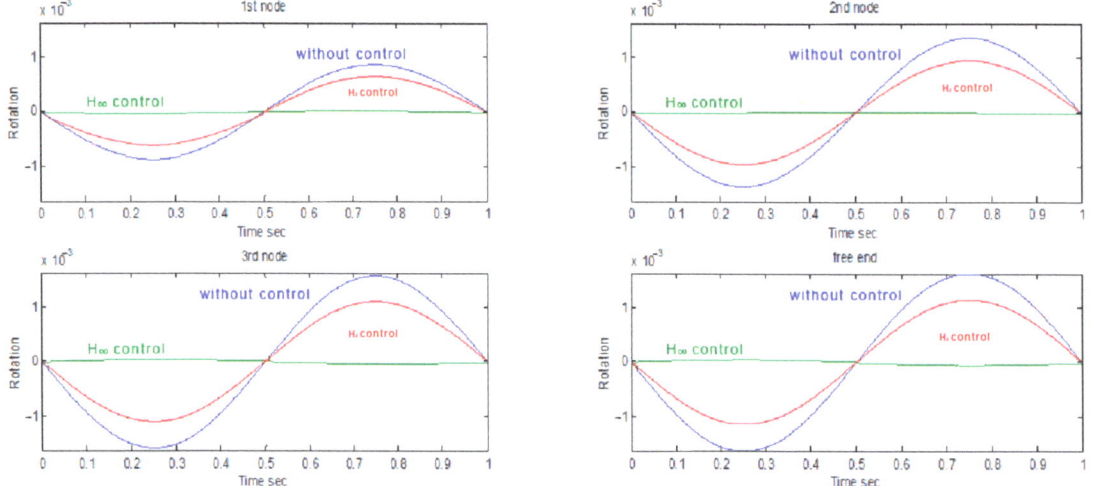

Figure 14. Comparing the nodes' rotations in the smart structures both with and without control.

In Figure 14, the four nodes of the smart structure rotations are depicted for three different scenarios: with H_2 control, H∞ (H-infinity) control, and without any control. The results clearly show that H∞ control provides the best performance, as the rotations are nearly zero. This indicates that the H∞ control method is highly effective in minimizing rotational movement systems [1,6,7,11,25–27,29–31,35].

Similarly, Figure 15 illustrates the displacements of the four smart structure nodes under the same three scenarios: with H_2 control, with H∞ control, and without control. The comparison reveals that H∞ control yields a superior outcome. The displacements were almost zero when the H∞ control was applied, demonstrating its effectiveness in minimizing positional deviations. Thus, the H∞ control proved to be the most effective method for reducing both rotations and displacements in smart structures.

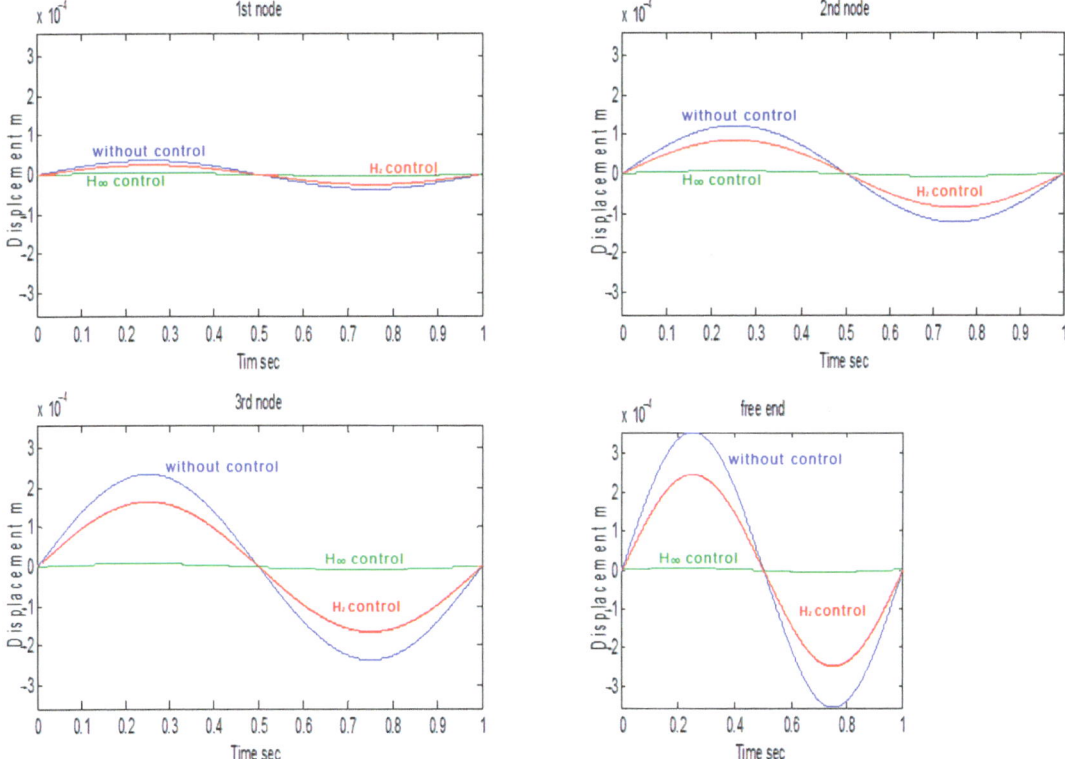

Figure 15. Analyzing and contrasting the smart structure node displacements with and without control.

The results are then provided in detail for the static loading of 12 N at the free end of the smart structure. In Figures 16–18, a concentrated force (12N) is applied to the edge of the carrier, and the displacement at the edge of the carrier quickly stabilizes at 0.015 sec. This shows the very good operation of the model. In addition, what is also the goal of the specific problem is achieved, i.e., a reduction in oscillation since with the blue line, we have a result with control where I is a reduction in distortion, while with the green line, I is the open loop in which the oscillation is much greater.

Figure 16 illustrates the displacements for all the nodes of the smart beam, where the H-infinity control criterion is employed. The results are highly impressive because the displacements were negligible. This illustrates how the H-infinity control strategy effectively reduces the displacements while maintaining the stability and structural integrity of the smart beam under static loading scenarios. The near-zero displacement highlights the superior performance and robustness of the control system [6,7,26,30,31].

Figure 17 depicts the rotations for all the nodes of the smart beam using the H-infinity control criterion. The findings were exceptionally impressive as the displacements were nearly imperceptible. This underscores the efficacy of the H-infinity control approach in reducing displacements to a minimum, thereby ensuring the structural integrity and stability of the smart beam under static loading scenarios. The minimal rotations for all the nodes of the smart beam highlight the superior performance and robustness of the implemented control system.

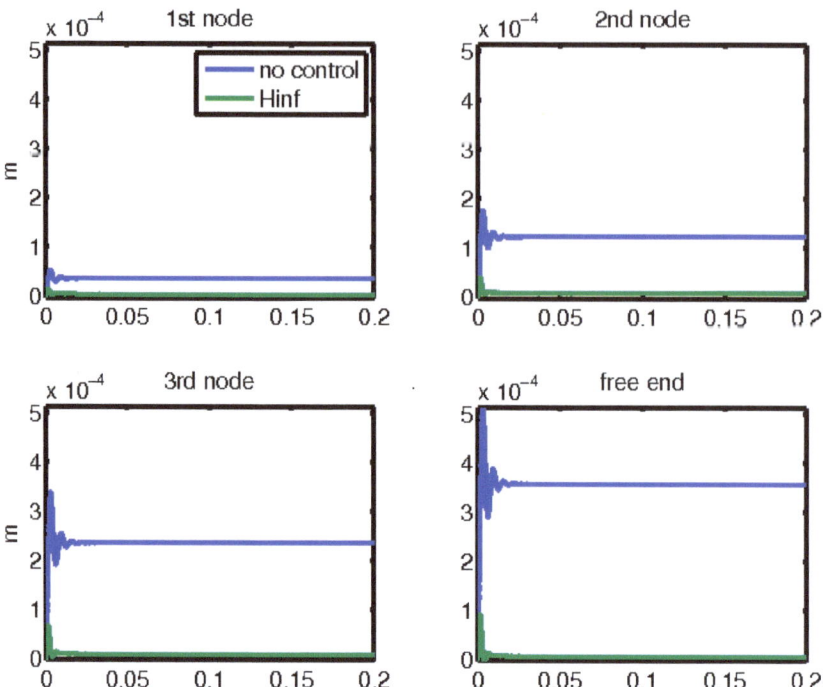

Figure 16. Results of displacements with and without control when applying static loading at the beam's free end.

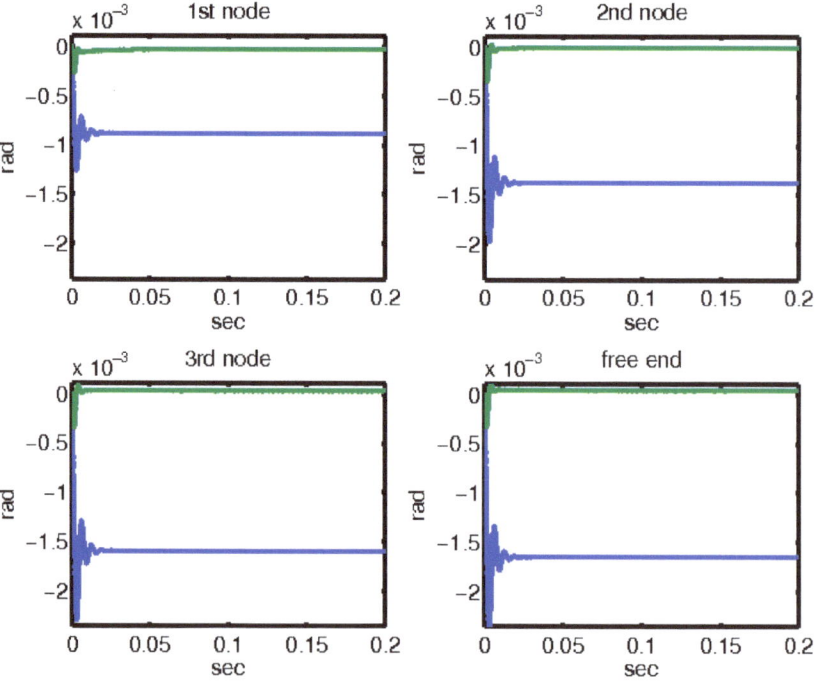

Figure 17. Results of rotations with and without control when applying static loading at the beam's free end.

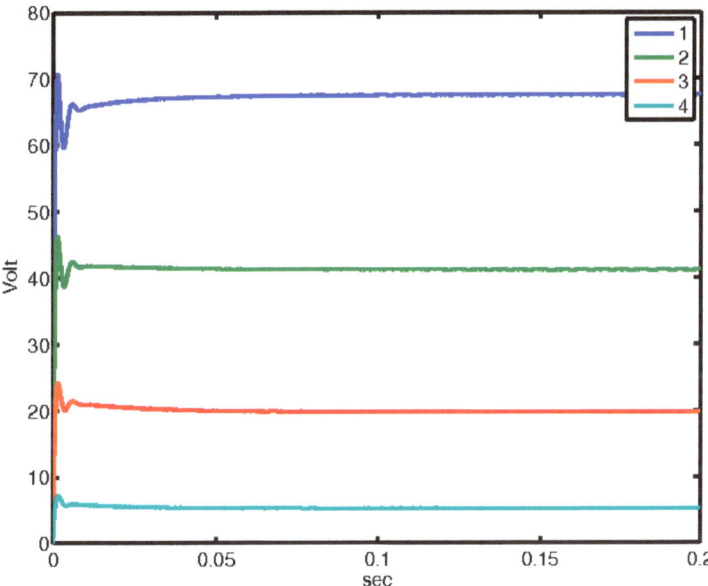

Figure 18. Control voltages for each smart structure node. The numbers 1, 2, 3, and 4 correspond to the four piezoelectric actuators (voltages) present in the smart beam.

The results for the four smart beam nodes are shown in Figure 18. This figure shows the piezoelectric stresses produced, which are necessary for damping oscillations. The data provided a clear insight into how piezoelectric elements contribute to reducing vibrational movement, highlighting the effectiveness of the smart beam design in mitigating oscillatory behavior through targeted stress generation.

Next, sinusoidal loading was applied while utilizing the H-infinity control theory. The results are highly impressive, as there is a noticeable reduction in oscillations. Figure 19 shows the displacement of the structural free end with and without the installed control system. These findings were remarkable, showing a complete reduction in oscillations when the control system was implemented. This highlights the efficacy of the H-infinity control theory in managing and mitigating vibrational movements and ensuring the structural stability and performance of smart structures under sinusoidal loading conditions. A comparison between the controlled and uncontrolled scenarios underscores the significant impact of the control mechanism on achieving optimal structural behavior. Figure 20 shows the displacement of the 3rd node of the structure with and without the control system. The results are remarkable, revealing the complete elimination of oscillations when the control system is active. This underscores the efficacy of the H-infinity control theory in reducing vibrational movements and ensuring the performance and stability of the smart structure under sinusoidal loading conditions. The comparison between controlled and uncontrolled scenarios highlights the crucial role of the control mechanism in optimizing the structural behavior. The control voltages under sinusoidal disturbances for all the nodes of the smart structures are shown in Figure 21. These voltages are crucial for counteracting disturbances and maintaining structural stability. By applying these control voltages, the system effectively mitigates the impact of sinusoidal disturbances, ensuring optimal performance and reducing oscillatory behavior in smart structures. A detailed analysis of these control voltages highlights their significance in achieving precise and efficient control over structural responses. Figure 21 shows the generated piezoelectric stresses, which are essential for damping oscillations. The data offer a clear understanding of how piezoelectric elements help reduce vibrational movement, emphasizing the effectiveness of smart beam design in mitigating oscillatory behavior through precise stress generation.

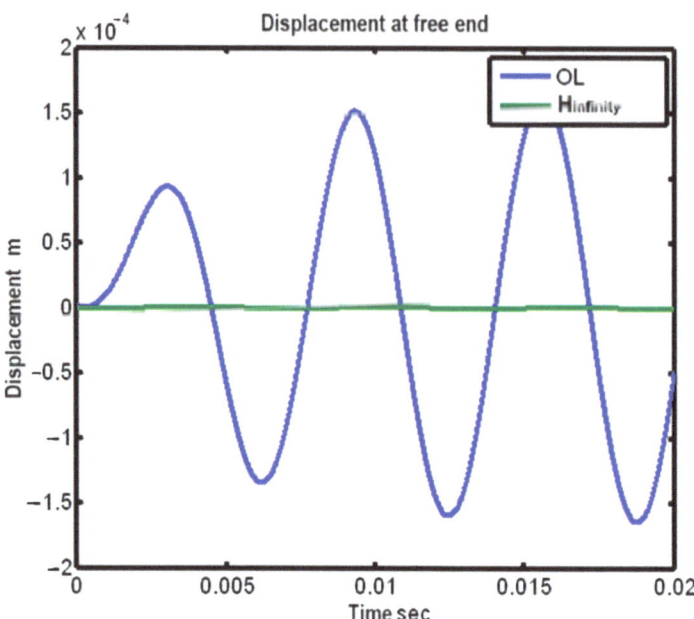

Figure 19. Smart structure's free end displacement with (H-infinity) and without control (open loop, OL).

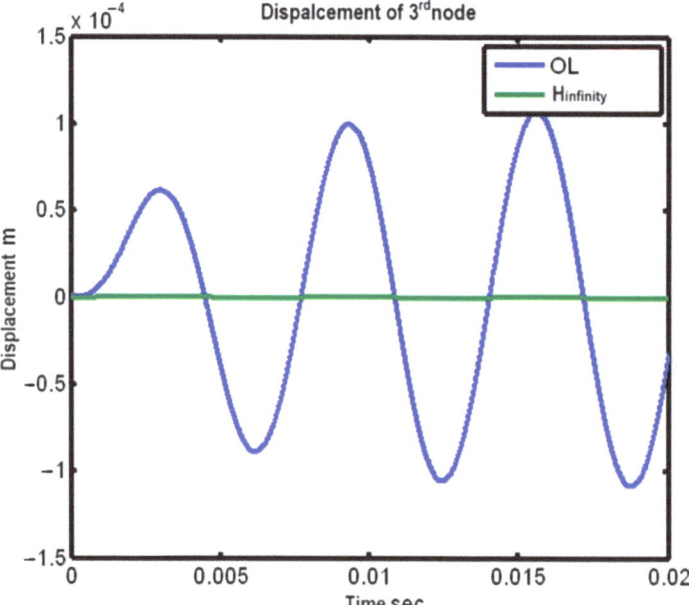

Figure 20. Displacement of the 3rd node of the smart structure presented with (H-infinity) and without control (open loop, OL).

Figure 22 presents a Bode diagram of the smart structure, which illustrates the frequency response of the system. This diagram provides critical insight into the gain and phase shift of a smart structure over a range of frequencies. By analyzing the Bode diagram, one can assess the performance and stability of the control system and identify how effectively it mitigates disturbances and responds to various frequencies. The Bode plot highlights key characteristics such as resonant frequencies and bandwidths, which are essential for understanding and optimizing the dynamic behavior of a smart structure.

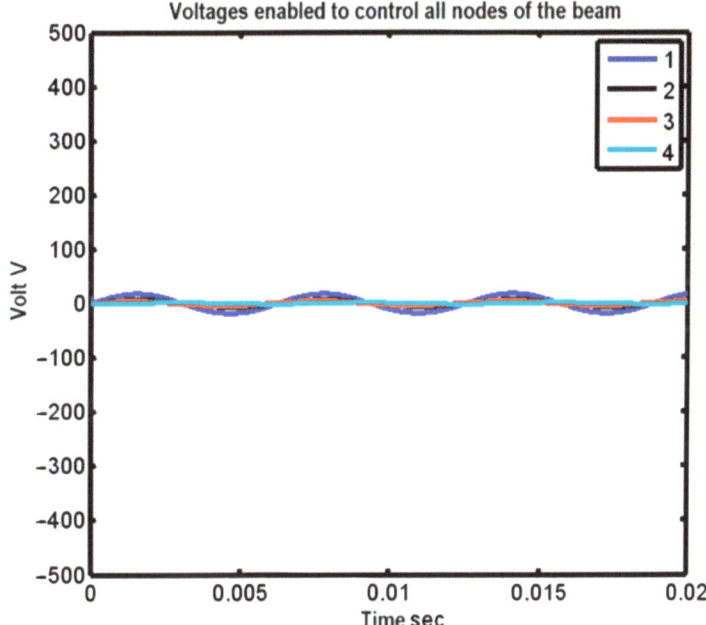

Figure 21. Control voltages for all the nodes of the smart structures under sinusoidal disturbances. The numbers 1, 2, 3, and 4 correspond to the four piezoelectric actuators (voltages) present in the smart beam.

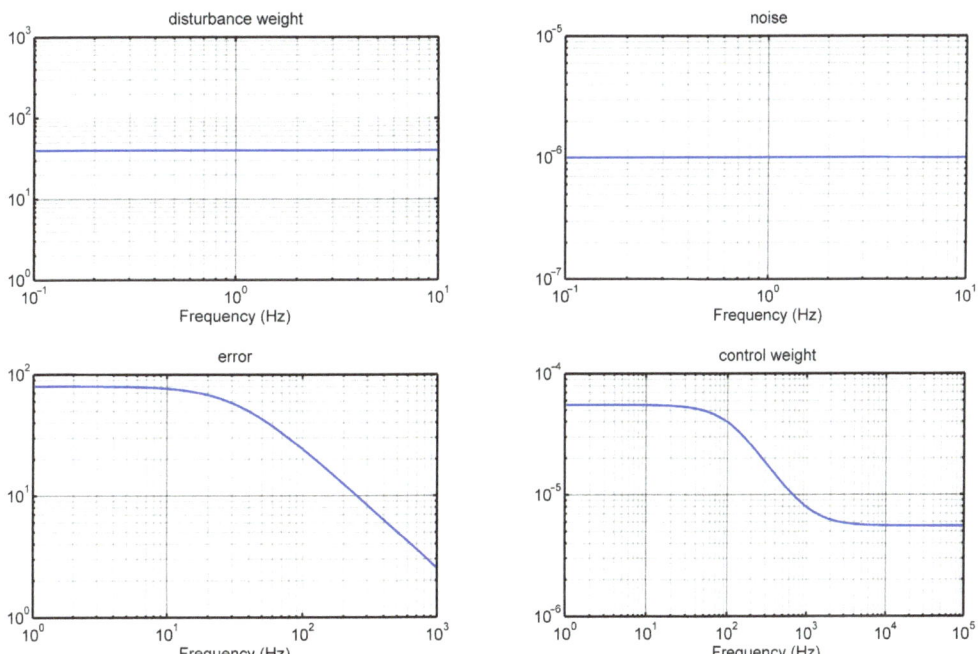

Figure 22. The Bode diagram of the smart structures. Υ axis is the magnitude (dB).

4. Discussion

This approach employs intelligent control techniques with a robust controller that minimizes the oscillations. Thus, a review of the parameters and their utilization in enhancing the system efficiency, as well as the system survey used to determine the crash resilience of the system. Considerable importance is attached to the disturbance rejection of smart structures that incorporate piezoelectric materials. This work contributes significantly to the reduction in oscillations. The initial modeling was performed using the finite element method. Subsequently, the equations for control theory are given. Equations (1)–(10) aid in the computation of the matrices for mass, damping, and stiffness as well as the matrices input to the electric charge matrix because of the piezoelectric patches.

All registers were calculated by the authors. Both state–space domain analysis Equations (10)–(14) and frequency domain analysis Equations (15)–(33) were used. The results first show us the comparison of the two controllers. Initially, both controllers should make a reduction in the oscillations in relation to the results without control (this is carried out by both). The two controllers are then compared to each other to see which achieves the greatest reduction.

By combining the H-infinity and H_2 methods within the simulated state–space and the frequency of characterization, this study examined the benefit of resilient control in intelligent systems. This study proposes a step-by-step method for generating and implementing stable controllers that are acceptable for intelligent structures. It proposes a robust approach for structural identification by strong control and deals with a state–space model and the frequency domain constructed from the output and input data of the structure. A controller for reducing vibrations is created using this control paradigm. The main concern of the theory is to control the variability of the system behavior. Vibration control techniques have been applied to minimize vibrations through dynamic disturbances, which are vital in mechanical systems, where operations might occur under stochastic loading scenarios. In this study, oscillations were completely suppressed, which was not achieved in earlier studies. In this work, two control techniques to suppress oscillations are employed, and a comparison is made. The results are good in both the frequency and state spaces. All calculations were performed with great accuracy owing to the optimized intelligent control systems. Although this topic has been discussed by several academics [1–3,11,35,36], the current study's findings are superior to those of prior research [2–4,14,33,36].

The advantages of this work include the following: MATLAB was used to program and manipulate the measurement noise from the beam condition to obtain the above results. The total oscillations were suppressed and simultaneously, the order of the controller was reduced. White noise was applied as the disturbance input, and its amplitude was described in terms of disturbances. This is aimed at the development of reliable controllers for smart structures with piezoelectric materials to address ambiguity and improve disturbance rejection. This study delves into the various methods and control techniques used to address this issue and provides a comprehensive description and analysis. The findings of this work hold substantial importance as they offer practical solutions to the widespread problem of oscillation reduction, which is a common concern in both the civil and mechanical engineering disciplines. The applications of this research are far-reaching, with potential uses in the stabilization of airplanes, metal bridges, and large metals. It should be noted that MATLAB codes are written by the article authors, and no code is off-the-shelf or taken from elsewhere. The finite element theory and advanced control theory were used. Initially, it was applied to a beam because the computational requirements for this model with infinite control are very large.

5. Conclusions

This study combined H_2 and H-infinity control to achieve complete vibration reduction in intelligent structures. Specifically, in vibration suppression applications, the resilience of the H-infinity controller to parametric uncertainty is emphasized. This study provides an excellent example of the benefits of active vibration suppression and robust control in the dynamics of intelligent structures. H-infinity control considers the modeling uncertainties that are difficult to introduce using different techniques. To do this, we used advanced programs written by the authors. The novelty of our work lies in the application of the H-infinity control theory specifically for oscillation damping, combined with its implementation using the finite element method. In our work, we managed to fully suppress the oscillations using the controller H-infinity. The piezoelectric material was inserted along the entire length of the beam. Reliable control systems can benefit from the many advantages of H-infinity control, which minimizes oscillations even when actuator placements vary. Numerical modeling validates that the suggested techniques are successful in lowering vibrations in piezoelectric smart structures. Herein, the benefits of robust control in intelligent structures are explored through the application of H-infinity regulation in both state and frequency domains.

The following are the key aspects of this work:

1. H_2 and H-infinity control are combined to achieve comprehensive vibration reduction in smart structures.
2. Demonstrating the resistance of H-infinity control to parametric uncertainties.
3. Highlighting the benefits of robust control and active vibration suppression in intelligent structures.
4. Showing that H-infinity control can minimize oscillations regardless of actuator placement.
5. Validating the effectiveness of the proposed vibration reduction methods through numerical modeling.
6. H-infinity regulation was used to investigate the advantages of strong control in intelligent structures in both state and frequency domains.
7. Results in the frequency domain and time–space domain: The study presents results in both the frequency domain and time–space domain, providing a comprehensive understanding of the system's dynamic behavior and control performance.

This study significantly advances the understanding and application of control methods in intelligent structures, thereby demonstrating the effectiveness of robust control techniques. In our research, we successfully managed to fully eliminate oscillations by employing the H-infinity control method. To achieve this, we incorporated piezoelectric elements along the entire beam length to ensure comprehensive coverage for optimal control. The modeling and simulation of the system were performed using custom codes, specifically compiled and developed by the authors, to accurately represent the dynamics of the system. A detailed description of the experimental setup, as well as the outcomes of the physical tests, will be presented in future work and publications.

Author Contributions: A.M. and M.P.: software, formal analysis, writing review, and editing; G.E.S.: methodology; A.P.: investigation and software; N.V.: validation. All authors have read and agreed to the published version of the manuscript.

Funding: This research received no external funding.

Data Availability Statement: The data presented in this study are available upon request from the corresponding author.

Acknowledgments: The authors are grateful for the support from the Hellenic Mediterranean University and the Technical University of Crete.

Conflicts of Interest: The authors declare no conflicts of interest.

References

1. Benjeddou, A.; Trindade, M.A.; Ohayon, R. New Shear Actuated Smart Structure Beam Finite Element. *AIAA J.* **1999**, *37*, 378–383. [CrossRef]
2. Bona, B.; Indri, M.; Tornambe, A. Flexible Piezoelectric Structures-Approximate Motion equations and Control Algorithms. *IEEE Trans. Autom. Control* **1997**, *42*, 94–101. [CrossRef]

3. Okko, B.; Kwakernaak, H.; Gjerrit, M. *Design Methods for Control Systems*; Course Notes, Dutch Institute for Systems and Control; Dutch Institute of Systems and Control: Delft, The Netherlands, 2001; Volume 67.
4. Burke, J.V.; Henrion, D.; Lewis, A.S.; Overton, M.L. Hifoo—A MATLAB Package for Fixed-Order Controller Design and H∞ Optimization. *IFAC Proc. Vol.* **2006**, *39*, 339–344. [CrossRef]
5. Yang, S.M.; Lee, Y.J. Optimization of Noncollocated Sensor/Actuator Location and Feedback Gain in Control Systems. *Smart Mater. Struct.* **1993**, *2*, 96. [CrossRef]
6. Ramesh Kumar, K.; Narayanan, S. Active Vibration Control of Beams with Optimal Placement of Piezoelectric Sensor/Actuator Pairs. *Smart Mater. Struct.* **2008**, *17*, 55008. [CrossRef]
7. Hanagud, S.; Obal, M.W.; Calise, A.J. Optimal Vibration Control by the Use of Piezoceramic Sensors and Actuators. *J. Guid. Control Dyn.* **1992**, *15*, 1199–1206. [CrossRef]
8. Song, G.; Sethi, V.; Li, H.-N. Vibration Control of Civil Structures Using Piezoceramic Smart Materials: A Review. *Eng. Struct.* **2006**, *28*, 1513–1524. [CrossRef]
9. Miara, B.; Stavroulakis, G.; Valente, V. Topics of Mathematics for Smart Systems. In Proceedings of the European Conference, Rome, Italy, 26–28 October 2006.
10. Karatzas, I.; Lehoczky, J.P.; Shreve, S.E.; Xu, G.-L. *Modeling, Control and Implementation of Smart Structures: A FEM-State Space Approach*; Springer: Berlin/Heidelberg, Germany, 1990; ISBN 9783540483939.
11. Moutsopoulou, A.; Stavroulakis, G.E.; Pouliezos, A.; Petousis, M.; Vidakis, N. Robust Control and Active Vibration Suppression in Dynamics of Smart Systems. *Inventions* **2023**, *8*, 47. [CrossRef]
12. Zhang, N.; Kirpitchenko, I. Modeling Dynamics of A Continuous Structure with a Piezoelectric Sensoractuator for Passive Structural Control. *J. Sound. Vib.* **2002**, *249*, 251–261. [CrossRef]
13. Zhang, X.; Shao, C.; Li, S.; Xu, D.; Erdman, A.G. Robust H∞ Vibration Control for Flexible Linkage Mechanism Systems with Piezoelectric Sensors and Actuators. *J. Sound. Vib.* **2001**, *243*, 145–155. [CrossRef]
14. Packard, A.; Doyle, J.; Balas, G. Linear, Multivariable Robust Control with a μ Perspective. *J. Dyn. Syst. Meas. Control* **1993**, *115*, 426–438. [CrossRef]
15. Stavroulakis, G.E.; Foutsitzi, G.; Hadjigeorgiou, E.; Marinova, D.; Baniotopoulos, C.C. Design and Robust Optimal Control of Smart Beams with Application on Vibrations Suppression. *Adv. Eng. Softw.* **2005**, *36*, 806–813. [CrossRef]
16. Chandrashekhara, K.; Varadarajan, S. Adaptive Shape Control of Composite Beams with Piezoelectric Actuators. *J. Intell. Mater. Syst. Struct.* **1997**, *8*, 112–124. [CrossRef]
17. Burke, J.V.; Henrion, D.; Lewis, A.S.; Overton, M.L. Stabilization via Nonsmooth, Nonconvex Optimization. *IEEE Trans. Autom. Control* **2006**, *51*, 1760–1769. [CrossRef]
18. Burke, J.V.; Lewis, A.S.; Overton, M.L. A Robust Gradient Sampling Algorithm for Nonsmooth, Nonconvex Optimization. *SIAM J. Optim.* **2005**, *15*, 751–779. [CrossRef]
19. Choi, S.-B.; Cheong, C.-C.; Lee, C.-H. Position Tracking Control of a Smart Flexible Structure Featuring a Piezofilm Actuator. *J. Guid. Control Dyn.* **1996**, *19*, 1364–1369. [CrossRef]
20. Culshaw, B. Smart Structures—A Concept or a Reality. *Proc. Inst. Mech. Eng. Part I J. Syst. Control Eng.* **1992**, *206*, 1–8. [CrossRef]
21. Tzou, H.S.; Gabbert, U. Structronics—A New Discipline and Its Challenging Issues. *Fortschr. -Berichte VDI Smart Mech. Syst.—Adapt. Reihe* **1997**, *11*, 245–250.
22. Zhou, K.; Doyle, J.C.; Glover, K. *Robust and Optimal Control*; Feher/Prentice Hall Digital and Wireless Communication Series; Prentice Hall: Saddle River, NJ, USA, 1996; ISBN 9780134565675.
23. Skogestad, S.; Postlethwaite, I. *Multivariable Feedback Control: Analysis and Design*, 2nd ed.; John Wiley and Sons Ltd., Ed.: Chichester, UK, 2005; ISBN 0-470-01167-X.
24. Doyle, J.C.; Francis, B.A.; Tannenbaum, A. *Feedback Control Theory*; Macmillan Publishing Company: New York, NY, USA, 1992; ISBN 9780023300110.
25. Guran, A.; Tzou, H.-S.; Anderson, G.L.; Natori, M.; Gabbert, U.; Tani, J.; Breitbach, E. *Structronic Systems: Smart Structures, Devices and Systems*; World Scientific: Singapore, 1998; Volume 4, ISBN 978-981-02-2652-7.
26. Tzou, H.S.; Anderson, G.L. *Intelligent Structural Systems*; Springer: Dordrecht, The Netherlands, 1992; ISBN 978-94-017-1903-2.
27. Gabbert, U.; Tzou, H.S. IUTAM Symposium on Smart Structures and Structronic Systems. In Proceedings of the IUTAM Symposium, Magdeburg, Germany, 26–29 September 2000; Kluwer: Dordrecht, The Netherlands, 2001.
28. Tzou, H.S.; Natori, M.C. *Piezoelectric Materials and Continua*; Braun, S.B.T.-E.V., Ed.; Elsevier: Oxford, UK, 2001; pp. 1011–1018. ISBN 978-0-12-227085-7.
29. *Walter Guyton Cady Piezoelectricity: An Introduction to the Theory and Applications of Electromechanical Phenomena in Crystals*; Dover Publication: New York, NY, USA, 1964.
30. Tzou, H.S.; Bao, Y. A Theory on Anisotropic Piezothermoelastic Shell Laminates with Sensor/Actuator Applications. *J. Sound. Vib.* **1995**, *184*, 453–473. [CrossRef]
31. Moutsopoulou, A.; Stavroulakis, G.E.; Petousis, M.; Vidakis, N.; Pouliezos, A. Smart Structures Innovations Using Robust Control Methods. *Appl. Mech.* **2023**, *4*, 856–869. [CrossRef]
32. Cen, S.; Soh, A.-K.; Long, Y.-Q.; Yao, Z.-H. A New 4-Node Quadrilateral FE Model with Variable Electrical Degrees of Freedom for the Analysis of Piezoelectric Laminated Composite Plates. *Compos. Struct.* **2002**, *58*, 583–599. [CrossRef]
33. Kwakernaak, H. Robust Control and H∞-Optimization—Tutorial Paper. *Automatica* **1993**, *29*, 255–273. [CrossRef]

34. Blondel, V.D.; Tsitsiklis, J.N. A Survey of Computational Complexity Results in Systems and Control. *Automatica* **2000**, *36*, 1249–1274. [CrossRef]
35. Bandyopadhyay, B.; Manjunath, T.C.; Umapathy, M. *Modeling, Control and Implementation of Smart Structures A FEM-State Space Approach*; Springer: Berlin/Heidelberg, Germany, 2007; ISBN 978-3-540-48393-9.
36. Kimura, H. Robust Stabilizability for a Class of Transfer Functions. *IEEE Trans. Autom. Control* **1984**, *29*, 788–793. [CrossRef]

Disclaimer/Publisher's Note: The statements, opinions and data contained in all publications are solely those of the individual author(s) and contributor(s) and not of MDPI and/or the editor(s). MDPI and/or the editor(s) disclaim responsibility for any injury to people or property resulting from any ideas, methods, instructions or products referred to in the content.

 algorithms

Article

A VIKOR-Based Sequential Three-Way Classification Ranking Method

Wentao Xu [1], Jin Qian [1,*], Yueyang Wu [1], Shaowei Yan [1], Yongting Ni [1] and Guangjin Yang [2]

1. School of Information and Software Engineering, East China JiaoTong University, Nanchang 330000, China; 2023218083500005@ecjtu.edu.cn (W.X.); 2023218083500008@ecjtu.edu.cn (Y.W.); 2023218083500021@ecjtu.edu.cn (S.Y.); 2023218085405028@ecjtu.edn.cn (Y.N.)
2. School of Computer, Jiangsu University of Science and Technology, Zhenjiang 212000, China; 231110701106@stu.just.edu.cn
* Correspondence: qianjin@ecjtu.edu.cn; Tel.: +86-17375239306

Abstract: VIKOR uses the idea of overall utility maximization and individual regret minimization to afford a compromise result for multi-attribute decision-making problems with conflicting attributes. Many researchers have proposed corresponding improvements and expansions to make it more suitable for sorting optimization in their respective research fields. However, these improvements and extensions only rank the alternatives without classifying them. For this purpose, this text introduces the three-way sequential decisions method and combines it with the VIKOR method to design a three-way VIKOR method that can deal with both ranking and classification. By using the final negative ideal solution (NIS) and the final positive ideal solution (PIS) for all alternatives, the individual regret value and group utility value of each alternative were calculated. Different three-way VIKOR models were obtained by four different combinations of individual regret value and group utility value. In the ranking process, the characteristics of VIKOR method are introduced, and the subjective preference of decision makers is considered by using individual regret, group utility, and decision index values. In the classification process, the corresponding alternatives are divided into the corresponding decision domains by sequential three-way decisions, and the risk of direct acceptance or rejection is avoided by putting the uncertain alternatives into the boundary region to delay the decision. The alternative is divided into decision domains through sequential three-way decisions, sorted according to the collation rules in the same decision domain, and the final sorting results are obtained according to the collation rules in different decision domains. Finally, the effectiveness and correctness of the proposed method are verified by a project investment example, and the results are compared and evaluated. The experimental results show that the proposed method has a significant correlation with the results of other methods, ad is effective and feasible, and is simpler and more effective in dealing with some problems. Errors caused by misclassification is reduced by sequential three-way decisions.

Keywords: ideal solution; sequential three-way decisions; VIKOR method; domain; muti-attribute decision making

1. Introduction

Multi-attribute decision making is a key part of modern decision science, which is used to solve the problem of optimal selection and ranking. It is widely used in technology, engineering, management, and other fields, and mainly deals with evaluation and selection. The VIKOR method is a powerful tool to help decision makers find the best compromise solution between multiple attributes or objectives. It takes into account the concepts of compromise and balance, as well as the subjective tendencies of relevant decision makers, which can provide valuable solutions in complex decision problems. Many researchers have developed various extensions and improvements of the VIKOR method, which can play a more effective role in various application scenarios. Chiranjibe et al. [1] proposed an improved

Citation: Xu, W.; Qian, J.; Wu, Y.; Yan, S.; Ni, Y.; Yang, G. A VIKOR-Based Sequential Three-Way Classification Ranking Method. *Algorithms* **2024**, *17*, 530. https://doi.org/10.3390/a17110530

Academic Editors: Sheng Du, Zixin Huang, Li Jin and Xiongbo Wan

Received: 14 September 2024
Revised: 2 November 2024
Accepted: 13 November 2024
Published: 19 November 2024

Copyright: © 2024 by the authors. Licensee MDPI, Basel, Switzerland. This article is an open access article distributed under the terms and conditions of the Creative Commons Attribution (CC BY) license (https://creativecommons.org/licenses/by/4.0/).

version of the improved type-2 fuzzy interval VIKOR method (IT2FVIKOR) in order to obtain better ranking results for the MCDM problem. Alhadidi et al. [2] introduced the FAHP weight into the VIKOR and proposed a new FAHP-VIKOR method. Zhang et al. [3] proposed a VIKOR method According to regret theory. Yu et al. [4] proposed a novel T-SF VIKOR method for tradeoff ranking in multicriteria analysis to adapt to complex real-world environments. Arunodaya et al. [5] proposed an innovative multi-attribute decision making method by combining FHFSs and improved VIKOR. Although these extended VIKOR methods have their own characteristics, they all follow the basic principle of calculating individual regret value, group utility value, and decision index value, so as to obtain the final ranking. These methods improve the steps of VIKOR and introduce other concepts. At the same time, some studies have pointed out that the traditional MCDM method can only rank schemes, but not classify them. Zhang et al. [6] saw unity in multi-attribute and three-way decisions as a viable research path, proposing a new TOPSIS method based on three-way decisions. Bisht et al. [7] also believed that three-way decision making increases delayed decision and can efficiently cope with multi-attribute decision making by reducing decision risk. Therefore, the VIKOR method can be considered to combine with the three-way decisions to take into account both classification and ranking.

Based on human cognitive processes, a three-way decision model is constructed. People often put off making decisions that require deliberation. Three-way decisions solve complex problems by dealing with three different parts, so that the VIKOR method can deal with decision complexity, consider cost and uncertainty, and complete classification and ranking. Wang et al. [8] proposed a three-way decision model on account of the third-generation prospect theory, introduced the α model and β model optimization of digital threshold solution, and simplified the three-way decision rules. Yang et al. [9] generalize the related work of three-way decisions through complex network analysis. Zhan et al. [10] combined regret theory with IIS prospect theory and proposed a new three-way decision method to further combine three-way decisions with behavioral decisions. Subhashini et al. [11] proposed an opinion classification method combining three-way decisions with fuzzy concepts and semantic concepts to solve the problem of reducing the boundary area and maintaining high accuracy. In order to deal with the stability of the conflict system being affected by different preferences of decision makers, Jiang et al. [12] combined three-way decisions and conflict analysis with a grey system to establish a new conflict analysis model. In order to reduce the risk of decision-making errors and express linguistic uncertainty, Luo et al. [13] combined double-layer hesitant fuzzy term sets with multi-attribute three-way decision making. Recently, researchers focused on making reasonable decisions with limited info to reduce decision risks. Qi et al. [14] combined the fuzzy attribute concept with the three-way decision model and utility theory and proposed the three-way utility decision model. In multilevel data, obtaining acceptable decisions at various granularities is crucial. Qian et al. [15] proposed a multi-granularity hierarchical sequential three-way decision model to advance three-way decisions. Yi et al. [16] combined Sigmoid utility with three-way decisions using Pythagorean fuzzy sets to solve related problems. Wang et al. [17] constructed three fuzzy hesitant three-way decision methods to calculate the contingent probability of the target in the fuzzy hesitant information decision system without class labels. Pan et al. [18] combined three-way decisions with interval values to propose a new method for solving multi-attribute decision-making problems in uncertain environments. In order to reduce the influence of different attribute types on decision results, Yan et al. [19] integrated TOPSIS and regret theory into three-way decisions to settle multi-attribute decision-making difficulties in fuzzy environments without changing attribute types. The integration of three-way decisions and granular computing offered a befitting idea and method for the thinking of cognitive science and the trialization of information processing. Sequential three-way decisions are a classic representation of three-way granular computing, which makes multi-stage decisions through a series of transaction-optimization (TAO) models. Yang et al. [20] integrated three-way decisions and multiple granularities to enhance the domain system's hierarchy and structure. Creating a sequential three-way decisions model that combines three-way decisions and granular computing is becoming more and more important in classification. Pei et al. [21] proposed four three-way sequential classifiers in order to solve the issue of the coarse and fine granularity of objects potentially causing conflict and thus affecting the decision accuracy. S3WD uses coarse-to-fine information granularity. Yu et al. [22] addressed granularity construction and decision cost in the three-way sequential decision model, verified the model's correctness and algorithm's feasibility, and solved the double constraint problem. The sequential three-way decision method, enhanced by multi-level granularity, is proven effective for solving human problems. Ju et al. [23] introduced a novel rational subspace classifier that outperforms advanced classifiers with fewer attributes. Combining granularity and multi-levels, this method efficiently handles uncertainty and dynamics in decision making.

The aforementioned researchers proposed improvements and extensions to the VIKOR method and three-way decisions to tailor them to their research fields. However, these enhancements did not integrate VIKOR with three-way decisions; VIKOR improvements focused solely on prioritization without classification. Similarly, three-way decision enhancements neglected ranking alternatives. This paper combines sequential three-way decisions with an improved VIKOR method, incorporating decision-makers' subjective tendencies and considering both maximizing team utility and minimizing individual regret. It argues that relying solely on team utility or individual regret for classification and judgment can lead to significant errors. Instead, it constructs a sequential three-way decision model considering both values. VIKOR classifies schemes into three regions using three-way sequential decisions. Ranking rules and formulas based on intradomain and cross-domain comparisons are proposed, and their correctness and applicability are demonstrated through an example.

Section 2 introduces the basics of three-way sequential decisions and multi-attribute decisions. Section 3 proposes the sequential three-way VIKOR method based on individual regret or group utility values, studying ordering rules within and across different areas. Section 4 introduces the sequential three-way VIKOR method considering both individual regret and team utility values, verifying its feasibility. Section 5 assesses the method's reliability and usefulness using a real-world engineering investment case study. Section 6 concludes the paper.

2. Preliminaries

In this chapter, we introduce the basic concepts of three-way sequential decisions and multi-attribute decision making.

2.1. Sequential Three-Way Decisions

Multi-step three-way decisions are three-way sequential decisions. The main concept of three-way sequential decisions is to obtain preliminary decisions at a coarse-grained level, and gradually obtain the final decisions by adding information and updating the universe. It is well known that multi-step classical sequential three-way decisions are gradually improved to form a three-way sequential decision model [24,25]. Next, we briefly introduce the contents of three-way sequential decisions.

Definition 1 ([26]). *For the decision table $S = \{U, At = C \cap D, V, I\}$, a dynamic threshold is given $(\alpha, \beta) = \left\{(\alpha^1, \beta^1), (\alpha^2, \beta^2), \cdots, (\alpha^l, \beta^l)\right\}$, E is a relation of equivalence. The lower approximation of the l-level granularity $\underline{apr_E}^{(\alpha^l,\beta^l)}(D_i^l)$ and upper approximation $\overline{apr_E}^{(\alpha^l,\beta^l)}(D_i^l)$ $(i = 1, 2, \cdots, s, l = 1, 2, \cdots, L)$ as defined below:*

$$\overline{apr_E}^{(\alpha^l,\beta^l)}(D_i^l) = \left\{x \in U^l \middle| p(D_i^l | [x_E] \geq \alpha^l\right\}$$
$$\underline{apr_E}^{(\alpha^l,\beta^l)}(D_i^l) = \left\{x \in U^l \middle| p(D_i^l | [x_E] > \beta^l\right\}$$

(1)

where D_i^l, $[x_E]$ denotes the object, x is contained in the partitions by the equivalence classes $U^l/D = \{D_1^l, D_2^l, \cdots, D_s^l\}$ and U^l/E, respectively. Dynamic updating of universe is an important part of sequential three-way decisions.

Unlike the seven different combinations for three regions proposed by Yang et al. [27], our next sequential decision uses boundary regions as the universe of discourse. $U^1 = U$, $U^{l+1} = \overline{apr_E}^{(\alpha^l,\beta^l)}(D_i^l) - \underline{apr_E}^{(\alpha^l,\beta^l)}(D_i^l)$. By upper and lower approximation of the l-rank granularity, we can obtain three probability regions as:

$$POS_E^{(\alpha^l,\beta^l)}(D_i^l) = \underline{apr_E}^{(\alpha^l,\beta^l)}(D_i^l)$$
$$BND_E^{(\alpha^l,\beta^l)}(D_i^l) = \overline{apr_E}^{(\alpha^l,\beta^l)}(D_i^l) - \underline{apr_E}^{(\alpha^l,\beta^l)}(D_i^l) \quad (2)$$
$$NEG_E^{(\alpha^l,\beta^l)}(D_i^l) = U - \overline{apr_E}^{(\alpha^l,\beta^l)}(D_i^l)$$

2.2. Multiple Attribute Decision Making

Multi-attribute decision making is very common in daily life, as shown in Table 1. The n alternatives are represented by the variable $A = \{a_1, a_2, \cdots, a_n\}$, and the evaluation of each alternative involves m criteria. The set of m criteria is denoted by the variable $V = \{v_1, v_2, \cdots, v_m\}$. The value of the object a_i under the criterion $v_j (1 \leq j \leq m)$ is represented by the variable $e_{ij}(e_{ij} \in [0,1])$. The importance of each criterion is represented by the corresponding weight, which can reduce the impact of the differences of different criteria on the final decision. The variable $W = \{w_1, w_2, \cdots, w_m\}$ denotes the set of m weights, where $w_j \in [0,1]$, $\sum_{j=1}^{m} w_j = 1$. The decision maker needs to rank each objective and combine the corresponding ranking information in the selection of the optimal scheme.

Table 1. Multi-criteria evaluation of information systems $S = (A, V)$.

	v_1	v_2	$\cdots$	v_m
a_1	e_{11}	e_{12}	$\cdots$	e_{1m}
a_2	e_{21}	e_{22}	$\cdots$	e_{2m}
$\vdots$	$\vdots$	$\vdots$	$\cdots$	$\vdots$
a_n	e_{n1}	e_{n2}	$\cdots$	e_{nm}
W	w_1	w_2	$\cdots$	w_m

The VIKOR method mainly includes five steps: calculating weight, calculating positive and negative ideal solutions, calculating individual regret value and group utility value, calculating decision index value, and sorting. The Lpmetric aggregation function is integrated into the calculation of "negative ideal solution" and "positive ideal solution" to obtain the compromise solution for each alternative. In the sorting process, the stability conditions and advantages are considered to obtain the ranking results according to the specific measurement between the ideal solution and each scheme. In recent years, many researchers [1–5] have carried out various types of expansion and improvement of the VIKOR method and combined it with other ideas and methods, showing better application effects compared with past methods. However, in addition to improving the decision results, these methods still have shortcomings in other aspects. In this paper, by introducing the VIKOR method into the three-way sequential decisions, a new VIKOR method combined with the sequential three-way decisions is proposed, which can classify and rank the alternatives.

In order to easily compare and process the attribute information of the alternatives, it is necessary to normalize the attribute evaluation value of the multi-attribute information table.

$$Y = (y_{ij})_{m \times n} \quad (3)$$

where $y_{ij} = \dfrac{x_{ij}}{\sqrt{\sum\limits_{j=1}^{m} x_{ij}^2}}$, x_{ij} is the element of set in the multi-attribute information table.

3. VIKOR Model of Sequential Three-Way Decisions Based on Individual Regret Value or Group Utility Value

Group utility value is a quantitative representation of decision-makers' views and attitudes towards gain and loss effects, which is used to measure decision-makers' subjective tendencies and preferences for certain things. The loss caused by the decision maker's mistake is represented by the individual regret value, which is a special measure of the optimal value compared to other values in the scheme. In the VIKOR method, the individual regret value and group utility value are obtained by calculating the "specific measure" between the ideal solution and each alternative. The smaller value of the group utility value means the greater group utility of the corresponding alternative, and the larger value of the individual regret value means the greater individual regret of the corresponding alternative. In practical decision problems, more values can be deduced and calculated based on one or two ideal alternatives to rank all alternatives, but the ranking results must follow certain rules.

For example, if the group utility value of scheme A_i is smaller than scheme A_j, it means that scheme A_i has greater group utility than scheme A_j, and then A_i should be better than A_j. Conversely, if the individual regret value of A_j is less than that of A_i, the result should be that A_i is inferior to A_j.

In order to easily determine the importance degree of an alternative, this study first considers a single individual regret value or group utility value. It classifies the alternatives by the single value calculated for each alternative, as well as the ideal alternative using three-way sequential decisions. Different regions are assigned corresponding alternatives according to the maximum individual regret value or minimum group utility value among the alternatives. Finally, all the schemes are ranked based on the ranking rules of the different region or same regions. Next, the three-way sequential VIKOR model according to the minimum group utility value and the three-way sequential VIKOR model according to the maximum individual regret value are introduced.

3.1. Squential Three-Way VIKOR Model Based on Minimum Group Utility Value

The key step of this model is to derive the group utility value corresponding to each alternative through alternatives, NIS, and PIS, and then classify the alternatives through three-way sequential decisions. The decision index value is calculated according to the measurement formula, and the ultimately ranking result is obtained through the ranking regulations of different regions and the same region. Therefore, the next step is to give the definition of PIS and NIS, as well as the measurement formula and the corresponding scheme comparison process.

Definition 2. *Worst solution (NIS) and optimal solution (PIS) of the alternatives attribute matrix.*

Where j is the condition attribute, the cost attribute set is J, the benefit attribute set is I, and the alternative and attribute sets are i and j.

According to the calculation results of the above formula, the NIS and PIS of all alternatives can be obtained, and then the group utility value of each alternative can be obtained on the basis of NIS and PIS. A smaller group utility value means that the corresponding scheme has better group utility.

Definition 3. *Let there be m alternatives, $PIS = \{e_1^*, e_2^*, \cdots, e_n^*\}$, $NIS = \{e_1^-, e_2^-, \cdots, e_n^-\}$, and a weight set $W = \{w_1, w_2, \cdots, w_n\}$, then the group utility value of alternative A_i is defined as follows:*

$$S_i = \sum_{j=1}^{n} w_j \frac{e_j^* - e_{ij}}{e_j^* - e_j^-} \qquad (4)$$

where S_i is the group utility value of the ith scheme.

Theorem 1. *The schemes in the negative region are inferior to the schemes in the positive region, that is, the ranking rules belonging to the schemes in different regions are derived from the group utility values of all the schemes calculated.*

Proof of Theorem 1. The alternatives in the positive region have relatively small group utility values and relatively large group utility. The alternatives that are in the negative region have larger group utility values and smaller group utility values. Therefore, the scheme for the negative region is inferior to the scheme for the positive region. To sum up, $POS\{A\} \succ NEG\{A\}$. □

Since three-way sequential decisions can only classify the alternatives, it is necessary to introduce an integral operator to rank the schemes in the different region and same regions. Opricovi et al. [28] used the decision index value combining individual regret value and group utility value to rank, and the decision-making mechanism coefficient could help realize the minimization of single regret and the maximization of group utility. The larger the mechanism coefficient of decision-making process is, the more attention should be paid to the group maximum utility rather than the single regret. A smaller value of the decision index indicates a better alternative. By maximizing the team utility and minimizing the single regret, the compromise solution of each attribute of the alternative is obtained. The decision index value is defined as follows:

$$Q_i = v \frac{(S_i - S^*)}{(S^- - S^*)} + (1 - v) \frac{(R_i - R^*)}{(R^- - R^*)} \quad (5)$$

where, Q_i denotes the decision index value of the ith alternative, $S^* = \min_i S_i$, $S^- = \max_i S_i$, $R^* = \min_i R_i$, the weights of maximum team utility and decision index coefficients are v, and $v = 0.5$ is usually assumed. According to Equation (5), the magnitude of Q_i value is related to the difference between S_i and S^*, R_i and R^*. S_i is closer to S^* and R_i is closer to R^*. That is, the single regret value of the scheme is closer to the minimum value in the set of single regret values, and the team utility value is also closer to the minimum value in the set of team utility values. Currently, the team utility of the alternative is larger, and the single regret is smaller, and the value of Q_i is smaller. This indicates that the individual regret value and group utility value of the better decision alternative are always as small as possible.

The steps of the three-way sequential VIKOR model according to minimum group utility value are as follows (where Algorithm 1 is used to Step 3):

Step 1. According to Definition 2, the NIS and PIS of the schemes are deduced from the multiple property message table.

Step 2. Calculate the group utility value for each alternative based on Definition 3.

Step 3. Algorithm 1 is used to classify the decision regions of the scheme.

Step 4. The decision index values of each scheme are calculated according to Equation (5).

Step 5. Sort the schemes belonging to the identical decision area in ascending order of their decision index values.

Step 6. The final ranking result is obtained by sorting the ranking rules about different regions shown in Figure 1.

Figure 1. Connections between decisions regions, $\rightarrow$ denotes $\succ$.

We will illustrate the time sophistication of Algorithm 1 as follows:

$A_{\max}$ and $A_{\min}$ are obtained in step 4 with a corresponding time sophistication of $O(|S|)$. Adding $A_{\max}$ and $A_{\min}$ to POS and NEG in steps 5 to 8, respectively, has a corresponding time sophistication of $O(\frac{|S|}{2})$. Steps 9 and 10 are the sequential process of processing S and BND.

This time sophistication is $O(|k|)$. Lastly, $O(|k||S|)$ is the time complexity of Algorithm 1. Next, the working process of the proposed model is briefly explained by an example.

Example 1. *Suppose there are 8 alternatives $A_m = \{A_1, A_2, A_3, A_4, A_5, A_6, A_7, A_8\}$. The attribute set $C = \{C_1, C_2, C_3\}$ of alternatives consists of two benefit attributes $\{C_1, C_2\}$ and one cost attribute $\{C_3\}$, and the corresponding weight set is $w = \{0.3, 0.5, 0.2\}$. The normalized attribute evaluation value table is shown in Table 2, and the uniformized determination matrix is expressed as $X = ((X_{mn})_{8\times 3})(m = 1, \cdots 8; n = 1, 2, 3)$.*

Table 2. Normalized decision matrix.

	C_1	C_2	C_3
A_1	0.9000	0.5000	0.4000
A_2	0.2000	0.1000	0.8255
A_3	0.7465	0.9000	0.1000
A_4	0.4525	0.6000	0.4000
A_5	0.6000	0.3565	0.6000
A_6	0.4000	0.4000	0.5575
A_7	0.3000	0.2000	0.7000
A_8	0.1000	0.1500	0.9000

(1) calculate PIS and NIS according to Definition 2 from the nature assessing values of all schemes in Table 2, which can be obtained by $PIS = \{0.9, 0.9, 0.1\}$, $NIS = \{0.1, 0.1, 0.9\}$.

(2) obtain the team utility value $S_i(i = 1,2,3,4,5,6,7,8)$ of each alternative by PIS and NIS according to Definition 3. $S_1 = 0.3250$, $S_2 = 0.9434$, $S_3 = 0.0576$, $S_4 = 0.4303$, $S_5 = 0.5772$, $S_6 = 0.6144$, $S_7 = 0.8125$, $S_8 = 0.9688$.

(3) classify all alternatives regionally according to Algorithm 1.
$POS^4 = \{A_3, A_1, A_4, A_5\}$, $NGE^4 = \{A_8, A_2, A_7, A_6\}$.

(4) calculate the decision index values of all schemes according to Equation (5) where Q_i represents the decision index value of the ith scheme, which can be obtained by $Q_1 = 0.3642$, $Q_2 = 0.9861$, $Q_3 = 0$, $Q_4 = 0.3513$, $Q_5 = 0.6039$, $Q_6 = 0.5936$, $Q_7 = 0.8436$, and $Q_8 = 0.9647$.

Algorithm 1 Compute the decision region based on the lowest sequential three-way VIKOR of the group utility value

input: Group utility values for m alternatives
$k^{th}-level$, $k = 0$.
output: Three decision regions, POS^k and NEG^k;
1   POS = ∅, BND = {Am}, NEG = ∅, k = 0, S = {Sm};
2   while $BND^k \neq \emptyset$
3       $k++$, $POS_{new} = NEG_{new} = \emptyset$;
4       $A_{\max} = \min(S)$, $A_{\min} = \max(S)$;
5   Add $A_{\max}$ to POS_{new}
6         $POS^k = POS^{k-1} \cup POS_{new}$;
7   Add $A_{\min}$ to NEG_{new}
8         $NEG^k = NEG^{k-1} \cup NEG_{new}$;
9       $BND^k = BND^{k-1} \cup (POS_{new} \cup NEG_{new})$;
10    $S = S - (A_{\max} \cup A_{\min})$;
11   end
12   Output $POS^k(A_m)$, $NEG^k(A_m)$.

(5) sort the alternatives in the same region according to the decision index value in ascending order, so that the ranking result in the POS domain is $\{A_3 \succ A_4 \succ A_1 \succ A_5\}$ and the ranking result in NEG domain is $\{A_6 \succ A_7 \succ A_8 \succ A_2\}$.

(6) through the ranking rules of different regional alternatives, $POS\{A_m\} \succ BND\{A_m\} \succ NEG\{A_m\}$, $\{A_3 \succ A_4 \succ A_1 \succ A_5 \succ A_6 \succ A_7 \succ A_8 \succ A_2\}$ is the final sorting result.

3.2. Sequential Three-Way VIKOR Model Based on Minimum Individual Regret Value

Like the three-way sequential VIKOR model according to the minimum group utility value, the key steps of the ordinal three-way VIKOR model according to the minimum single regret value are to calculate the individual regret value for all alternatives, classify the alternatives using the sequential three-way decision method, calculate the decision indicator value of each scheme, and then sort schemes in the identical area. The final ranking results are acquired through the alternative ranking rules of different regions.

Definition 4. *Let there be m alternatives $A = \{A_1, A_2, \cdots, A_m\}$, $PIS = \{e_1^*, e_2^*, \cdots, e_n^*\}$, $NIS = \{e_1^-, e_2^-, \cdots, e_n^-\}$, and a weight set is $W = \{w_1, w_2, \cdots, w_n\}$, then the individual regret value of alternative A_i is defined as follows:*

$$R_i = \max_j w_j \frac{e_j^* - e_{ij}}{e_j^* - e_j^-} \qquad (6)$$

where R_i denotes the individual regret value of the ith alternative.

The ordinal three-way VIKOR model based on minimum individual regret value is illustrated as follows:

Step 1. Derive the NIS and PIS of schemes from the multi-attribute information table based on Definition 2.

Step 2. The individual regret value is calculated for each scheme according to Definition 4.

Step 3. Classify the alternatives by a similar procedure as in Algorithm 1.

Step 4. The decision index values of each scheme are calculated according to Equation (5).

Step 5. The schemes belonging to the identical decision area are sorted by the decision index value in ascending order.

Step 6. According to the ordering regulation of different areas, the schemes of different areas are ordered to obtain the final ranking results.

Example 2 (like Example 1). *The alternatives in Table 2 are calculated according to the above steps, and the final ranking result of the three-way sequential VIKOR model on account of the minimum individual regret value is $\{A_3 \succ A_4 \succ A_1 \succ A_6 \succ A_5 \succ A_7 \succ A_8 \succ A_2\}$. It can be acquired through the ranking solutions of all alternatives in Table 2 by the two models, which are different. The final ranking result of the three-way sequential VIKOR model on account of the minimum group utility value is $\{A_3 \succ A_4 \succ A_1 \succ A_5 \succ A_6 \succ A_7 \succ A_8 \succ A_2\}$. However, the final ranking result of the three-way sequential VIKOR model on account of the minimum individual regret value is $\{A_3 \succ A_4 \succ A_1 \succ A_6 \succ A_5 \succ A_7 \succ A_8 \succ A_2\}$. In the three-way sequential VIKOR model on account of the minimum group utility value, A_5 is divided into the POS and A_6 is divided into the NEG, but in the three-way sequential VIKOR model on account of the minimum individual regret value, A_5 is divided into the NEG and A_6 is divided into the POS, which eventually leads to diversities in the ultimate classification of results for the two models. At the same time, the diversity between the final ordering consequences of the two models also verifies this paper's idea that only considering the single regret value or group utility value to classify and judge the alternatives will lead to large errors, and a single individual regret value and group utility value can only afford incomplete decision information. Thus, to make the ordering consequences of all schemes more accurate, this paper will simultaneously consider the single regret value and group utility value to sort through the three-way sequential decision method.*

4. Sequential Three-Way VIKOR Model Based on Group Utility Value and Individual Regret Value

The two models mentioned above mainly classify the alternatives based on the minimum single regret value or group utility value, and then rank the same and different regions by calculating the integral operator formula. Therefore, in the model proposed next, the single regret value and group utility value of alternatives will be considered simultaneously. The three-way sequential VIKOR model will be established on account of the maximum individual regret value and the minimum group utility value. Finally, the sequential three-way VIKOR model will be established on account of the minimum single regret value and the maximum group utility value.

A good scheme should have a small single regret and a large group utility. The previous and the following models are classified on account of the three-way sequential decision method by calculating the single regret value and the group utility value of the scheme. Through the idea of three-way sequential decisions, all the schemes are reasonably and effectively separated into positive, boundary, and negative areas. The alternative is separated into the positive area, which signifies that it should be a good decision scheme and easy to be accepted by the decision maker. Dividing an alternative into a boundary region means that it has a large individual regret value and a small group utility value in the sequential three-way decision process, or on the contrary, that the decision maker needs to delay acceptance or rejection. The alternatives are classified into the negative region, which indicates that they should be inferior decision alternatives and easy to be rejected by decision makers. In the following part, all alternatives are separated into three areas—negative area, boundary area, and positive area—through three-way sequential decisions. Uncertain alternatives are put into the boundary region and the decision is delayed until more basis and support is obtained, to avoid misclassification and avoid the risk caused by directly accepting or rejecting alternatives. After that, the final sorting result is calculated according to the integral operator and the sorting rules of the different region and same regions. Next, the sequential three-way VIKOR model, based the maximum individual regret and the minimum group utility value, and the sequential three-way VIKOR model, based on the minimum individual regret value and the maximum group utility value, will be discussed.

4.1. Sequential Three-Way VIKOR Model Based on Minimum Group Utility Value and Maximum Individual Regret Value

Unlike the previously proposed model according to a single value, the proposed model comprehensively considers the single regret value and the group utility value. In most cases, it is impossible to obtain an accurate decision scheme by only considering the partial decision information corresponding to a single value. The alternative with larger group utility does not necessarily have smaller individual regret, and the decision scheme with smaller individual regret does not necessarily have larger group utility. When dealing with these alternatives, a new method is needed to identify the classification results of the schemes by considering both the single regret value and the group utility value of the alternatives.

Theorem 2. *The alternatives with the largest single regret value and group utility value or vice versa are classified as boundary regions in the model. Based on the concept of three-way decisions, a ranking rule considering the alternatives in different regions of the boundary domain is proposed, as shown in Figure 2.*

Figure 2. Ranking rules for different decision regions.

Proof of Theorem 2. The individual regret of the alternatives divided into the positive region is relatively small and the group utility is relatively large, which is easy to be accepted by the decision maker. The schemes divided into the negative region have large single regret and relatively small group utility, which are easy for decision makers to reject. The single regret and group utility of the schemes separated into the boundary area are equivalent, so the decision maker needs to delay the decision. Therefore, the boundary region scheme is better than the negative region scheme and the boundary region scheme is inferior to the positive region scheme; this can be obtained by:□

$$POS\{A\} \succ BND\{A\} \succ NEG\{A\}$$

The overall steps of the proposed model are the same as those of the model considering a single value, the main difference being that the proposed model considers both the single regret value and the group utility value. In the classification of the alternatives by each round of sequential three-way decisions, the scheme with the minimum group utility value is divided into the positive region, the alternative with the maximum individual regret value is separated into the negative region, and the alternative with the maximum individual regret value and the minimum group utility value is divided into the boundary region.

The steps of sequential three-way VIKOR model according to maximum individual regret value and minimum group utility value are as follows (where Algorithm 2 is used in Step 3):

Step 1. Derive the NIS and PIS of schemes from the multi-attribute information table based on Definition 2.

Step 2. Calculate the single regret value and group utility value for each alternative based on Definitions 3 and 4.

Step 3. Algorithm 2 is used to classify the alternatives.

Step 4. Calculate the decision index value for each alternative according to Equation (5).

Step 5. Sort the schemes belonging to the same decision area in ascending rank of their decision index values.

Step 6. According to the ordering regulations of different areas, the results of different areas are ordered to obtain the final ordering results.

We illustrate the time sophistication of Algorithm 2 as follows: In Step 4, the extraction of the minimum value in S is denoted as A_{max} and the extraction of the maximum value in R is denoted as A_{min}, and the time sophistication is $O(|S|)$. Steps 6 to 11 add the alternatives to the corresponding domain, respectively, with time sophistication $O(|k|)$. Steps 12 to 13 are sequential processing of the boundary region, S and R, and the time complexity is $O(|k|)$. In general, $O(|k||S|)$ is the time sophistication of Algorithm 2.

Example 3. *The process of using this model to process the normalized attribute matrix $X = ((X_{mn}))_{8 \times 3}$ ($m = 1, \cdots 8; n = 1, 2, 3$) and the corresponding weight set $W = \{0.3, 0.5, 0.2\}$ shown in Table 2 is as follows:*

(1) derives the NIS and PIS of alternatives from the multiple message attribute information table on account of Definition 2.

(2) calculates the individual regret value and group utility value of each scheme on account of Definitions 3 and 4, where R_i denotes the individual regret value of the i scheme and S_i represents the group utility value of the ith scheme.

$S_1 = 0.3250$, $S_2 = 0.9434$, $S_3 = 0.0576$, $S_4 = 0.4303$, $S_5 = 0.5772$, $S_6 = 0.6144$, $S_7 = 0.8125$, $S_8 = 0.9688$. $R_1 = 0.2500$, $R_2 = 0.5000$, $R_3 = 0.0576$, $R_4 = 0.1875$, $R_5 = 0.3397$, $R_6 = 0.3125$, $R_7 = 0.4375$, $R_8 = 0.4688$.

(3) divides all the alternatives into corresponding regions according to Algorithm 2. $POS^3 = \{A_3, A_1, A_4\}$, $BND^3 = \{A_5, A_6\}$, $NEG^3 = \{A_2, A_8, A_7\}$.

(4) calculates the decision indicatrix value of each scheme according to Equation (5), where Q_i denotes the decision index value of the ith alternative.

$Q_1 = 0.3642$, $Q_2 = 0.9861$, $Q_3 = 0$, $Q_4 = 0.3513$, $Q_5 = 0.6039$, $Q_6 = 0.5936$, $Q_7 = 0.8346$, $Q_8 = 0.9647$.

(5) sorts alternatives for the same region in ascending order of decision index values based on the ordering regulations of alternatives in the identical area. The ordering result in the positive region is $\{A_3 \succ A_4 \succ A_1\}$, the ranking result in the boundary area is $\{A_6 \succ A_5\}$, and the ranking result in the negative area is $\{A_7 \succ A_8 \succ A_2\}$.

(6) Finally, the ranking rules use different regions when ranking the alternatives are shown in Figure 2. The final sorting result is $\{A_3 \succ A_4 \succ A_1 \succ A_6 \succ A_5 \succ A_7 \succ A_8 \succ A_2\}$.

4.2. Sequential Three-Way VIKOR Model Based on Maximum Group Utility Value and Minimum Individual Regret Value

In the sequential three-way decision classification, the scheme with the largest group utility value is separated into the negative area, and the scheme with the smallest individual regret value is divided into the positive region. If the alternative with the minimum single regret value and the maximum group utility value is also divided into the boundary region, the other steps of the proposed model are roughly like the sequential three-way VIKOR model according to the maximum individual regret value and the minimum group utility value.

Algorithm 2 Sequential three-way VIKOR model based on minimum group utility value and maximum individual regret value

---

Input: Group utility values and individual regret values for m alternatives
$k^{th}-level, k = 0$;
output: Three decision regions, POS^k BND^k_{new} and NEG^k;
1   POS = ∅, BND = {Am}, NEG = ∅, k = 0, S = {Sm}, R = {Rm}
2   **while** $BND^k \neq \emptyset$ **do**
3        $k++$, $POS_{new} = NEG_{new} = \emptyset$;
4        $A_{max} = \min(S)$, $A_{min} = \max(R)$;
5   if $A_{max} = A_{min}$
6   Add A_{max} to BND_{new}
7            $BND^k_{new} = BND^{k-1}_{new} \cup BND_{new}$;
8   else Add A_{max} to POS_{new}
9            $POS^k_{new} = POS^{k-1}_{new} \cup POS_{new}$;
10   Add A_{min} to NEG_{new}
11       $NEG^k = NEG^{k-1} \cup NEG_{new}$;
12       $BND^k = BND^{k-1} - (POS_{new} \cup BND_{new} \cup NEG_{new})$;
13       $S = S - (A_{max} \cup A_{min})$;
14   **end**
15   Output $POS^k(A_m)$, $BND^k_{new}(A_m)$, $NEG^k(A_m)$.

Example 4. *(Similar to Example 3), Using this model to process Table 2 can acquire the final ordering result of the schemes of the three-way sequential VIKOR model according to the minimum single regret value and the maximum group utility value as* $\{A_3 \succ A_4 \succ A_1 \succ A_6 \succ A_5 \succ A_7 \succ A_8 \succ A_2\}$. *It can be seen that the ranking results of the sequential three-way VIKOR model according to the maximum individual regret value and the minimum group utility value and the sequential three-way VIKOR model according to the minimum single regret value and the maximum group utility value are both* $\{A_3 \succ A_4 \succ A_1 \succ A_6 \succ A_5 \succ A_7 \succ A_8 \succ A_2\}$. *It shows the effectiveness of considering the group utility value and single regret value and the stability of the final ranking result. Unlike the sequential three-way VIKOR model, according to a single individual regret value or group utility value, the three-way sequential VIKOR model based on individual regret value and group utility value separated the schemes into the negative area and positive area and divides the schemes that are difficult to judge into the boundary area.*

From Example 1 and Example 2, it can be seen that there is A_5 difference in the final ranking results of A_5 and A_6. Example 1 divides A_5 into the positive area and A_6 into the negative area, while Example 2 divides A_6 into the positive area and A_5 into the negative area, which eventually leads to the difference in the ranking results. Therefore, it is difficult to acquire an accurate ranking consequence by only considering the partial decision information of A_5 single individual regret value or group utility value. By comprehensively considering the single regret value and group utility value, the result that A_6 is better than A_5 is consistent with the result obtained by VIKOR method.

The alternatives for these two models to be separated into the positive area are consistent with the alternatives to be classified into the negative area, $\{A_3 \succ A_4 \succ A_1\}$ and $\{A_8 \succ A_2 \succ A_7\}$, respectively. It shows that these two models also follow the principle that the smaller the single regret, the larger the group utility, and the better the scheme, and the larger the single regret, the smaller the group utility, and the worse the scheme. Through sequential three-way decisions and considering both single regret value and group utility value, decision makers can obtain more decision information to classify alternatives. The sequential three-way VIKOR model based on single regret value and group utility value reduces the range of the positive area and negative area, and divides the difficult solutions into the boundary area, which avoids the difference in ranking results due to misclassification to a certain extent.

5. Experiment and Analysis

In this chapter, the ranking results of the proposed two models in two examples are compared with other existing multi-attribute ranking methods to further illustrate the VIKOR-based sequential three-way model. The first example is from Zhang [6] and the second example is from Ye [29]. The selected examples are from other papers on the combination of multiple attribute decision-making methods and sequential three-way decisions, and papers on the combination of fuzzy information systems and sequential three-way systems. These are representative in terms of multiple attribute decision-making methods and sequential three-way decisions, and the selected examples are also classic in terms of decision ranking and investment decision problems. Therefore, the selected examples are representative.

Example 5. *In order to the usefulness and feasibility of the newly proposed multiple attribute decision-making method related to TOPSIS, Zhang et al. [6] used the data related to an investment plan. The company needs to comprehensively consider the expected benefit, market saturation, environmental impact, social benefit, and energy saving degree of the eight investment plans proposed and select the best investment plan. The set of eight investment plans is $A = \{A_1, A_2, A_3, A_4, A_5, A_6, A_7, A_8\}$, the corresponding attribute set of investment plans is $C = \{C_1, C_2, C_3, C_4, C_5\}$, the benefit attribute is $\{C_1, C_4, C_5\}$, and the cost attribute is $\{C_2, C_3\}$. The set of weights corresponding to each attribute is $W = \{0.3, 0.1, 0.15, 0.25, 0.2\}$, and the uniformized decision matrix corresponding to the eight investment alternatives is $X = ((X_{mn}))_{8 \times 5}$ $(m = 1, \cdots, 8; n = 1, 2, 3, 4, 5)$, as shown in Table 3. The visualization of Example 5 is presented in Figure 3.*

Table 3. Normalized decision matrix corresponding to investment alternatives.

	C_1	C_2	C_3	C_4	C_5
A_1	0.8	0.4	0.3	0.8	0.9
A_2	0.9	0.5	0.5	0.7	0.6
A_3	0.3	0.4	0.6	0.4	0.3
A_4	0.5	0.2	0.2	0.7	0.6
A_5	0.7	0.6	0.6	0.5	0.8
A_6	0.4	0.8	0.7	0.7	0.3
A_7	0.9	0.5	0.1	0.8	0.7
A_8	0.6	0.8	0.8	0.3	0.4

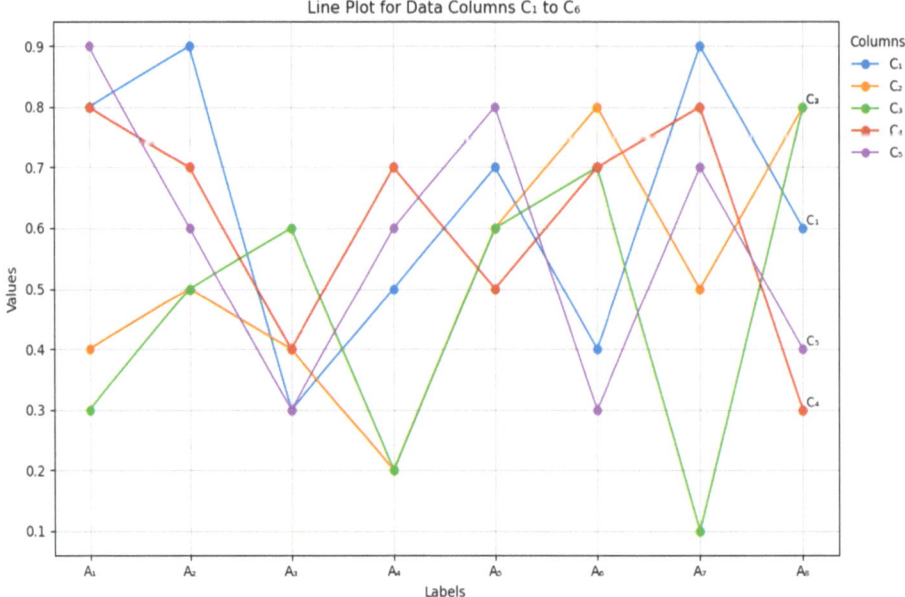

Figure 3. Visualization of Example 5.

Method 1. Sequential three-way VIKOR model according to maximum individual regret value and minimum group utility value:

Step 1. Calculate the PIS and NIS of all investment plans according to Table 3, the larger value of benefit attribute.

Step 2. Calculate the single regret value and group utility value of all schemes on account of (4) and (6), where R_i denotes the individual regret value of the ith scheme and S_i denotes the group utility value of the ith alternative.

$S_1 = 0.1262$, $S_2 = 0.2857$, $S_3 = 0.8404$, $S_4 = 0.5642$, $S_5 = 0.4571$, $S_6 = 0.6911$, $S_7 = 0.1167$, $S_8 = 0.8167$. $R_1 = 0.0500$, $R_2 = 0.1000$, $R_3 = 0.3000$, $R_4 = 0.2000$, $R_5 = 0.1500$, $R_6 = 0.2500$, $R_7 = 0.0667$, $R_8 = 0.2500$.

Step 3. Classify the alternatives based on Algorithm 2 by the maximum single regret value and the minimum group utility value, which can be obtained $POS^4 = \{A_7, A_1, A_2, A_5\}$, $NEG^4 = \{A_3, A_6, A_8, A_4\}$. The boundary region BND^4 is empty because there is no alternative that has both the maximum single regret value and the minimum group utility value when classifying the alternatives by sequential three-way decisions.

Step 4. Calculate the decision index values of all schemes according to Equation (5), and Q_i represents the decision index value of the ith scheme, which can be obtained by

$Q_1 = 0.0066$, $Q_2 = 0.2168$, $Q_3 = 1$, $Q_4 = 0.6092$, $Q_5 = 0.4352$, $Q_6 = 0.7969$, $Q_7 = 0.0334$, $Q_8 = 0.8836$.

Step 5. On the basis of the ordering regulations of alternatives in the identical area, the alternatives in the identical area are sorted in ascending rank of decision index values, and the ranking result in the positive region is $\{A_1 \succ A_7 \succ A_2 \succ A_5\}$, and the ranking result in the negative region is $\{A_4 \succ A_6 \succ A_8 \succ A_3\}$.

Step 6. The final ranking result $\{A_1 \succ A_7 \succ A_2 \succ A_5 \succ A_4 \succ A_6 \succ A_8 \succ A_3\}$ is obtained through the ordering regulations $POS\{A\} \succ BND\{A\} \succ NEG\{A\}$ of different regions.

Method 2. Sequential three-way VIKOR model based on minimum individual regret value and maximum group utility value:

Step 1. This step is the same as in Method 1.

Step 2. This step is the same as in Method 1.

Step 3. According to Algorithm 2, the alternatives are classified by the maximum individual regret value and the maximum group utility value. $POS^4 = \{A_1, A_7, A_2, A_5\}$, $NEG^4 = \{A_3, A_8, A_6, A_4\}$.

Step 4. is the same as in Method 1.

Step 5. Similar to Method 1, it can be observed that the ranking result in the positive domain is $\{A_1 \succ A_7 \succ A_2 \succ A_5\}$, and the ranking result in the negative domain is $\{A_4 \succ A_6 \succ A_8 \succ A_3\}$.

Step 6. The final ranking result $\{A_1 \succ A_7 \succ A_2 \succ A_5 \succ A_4 \succ A_6 \succ A_8 \succ A_3\}$ is obtained through the ranking rules of different regional alternatives.

Through the final ranking results of the above two models, it can be found that the ordering consequences of the two models are consistent. This shows that the comprehensive consideration of single regret value and group utility value makes the decision information considered by decision makers more complete and shows the effectiveness and the stability of the final ranking results. In three-way sequential decisions, the individual regret value and group utility value are used to provide more effective ranking information for the alternatives. Three-way sequential decisions divide the alternatives into different domains to obtain preliminary ranking information, which avoids some unreasonable ranking results to a certain extent.

The weight information of Example 5 is changed to $W = \{0.3, 0.1, 0.3, 0.2, 0.1\}$, and the final ranking result is changed to $\{A_7 \succ A_1 \succ A_2 \succ A_4 \succ A_5 \succ A_6 \succ A_3 \succ A_8\}$, as shown in Table 4 and in the visualization of comparison results with other methods shown in Figure 4. The ordering consequences of this method are consistent with other schemes or slightly different.

Table 4. Comparison results with other methods (Example 5).

Different Methods	Ranking Results	The Optimal Candidate	The Inferior Candidate
ours	$A_7 \succ A_1 \succ A_2 \succ A_4 \succ A_5 \succ A_6 \succ A_3 \succ A_8$	A_7	A_8
Zhang et al.' s method [6]	$A_7 \succ A_1 \succ A_4 \succ A_2 \succ A_5 \succ A_6 \succ A_8 \succ A_3$	A_7	A_3
Ye et al.'s method [29]	$A_7 \succ A_1 \succ A_2 \succ A_4 \succ A_5 \succ A_3 \succ A_8 \succ A_6$	A_7	A_6
Jia et al.'s method [30]	$A_7 \succ A_1 \succ A_4 = A_2 \succ A_5 \succ A_6 \succ A_3 \succ A_8$	A_7	A_8
Wang et al.' method [31]	$A_7 \succ A_1 \succ A_2 \succ A_4 \succ A_5 \succ A_6 \succ A_8 \succ A_3$	A_7	A_3
VIKOR method [28]	$A_7 \succ A_1 \succ A_2 \succ A_4 \succ A_5 \succ A_6 \succ A_3 \succ A_8$	A_7	A_8
TOPSIS method [32]	$A_7 \succ A_1 \succ A_2 \succ A_4 \succ A_5 \succ A_6 \succ A_8 \succ A_3$	A_7	A_3

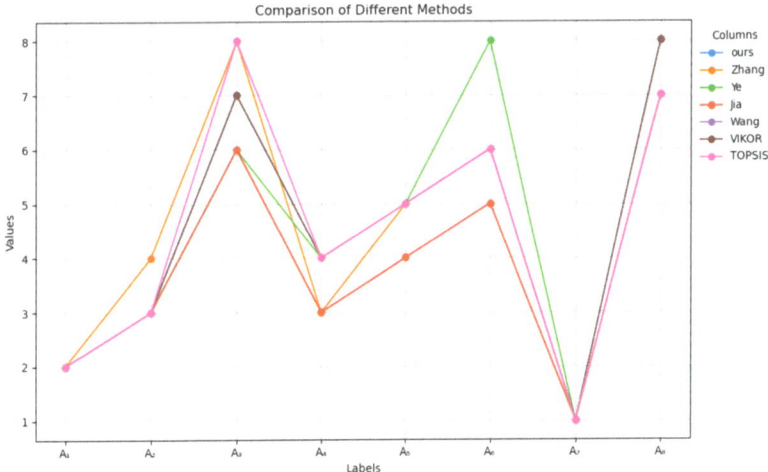

Figure 4. Visualization of comparison results of Example 5 with those of other methods.

The imparity between the proposed method and other comparison methods is that the positions of alternatives with similar rank are exchanged with each other, and the overall ranking information is only slightly different. On the premise of ensuring the accuracy of the experimental consequences, the usefulness and availability of the proposed method are verified.

Example 6. *Ye et al. [29] considered the information of six manager candidates in the company and selected the manager candidates according to their health status, educational background, social ability, work style, writing ability and work experience, which were all benefit attributes. The set of manager candidates is $A = \{A_1, A_2, A_3, A_4, A_5, A_6\}$, the corresponding set of attributes is $C = \{C_1, C_2, C_3, C_4, C_5, C_6\}$, and the corresponding set of attribute weights is $W = \{0.1545, 0.1545, 0.19, 0.19, 0.1555, 0.1555\}$, as shown in Table 5 and Figure 5.*

Table 5. Attribute evaluation values of manager candidates.

	C_1	C_2	C_3	C_4	C_5	C_6
A_1	0.68	0.74	0.64	0.83	0.65	0.75
A_2	0.48	0.83	0.62	0.78	0.48	0.72
A_3	0.83	0.48	0.78	0.58	0.75	0.48
A_4	0.74	0.68	0.83	0.64	0.75	0.65
A_5	0.76	0.66	0.48	0.62	0.72	0.83
A_6	0.66	0.76	0.58	0.48	0.83	0.75

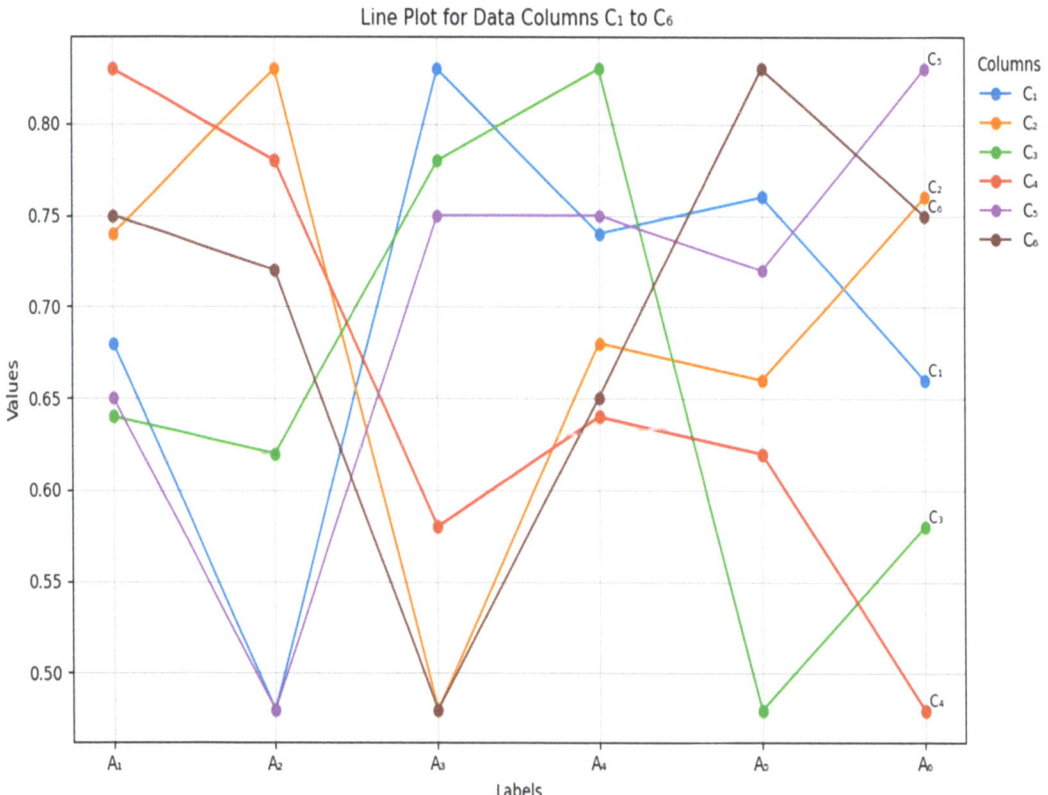

Figure 5. Visualization of Example 6.

The final ordering result acquired by the proposed method is $\{A_1 \succ A_4 \succ A_5 \succ A_6 \succ A_2 \succ A_3\}$ and is compared with other methods, as shown in Table 6 and visualization of comparison results with other methods shown in Figure 6.

Table 6. Comparison results with other methods (Example 6).

Different Methods	Ranking Results	The Optimal Candidate	The Inferior Candidate
ours	$A_1 \succ A_4 \succ A_5 \succ A_6 \succ A_2 \succ A_3$	A_1	A_3
Ye et al.'s method [29]	$A_1 \succ A_4 \succ A_5 \succ A_6 \succ A_2 \succ A_3$	A_1	A_3
TOPSIS method [32]	$A_1 = A_4 \succ A_5 \succ A_2 \succ A_6 \succ A_3$	A_1, A_4	A_3
WAA operator method [33]	$A_1 = A_4 \succ A_5 \succ A_6 \succ A_2 \succ A_3$	A_1, A_4	A_3
EDAS method [34]	$A_1 = A_4 \succ A_5 \succ A_6 \succ A_2 \succ A_3$	A_1, A_4	A_3
Jia et al.'s method [30]	$A_1 = A_4 \succ A_5 \succ A_6 \succ A_2 \succ A_3$	A_1, A_4	A_3
Zhang et al.'s method [6]	$A_5 \succ A_6 \succ A_1 = A_4 \succ A_2 \succ A_3$	A_5	A_3
VIKOR method [28]	$A_1 \succ A_4 \succ A_5 \succ A_6 \succ A_2 \succ A_3$	A_1	A_3

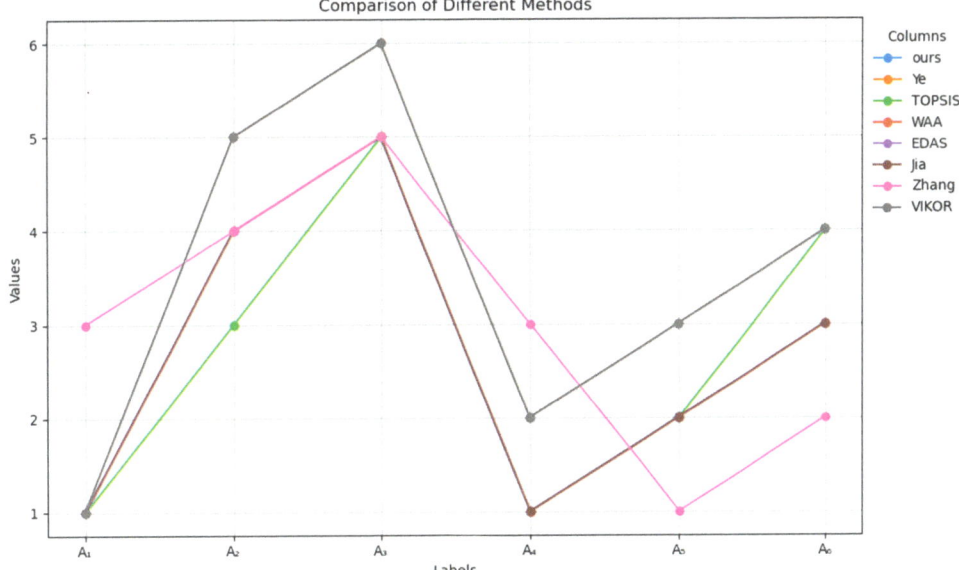

Figure 6. Visualization of comparison results with other methods of Example 6.

Table 6 shows that the ordering consequences of the proposed method are consistent with those of most methods. The ordering consequences of the proposed method are identical as those of Ye [29] and VIKOR method [28]. The imparity between the proposed method and other methods is that A_1 is used as the optimal solution in this paper. In addition to Zhang [6]'s method, other methods take A_1 and A_4 as optimal solutions at the same time. Table 6 shows that the proposed method has the same worst and optimal alternatives as most of the reference methods. According to Table 5, attributes $\{C_1, C_3, C_5\}$ and $\{C_2, C_4, C_6\}$ are evaluated by A_1 and A_4 with opposite values. Since the weights of $\{C_1, C_2\}$, $\{C_3, C_4\}$, and $\{C_5, C_6\}$ are the same, there is intuitively no difference between A_1 and A_4. Other methods mainly use TOPSIS for ranking, which is based on the set of distances from the ideal solution, and a compromise scheme with dominance ratio is improved by VIKOR, which is the basis of the TOPSIS method. The VIKOR method makes the decision of decision makers more conservative or radical by adding the decision mechanism coefficient since TOPSIS method. The process of TOPSIS method does not incorporate any subjective factors, so there are slight differences in the priority of A_1 and A_4. Besides that, most methods are consistent with the ranking results of the proposed method. The consequences show that the proposed method is as effective as other methods in dealing with the above examples, and is more effective and simpler than other methods, which extends the application scope of sequential three-way decisions and VIKOR methods.

To further test the proposed method, Example 5 is used to quantitatively analyze the proposed method. Firstly, the sensitivity analysis of the decision-making mechanism coefficient v in Equation (5) is carried out, and the values in the interval $[0, 1]$ are taken in turn with a step of 0.1 to analyze the decision index value Q corresponding to the alternatives and the ranking order of the schemes. It can be observed from Figure 7 that with the continuous increase of v, the proportion of the relative distance calculated by the group utility value becomes larger and larger. This means that the decision index value corresponding to the alternative with the smaller group utility value and the decision index value corresponding to the alternative with the larger single regret value and the group utility value corresponding to the alternative with the larger group utility value becomes larger and larger.

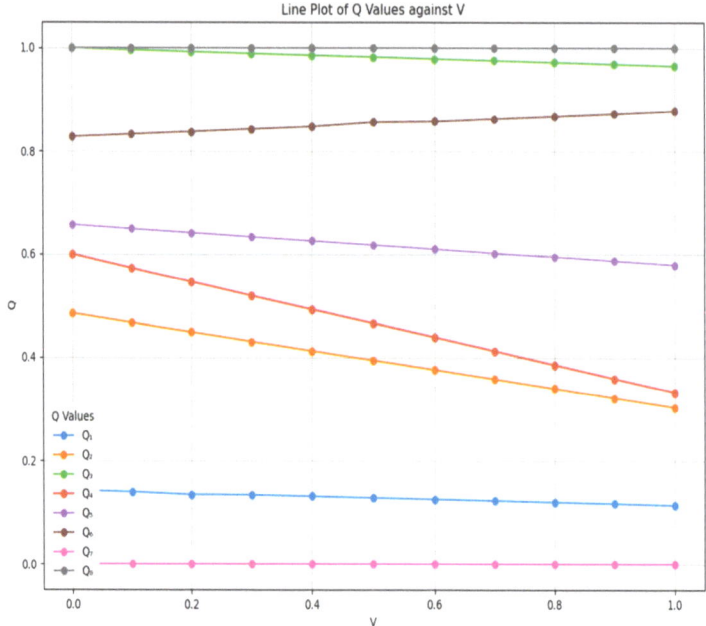

Figure 7. Influence of decision mechanism coefficient v on decision index value Q.

However, the relative order of all schemes is not changed, and only when $v = 0$, the ranking result is $\{A_7 \succ A_1 \succ A_2 \succ A_4 \succ A_5 \succ A_6 \succ A_3 = A_8\}$, and A_3 and A_8 are in the same priority. When $v = 0$, the group utility value is not considered in the calculation of the decision index value, and the individual regret values R_3 and R_8 of A_3 and A_8 are both 0.3 at this time. This possible decision error is caused by only referring to partial decision information, as mentioned in this paper. When $V \neq 0$, because the group utility values of A_3 and A_8 are not the same and the group utility value is considered in the calculation of the decision index value, the ordering consequence is $\{A_7 \succ A_1 \succ A_2 \succ A_4 \succ A_5 \succ A_6 \succ A_3 \succ A_8\}$, which is consistent with the ordering consequences of other cases. Therefore, the proposed method is stable.

Next, the correlation between other methods and the ordering consequences of the proposed method is calculated by Example 5 as shown in Table 7 and Figure 8. It can be seen from Table 7 that the proposed method is significantly correlated with other methods and has high consistency in the ranking results.

Table 7. Spearman correlation coefficient between the proposed method and other methods.

Different Methods	Ours	Zhang [6]	Ye [29]	Jia [30]	Wang [31]	VIKOR [28]	TOPSIS [32]
ours	1	0.952	0.922	0.994	0.976	1	0.976
Zhang's method [6]	-	1	0.898	0.970	0.976	0.952	0.976
Ye's method [29]	-	-	1	0.916	0.922	0.922	0.922
Jia's method [30]	-	-	-	1	0.970	0.994	0.970
Wang's method [31]	-	-	-	-	1	0.976	1
VIKOR method [28]	-	-	-	-	-	1	0.976
TOPSIS method [32]	-	-	-	-	-	-	1

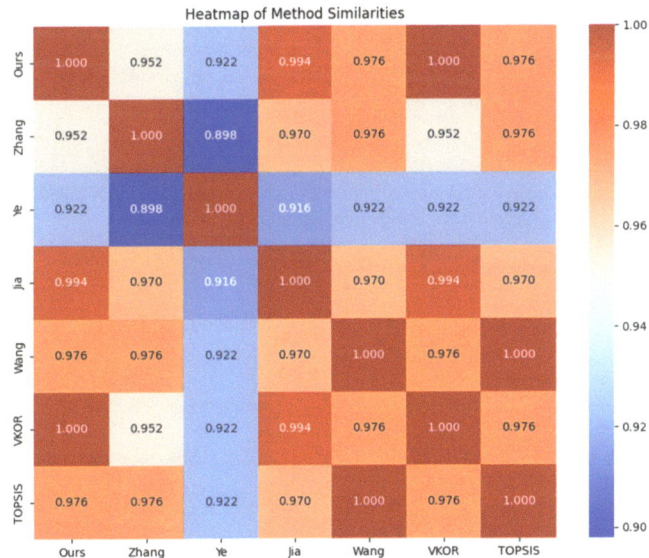

Figure 8. Heatmap of Spearman correlation coefficient.

In addition, it can be observed that the correlation coefficients between the method proposed in this study and other methods are higher than or equal to the correlation coefficients between other methods. This indicates that the method proposed in this study is comparable to the other methods to some extent. In summary, the proposed method demonstrates a certain level of superiority and effectiveness.

6. Conclusions

This paper proposes a three-way sequential classification ranking method based on the VIKOR method. Firstly, based on the single regret value and group utility value, two different sequential three-way VIKOR models based on single regret value or group utility value are proposed. One shortcoming of the two models is that referring to partial decision information may bring errors in classification and ranking. This paper proposed a three-way sequential VIKOR model according to individual regret value and group utility value to compensate for the errors in classification and ranking. Secondly, the VIKOR method is introduced into three-way sequential decisions to design a three-way VIKOR method that can deal with both ranking and classification. This can effectively solve the problem of classification ranking and divide alternatives that are difficult to judge into the boundary region, reducing the possibility of misclassification leading to differences in ranking results. This study extends the application scope of the VIKOR method and sequential three-way decisions. Based on the experimental results, the effectiveness and feasibility of the method are confirmed. In the decision-making process, the advantages of the two methods are combined. By comprehensively considering the ranking index of the VIKOR method and the hierarchy and the division of decision domains for sequential three-way decisions, the possibility of misclassification and discrepancies in ranking results is reduced, leading to more scientific decision making.

Next, the related models were improved and supplemented in terms of weight allocation, multi-criteria preference, extension, and improvement of the VIKOR method. The VIKOR method based on sequential three-way decisions in more complex decision problems is further explored and applied to solve sequencing and investment decision problems. In addition, the effective integration of other multi-attribute decision-making methods and three-way decisions will continue to be explored.

Author Contributions: Conceptualization, W.X. and J.Q.; methodology, W.X.; software, S.Y.; validation, W.X.; formal analysis, Y.W.; investigation, Y.N.; resources, J.Q.; data curation, G.Y.; writing—original draft preparation, W.X.; writing—review and editing, W.X.; visualization, W.X.; supervision, J.Q.; project administration, J.Q.; funding acquisition, J.Q. All authors have read and agreed to the published version of the manuscript.

Funding: This research was funded by [National Natural Science Foundation of China] grant number [62466017, 62066014, 62163016] and [Double thousand plan of Jiangxi Province of China, the Natural Science Foundation of Jiangxi Province] grant number [20232ACB202013]. And The APC was funded by [National Natural Science Foundation of China].

Data Availability Statement: All data generated or analyzed during this study are include in this published article.

Conflicts of Interest: The authors declare no conflict of interest.

References

1. Jana, C.; Mohamadghasemi, A.; Pal, M.; Martinez, L. An improvement to the interval type-2 fuzzy VIKOR method. *Knowl.-Based Syst.* **2023**, *280*, 111055. [CrossRef]
2. Alhadidi, T.I.; Alomari, A.H. A FAHP-VIKOR model for evaluating single point interchange operational performance. *Expert Syst. Appl.* **2024**, *248*, 123386. [CrossRef]
3. Zhang, N.; Zhou, Y.; Liu, J.; Wei, G. VIKOR method for Pythagorean hesitant fuzzy multi-attribute decision-making based on regret theory. *Eng. Appl. Artif. Intell.* **2023**, *126*, 106857. [CrossRef]
4. Chen, T.-Y. An evolved VIKOR method for multiple-criteria compromise ranking modeling under T-spherical fuzzy uncertainty. *Adv. Eng. Inform.* **2022**, *54*, 101802. [CrossRef]
5. Mishra, A.R.; Chen, S.-M.; Rani, P. Multiattribute decision making based on Fermatean hesitant fuzzy sets and modified VIKOR method. *Inf. Sci.* **2022**, *607*, 1532–1549. [CrossRef]
6. Zhang, K.; Dai, J.; Zhan, J. A new classification and ranking decision method based on three-way decision theory and TOPSIS models. *Inf. Sci.* **2021**, *568*, 54–85. [CrossRef]
7. Bisht, G.; Pal, A. Three-way decisions based multi-attribute decision-making with utility and loss functions. *Eur. J. Oper. Res.* **2024**, *316*, 268–281. [CrossRef]
8. Wang, T.; Huang, B.; Li, H. Optimized third-generation prospect theory-based three-way decision approach for conflict analysis in multi-scale Z-number information systems. *Inf. Sci.* **2024**, *663*, 120309. [CrossRef]
9. Yang, B.; Li, J. Complex network analysis of three-way decision researches. *Int. J. Mach. Learn. Cybern.* **2020**, *11*, 973–987. [CrossRef]
10. Zhan, J.; Wang, W.; Alcantud, J.C.R.; Zhan, J. A three-way decision approach with prospect-regret theory via fuzzy set pair dominance degrees for incomplete information systems. *Inf. Sci.* **2022**, *617*, 310–330. [CrossRef]
11. Subhashini, L.; Li, Y.; Zhang, J.; Atukorale, A.S. Integration of semantic patterns and fuzzy concepts to reduce the boundary region in three-way decision-making. *Inf. Sci.* **2022**, *595*, 257–277. [CrossRef]
12. Jiang, Q.; Liu, Y.; Yi, J.-H.; Forrest, J.Y.-L. A three-way conflict analysis model with decision makers' varying preferences. *Appl. Soft Comput.* **2024**, *151*, 111171. [CrossRef]
13. Luo, N.; Zhang, Q.; Yin, L.; Xie, Q.; Wu, C.; Wang, G. Three-way multi-attribute decision-making under the double hierarchy hesitant fuzzy linguistic information system. *Appl. Soft Comput.* **2024**, *154*, 111315. [CrossRef]
14. Qi, Z.; Li, H.; Zhang, K.; Dai, J. An attribute fuzzy concept-oriented three-way utility decision model in multi-attribute environments. *Appl. Soft Comput.* **2023**, *143*, 110353. [CrossRef]
15. Qian, J.; Hong, C.; Yu, Y.; Liu, C.; Miao, D. Generalized multigranulation sequential three-way decision models for hierarchical classification. *Inf. Sci.* **2022**, *616*, 66–87. [CrossRef]
16. Yi, J.-H.; Liu, Y.; Forrest, J.Y.-L.; Guo, X.-G.; Xu, X.-J. A three-way decision approach with S-shaped utility function under Pythagorean fuzzy information. *Expert Syst. Appl.* **2022**, *210*, 118370. [CrossRef]

17. Wang, J.; Ma, X.; Xu, Z.; Zhan, J. A three-way decision approach with risk strategies in hesitant fuzzy decision information systems. *Inf. Sci.* **2022**, *588*, 293–314. [CrossRef]
18. Pan, X.-H.; Pan, X.-H.; He, S.-F.; He, S.-F.; Wang, Y.-M.; Wang, Y.-M.; Martínez, L.; Martínez, L. A novel interval-valued three-way decision theory under multiple criteria environment. *Knowl.-Based Syst.* **2022**, *253*, 109522. [CrossRef]
19. Yan, K.-Y.; Yang, H.-L.; Guo, Z.-L. A novel three-way classification and ranking approach based on regret theory and TOPSIS. *Inf. Sci.* **2024**, *666*, 120443. [CrossRef]
20. Yang, X.; Li, T.; Liu, D.; Fujita, H. A multilevel neighborhood sequential decision approach of three-way granular computing. *Inf. Sci.* **2020**, *538*, 119–141. [CrossRef]
21. Liang, P.; Cao, W.; Hu, J. A sequential three-way classification model based on risk preference and decision correction. *Appl. Soft Comput.* **2023**, *149*, 110978. [CrossRef]
22. Fang, Y.; Gao, C.; Yao, Y. Granularity-driven sequential three-way decisions: A cost-sensitive approach to classification. *Inf. Sci.* **2020**, *507*, 644–664. [CrossRef]
23. Ju, H.; Pedrycz, W.; Li, H.; Ding, W.; Yang, X.; Zhou, X. Sequential three-way classifier with justifiable granularity. *Knowl.-Based Syst.* **2019**, *163*, 103–119. [CrossRef]
24. Yao, Y. Granular computing and sequential three-way decisions. In *International Conference on Rough Sets and Knowledge Technology*; Springer: Berlin, Germany, 2013.
25. Yao, Y. Rough sets and three-way decisions. In *Rough Sets and Knowledge Technology: 10th International Conference, RSKT 2015, Held as Part of the International Joint Conference on Rough Sets, IJCRS 2015, Tianjin, China, 20–23 November 2015, Proceedings 10*; Springer International Publishing: New York, NY, USA, 2015.
26. Yao, Y.; Deng, X. Sequential Three-Way Decisions with Probabilistic Rough Sets. In Proceedings of the 10th IEEE International Conference on Cognitive Informatics and Cognitive Computing, Banff, AB, Canada, 18–20 August 2011; IEEE: New York, NY, USA, 2011.
27. Yang, X.; Yang, X.; Fujita, H.; Liu, D.; Yao, Y. A unified model of sequential three-way decisions and multilevel incremental processing. *Knowl.-Based Syst.* **2017**, *134*, 172–188. [CrossRef]
28. Opricovic, S.; Tzeng, G.-H. Extended VIKOR method in comparison with outranking methods. *Eur. J. Oper. Res.* **2007**, *178*, 514–529. [CrossRef]
29. Ye, J.; Zhan, J.; Xu, Z. A novel decision-making approach based on three-way decisions in fuzzy information systems. *Inf. Sci.* **2020**, *541*, 362–390. [CrossRef]
30. Jia, F.; Liu, P. A novel three-way decision model under multiple-criteria environment. *Inf. Sci.* **2019**, *471*, 29–51. [CrossRef]
31. Wang, Y.; Liu, P.; Yao, Y. BMW-TOPSIS: A generalized TOPSIS model based on three-way decision. *Inf. Sci.* **2022**, *607*, 799–818. [CrossRef]
32. Wang, Y.; Liu, P.; Yao, Y. Decision making framework based Fermatean fuzzy integrated weighted distance and TOPSIS for green low-carbon port evaluation. *Eng. Appl. Artif. Intell.* **2022**, *114*, 105048.
33. Harsanyi, J.C. Cardinal welfare, individualistic ethics, and interpersonal comparisons of utility. *J. Political Econ.* **1955**, *63*, 309–321. [CrossRef]
34. Mehdi, K.G.; Edmundas Kazimieras, Z.; Laya, O.; Zenonas, T. Multi-criteria inventory classification using a new method of evaluation based on distance from average solution (EDAS). *Informatica* **2015**, *26*, 435–451.

Disclaimer/Publisher's Note: The statements, opinions and data contained in all publications are solely those of the individual author(s) and contributor(s) and not of MDPI and/or the editor(s). MDPI and/or the editor(s) disclaim responsibility for any injury to people or property resulting from any ideas, methods, instructions or products referred to in the content.

MDPI AG
Grosspeteranlage 5
4052 Basel
Switzerland
Tel.: +41 61 683 77 34

Algorithms Editorial Office
E-mail: algorithms@mdpi.com
www.mdpi.com/journal/algorithms

Disclaimer/Publisher's Note: The title and front matter of this reprint are at the discretion of the Guest Editors. The publisher is not responsible for their content or any associated concerns. The statements, opinions and data contained in all individual articles are solely those of the individual Editors and contributors and not of MDPI. MDPI disclaims responsibility for any injury to people or property resulting from any ideas, methods, instructions or products referred to in the content.

www.ingramcontent.com/pod-product-compliance
Lightning Source LLC
LaVergne TN
LVHW072328090526
838202LV00019B/2372